DOCUMENTALITY

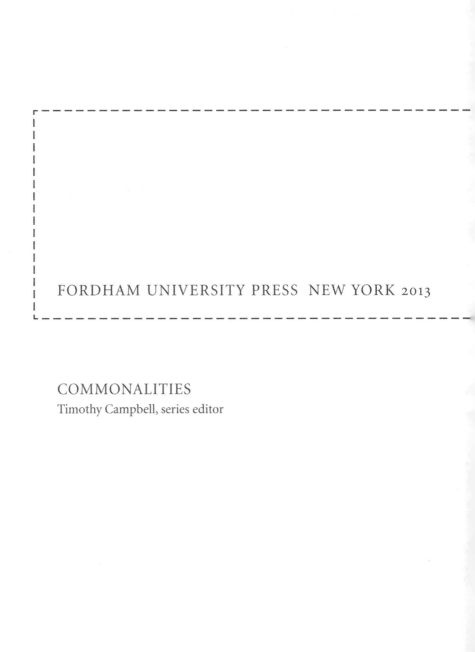

FORDHAM UNIVERSITY PRESS NEW YORK 2013

COMMONALITIES
Timothy Campbell, series editor

DOCUMENTALITY

Why It Is Necessary to Leave Traces

MAURIZIO FERRARIS

Translated by Richard Davies

Acknowledgment

The translator would like to thank Davide Grasso for his invaluable help in hunting down English versions of many of the sources cited in the footnotes.

Printed in the United States of America
15 14 13   5 4 3 2 1
First edition

To my friends in Labont

CONTENTS

Introduction: Marriages and Years in Jail 1

1 Catalog of the World 7
1.1 Samples 7
1.2 Subjects 22
1.3 Objects 13

2 Ontology and Epistemology 55
2.1 The Transcendental Fallacy 57
2.2 Ontological Differences 84
2.3 Theory of Experience 102

3 Social Objects 120
3.1 Social Epistemology .121
3.2 Realism and Textualism 138
3.3 Objects, Acts, and Inscriptions 164

4 Ichnology 175
4.1 Registration and Imitation 178
4.2 Writing, Archiwriting, Thought 197
4.3 Genesis and Structure of Inscriptions 224

5 Documentality 247
5.1 Documents 249
5.2 Works 271
5.3 The Phenomenology of the Letter 281

6 Idioms 297

6.1 What Does a Signature Mean? 298

6.2 *Le Style C'est l'Homme* 305

6.3 Epilogue: Eleven Theses 316

Notes 321

Index 371

Ton acte toujours s'applique à du
papier, car méditer, sans traces,
devient évanescent

Your act is always stuck to a piece of paper,
for meditation without traces
becomes evanescent
—Stéphane Mallarmé, "L'Action réstreinte"

INTRODUCTION
Marriages and Years in Jail

In this book I discuss social objects, which is to say things like money and works of art, marriages, divorces and shared custody, years in jail and mortgages, the price of oil and tax codes, the Nuremberg Trials and the Swedish Academy of Sciences, and then economic crises, research projects, lectures, degrees and students, the clergy, hirings, elections, revolutions and firings, trades unions, parliaments and limited companies, restaurants, lawyers and wars, humanitarian missions, taxes and weekends, medieval knights and the "knights" of the Italian Republic.

We do not need philosophy to see that these objects abound in our world, much more than do stones, trees, and coconuts, and that they are much more important for us, given that the most part of our happiness or unhappiness depends on them. All the same, we do not always notice them, and even more rarely do we ask what they are made of, taking stock of them only when we lose our wallet, train ticket, passport, or credit card and try to pay for something, to make a phone call, to send an email, or to join a line in any government office. It is only then that we grasp (though it is often too late) that social objects are made of *inscriptions*, impressed on paper, on some magnetic medium, or even only (for instance, in the promises we make to each other every day) in people's heads.

This is the reason why I have called this theory of the social world "documentality":[1] The ontology of social objects is made up of traces, registrations, and documents, and it manifests itself in those bits of paper that accumulate in our pockets, in the pieces of paper or plastic that we hold onto more carefully in our wallets, and then in the mass of registrations that fill up computers, archives, cell phones, and banks.

HOW TO READ THIS BOOK

The parts in italics (beginning with this one) summarize the argument. If the reader is in a hurry, they can be skipped, or, if the hurry is compelling, they can be read as an alternative to the text in roman, which is to say the rest of the book. The basic theses that I propose can be grasped by reading the epilogue in Chapter 6.3; and someone who is interested specifically in the theory of documents, whose constitutive law is Object = Inscribed Act, may begin by reading Chapter 3.

Overall, the book is made up of two main blocks. The first, which is analytic, proposes two distinctions that are fundamental for my theory: the difference between families of objects and that between being and knowing or between ontology and epistemology. The other, which is dialectical, argues for the constitutive law of social objects, its foundation in a general theory of traces, and its development into a theory and practice of documents and signatures. With an eye to articulating these themes, I have sought to impose a systematic structure on the book and have divided it into six chapters, each subdivided into three main sections.

Chapter 1 begins by justifying a generous ontology that, in addition to natural objects, admits ideal objects and social objects. The reason for setting out a catalog of all the things that there are in the world is very straightforward. On the heels of certain eighteenth-century manuals of ontology, and rather in the spirit of Georges Perec, I have tried to take account of all the objects—or at least of all the types of objects—that furnish our lives, of their common characteristics but especially of the differences among them. This derives from the unoriginal but I think well-founded conviction that a good many of the problems that assail us not only in everyday life but also in philosophy derive from our taking one sort of object for another. It would be an obvious mistake, of a sort that we are well aware of and are able to avoid, to use a screwdriver as a toothpick or to blow our noses on a banknote. But, given that we do not all do philosophy—and even those who do philosophy don't do it all the time—there are more hifalutin mistakes, of a sort to which we tend to be oblivious, such as treating natural objects as if they were socially constructed or a hundred ideal dollars as if they were equivalent to a hundred real dollars, but that carry heavy consequences. How can we avoid these mistakes and save ourselves from all sorts of nonsense?

My proposal is that, in the first instance, we should proceed to a clear distinction that separates natural objects, which exist in space and time independently of subjects, from social objects, which exist in space and time and depend on subjects, on the one hand and on the other, ideal objects, which exist outside space and time and are independent of subjects. On this basis, it will no longer be possible to maintain that natural reality is constructed by scientists' theories, as many postmodernists claim. But it will also become fairly difficult to assert that, in the absence of conceptual schemes, we have no relations with the physical world, as has been claimed by perfectly reasonable philosophers who have not, however, considered that, unlike social objects, natural objects exist independently from subjects and hence have no use for conceptual schemes. Of course, we will still be able to clean our teeth with a screwdriver, but, as I have already hinted, this is would be a rarer and, despite appearances, a more benign mistake than the misunderstandings regarding conceptual schemes.

Why, then, does it seem so natural to confuse the existence of things with the knowledge we have of them? To confuse ontology with epistemology? In Chapter 2, I clarify what I mean by ontology (the theory of what there is) and how it differs from epistemology (the theory of how we know what there is). In 6.1, 6.2, and 6.3, I essentially take on Kant, whose philosophy—as I see it—is marked by a collapse of being into knowing, which was since recurred in the though of pragmatists and postmodernists. After setting out the fallacy that I call transcendental, because it forms the basis of the transcendental philosophy, I offer the groundwork of an ontology that is independent of epistemology and outline the foundations of a theory of experience that, in my view, is the proper level at which to carry out a descriptive metaphysics of the sort that I propose. In conclusion, I observe that this superposition turns out to be entirely inappropriate for natural objects, which have their existence separate from and independent of being known, while it is perfectly applicable to social objects. In other words, there is a realm in which the transcendental philosophy can be reinstated, and this is the realm of social objects, of whose existence, however, Kant did not have the slightest inkling.

Chapter 3 is dedicated to social objects themselves. Chapter 3.1 sets out the general scheme of what I call a critique of social reason, which is to say a critique of pure reason as applied to social objects. 3.2 takes on the theories that have been proposed on the matter, concentrating on the most recent and widely accepted social ontology, that of John Searle, according to which social objects are higher-level objects relative to natural objects in such a way that their constitutive rule is "X counts as Y in C": a physical object X, such as a piece of paper, counts as the social object Y, such as a ten-euro banknote, in C, namely the European Union in 2009. Searle's theory seems to me nevertheless inadequate on two grounds. One is that it cannot explain a very wide range of social objects: it is hard to pick out the X that counts as the University of Turin, or, even worse, the X that counts as the public debt in 2009. The other is that it *makes social objects depend on a mysterious entity, namely collective intention-ality, which seems to be a sort of common spirit that precedes individuals and makes society possible.*

After criticizing Searle's proposal, I present my own theory, which I call weak textualism *because it arises out of a weakening of Derrida's principle that "there is nothing outside the text." On my version, the principle becomes "there is nothing social outside the text." And the constitutive rule of social objects is: "Object = Inscribed Act," by which I mean that social objects are social acts (that is, they arise among at least two persons) and are characterized by being written on a piece of paper, a computer file, or at least in the heads of the people involved. Thus, banknotes are social objects because they have been issued by a public act and are written on paper, and the rule "Object 5 Inscribed Act" explains what the rule "X counts as Y in C" leaves obscure, namely, how come we can carry out financial transactions simply by typing on the keyboard of a computer. The ap-peal to inscription also explains—and it is a matter on which I shall have much to say—how to found complex social objects, such as the University of Turin, the European Union, and negative entities such as debts. These do not require bulky objects, because inscriptions and documents will suffice.*

Given that in the weak textualism I propose, inscriptions constitute the condi-tions for the possibility of social objects, Chapter 4 analyzes the function and field of action of inscriptions in what I call an ichnology, *which is to say, a "theory of traces."[2] Chapter 4.1 is given over to considering the role of registration and imitation in constructing social reality. We can imagine a society that does with-out very many things, but not without memory and registration. For every role and every agreement depends on memory, and every behavior on imitation, and this explains why archives and documents are so central to the lives of persons and societies. This consideration holds good for every era and is all the more obvious when we look at the huge changes of the last thirty years, in which we have witnessed an explosion in the systems of registration and of writing, from computers to mobile phones and the Web. On the one hand, these have radi-cally transformed our ways of living and working while, on the other, they have helped to bring out the essence of social reality, namely, the fact of being based in a nonaccidental but rather essential way on inscriptions and registrations. A historical accident thus manifests a theoretical essence. 4.2 focuses on this es-sence and examines the ways that inscriptions ensure the passage from nature to culture, both in the usual sense of writing as well as in the mere possibility of registration in general (which I call* archiwriting*) and as the condition of the* *possibility of thought. 4.3 then proposes a formalized hierarchy of inscriptions, which rises from traces though registrations to reach the level of inscriptions in the technical sense.*

Coming, then, to the core of my theoretical proposal, Chapter 5 illustrates the notion of documentality *and its role in the construction of that extreme point of social reality, which is institutional reality. Here we find not only the objects of economics, of politics, of the law, and of the bureaucracy (which Hegel would have called "objective spirit"), but also the objects of art, of religion, and of philosophy (that sphere that for Hegel makes up "absolute spirit). 5.1, I take the specific case of the constitution of the European Union on the basis of a series of documental acts, with a view to making a claim that completes the view set out in Chapter 4. The basic thesis is that it is a mistake to presuppose something like a spirit (such as Searle's collective intentionality) behind the letters that make up social reality and, a fortiori, institutional reality. These realities grow and feed themselves on the basis of a system of inscriptions that, by allowing the fixity of acts, contribute to the creation of what, in the social world, appears meaningful, worthy of being pursued or avoided, praised or blamed, shared or not.*

If a man were deprived of language, of habits, and of memory, that is to say, deprived of inscriptions and documents, he would hardly be able to cultivate social aspirations, because he would not know what to aspire to, and the aspiration would not occur to him. This priority of the letter over the spirit, just like that of technique over meaning, is particularly clear in the case of artworks, which I consider in 5.2. From the perspective I am suggesting, works are inscriptions that acquire meaning only once they have been brought about and, paradoxically, illustrate in the best possible way the deep nature of documents. Thinking of writing a poem is not writing a poem; imagining the Mona Lisa is not painting it. There needs to be an exteriorization, and this in turn needs to be made permanent in an inscription. But even the mere thought of writing a poem or of marrying would have no sense if there were not a world of inscriptions, a social world in which there exist things like poems and marriages. Robinson Crusoe or a person deprived of memory would not be able to sign checks or take out a mortgage for the same reason that he would not be able to collect mannerist paintings or attend rock concerts. Chapter 5.3 is dedicated to the phenomenology of the letter *and proposes, in line with what has already been said, a generalization of the sphere of documentality as the key for reading the whole of the realm of objective spirit an absolute spirit.*

Finally, Chapter 6 brings to light a feature that is constitutive of the theory of documents and that presents itself as an indispensable ingredient both for paperwork and for artworks. This is the signature, which is a trace that is not necessarily the name of the signatory but that manifests the identity and authoriality of the document. In the signature and in its style absolute individuality is manifested, even if it is the upshot of a social convention: Only I sign this way and with this handwriting, whose salient characteristic is to deviate more or less from the calligraphic standard. Our individuality is in this way a production defect, just as we find with the Golem, but fortunately not always with the same results.

1

CATALOG OF THE WORLD

1.1 SAMPLES

1.1.1 Mundaneum and Panopticon

Lying at about sixty kilometers to the southwest of Brussels, the city of Mons is pure Simenon: fog, brick houses, and, early in the morning at the station bar, the smoke, the beers, the coffees, and the barmaid who is too good-looking for her husband. I've come here because 76 rue de Nimy houses what is left of an actual Library of Babel, the Mundaneum, a gigantic archive that, in the 1930s, held twelve million documents, from bibliographical indications to maps, manifestos, postcards, photographs, and phonograph disks. It is a project that stands somewhere between Christian Wolff and Tintin, between the universal encyclopedia and the childish passion for collecting things.

What has this outing got do to with philosophy? Or at least with this book? To get a handle on it, allow me first to tell a true story. In 1895, two Belgian lawyers decided to bring together everything that was known and to catalog it with the system known as the Universal Decimal Classification (which is still in use in libraries), setting up the standard and the format of the bibliographical slips as well as the filing cabinets that would hold them. They were Paul Otlet, son of a big industrialist, and Henri-Maire La Fontaine, who won the Nobel Peace Prize in 1913. Their undertaking was guided by a theory set out in 1934 in Otlet's *Traité de Documentation*,[1] based on the principle that everything could be a document. The idea was that the world exists so as to find its place in a catalog that would bring order to knowledge

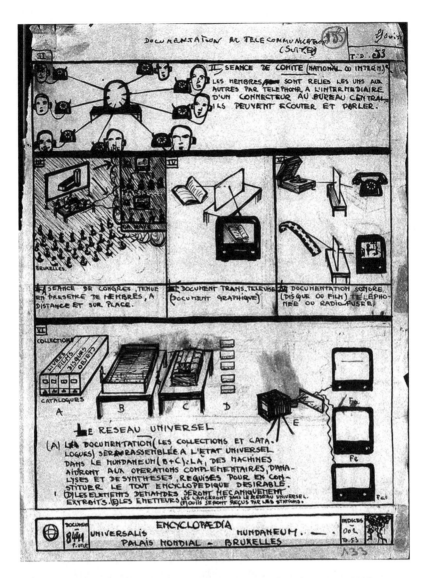

Illustration of the Mundaneum by Paul Otlet (courtesy of Stéphanie Manfroid, Director of the Mundaneum Archive, Mons, Belgium)

in such a way as to favor understanding among different peoples and promote universal peace. It was in this spirit, trying to move from word to deed, that the two men projected an international city with representatives from every country, itself a sort of catalog; given that parliamentary governments wouldn't listen to them, they even tried to propose their scheme to Mussolini and Hitler, but in vain. This was not the only time that the destiny of the Mundaneum intersected with that of the Third Reich. The Mundaneum had originally been housed in the Palais du Cinquantenaire in Brussels, but it underwent its first setback in the 1930s when some of the rooms were dismantled to make room for an exhibition of rubber. Otlet hoped to transfer to Geneva into a building designed by Le Corbusier, but what happened in the 1940s was the German occupation of Belgium and, in the case in hand, a triumphalist exhibition of the art of the Third Reich which took the place of the Mundaneum. Otlet died in 1944, forgotten by everyone, which seems an ironic fate for an archivist. His filing cabinets with their cards had a hard time of it in inadequate housing until they were finally taking in at Mons. Visiting it today gives the feeling of one of the oddest museums, a museum that collects everything because everything can be a document.

So much for the history. Let us turn to the theory. Little by little, the visitor grasps the family resemblances in those old-fashioned papers, and, at a certain point, there comes the illumination: the dream of Otlet and La Fontaine became a reality just few years ago, and it is the Web. Vice versa, we find in the two Belgians, who could have taken the motto of Monsieur Teste, "*transit classificando*," what we might call the missing link between, on the one hand, encyclopedias and libraries and, on the other, that immense paper-free catalog that is proffered to us today by the Internet. Otlet dreamed of the day when everyone could access this immense archive from home, as we can seen from the drawing he made (see above):[2] books, catalogs, and documents would have been accessible by means of the television, which was making its first showing in the 1930s. From this point of view, the Mundaneum becomes a Panopticon, the ideal prison that Jeremy Bentham had dreamed of at the end of the eighteenth century and that was given a philosophical reading by Michel Foucault in the twentieth.[3] But here we have a Panopticon turned back to front: rather than a tower that spies on everyone, televisions by which everyone can see, as in Internet, everything, or *nearly*.

And here is a peculiarity to which to give a thought, and that does not have to do with the obvious fact that the Mundaneum's archive is over-whelmingly on paper, even though it includes also microfilms, photographs, and records (on one of these, which is currently being restored, Otlet can be heard setting out his principles of classification). Rather, it is that Otlet did not foresee in his prophecy—what, on the contrary, is central to my cata-log—that *access to the documents would be by means of writing.* If we take note, we can see that what is missing from Otlet's drawing are the keyboards of the computers: he drew only the screens. And, after all, this changes ev-erything: when we use Internet, we are not channel-surfing; we type on a keyboard, we write, just as we do when we use a cell phone or a smart phone, which, relative to their poor relations (as regards memory), offer the ad-vantage of having a fuller keyboard. It is curious that a great archivist like Otlet should not have thought the thing through[4] and should have failed to consider that a future and fully realized Mundaneum would have done away with paper for good, replacing it at least in principle by other media, but that this would have certainly led to an explosion in writing.

These are initiatives that recur. I recall an occasion in April 2007 when I was introduced in Bogota to the gigantic undertaking of the *Libro total*, meant to bring to fruition Mallarmé's dream of the *Livre*. From this follows the idea of the devil of the system: a classification of everything that there is in the world. But, in the first place, what is there in the world? What is there to catalog? In my view, the answer is that what we catalog are *samples*, that is to say individuals with generalizable features just as in Leporello's catalog,[5] which is philosophically instructive because it collects individuals who give rise to classes:

> Among these are peasant-girls,
> Waiting-maids and city-girls,
> There are countesses, baronesses,
> Marchionesses and princesses.
> And there are women of every rank,
> Of every shape and every age.

We can make catalogs of plates and forks, of banknotes and mail stamps, of butterflies and jellyfish, of Indian chiefs and Egyptian dynasties. Yet, while we cannot catalog virtue in itself, nor musicality in itself, nor redness, nor sound as such, we can catalog samples or cases of virtue, of musicality, of colors, and of sounds. In short, we can catalog things that are, but not their being as such. And when we list the titles of books, as in a publisher's catalog, or animal species in a zoological treatise, what we are classifying are samples, which is to say examples or generalizable single cases in line with a logic of exemplariness that I try to develop shortly.

In addition to giving samples pride of place as a subspecies of individuals, my proposal for how to classify the world also presents a second variation relative to a standard characterization of individuals.[6] Rather than subdivide individuals into persons and things or bodies, I would suggest distinguishing between subjects and objects. The reason for this preference is the difficulty of defining the concept of *person*, with its freight of moral and juridical meanings, and the simplicity of defining the concept of *subject* and, correlatively, of *object*. A subject is what has representations; an object is what does not have any, though it can obviously be represented.[7] What is more, I mean to give pride of place to the object within the subject-object polarity, and in doing so I opt for an anti-Kantian position. Where most modern systems have been constructed starting from a Kantian base (from the pure Self and its transformations down to Heidegger's Dasein and Sartre's situated being), my proposal is rather an Aristotelian view giving preeminence to objects and replacing the transcendental Self with the idea of the catalog. Furthermore, if, as I have said, the world is the totality of individuals and of their relations, namely the set of all samples, then space and time are not two pure forms of intuition but rather, in Leibnizian vein, the order of compresence and of succession of individuals.

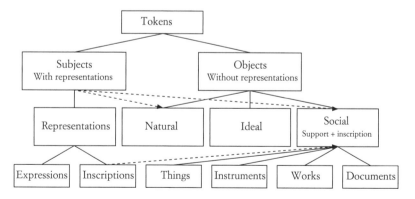

Summary of ontology

There are five rules that I have set myself in drawing up my catalog: classify, not construct; objects, not subjects; exemplify, not simplify; describe, not prescribe; experience, not science. I suppose that, put that way, these rules will appear fairly cryptic and—at least relative to Descartes's *Rules*—have only the undoubted but inadequate advantage of being few in number. I shall try to make them clearer.

1.1.2 *Classify, Not Construct*

Let us begin with the first rule. Against the idea that the world is nothing but a pure construction of the subject, I claim that the world has its own rules and it enforces them, and hence that the philosopher's job is in the first instance that of classifying. From Kant down to the postmodernists, passing through the transcendental idealists and the Nietzschean hermeneuticists (all groups that will be discussed in Chapter 2.1), the constructionists claim that reality is determined by truth, as established by our judgments and conceptual schemes,[8] and some assert[9] that the list of schemes is not exhausted by science, but extends to many other human practices, and particularly artistic enterprises. They maintain, in short, that ontology, what there is, is determined by epistemology, the set of our justified beliefs.

In my view, the correct strategy is different. In the first place, we should recognize that reality precedes and is independent of truth, that ontology is not determined by epistemology, any more than our bare hope to assemble an Ikea bookcase coincides with our effectively assembling it. Directly following on from this, we should observe that our inventiveness is less occupied with creating worlds than it is with introducing—and rather more often with recognizing—an order that is plausible and not always in line with what science says. Rather the suggestions of Proust and Picasso are welcome along with those of Livy, Machiavelli, Montaigne, and many other people who have never had anything to do with quarks but who have not been merely promenading in invented worlds.

It is against this background that ontology is the foundation of a theory of the human sciences and of the world in which we live, but the idea of the catalog is much older.[10] In the baroque period, "ontological catalogs" were drawn up to classify and in such a way as to respond to the emergence of the modern order, for instance, everything that was to be found in a given state or a given region: from crockery to noble titles, from domestic animals to cities. They offered a sort of map of the empire that would have made Borges happy; and the eighteenth-century philosopher Alexander Gottlieb Baumgarten, the coiner of the word *esthetics*, advised artists who were short of subject matter to seek inspiration in manuals of ontology, which is to say in catalogs. In some measure, then, to think of philosophy as classification is a return to our origins, under the aegis of an ideal of philosophy as description (a point we return to shortly). In some measure, though, it is also a response to a much more recent pressure. For, over the last thirty years, the world has been filled with new physical objects, namely computers, which have given rise to new social objects, such as websites. Precisely with a view to handling the potential chaos of the Web and to avoid the Babel effect, computer scientists have felt the need for an ontology, of what there is, that, ever since the seventeenth century was an instrument for cataloging the objects present in the world. Sites, the new states of ontological catalogs, are connected one to another in "webs" or "nets" and refer to an enormous variety of objects and events: the medicines produced by a pharmaceutical company, the rulings of circuit courts, tourist packages for a week in Finland, a customer's purchases at the supermarket, the tax dodgers in the province of Belluno, and so on. So why not do the same with the world taken as a whole? After all, the success of Google is nothing but a proof of the extent to which searching and classifying samples is a primary need in our lives, a necessity to which we rarely pay adequate attention (at least as a point of theory).

1.1.3 Objects, Not Subjects

Let us move on to the second rule, namely the choice of giving pride of place to objects relative to subjects, which we might more pompously express by talking of the affirming the priority of ontology over theory of knowledge. If we assumed, as constructionists do, that the subject creates the world, then it would be very natural to suppose that the most important part of philosophy is the theory of knowledge, understood as the examination of the conceptual schemes through which the world is created. I, on the other hand, claim that what matters most are the objects that are in the world, the things we find ourselves having to organize and that in any case we encounter in our experience; the fact that these objects can receive determinations (let us suppose) from unconscious processes that take place in us, is an epistemological or psychological matter and not an ontological one.[11] I assert therefore that philosophy must begin not with the theory of knowledge, but with ontology, considered as a theory of objects.[12] From the epistemological point of view, my basic claim is that objects appear much more clearly and definitely than subjects do; they are endowed with immanent laws.[13] At least in the overwhelming majority of cases, they are recognizable without complex or sophisticated categorical apparatus. In this sense, they incorporate three main advantages.

The first has to do with evolution. Even before they learn to speak, babies recognize objects,[14] because the attention given to objects responds to the need to recognize obstacles and to pick out prey.[15] We are extremely well equipped for objects, and we have much better eyes for them than we do for concepts, since we can grasp by considering how much more frequent are conceptual confusions than confusions arising out of objects. Obviously, the constructionist may well object that it is not true that stones and branches exist independently, and that it was evolutionarily advantageous to be equipped for objects because the world is full of objects, but in fact objects exist because brains, ours and those of animals, for all their differences, show themselves to be able to transform bundles of stimuli and swarms of particles into coordinated and coherent objects, such as the very same ball that I throw to Fido and that Fido picks up. This objection has its precedents, not least in Malebranche's hypothesis of the preestablished harmony, according to which the world is created and maintained in being with all the objects and events that it contains moment after moment by divine effulgences and hence by an omnipotent principle. But the constructionist makes life harder for himself even than the Malebranchean does, because, in place of the divine intellect, he puts my and Fido's brains at the origin of the universe—and, in that case, why not only mine, or only Fido's, or indeed, only that of the constructionist?

The second epistemological advantage concerns reification.[16] As I have already said, relative to the subject, an object is stable and clear, with sharp outlines. It is precisely this clarity of the borders and limits and the way that the object speaks, and some speak better than others, that makes reification so splendid. In this way, objects give visual evidence to concepts. Just think of what happens on the desktop of a computer: in order to make abstract functions clear, objects are used: trash baskets, scissors, brushes, books, printers, diskettes—things that have almost disappeared from the real world but that have survived as icons on the desktop, which in its turn is represented as the very desk on which the computer is standing. Moreover, objects have a way of capturing and preserving those more fluid things that are events. Investigators, historians, and archaeologists are essentially looking for objects, and they could not be looking for anything else. Last, they give depth to the impalpable things that are social relations, presenting themselves as social relations become lasting and, above all, visible out there.

The third reason—which is at once epistemological and ontological—for privileging objects relative to subjects concerns precisely the catalog. One fine feature of objects is that we can classify them, collect them, and make archives of them; it is the most natural thing in the world, given that ontology, considered as a theory of objects shows a spontaneous tendency toward the collection and the catalog.[17] Let us clarify this point. On the one hand, as we have seen, taking ontology as the theory of objects is one of the most common and widely agreed choices, which favors my proposal of a philosophical catalog. On the other hand, as we have also seen, catalogs include samples, which is to say not just individuals (a box) but also samples (this box with its determinate individual features, considered as an example of boxness). Now it seems to me that the sample is a great philosophical resource, because it allows us to generalize about individuals without having to appeal to universals. This is, typically or exemplarily, the point of Berkeley's objection to general ideas.[18] It is hard to see how we could have a general idea of a dog, though we can easily understand how, to explain what a dog is in general, I can point to a dog (an individual) using it as an example of many individuals with different features, such as size, color, and shape. The example thus allows us to keep to individuals and to refer to classes (which are formed later, starting from the individuals), as is implicit in the meaning of "sample." These are the thoughts that underlie my second rule of method.

1.1.4 Exemplify, Not Simplify

As Hamlet says, "There are more things in heaven and in earth, Horatio, than are dreamt of in your philosophy."[19] I take it he was standing up for exemplification and abundance. After all, the choice between exemplification and simplification is one that divides philosophers between those who prefer deserts and those who love the jungle. In the first camp, there are those, such as Willard Van Orman Quine, who have declared themselves in favor of a stripped-down ontology. He wrote of having a "taste for desert land-scapes,"[20] and he acted accordingly both in life (he took holidays in Arizona) and in his ontology: The world is made of particles, which are atomic, and the rest is just words. The problem, however, is that Ockhamitis—I suggest this term for the abuse of Ockham's razor, which in pruning useless entities ends up chopping out useful ones[21]—is a nasty disease, at least if your have set your heart on accounting for what there is in heaven and in earth: you will only have particles disposed tablewise, chairwise, professorwise, but the fact of knowing that they are particles will not tell you much about the table, the chair or the professor. It is rather like explaining the plot of a novel by talking about cellulose and grammar.

This is the advantage of a richer ontology, namely the jungle of Alexius Meinong.[22] The sphere of being is broader than that of the real, and there are not only physical objects, such as stones and trees, there are also objects that are no longer (ex-existent objects such as the Roman Empire), those that do not exist as a matter of fact (a Golden Mountain), those that do not exist as a matter of law (the round square) and the subsistents, such as numbers and relations. This seems to be an uncalled-for multiplication, a baroque pas-sion; yet—as we have just seen—it is hard to make much sense of the social world with nothing but particles. It is clear that the more objects there are, the easier it is to understand a world that is, as we often hear, complicated, and it is so precisely because there are so many objects. The conciliatory spirit of Leibniz bore this in mind in recalling that someone who has looked carefully at the shapes of plants and animals, of castles and houses, who has read more novels and clever stories will have more knowledge than someone else even if, in everything that has been shown or recounted to him, there is nothing true whatever.[23] He added, with a fine example connected to objects, that Egyptian vases can be used perfectly well in the service of God. In short, the jungle is preferable to the desert, but the catalog is best of all.

The objection to abundance is that the catalog will be disorderly, but this does not seem to me to be necessarily so given what I call the "exemplar-ity of the sample,"[24] for this refers to the possibility of generalizing about individuals on the basis of considering them precisely as samples. By way of criticism of this view, it can always be argued that, when we take something as a sample of a class, we select certain features of it and not others: if we use an oblong of material as a sample of the material that we want to cover the divan, then we are assuming that the exemplarity refers tot he material and not the oblong shape of the sample.[25] But I am sincerely puzzled at how this can be an objection to the exemplarity of the sample. If, faced with a sample of material, someone thinks that its shape or its size is important rather than the weave or the pattern, then either he is living in a different culture from ours or he is being to say the least bizarre; for philosophical theories should not be built on limiting cases, at most objections can be so constructed, to which, as in this case, we can make counterobjections.

When I recognize an individual as a sample, I grasp features of it that can be generalized to other individuals. But the most interesting thing here is that there is not a priori operation that precedes the sample, but rather a judgment that can be formulated on the basis of the existence of a concrete individual. Consider artworks that can become "canonical," which is to say exemplary, but only once they have made their concrete appearance in the world. Or technical inventions: the way in which they affect our lives, and hence their genuine function, could not preexist their concrete exemplification, and often enough it is the inventors themselves who are most surprised. Should we infer that truth is the daughter of time, that there are no nonempirical questions, that everything is relative or something of that sort? Not at all: Things embody their own intrinsic laws, which make them canonical or typical without thereby making them knowable a priori.

Insofar as it is contrasted with "determinative judgment," Kant's notion of "reflective judgment" seems to capture what we are after here. And it is a matter to which I return at length in 1.3.3.1, but what I want to stress here is that, while determinative judgment passes from the rule to the case, so that it is the universal that constructs the individual (starting with the notion of *substance*, I get, by way of a series of complicated and implausible mechanisms to be discussed in 2.1.1, to the mouse I have in my hand), in reflective judgment we have the passage from the individual (the case) to the general, even if not necessarily to the universal, because I am not certain that I have exhausted all the cases. Thus, starting with this single mouse, considered as a sample, I can rise to "mouse in general," which would then be the rule by which to distinguish mouses (rather than mice) from bars of soap or cell phones, even though those who think that a sample of material is exemplary of its shape can make a mistake also this time round.

We can see then that, within a sample, an individual that is at once a principle for generalizing, a case and a rule (consider the notion of a classic), but also a rule and an exception (consider the "sample" that is without commercial value because part of a sampler[26]), and sometimes even both real and idea (though it is unlikely that an example of a father is an exemplary father). This is how the examination of objects and their exemplarity opens up to us a wide variety of essences that are unimaginable in an ontology that admits only the two or three that come to mind when we shut ourselves up in a room to reason about how the world is constituted. We would do well to remember that the philosopher who retreats from the world begins by exemplifying what he has on his table, "this paper, this sheet, this fire," as Descartes said. And so do all of us.

1.1.5 Describe, Not Prescribe

Thus we come to the fourth rule: the aim of classification ought to be, so far as possible, rather a description than a prescription, thus realizing the ideal of a descriptive metaphysics[27] as opposed to a revisionary metaphysics that seeks to reform our conceptual schemes.[28] I do not see that descriptivism is necessarily a parochial or merely domestic choice.[29] What I envisage is a project parallel to that of ethnology. Indeed, both in ethnology and in a descriptive metaphysics we have to do with a distanced view: the ethnologist rediscovers Oedipus or Cinderella in Alaska or in the Mato Grosso, while the descriptive metaphysician throws light on the world that we inhabit and that, in virtue of being too close up, has become conceptually opaque to us. All that the philosopher has to add is reflective awareness, which is quite a different thing from being able to move at ease in the world. In this exercise, you come across a case and you look for the rule to which it refers or, more concretely, you find an object and you look for the shelf on which to put it, as if you were in a hardware store or a supermarket. This is done with the awareness that, exactly as happens in the supermarket, logical form or physical theories do not necessarily provide the right way to understand the world. Naturally, there can be cases in which a commonsense solution can, on inspection, turn out incoherent or unsatisfactory; in such cases, reflective awareness should either replace it or correct it in line with the revisionary project. But these are exceptions not the rule; in general, ontological Jacobins should be resisted on the grounds of the bizarre ideas that inspire them. And vice versa, many of the old solutions of common sense, even if not accepted outright, should be taken account of and checked out for their legitimacy, because they have been tried and tested by the usage of generations and generations rather than being thought up one afternoon in an armchair by a revisionary philosopher.

For sure, one might reasonably think that the metaphysician's job today should be to build up a theory informed by (and compatible with) the very knowledge of the foundations that is passed on from physical theories. In that case, bizarre ideas would be the price to be paid from constructing a general theory that tries to explain the status of things like oranges, chairs, and mortgages in a world of fermions, bosons, and so on. On the one hand, we might wonder whether fermions and bosons are the fundamental ontological level and oranges and chairs are mere appearances.[30] On the other hand, a pragmatic argument seems to me to be decisive here: Revision should come into play only once description has shown itself to be insufficient. For instance, we have excellent reasons for discussing anew the notions of the beginning and the end of life, of the family, of paternity and maternity, in the light of current biotechnology and of the controversies that it gives rise to. In these areas, it is not merely legitimate but desirable to proceed to revisions, given that the notions handed down by the tradition show themselves to be obviously lacking. It is obvious that these revisions should be conducted as far as possible in the light of current scientific knowledge and not by following prejudices that have only their antiquity to recommend them. But there is no reason to apply this sort of approach to the whole of our experience, even to the cases that do not appear problematic. In other words, just like the use of hermeneutics, the use of revisionary metaphysics is legitimate when it is local. In hermeneutics the rule "*in claris non fit interpretatio*" is utterly reasonable: only obscure expressions call for interpretation; but it is much less reasonable, as we will see in 2.1.2, to claim that there are no facts, but only interpretations. In the same way, it is utterly reasonable in ontology to say that, when some part of our experience appears problematic, it needs to be revised; but it is senseless to call for *everything* to be revised, otherwise, we would find ourselves faced with a nihilistic "there are no objects, but only revisions."

In the end, the mere fact that something turns out to be secondary or less fundamental in our classification of the world (granting for the sake of argument, as I suggested, that a fundamental level can be reached and justified) does not mean that the thing has to be rejected. Rather, it should be placed in its right position in a correct hierarchy. There very well may be ontologically secondary features that should not, on those grounds, be thrown out but rather put in their rightful place. If for no other reasons than that, in all probability, the idea of holding on to only the primary ontological properties is not that different from the idea of a life given over only to the essence, of someone who lives on a diet of masterpieces and eats only the most delicate dishes. Above all—just like Leibniz's Egyptian vases—old concepts can be taken up anew and put to new uses, being recovered, repaired, dusted off, and, for this very reason, renewed.[31]

1.1.6 Experience, Not Science

There remains the fifth rule: experience, not science. Descriptive metaphysics bears the inherently fragile burden of defending ordinary language. When Quine observed that ordinary language should not be considered sacrosanct,[32] J. L. Austin did well to reply that ordinary language should still have the first word.[33] In so doing, he was implicitly allowing that the final word should belong to someone else. Now, from the viewpoint of the catalog that I am proposing, this matter does not arise, because we are dealing with things, not with words, and with classifications, not with explanations. Against this background, it is not at all obvious that classification has to be responsible in the end to what science tells us.

As I said in the last section, it is an open question whether, even as regards physical objects, physics will supply the fundamental level of description, especially when the relation we enter into with these objects is not theoretical but rather pragmatic. Tomato juice is a case in point,[34] a typical example of those "moderate-sized specimens of dry goods" to which Austin drew attention as the paradigmatic physical objects for common sense.[35] Some years ago, tomato juice disappeared, or seemed to, from the supermarkets. It could not longer be found where it had usually been displayed, along with fruit juices. This was a fairly intuitive, if not overly precise classification (are tomatoes really fruit in the same way that apples and pears are?), which corresponded to the principles of merceology (the science of marketing goods) if not of mereology (the science of the part-whole relation) or of botany, but it was underpinned at least by a certain tradition. So I went looking for it on the shelves given over to prepared pasta sauces. In doing so, I was reasoning like a physicist or a chemist: The molecules are the same, so the tomato juice should be there. No dice. I gave up looking. So I ordered it at the bar, but there I obviously couldn't ask the barman, "Where do you find tomato juice?," because the reply would have been, "At the wholesaler's." Then, after I had given up all hope, I found the tomato juice by chance. It was alongside the aperitifs, which does not correspond at all to the way we encounter the physical world, given that tomato juice is not an alcoholic beverage, unlike most aperitifs. So what did it respond to? After a bit of thought, I reckoned that the classification was dictated by the ends that the products served, their use or their context—philosophers might say that the classification was teleological. Granting the anecdote, we may try to draw some lessons from it, which will be developed in Chapter 2.3.

The tomato juice was neither an artwork nor a moral act, which are traditionally territories that the sciences have no grip on. Nor, within my search, did it give me pleasure or displeasure, or contribute to my moral action, because, in the end, I was just looking for a physical object—to wit, a can of tomato juice. Once found, it would surely have given me an interested physical pleasure insofar as it satisfied a heteronomous desire and, so, did not fulfill the requirements either of esthetics or of ethics, as Kant understood them. As already pointed out, in looking for the disappeared juice among the pasta sauces, I was reasoning like a baby chemist, allowing myself to be guided by the sameness of the tomato molecules in the juices and in the sauces, and thus falling victim to the transcendental fallacy that I discuss in 2.1. The teleological classification was not guided in the least by science, but it does not at all seem to be the sort of superstition that will sooner or later be swept away by the progress of the human spirit, even though it might be set at naught by a change in culinary fashion.

Let me hazard a prediction. The discrepancies between these various approaches will not lessen with the passage of time, nor will they disappear. On the contrary, they will probably grow. I say so because, over the last two centuries, this is just what has been happening: There has been an increasing rift between ontology and epistemology that has not involved an increase in superstition, but rather a growing awareness of the differences that previously, in a more primitive state of the sciences, did not stand out so clearly. In summary, if no one in the eighteenth century thought of constructing the sciences of the spirit (*Geisteswissenschaften*) or the phenomenology of perception, it was because, in the end, a physics like Newton's gave a satisfactory account of the phenomena of the ecological world. Today, we know more about the limits of that science because Newtonian mechanics provides exact predictions only for cases in which the velocities are not too high and the bodies are macroscopic. It does not hold for velocities close to that of light (where relativistic mechanics applies) or for subatomic particles (where it has been replaced by quantum mechanics). Today, therefore, we know something that Newton did not about the fundamental level for describing the world, namely that the laws of our experience are limited both in space and in time. Against the last remaining reductionist, this does not at all mean a transcription of the whole world of experience into the terms of fundamental physics, because it is obvious that supermarkets (and the rest of our traffic with the world) cannot be organized on the basis of quantum physics. Rather, today even more than in the eighteenth century, it offers an argument in favor of the renewed need for catalogs. Let us then proceed to our list, beginning with the highly valued samples that are subjects.

1.2 SUBJECTS

1.2.1 Representations

I am sorry to say so, but there is not much to be said about subjects. They are not the origin of the world, or the I-think that is the proprietor of the universe, or anything of that sort. They are individuals whose prime characteristic is to have a central nervous system that is sophisticated enough to capture and fix representations. Crudely, I have a representation of the table, but the table does not have a representation of me, nor indeed do mirrors or cameras, which bear reflections or impressions but not "representations."

This state of affairs is crucial. Having representations is necessary for acting and thinking, which are the characteristics generally attributed to subjects. That is to say, every action with a view to something or other presupposes the ability to represent the objective of the action; but representing is also the basis of thinking and of having feelings, hopes, and suffering, which are all characteristic of human being (and some animals) and not of things.[36] Thinking is always thinking of something, a something that, within the mind of the thinker, has what philosophers call *intensional existence*[37]— which we may also express by saying that it exists as a representation. The same holds also for desire, fear, love, hate, and the whole gamut of feelings that call for images. In this respect, representations are the causes of desires and states of mind (with the possible exceptions of depression, anguish, and boredom), and should not be confused with them given that, if they were identical, there would be no difference between representing happiness and being happy, between representing pain and feeling pain.

A crucial consequence of having representations is that two subjects can enter into reciprocal relations in a way that is not possible between two objects or between a subject and an object. If I look at the table, I do not suppose that it will look at me; nor do I really think that when I plug my memory stick into the computer there is an exchange of representations. I do not feel looked at by CCTV cameras, but rather by the security staff behind them, and if I am afraid of being recorded, it is because I suspect that sooner or later there will be someone who will look at or listen to the recording. On the other hand, if I look at a monkey at the zoo, it can happen that our looks meet; and this is even more normal among people, and what happens when I meet the gaze of a monkey or of a driver who does not want to give way even though I am on the pedestrian crossing is not merely that I see the monkey or the driver but that the monkey or the driver sees me. This "seeing" can take on all sorts of meanings, and in the end it can become that sort of highly aware representation that we call *consciousness*; but at the very root of it there is in any case the possibility, which is exclusive to subjects, of having representations.

From this it follows that, even if we can have feelings toward objects, the feeling we have cannot require reciprocity, which is to say feelings that call on me not merely to represent an object but to represent a subject.[38] For instance, if the ATM wishes me a happy birthday at the end an operation, I might feel a certain unease, not because I think that the ATM is wishing me a happy birthday, but rather because I reflect on how much the people in the bank know about me and how they are keeping tabs on me. Likewise, it would be very odd if, at the tollbooth, someone were to reply to the machine's saying, "Thank you, and see you again soon" (and it would be odder still if someone were to point out that, given that it does not have eyes, it should not talk about "seeing" at all). Even when they have scanners and cameras, objects are blind.

It also seems obvious that, on their own, representations are not enough to define what a subject is; that is to say, they are a necessary but not a sufficient condition. The crippled orphan child who cannot speak and who is one of the saddest and most tragic figures in Primo Levi's book *If This Is a Man* surely has representations, but it is hard to say that he is a subject in the full juridical sense—suffice it to think of formulae like "able to intend and to wish" or "in full possession of my faculties." For a natural object to become a subject endowed with representations requires, as I argue at length in 4.1.2, a system of inscriptions that transforms a natural being into a social being. From this perspective, a subject is constitutively a social being; it is, so to say, a Hegelian subject whose development is manifested in a phenomenology of the spirit rather than a Cartesian subject which, as Descartes himself would have been the first to admit, though not everyone has noticed, is nothing but a methodological abstraction (his isolation is a spiritual exercise and not a rule for living). The relation with the mother, the mirror stage, and the entry into language are just so many phases in the constitution of subjectivity. Granted, subjects can have monological functions that, as we shall see shortly, constitute some rather shadowy objects, such as thoughts and imaginings, but that do not constitute social objects precisely because they are merely motions that take place in the heads of single individuals. The thought "I want a divorce" certainly has a social dimension, because divorce exists only in a society; but the thought is not a social object until it is expressed to someone who has the appropriate rights and duties.

Psychic objects. At this point someone might ask whether we can find a place in our catalog of the world for psychic objects, by which I mean those objects that exist in the mind of just one person. On the one hand, there is no doubt that we can, given that they are objects endowed with a certain thickness in virtue of being inscribed in a mind, in the forms that I make clear in 4.2.3. On the other hand, as long as they remain in the mind of a single person, they can easily be removed or altered, either consciously or not. To be sure, it might be objected that there are many thoughts that, even before they are made public, are in some measure not subject to the will; for instance, phenomena such as psychoses, phantom limbs, and hallucinations (which take on objective form in the ontologies of films like *A Beautiful Mind* and *Fight Club*), but also, less elaborately, traumas, guilt feelings, pangs of remorse, desires and fears, and so on. Even though people would happily do without some of these psychic states, they have to put up with them and sometimes take them to the grave without ever communicating them to anyone; often enough, the omniscient narrators of novels treat secret thoughts of this sort as having objective existence. Then we should bear in mind states of mind such as jealousy or unhappiness. While admiration, suffering, and happiness can be known only when they are made public, the epistemological fact of their being made known should not be confused with the ontological fact of their existence: The expression of envy is not envy; the interpretation of a dream is not a dream; and the behavior of a mental defective is not itself a juridical impediment, otherwise courts of law would have to grant exemptions to actors who are known to be sane.

In some cases, psychic objects of the sort we are discussing can take on all the properties of a text. There is no doubt that the poem "March 1821," which Alessandro Manzoni composed in honor of the liberal rebellions, but that he destroyed and conserved only in his memory out of fear of the police, was an object, but it depended entirely on a single subject: If Manzoni had died without ever writing it out, it would no longer have existed. Conversely, the books that are committed to the memories of individuals in *Fahrenheit 451* are, so to speak, objects that have been privatized and, for the time being, transformed into subjective memories; in that condition, their existence is much more fragile because dependent on what happens to the subjects in question. This point applies all the more to those thoughts that have never been expressed in writing. In such cases, the subject is, in the end, omnipotent in regard to the mental object, and is so all the more because he is weak and subject to mystifications and to self-deception. And even when a subject believes that he is put upon by a thought, as in cases of obsession, he is nevertheless its owner: If the subject disappears, so does the obsession or the hallucination. This is not how things stand with objects in the narrow sense, which exist both before and after us and, at least as regards many of their features, independently of us. This is why, on the scheme proposed earlier in this chapter, the items placed on the left-hand side are not objects, but rather properties of subjects. There are not really perceptions, representations, or memories in the world, but only subjects that have perceptions, apperceptions, memories, fantasies, and thoughts, which become objects only when they are expressed and are inscribed in the world. Let us look briefly at this phenomenology of the spirit, regarding the representations that pass through our minds, and whose genuine realization will be found in the phenomenology of the letter, which I will set out in 5.3.

1.2.2 Perceptions and Apperceptions

I divide representations into perceptions and apperceptions. The former are not present to consciousness, while the latter are, so I shall call perceptions *presentations* and reserve the term *representations* in the technical sense for only those apperceptions that are accompanied by consciousness, as I shall clarify shortly. Insofar as they are peculiar to subjects, representations are *psychisms*, a term by which I mean everything that, at least in the first instance, would seem to be inside the head of a person without leaving it. In the case of vague thoughts, we have something that cannot by rights be an object because it lacks any sort of constancy. In that of clear and distinct thoughts, what we have are representations situated in the mind of a person, even if, on contingent grounds, they happen not to get expressed.

Perception, then, is any kind of presentation, even a vague one, and not accompanied by consciousness: the dreary unease that precedes a toothache, a noise below the attention threshold, and vision at the corner of the eye. These are impoverished phenomena, which nevertheless call for a subjectivity as their bearer. On the other hand, *apperception* is any presentation accompanied by consciousness: the full-frontal toothache, the car alarm that stops me sleeping, the photograph I am looking at on the front page of the newspaper. Perhaps *consciousness* is too fancy a word.[39] We might equally well speak of *attention*, which can be more or less fluctuating. In any case, it might be wondered if and when it is right to speak of *consciousness* in apperception, and I believe that the safest criterion is that of recoverability: if I can repeat a certain image with a certain degree of clarity, then I can represent it—and in such cases, we have to do with *representations* in the etymological sense (*re-ad-praesentare*, to make present anew).

As I have said, all apperception has a conscious element, even if this is not necessarily a voluntary element. From the point of view of what happens in the subject, apperception can be subdivided into three constituents: the *act*, or the individual process; the *content*, of the idiomatic representation of the particular mod in which the object of apperception presents itself; and the *object*, or the common referent. I shall clarify this tripartition,[40] which has a certain importance for the subject of this book. The act is the psychological process by which we think of a thing, such as a dog; the content is the individual representation that each person forms in his or her mind as a result of the act (one person will have thought of a poodle, another a bulldog or a German shepherd standing, sitting still, or running, and so on); the object is the element that is in common and to which we all refer when we say "dog," and therefore is distinct from the individual contents. This object stays the same despite the variation of the intrasubjective representations (today I think of a white dog, tomorrow a black one, but it is still a dog I am referring to), and it is, so to say, exportable in intersubjective form (I say "dog" and one person represents a "white dog" and another "black dog," but both are thinking of a dog). This is how it takes on objective value.

Thus, on the theory I am proposing, the object in the primary sense is external and, at a first approximation, can be concrete or abstract (natural or ideal). In particular, social objects have among their necessary conditions the existence of subjects endowed with the capacity for representations that are at least complex enough to be described in terms of the distinction among act, content, and object. In such cases, there are two main stages in the process whereby we depsychologize, and hence stabilize, the object. The first is constituted of fantasies, memories, and thoughts, where the object is progressively fixed within the subject; the second is that of expression, in which the object being thought of is manifested on the outside and becomes a shared object.

1.2.3 *Fantasies, Memories, and Thoughts*

At the outset, the object is so fluctuating that it can very often be identified with the content, which is to say with my own idiomatic representation. If I tell someone that I have imagined or dreamed about Ghirardelli Square in San Francisco, it makes little sense to query whether it was really Ghirardelli Square and not some other square that looks very much like it. Things are different if I say that I *remember* that there is an obelisk in Ghirardelli Square. In that case, it is quite legitimate to ask whether I am not mixing it up with some other square, such as the Place Vendôme or the Piazza del Popolo. For in memory, the idiomatic side, which is precisely the subjective representation, demands a correspondence with the object; this in why, unlike a fantasy, a memory can be false. All the more so in the case of a thought, which can be defined as a representation accompanied by a judgment: a thought that is neither true nor false is an experimental abstraction that lacks the concreteness of what we call *thought*. In thought, then, there is an essential relation with the object and with the truths about it. Yet, as we shall see, thought is liberated from its subjective bearer and takes on genuine objectivity only when it is expressed externally.

Fantasies are vague images, and above all images that do not require anything actually existing outside the head. On the whole, many fantasies pass through our heads that are inconstant and that often change direction following what is rightly called the *stream of consciousness*, given that we are aware of what is going on in our heads but we are unable (and not particularly concerned) to stabilize the succession of the phantasmagoria. The most evanescent of all fantasies is the sort that I propose to call *shadows*,[41] a sort of mental analogue of motes in the eye. It is hard to say that these fantasies are objects precisely because it is not easy to be sure that we are referring to them, and there is a sort of flattening of the object into its content in such a way that a shadow is a weak object. They are such stuff as dreams are made if: confused and mutable desires, sketches of thoughts, images that go round in our minds when we are listening to a boring lecture, or when we are awake before alarm and we can stay for a while aimlessly in bed. The vagueness of these psychisms can be seen from the way that, if someone asked what we were thinking and we replied that we did not know, the reply would be sincere, and not an attempt to hide our thoughts.

Memories, on the other hand, are representations that we can repeat and that, if we want to split hairs,[42] can be divided into rememberings (representations that repeat themselves without an effort of will on our part) and reminiscences (that we have to look for with the will and that we can if need be fix with mnemonic tricks). Though I drew a distinction between fantasies and memories, in that the former can be neither true nor false, while the latter can (at least as regards their adequacy or exactitude), I have decided to treat them together for a reason that is well founded in the philosophical tradition, namely the way that the imagination is the free reelaboration of memory traces and is thus closely related, as a matter of their genesis, to remembering.[43] As I just noted, imagination is when something goes round in our minds, especially as regards the future. On the way to a dinner, we fantasize about how splendid a figure we will cut; at the end of the evening, coming down the stairs, we imagine a memorable quip we could have made. Thus we might say that imagination is a memory that intentionally modifies the past but that, more often, is forward-looking: the traces of the past (to which I will return at greater length in 4.3.1) become traces of the future, rather as we speak of the notes for what we will say tomorrow are the trace of a speech. Recalling last summer's holiday and planning next summer's are functions that are not so different one from the other, so much so that, after a while, the memory takes on a pinkish tinge, becomes fuzzy and sweeter.

This then is why imagination turns out to be a close relation of memory. In themselves, the two functions can hardly be differentiated and it is the outside world that determines whether what we have is an imagining or a truthful memory. Unless, of course, we have set ourselves deliberately to imagining something. Even here we can encounter a symmetrical phenomenon, which often afflicts involuntary plagiarists (we thought we were creating something, but in reality we were remembering), but at least from our point of view, the film that runs in our minds really is a work of the imagination. We could put it in the credits at the end of the film to avoid misunderstanding and lawsuits. As regards creators, theirs is only a dilated and compound memory that celebrates illicit marriages among things; this is no small matter, though the discovery of it may be disappointing. After all, when we are criticized for having limited imagination, the criticism is different from that of having limited memory. It is easy to respond to the latter, "What can I do about it?" But it seems that someone can always, with a bit of good will, make an effort to have some imagination. If we observe creators, or at least creative types, we discover that getting the imagination to work is generally a matter of ransacking archives, quoting, recovering, setting things out a bit differently.

So much for imagination and memory. If fantasies are representations that are neither true nor false and that face the future, thoughts are representations that aspire to be true, even though they are not always concerned with the past, as memories are.[44] For a thought to count as an object, then, it must be distinguished from the mere psychological act of thinking, and from the specific manifestation that this act can take on in the mind of an individual. It is nevertheless a fact that, considered as such, a thought presents itself as something that points outside the subject. By means of simple psychological introspection, I know that the act is in my mind, as is its content. This is not how things stand with the object. This holds literally for natural and ideal objects, given that Mont Blanc and the equilateral triangle are not merely in my mind. It is rather different in the case of social objects, which go beyond their purely psychological dimension and enter into the realm of genuine objects only by being expressed.

1.2.4 Expressions and Inscriptions

Expressions and inscriptions transform thoughts into objects. At the beginning of Italo Svevo's *Confessions of Zeno*, the main character writes on the wall of his room his solemn resolution, appropriately dated, to give up smoking. An individual resolution seems to become stronger when it is transferred onto the medium of an external writing, even if, in the case in hand, it might be suspected that Zeno writes his vow down so as to offload his conscience and to lighten the weight of maintaining it. Conversely, it seems that Napoleon had the habit of writing his reminders to himself down on pieces of paper that he then threw away: it was the act of writing and the visualization of the paper that fixed the memory, which no longer stood in need of an external medium. We return to consider at length the correspondence between writing and the mind in 4.2.3. For now, I would like to stress this point: sometimes something that has been thought is expressed and is said to another person; it is only when this happens, hoping that the person is listening attentively and has understood, that the thought becomes a *genuine* object, which is to say no longer at the exclusive whim of the subject. He can take back what he has said, of course, or claim to have been misunderstood—but this would always be relative to an object that is by now out there, with an ontological status quite different from what it had so long as it remained within the perimeter of the subject. It is for this reason that we say that he is "eating" his words: They have become an object, and a word spoken is always potentially a word given to someone else.[45] This holds good for judgments, which is to say for the linguistic acts that most philosophers have regarded as being thoughts in the full sense (how can we be sure, without an expression, that the thought remains the same or that it is true?), but it takes on a special importance for orders and performatives ("I pronounce you doctor in philosophy," "You are under arrest"), which I discuss at more length in 2.3.2.2: an order or a promise that is merely thought is not an order or a promise, but merely resembles one.

Let us look more closely at the difference between, on the one hand, natural and ideal objects and, on the other, social objects, which I discuss in detail in the next chapter. As regards the first two, which have their existence independently of subjects, it is not necessary for them to be thought for them to exist. Mont Blanc and the equilateral triangle exist even without thoughts that refer to them. On the other hand, a promise, a bet, a federal state, a football team, or an epic poem bear two essential characteristics: They do not exist unless someone thinks of them, and they begin to exist only when they exit from the mind of one person, are made manifest, and are then inscribed in the external world, in line with the law "Object = Inscribed Act," which is set out in full in the course of the book as a whole. It is thus not surprising that oral, written, or merely gestural expression is so important in the constitution of social objects. There is a crucial difference between: (1) thinking of declaring war, of getting married, of promising, or of buying something; and (2) saying (writing, meaning on the outside) that war is declared, that one is married, that one promises, that one is buying; in (2) there is an expression and, unlike (1), there is an object in the world, because it does not depend only on the subject. In (1) we have a movement of the soul, which can be as vague, fleeting and insubstantial as can be; in (2)—and it is easy to understand why it makes so much difference to us—we already have a shared object, one whose existence does not depend only on one or other of us.

It is hard to overemphasize the importance of this point. It is easy to say that something is easier said than done. But we are prone to forget that sometimes saying *is* doing. And we are even more prone to forget that something is easier thought than said (or written, or communicated by whatever means, even the click of a mouse to make a purchase online). It is precisely this situation, of what happens when what was merely thought enters into the world, that Hegel captured with his notion of "objective spirit," the spirit that is manifested and made concrete in institutions, and that, for the purposes of this book's argument, I conceive of as the role of the letter and the inscription in the constitution of consciousness and of the human world.

Let us put the matter in Hegelian terms, then. Everything begins with the soul that feels, and the first element of the spirit to emerge is the imagination and then memory, which frees perception from the here and now in which it finds itself in the world, transforming it into something more spiritual because freer. It is at this point that within the soul there unfurls a phantasmagoria of images, which is what makes Hegel say that, in the eye of man can be seen the night of the world,[46] one of those Gothic turns of phrase that have turned the commentators on. The real leap is made when these images of a fluctuating world turn into language, which gives them stability and makes them available for communication on the outside. How often does it happen that the verbalization of our states of mind allows us to discover what they are, even when that comes out as an expression such as, "I can't put up with that," not to mention the greater stability and explicitness that come when it is fixed in writing. When some fixing has been brought about, though, even if it is only in the head of an interlocutor or witness, what we have is no longer the property of a subject. It has become an object.

This is why we cannot live without bureaucracy, without paperwork or inscriptions, even if we do not always notice the fact. While it is straightforward enough that a promise that is not made to someone is not a promise, it seems less straightforward that a promise that is not registered (at least in the minds of the promiser and of the promisee) is not a promise. Or, at least, this is a point that philosophers have paid little attention to, given that the common practice of drawing up documents and of sayings such as *verba volant, scripta manent* are signs of how this principle is at work in everyday life. Expressions would lose their objectivity and would regress to the status of fantasies were they not registered; and if it is true that there is no entity without identity, which is to say that it is part of an object's objectivity that it is identical with itself then it is equally true that it is part of an object's identity that that identity can be repeated, namely that it is written, in line with what I say in 1.3.2.2. A merely psychological event that is not communicated to anyone, such as a desire I had five minutes ago or the dream I had the other night, is too unstable to count as an object; I could convince myself that I did not have that desire or involuntarily change the dream in my memory. Spirit would regress into nothingness, as when a man dies leaving no documents regarding himself.[47] If this is how things stand (and it is the intuition underlying the whole book) the letter constitutes the possibility from which the spirit begins and in which it takes its ultimate refuge. By that I mean, as I will set out in 5.3, the phenomenology of the spirit is the phenomenology of the letter, of the very basis on which the social world is founded and that makes intentions possible.

1.3 OBJECTS

When an expression creates a thought and brings it into the world, we have a social object, which depends on the subjects from which it arises and to which it is directed. Within the world there are other objects that have nothing to do with subjects. These are natural objects. Last, outside the world there are yet other objects, likewise independent of subjects—namely, ideal objects. All objects have two features in common. In the first place, as we have seen, they do not, unlike subjects, have representations; in the second place, they can be for more than one person, and in this they are unlike thoughts, which can be for just one person.

What I suggest,[48] then, is that we repopulate Kant's ontology, which is limited to only natural objects, and thin out Meinong's jungle by distinguishing three types of objects: *Natural objects*, which occupy positions in space and in time and do not depend on subjects; *ideal objects*, which do not occupy any position either in space or in time and do not depend on subjects; and, last but not least, *social objects*, which do occupy a positions in space and in time and do depend on subjects, though they are not themselves subjective. A word is called for on space and time. It is only for ease of exposition that I say that natural and social objects are in space and time and that ideal objects are outside them. This formulation has a Kantian flavor to it and might lead one to think of there being two pure forms of intuition and, in the long run, of the absorption of objects inside subjects, as happens in Kant. To be more precise, we should say that natural and social objects are spatiotemporal, while ideal ones are not; but I suspect that this would be less clear, so I restrict myself to the observation to allay misunderstanding.

The introduction of social objects involves favoring a realism according to which taxes and promises are real things. Social objects, such as marriages and academic degrees, occupy a modest portion of space—roughly the extent taken up by a document[49]—and an amount of time that can be longer or shorter, but never infinite. Unlike ideal objects, social objects seem to tend towards their own ending: while the Pythagorean theorem has its meaning because precisely because it is eternal, a bill of exchange has its for precisely the opposite reason, namely that it will become due sooner or later—even if there can obviously be social objects, such as the Holy Roman Empire or the Egyptian dynasties, that last much longer than the life of any individual. Thus social objects seem to be placed halfway between the materiality of natural objects and the immateriality of ideal objects. As I explain in 3.3, social objects consist of a medium and an inscription; but the predominant role is played by the inscription, given the way that (as we see with money or a document), for a given documental value, the medium can be metal, paper, plastic, or silicon.

What I want to stress in the second place, both to explain why philosophers and ordinary people have been so slow to discover social objects and to bring to light their most singular feature, is this: *Unlike natural and ideal objects, social objects exist only insofar as people think that they do.* Without human beings, mountains would stay as they are, and numbers would continue to have the properties they do, but it would make no sense to talk of offenses and mortgages, of viscounts or corporals, of artworks or pornographic material. As I hinted earlier, this singularity has led to a widespread conceptual misunderstanding, namely the idea that social objects are entirely relative, or that they are a mere manifestation of the will. In this way, what is denied is that social objects are objects, and they are reduced either to something that is endlessly interpretable or to a mere psychological event. But this is clearly not so, and everyday life provides countless examples. When a word is expressed and registered, it becomes a thing, a social object that can weigh very heavily: A promise exists even when I am not thinking about it, and I cannot change the terms of my mortgage by a mere act of the will, even though I can do something about it by means of a social action, namely by other documents and expressions.

1.3.1 *Natural Objects*

1.3.1.1 *EIDE*, MORPHIC UNITIES, AND AGGREGATES   I do not have an original theory about natural objects and restrict myself to adopting, with slight amendments, the classification proposed by the realist phenomenologist Dietrich von Hildebrand.[50] This view seems to be a fair middle way between an ecological or pragmatic classification, to which it could be objected that it does not do justice to the assumption that natural objects are independent of subjects, and a physical or biological classification, to which it might be rightly objected that it falls on epistemological rather than ontological criteria. In Hildebrand's taxonomy, natural objects are divided into *eide*, morphic unities, and aggregates.

Eide are endowed with an intrinsic and necessary unity that we can grasp immediately: A drop of water is an *eidos*, as are a grain of wheat, a grain of sand, and a flake of snow. *Eide* are the ontological counterpart of what the elements are in epistemology, namely the substances that cannot be broken down into simpler parts by any chemical transformation. In light of the distinction between ontology and epistemology, we can see the notion of an *element* is rather epistemological than ontological, given that we rarely meet elements in ordinary experience. On the other hand, we sometimes do have to do with *eide*, as when we see raindrops falling on the windscreen or when a grain of sand is irritating our eye.

Morphic unities are endowed with intrinsic unity, but this unity is contingent: The tail is part of the cat, but we can easily imagine a cat without a tail, while half a grain of sand is still a grain of sand and half a raindrop is still a raindrop. Typically, organisms (animals and plants) that make up an important part of the world of natural objects are morphic unities.

Last, *aggregates* are those mostly inanimate natural objects with which we have most traffic. In Hildebrand's view, aggregates possess a unity that is both extrinsic and contingent and is generally imposed by knowing subjects, and they are things such as flocks, forests, and heaps. Without exaggerating the role of the knowing subject, which does not create flocks, forests, or heaps, because they are very different things, for instance, from football teams, we should not forget that the sphere of aggregates involves the subject's agency, which is not epistemological (it is not science that tells us what a flock, a forest, or a heap is). Nor is this dependence of the kind we find in social objects. Rather, aggregates depend on subjects if certain of their properties, which they have independently of subjects, allow them to be used as unities. If, on the one hand, their unity conditions include objective characteristics, such as connectedness and continuity among the parts, on the other, there are reasons of ecological adaptation that mean that we and a mouse experience the unity of a heap of stones that is a house differently. The mouse experiences the unity of this heap much as we do the unity of a forest we are walking through, in terms of the uniformity of the environment, and the same goes for a woodworm and a piece of furniture.

And that is all. That I say so little about natural objects follows as a matter of course from the fact that I do not have much to say about them. I am neither a physicist nor a biologist, and natural objects are of account in my ontology in the first instance insofar as they play a role, as socialized objects, within the world of human beings (for instance, when those objects raise questions of a bioethical nature). Nevertheless, getting clear about the features of one class of objects that exist in time and space independently of subjects is, along with the distinction between ontology and epistemology, a necessary and preliminary condition for setting up the problem of social objects. This point will become clearer when I set out, in 2.2.1.1, the notion of *unemendability*. If there were no objects external to our conceptual schemes and resistant to their action, then we would run into serious difficulties both in grasping the essence of social objects (which appear to be more dependent on conceptual schemes) and in understanding science as the search for truth—and not as a play of conceptual schemes.

1.3.1.2 PHYSICAL OBJECTS AND NATURAL OBJECTS Before moving on to ideal objects, I would like to make a few points about natural objects. To begin with, I called these objects *physical objects*, but then I took account of the ways that chairs and tractors, and artifacts in general, are physical objects even thought their coming to be depends on subjects. The realm of natural objects seems to me less ambiguous, even though it still raises a few problems, which it is worth setting out and discussing.

Socialized objects. The first is this: On the one hand, a chair seems to have many more properties in common with a tree than it does with a check, even though it belongs (in a broad sense as we shall see) with social objects. To avoid this paradox, I propose to consider artifacts, which I discuss at greater length in 1.3.3.3, a mixed form between natural and social objects; like natural objects, they exist as merely physical objects whether we think of them or not; like social objects, they have human intentionality at their origin. Chairs, like passports but unlike equinoxes, originate in human agents. In some cases they can take on a high social charge, if, for instance, the chair is a throne. If the whole of humanity disappeared, though, the throne (the social function) would disappear, but the chair would not. Likewise, Robinson Crusoe could make himself a chair and a table, but not a passport or, for obvious reasons (at least until he meets Man Friday), a throne or a professorial chair. It makes sense to ask whether a seat that Robinson uses is a genuine social object. In a strict sense, it is not, because a society exists only when there are at least two people. But I want to be fair to Robinson, who grew up in a social world and retains the memory of it, so that he would not appreciate owning totally useless banknotes, but he would not disdain being able to hear some music on an iPod so long as the batteries lasted. It remains to be asked whether a dog's bone, a cat's ball of wool or a hermit's secret diary are social objects. As to the misanthrope's diary, I would have no doubts because, as I explain in 4.3, every inscription is by definition a social object. As to the bone or the ball of wool, I might have to think about it, but the matter does not seem to be urgent.

Still regarding the differentiation between social and natural objects, it might be noted that shipping lanes or air routes, and indeed the oceans themselves, considered as geographical entities, are portions of natural space that have a precise social role. To this I respond that the institutional fact of giving a name to a region of sea or of setting up rules about how a part of it may be crossed should not be confused with the brute fact, independent of any society or subject, of the existence of a larger or smaller region of sea. Furthermore, there have been attempts of late to impose copyright on natural kinds, such as water or certain medicinal plants. This is an institutionalization of natural objects that is similar to the action whereby, in using a stone as a paperweight, it is thereby socialized and transformed into furniture; but the internal properties, as much of the stone as of the water or the medicinal plants, remain unchanged. For air routes and paperweights just as for chairs, then, I propose to speak of *socialized objects*.

What is "nature"? Other problems arise specifically about the class of natural objects as such. A first point regards the notion of "nature" that lies behind the definition of "natural objects." Is it not, after all, an epistemological notion (in the sense of a "justified belief" that I clarify in 2.1.0), deriving from what we know and hence subject to change over time in line with our knowledge? In light of this obvious consideration, not only is the *physis* of the Greeks very different from what we call "nature," but leprechauns are entities of nature for the ancient Irish (who had beliefs about leprechauns that were at least justified by popular tradition and legend), whereas for us they are social objects (given that our modern justified beliefs exclude the existence of leprechauns). I do not think this objection is, in the end, any more decisive or destructive than that concerning shipping lanes, and the response can be the same: Ponds exist and are part of nature, as much for the ancient Irish as for us. If the ancient Irish then put leprechauns next to the ponds, that is not the fault of the notion of "nature"; they simply made a mistake, as we all do from time to time.

Phenomena and things. A third objection that might be made regards the distinction between phenomena and things. After all, we might notice that even a reflection is in space and time independently of subjects, and that therefore, we have to bring in extra specification so as to narrow down the class of natural objects so as to distinguish them, for instance, from rainbows. Fortunately, such specifications exist and have classically been recognized by philosophers.[51] A natural object, insofar as it is physical, is an X endowed with three-dimensional existence (if it had only two dimensions, we would think of it as an image); it is coherent, or all stuck together (my arm is an object only with my body, unless it is cut off; in which case, there are two objects); it is individualized (I am able to distinguish it from its background: a green spot in a meadow is not a thing, but a clover plant is); and it is persistent, that is, it lasts at least some time.

It might be objected that a quark does not answer to this description, which is rather ecological than physical in the narrow sense. I agree entirely. Indeed,

I am not aiming to give a scientific description of the world, but rather a classification of the things we have to do with in ordinary experience. I get clearer about the reasons for this choice in Chapter 2, but the point in brief is this: The fact that natural objects, just like ideal ones, exist independently of subjects, and hence of the theories that subjects may formulate, prompts us to mark the distinction between ontology (what there is) and epistemology (the set of our justified beliefs about what there is).

1.3.2 Ideal Objects

Thus we come to the second class of objects, ideal objects, which exist outside time and space independently of subjects. Their prime features are *individuation*, their being capable of being recognized as such, their having an identity distinct from that of other objects; and *eternity*, their not having a beginning or an end in time. My underlying reason for isolating the sphere of ideal objects is classical.[52] We have to allow that ideal objects exist, distinct from our thoughts considered as psychological acts, otherwise we would not see how we could have common objects of thought. I would add to this way of putting the matter that, like Plato's Ideas, ideal objects do not have even an occasional origin in our thoughts; not only do they constitute the invariant content of our thoughts, but they would exist even if humankind had never existed, or indeed if the world or even one physical object had never existed. I am aware that this conception of ideal objects is anything but universally accepted, and that, together with the variety of meanings given to "idea" (as independent objective reality, as dependent psychological construct, as teleological ideal), that fact makes it hard to recognize the realm of ideal objects, but I hope that the following sketch will help to clarify.

1.3.2.1 SIMPLES, COMPOSITES, RELATIONS   In the catalog I am proposing, ideal objects can be subdivided into simples, composites, and relations. *Simples* are those ideal objects that have no parts: the point and zero. *Composites* are those ideal objects that do have parts and can thus be represented as constructions: lines, surfaces, numbers, propositions, and operations. *Relations* are ideal relations that hold among ideal and nonideal objects: the fact that the world is bigger than a table; that there is a window to my left; that $4 > 3$; and so on. These are spurious ideal objects because they depend on states of affairs and they are not simple because they relate to states of affairs.

Ideal objects are distinct from psychological acts and contents as well as from linguistic and social acts. If a person discovers a theorem or a relation, it is like discovering a continent, something that exists independently of him and that, in its very nature, could have been discovered by anyone else, so long as they had the necessary intellectual instruments. As regards linguistic and social acts, Derrida was misled into thinking that communication and writing are necessary for the constitution of ideal reality.[53] The fact of the matter is, as already suggested, that the ideal objectivities are not constituted but found; if anything, what is constituted is the *socialization* of ideal objects; but in that case, I am simply referring to the properties of social objects that reflect the law Object = Inscribed Act, and to which we return at length in Chapter 3 of the book.

1.3.2.2 PLATONISM AND CONSTRUCTIONISM   As already indicated, my Platonist vision of ideal objects is by no means the default view. In particular, there is broad and solid tradition of constructionism in mathematical thought. And it would seem altogether reasonable to argue as follows. We can admit that objects like the natural numbers or the Pythagorean theorem are so familiar that we have no problem regarding them as existing independently of their discoverers, but when we get to Goldbach's conjecture, Cantor's transfinite cardinals, Dedekind's cut, or the proof of Fermat's last theorem, we are dealing with very peculiar entities, for which it is hard to conceive of an existence outside their theoretical framework and separated from pragmatic contingencies: their discovery looks suspiciously like a creation. What should we say of Newton's laws, Maxwell's equations, or Einstein's relativity? Are they ideal objects or social ones? One might say that they are social objects that tend to liberate themselves more than others do from their dependence on subjects. This line of thought gives rise to two objections to my conception of ideal objects.

The first of these has to do with the very possibility of the existence of ideal objects. In some fields of mathematics, such as abstract algebra, it seems that the elaboration of a set of consistent axioms is a sufficient condition for the existence of the systems of (ideal) objects that satisfy the axioms, which is a view relative to which my Platonism appears decidedly excessive. At most, one might even conclude that, insofar as they are the result of consistent axioms, the ideal objects are not really objects in the full sense.[54] The second objection concerns the distinction between ideal and social objects. Even without wanting to deny the existence of ideal objects, they might be regarded as a sort of aristocracy among social objects, as free idealities that nevertheless belong to the same sphere in which we find the bound idealities, namely those that are tied up with their inscriptions, which are the middle- and low-class social objects. Or we might think of them as allographic social objects that, unlike autographic social objects (such as paintings), maintain their identity even when their inscriptions are very different from the originals.

It seems to me that these objections share two assumptions. The first is the identification of ideal objects with numbers, which is by no means obvious. The class of ideal objects is not limited to that of numbers and it would be hard to say, for instance, that relations are constructed. On the contrary, there seems to be a great deal of work (and not a little skill) behind transfinites—which are numbers—while no one would say that the relations "greater than," "to the right of," or of similarity between two triangles stand in need of a great work of construction. The second assumption is an underestimate of what we expect from ideal objects: *Even if it were a philosopher's mythology, we cannot get away from the need to draw a distinction between the objects that presuppose the existence of human beings* (as social objects do) *and those that, for various reasons, do not* (such as natural and ideal objects). There is a difference between the number 5, a chair, and a rental contract, and this difference seems to be more important than any of the possible affinities that might be dreamed up.

A further and rather different possible objection is as follows. If at least some ideal objects are universals, how can they find room in a nominalist ontology (as regards universals) of the sort I am proposing? To this objection, I reply that, like all the individuals that I handle in my ontology, ideal objects are *also* samples (a notion set out in 1.1.3 and to which I return in 3.3.2) and it is *insofar as they are samples* that they find their place in it. The triangle, the number 5 and the relation "to the left of" are individuals that are exemplified in the sense given of "having the value of an exemplar," in natural and social objects, and, in being exemplified, they receive their spatiotemporal articulation. To clarify this point, we may think of biological taxonomies: When a new species is named, its description is based on an exemplar know as the *type-exemplar*, which has to be deposited in a public collection. Just as in the case of zoological and botanical catalogs, our ontology is not interested in abstract universals, outside space and time, but in their type-exemplars.

1.3.2.3 IDEALIZATION, PSYCHOLOGIZATION, SOCIALIZATION If things stand as I have tried to illustrate, then we are faced with three main theses regarding the relation between inscriptions and ideal objects. One, of a constructionist sort, might be called the *idealization thesis*, because it claims that writing lies at the origin of idealization and so of ideal objects. Another, of a Platonist sort, is the one I defend and which I call the *socialization thesis*, because it claims that writing does not govern the *creation* of idealities, which are independent of it, but rather governs their *socialization*. In the middle, there is a further aspect of inscription-iteration, namely its ability to stimulate psychological constructs or *ideas* in the empiricists' meaning of the term, in line with what I call the *psychologization thesis*. It is worth looking more closely at these to stress the underlying differences between ideal and social objects.

The idealization thesis.[55] On this view, every form of inscription is a step forward towards idealization, which is to say toward emancipating the formulation (for instance, of a theorem) from its contingent and subjective status. Underpinning the idealization that is already under way in perception, spoken language frees the object from the subjectivity of its inventor or discoverer but keeps it within the bounds of the original community. For all that it appears as the most empirical and inanimate of means, it is writing that is able to carry through the idealization by removing the ideality from the spatiotemporal finitude of its inventor and his contemporaries. In this way, writing makes plain the senses' independence from the current community, and the perfection of the ideality resides precisely in this independence. On this sort of view, writing is the condition of the possibility of objectivity, even though the idealization thesis does not specify whether this is a necessary or a sufficient condition. Indeed, even within the idealization thesis, everything points to its being a necessary but not sufficient condition. By this I mean that, even if writing were a condition for idealization, that wouldn't imply that everything written is true, and so the Pythagorean theorem has a source of truth independent of being inscribed. Indeed, the system of idealization-iteration characteristically does not make $2 + 2 = 5$ true. For this reason, idealization-iteration is not

Platonic, because it makes no reference to true ideas. At most, it can be a way of explaining the genesis of ideas taken as psychological constructs in the empiricists' meaning of the term. But in that case, we are not dealing with the constitution of ideal objects, but only with a mental process, which I will examine at length in Chapter 4.

The psychologization thesis. Nevertheless, the idealization thesis can be put to work to explain the psychologization thesis. The argument, which I will set out more fully in 4.2, runs as follows. What is an idea, in the sense of a Fregean "thought"? It is an entity that is, in principle, independent of anyone who thinks is, and such as to exist even after someone has stopped, for a moment or forever, thinking it. Now, for such a condition to be realized, it is not enough to say that the idea is "spiritual," for in such a case, the thought could depend exclusively on the mental acts of individuals. Rather than concentrate on the spiritual nature of ideas, the idealization thesis invites us to take seriously the ways that an idea, in order to be such, must be indefinitely *iterable* by means of the sign-medium that fixes it, and that the possibility of repeating begins when a code is set up. The written sign provides the originary and underived archetypical form of the code, and the traces it leaves can be iterated even, but not necessarily, in the writer's absence. A piece of writing, even a laundry bill, represents the condition of ideality in its purest form because, unlike mental processes that have no external manifestation, it can take on an existence separate from its author. But here ideality should be understood in the empiricists' meaning of the term "idea"; the idealization thesis explains only how iteration applies both to the psyche (as in the psychologization thesis) and to society, where it appears as the socialization thesis.

The socialization thesis. The socialization thesis asserts that what is described in the analysis of inscription-iteration does not give birth to a Platonic idea. Rather, it is the socialization either of an idea that is a genuine ideal object, such as the Pythagorean theorem, with its preceding and separate existence, or of an act performed by two agents, such as a laundry bill, which had no existence independent of, separate from, or prior to the act and thus becomes a genuine social object. But to see how different social objects are from ideal ones, suffice it to consider a very simple case. When a recorded message on the telephone tells us, "The number does not exist," this would be an absurdity as regards numbers understood as ideal objects, given that there are no numbers that do not exist. Clearly, what is in play is a number considered as a social object, which is to say as a code. Indeed, as such, all the numbers exist, and it makes no sense to say, for instance that 011774573 does not exist or, as some American phone companies put it, "is no longer a working number";[56] as ideal objects, numbers cannot do any "work." It is quite another story for numbers as social objects, and for social objects taken together.[57]

1.3.3 Social Objects

As I have said, unlike ideal objects, social objects exist in space and time and are dependent on subjects.[58] Unlike both natural objects and ideal objects, social objects, insofar as they depend on subjects, obey the constitutive rule: Object = Inscribed Act. As already hinted, this rule holds also for the *socialization* of ideal objects. The basic features of social objects are that they persist in time and have a beginning and an end, they are constructed, and specifically this construction comes about by means of an inscription. Given that I provide a deeper analysis in Chapter 3 and an articulation in Chapters 4 and 5, I offer here a schematic presentation of social objects.

As I have already noted, the peculiarity of social objects resides in the fact that *unlike natural and ideal objects, social objects exist only insofar as at least two human beings are thinking about them.* I would like to make this point clearer. Right from the start of this book, I have insisted on the fact that social objects depend on subjects and this is what makes them different from other objects. But it is as well to clarify at once that this is a curious sort of ontological dependence, given that it calls on a before and an after, namely a before and an after of the inscription of the act by which they are constituted. This is tantamount to saying that they depend on subjects genetically rather than structurally. The existence of a contract depends on the contracting parties but once it has come into being, it is the parties—considered as entities with social status—that depend on it in virtue of being bound by it; an artwork derives from its author, but once it enters into circulation, the author is no longer the sole holder of its meaning (neither, in any case, is he or she the exclusive holder of its value). This fact seems to me to have a double significance.

In the first place, it puts right the misunderstanding according to which whatever depends on subjects must also be subjective. In 1.2.1 I set out the features of subject-dependence in relation to mental objects, and it is obvi-

ous that interest rates depend on subjects (and in particular on those subjects that pay them) in a wholly different way from that of the fantasies that
pass through our heads in the early hours of the morning. In the second
place, as I will set out at greater length in 4.1.2, this fact clarifies how the relation of subjects to objects in the case of social objects cannot be likened to
the traditional relation between body and soul: the duty that arises from a
social object, whether it be a contract, money, or family relations, is a letter
that, in point of fact, precedes or promotes the spirit. Trivially, a man con-
sumed by the ambition to become a rear admiral, a millionaire, or the poet
laureate is in subjective and spiritual states that derive from the presence of
institutions and inscribed social objects. It is precisely in light of this consideration that my fundamental speculative claim is that there is no spirit
without inscription, and that spirit is dependent on traces at least as much
as traces depend on spirit.

1.3.3.1 ARCHETYPES AND ECTYPES Let us proceed then to the concrete
examination of social objects, which, relative to natural and ideal objects,
carry with them a peculiar difficulty. For, given the way I have outline them,
social objects seem to confuse two things, one of which is the concrete social
object and the other is the model, which is to say, the *token* and the *type*.
Or rather, to be precise, they confuse three things, because also the act of
articulating them, which is a sort of event, is a social object. Let us take
marriage, a word that applies to the juridical institution of marriage to the
nuptial ceremony and to the state that follows from having contracted a
marriage with someone. I propose to call the juridical institution the
archetype because it is the model, the nuptial ceremony the *inscriber*, because
it is the act by which the juridical institution is actualized by registration in
the single concrete example of a marriage, which I call the *ectype*. Because,
as we shall see, there are three forms of archetype, we may summarize the
situation as follows:

Archetype	Archetype$_1$: ideal form Archetype$_2$: institution Archetype$_3$: abstract artifact
Inscriber	
Ectype	

Archetypes. Archetypes are *types*, the broad models that underpin the formation of a social object, just as the *exemplary* triangle underpins individual triangles. Examples of archetypes would be promises and bets.[59] The idea is that, just like continents, these objects can remain undiscovered and remain in the realm of possibility. But when they are uncovered—and I would say "encountered"—they reveal certain inner necessities. We can imagine a society in which there are no promises; yet, once promises are discovered, they manifest certain intrinsic structural laws, such as having a promisor, a promisee, an object and a time: "I promise" is not a promise; but "I (promisor) promise to you (promisee) that I will give you five euros (object) tomorrow (time)" is one. It is not hard to see in an archetype something similar to a Platonic form or a Kantian pure concept of the intellect, except that, unlike a Platonic idea, it does not have separate existence and, unlike a pure concept of the intellect, it is much more concrete; we might say it is an empirical concept endowed with the same necessity that characterizes pure concepts, even if the necessity can only come a posteriori. This last point calls for three clarifications that pick out three archetypical forms, namely archetypes 1, 2, and 3.

There is a temptation to regard archetypes as ideal objects: the promise considered as a possibility that can remain abstract has no need of a physical inscription; in that case, when I make or inscribe a promise concretely, am I not simply socializing it? No: we do not inscribe archetypes to socialize them, but rather to institute ectypes whose essential and interesting features are not exhausted by the necessary properties of the archetype. I think that this difference is enough to justify placing archetypes in the realm of social objects; nevertheless, to stress the peculiarity of such powerful archetypes as promises, bets, and obligations, I propose to call them *Archetypes₁*.

In the second place, it might be observed that there is an ambiguity in the word *archetype* and that, in the sense just described, an archetype is like an ideal object and, in another, it is a sort of inscription. Indeed, in one sense of the word, an *archetype* is a possibility, an ideal object with formal properties like those of the objects of mathematics and logic. But there is also a sense in which we can call a certain sort of social object an *archetype*, as in the case of the way in which the institution of marriage is embodied in a given society. This surely needs inscriptions, which are not the signatures of the bride and groom, but rather the laws of the land—and after all, there are many archetypes of marriage in this sense. The ectypes also depend on the archetypes in this second sense. Without the institution of marriage, the documents regarding individual marriages would have no role to play. Obviously, the archetypes can be nothing but inscriptions in the heads of the members of a community. There are no laws that make a party or a friendship valid, but there certainly are shared beliefs about what should happen at a party or in a friendship that "is successful." It should be borne in mind, however, that *in this second sense the archetypes are a type of ectype*; they are more fundamental and important ectypes than others, and further ectypes depend on them, which others are in general longer lived and not bound to individuals. In this case, however, we can also pick out an archetypal function, even though it is less clear than in the preceding case, for which reason, I propose to call them *Archetypes$_2$*.[60]

Finally, it is one thing to attribute archetypical reference to a promise, which necessarily has a promisor, a promisee, and object, and a time. But is not so easy to speak of a necessary structure for instance when it comes to institutions or to a certain model of automobile; these *types* are (abstract) artifacts, and for that reason, have no essences. Their definition derives from the function they fulfill, and this is arbitrarily imposed by a social group. For sure, we can make out empirical regularities, but these are not genuine necessities. If so, the discovery of these social objects is more properly regarded as a sort of creation—of a model of automobile or of a tax. I think we can here speak of *Archetypes$_3$*, taking as a model, for instance, literary works. The manuscript of *Madame Bovary* is an Archetype$_3$, from which derive all the ectypes: the concrete copies of the book, new editions, translations, and film treatments.[61]

Inscribers. In addition to that of fixing the act, we find a second function of inscriptions in the relation between archetypes and ectypes. By fixing the act, inscriptions individualize the archetype and inscribed it in the ectype. To continue the classical philosophical analogies, inscriptions are the mediators between the archetypical forms and the ectype. This is what brings the ectype into being in the full sense (in the example cited earlier, a marriage, considered as an inscription, is what actualizes the marriage institution in the concrete marriage).[62]

In this sense, inscriptions play a role similar to that of the geometrical forms in Plato's *Timaeus* in transmitting the Ideas to matter, and to that of the schemes in the *Critique of Pure Reason* in being the modes of construction by which one gets from the categories to the object. Here again, the crucial difference is that the constructions that depend on inscriptions are all social. Relative to the geometrical forms in the *Timaeus*, which are ideal objects that can hardly give rise to real objects, and relative to the schemes of the *Critique*, which can hardly be understood (or rather how they are supposed to work),[63] the advantage of social objects is that they are very concrete things: a marriage ceremony, a graduation, registries, and rites of various kinds. And we can even find concrete objects that play the role of "inscribers."

Let us look a bit deeper into this. There are things that have only one function and others that have more than one—and I am not referring only to Swiss Army knives. There are also objects that create other objects, specifically social objects (and in this they differ from toolmaking machines). Here the essential point is precisely the inscription and the technological means for registering inscribed acts. The continuous growth of these constructors of social reality is a matter that has been ignored by the enormous literature on technology, which has often put the emphasis on the dehumanizing role of technology, while we clearly have to do with humanizing functions. Humankind is humanized through its rites, which are forms of registration that can precede (and, in societies without writing, that can do without) formalizations in documents and that, in many cases, such as that of circumcision, show up as markings. Thus, the fact that public acts are accompanied by ceremonies, and that the ceremonies are followed by endless feasts, clearly derives from the way that what matters is not the pleasure of those present, but the inscription on their minds.

Ectypes. Last, there are the ectypes, tokens of various concrete exemplifications (regularly accompanied by an inscription) in which the archetype is actualized. As I have already mentioned, the ectypes stand in a curious relation with the archetypes (even in the case of Archtypes$_1$, and all the more clearly with Archetypes$_2$ and Archetypes$_3$), which make the archetype/ectype relation different from the Idea/thing relation in Plato or the pure concept/phenomenon relation in Kant.[64] If there were no ectypes in the social world, there would be no documents; in this they differ from the world of ideal objects, in which the equilateral triangle exists even if no one ever draws one. Nevertheless, we can see a relation of the ectype on the archetype: in social practice, a marriage as ectype presupposes a ceremony, and this presupposes marriage as an archetype that, in the case in hand, is an Archtype$_2$.

Given that the ceremony is, in turn, a sort of inscription, we have to do with a situation in which the archetype is not confused with the ectype, not the ectype with the inscription (my marriage is neither the ceremony nor the document), but relations of necessary interdependence are set up, and they will be set out more in detail in 4.3.3.2. In summary, the relations in question take the form of a triangle as follows:

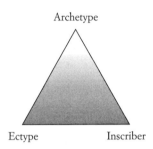

1.3.3.2 THE EXEMPLARINESS OF THE SAMPLE   Unlike the case of ideal objects, the fact that when we have anything to do with social objects it is the ectype that generates the archetype allows us to get clearer about the logic of the exemplariness of the sample that we proposed in 1.1.2. That is of central importance to the view proposed in this book. My idea is that samples are individuals used as principles of generalization: an example of a dog to recognize other dogs as such, rather than "the general idea" of dogs.

   In this way, we have individuals that produce classes. When we say of someone that they behaved in an exemplary manner in unexpected circumstances, we do not mean that they carried out a program (which in any case could not have foreseen those circumstances), but rather that they behaved in an entirely individual and innovative way that, given how things turned out, showed itself to be fitting, so much so as to suggest that it could be repeated in other circumstances. The logic of masterpieces in art is typical. An architect invents a new solution for a problem never previously encountered, a painter discovers a new form of expression, a writer introduces a new narrative technique, and so on: the value of the work derives in the first instance from its originality, from the fact of not having forerunners and of presenting itself as an absolute individual. At the same time, however, this individual stands at the head of a stream of works that are inspired by it, and it may even create a style. Now, this does not seem to be an exception, but rather the rule: Throughout the social world—from customary rights to fashion—the logic of the exemplarity of the sample rules, in line with the constitutive role of imitation in the formation of social reality, which I discuss in 4.1.2.

The sample then acts as a case from which to derive the rule, in line with Kant's model of the reflective judgment, as opposed to the determinant judgment, which, starting from the rule seeks the case that best fits it. As I have suggested elsewhere,[65] the passage from the determinant judgment to the reflective is, for Kant, a move from a strong schematism to a weak one. In the strong schematism, we have the concept (as universal) that is applied to the individual; in the weak schematism, on the other hand, we have the individual (as particular) that counts as a universal (or, rather, as the principle of a class), without ceasing, for that reason, to be an individual. It is the requirements of social life that bring certain social objects into being, whose first emergence is a concrete situation but that then count as samples for other social objects. In short, it is difficult to imagine the arising a priori of spaghetti alla carbonara or of quiche lorraine; but, once they have carved out their place in recipe books (which have their own normative role), we start saying that this or that dish has been prepared in the right way or, even—naming perhaps in vain an ideal-typical normativity—"as God commanded."

1.3.3.3 INSCRIBED ARTIFACTS   As we have seen, inscriptions are the social objects in the fullest sense. But the social world is full of objects that do not look at all like documents, but that nevertheless are charged with social importance. I propose to call them *inscribed artifacts* to pick out a range of objects that goes from things with a low density of inscription, such as stones used as paperweights, to things that are highly and purposefully inscribed, such as artworks and documents.

All artifacts are physical objects that have been made or modified by man, whether as archetypes (as in the case of the design for a model of motorcar) or as ectypes (instances of the model). We may leave to one side the distinction between existent and nonexistent social objects,[66] which I think can be assimilated to the distinction between strong documents, such as inscriptions of acts, and weak documents, which I discuss in 5.1.4.1; instead,

I propose a rising hierarchy of things, instruments, works, and documents. As we shall see, this hierarchy is ruled by the amount of inscription present in each artifact and obviously obeys the law Object = Inscribed Act, which is the basis of the construction of social reality. The more densely an object is inscribed, the less it can be conceived to have a role outside the social world; if we can imagine a cat sleeping in an armchair, it is hard to imagine one getting esthetic pleasure out of the *Mona Lisa* or being panicked by reading its bank statement.

For its part, an inscription is a physical trace or modification dependent on some medium. In some cases (such as those of money, novels, or symphonies) it can remain the same even though the medium varies, while in others (such as a painting) it cannot. Inscriptions are the quintessence of social objects insofar as they are present in various ways in every one of them. They can be divided into inscriptions in the broad sense (every kind of registration, including memories in the minds of persons) and those in the narrow sense (writings on paper or on computer files, and, within this class, documents understood as having special institutional value), and this explains why there is as much inscription in a notch on a stick as on a Post-It, in a pre-Raphaelite painting, in a gas bill, in a handshake, and in a football game. In 4.2.1 to explain and argue for the legitimacy of this extension of "inscription" to so wide a range of objects.

I need to make two observations in connection with what I said in 1.3.1.2 so as to set the scene for an analysis of inscribed artifacts. The first concerns the issue of artifacts in general. In considering things, instruments, and works, we can come across natural objects that fall outside the category of *artifacts*: a stone used as a paperweight or as a trinket is undoubtedly a thing, just like an apple or an eggplant, while a branch used as a lever is undoubtedly an instrument. Not to mention the skull of Cunimund, which the Lombard king Alboin is said to have made into a cup after he had killed him and from which he made his wife Rosamund (Cunimund's daughter) drink, or the equally grisly lampshade that Dr. Mengele is said to have made from human skin. In such cases, we have fully fledged instruments that are the result of a manipulation in such a way that the natural object is present only as the primary matter, just as in a leather briefcase, suede shoes, or buttons made of bone. Thus, Cunimund's skull and Mengele's lampshade are artifacts in the full sense. On the other hand, the stone paperweight, the fruit and vegetables, and the lever seem to be more independent of how they are handled. Nevertheless, there will have been a hand that picked up the stone and took it indoors, another that picked the fruit or the vegetables, and all the more so one that knew how to use the branch as a lever. This is not enough for them to be artifacts: An apple pie is much more of an artifact than an apple is. The decisive point is that we could choose these objects within the human sphere. We might say that they exemplify the necessary, though not the sufficient, conditions for becoming what they are, in such a way that I propose to call them *quasi-artifacts*, whose artifactuality depends on the context in which they are found.

The other observation concerns the distinction between *social objects* and *socializable objects*. There are objects that come into being as social, and these are inscriptions in the narrow sense. Others can become such and are thus subjected to socialization. As I mentioned, a chair can have a social function and can even become a throne, but given that a cat can use it too, it is not necessarily a social object. On these grounds, within the scheme I am proposing, we see the special status of artworks and documents relative to things and instruments: artworks and documents come into being with a social function. For this reason artworks and documents are social objects from the outset. Artifacts, on the other hand, are socializable, just as a natural environment can be socialized into a park, an English-style garden, or a golf course.

For the present purposes, I would like to remark on the social status of human and animal bodies. Human bodies are, obviously enough, natural objects that carry out functions that are perfectly natural. They live, they feel and are felt, they think, and they undergo pain and pleasure. Traditionally, they form a category distinct from that of artifacts, even though, to some extent, transplants and plastic surgery and, to a greater extent, genetic engineering have changed this. Nevertheless, both human and animal bodies undergo various kinds of social inscription, from the branding of animals, slaves, and prisoners (which is an indicator of ownership) to intentionally adopted signs (tattoos, ornaments, clothes) to sexual and food-related taboos, starting with that against incest (which presupposes a marking of social roles) or against cannibalism (within the clan or more in general), extending to vegetarianism. For this reason, I take bodies to be a palmary example of the *socialization* of natural objects, which takes its place alongside the use of conches as musical instruments, pebbles used for calculating, and chicken eggs painted for Easter.

Let us proceed to things, instruments, and artworks. I propose to think of things as the set of artifacts and quasi-artifacts; of instruments as the subset of things that have some external finality (a urinal is used for urinating); and artworks as the subset of things that do have an internal finality but do not have an external finality (Duchamp's urinal is not for urinating in).

Things. Things are the furniture of the human world or, less metaphorically, physical objects that stand in direct and perceptible relations with subjects. To do so—as I shall clarify in 2.2.3.3—they must be of medium dimensions, being neither too big nor too small.[67]

There are four essential properties of things, that make all things objects, but not all objects things: They must be available to the senses, manipulable, ordinary, and relational. Their being available to the senses means that they interact with the eyes, the ears, touch, smell, and taste. In this sense, there is no doubt that an atom is a physical object, but it is not a thing, because it is not perceived as such. Manipulability means that things should be within our grasp and usable with the hands or, as occasion demands, with the feet (bearing in mind that, with a handle, a button or a pedal, it is the handle, button, or pedal that is the object of our interaction, rather than, for instance, the particle accelerator that is activated by our movements). Things are ordinary in that they are banal parts of our daily lives. And they are relational in the sense that they correlate with other things and with us, which is to say (I suppose) with persons. While there is no difficulty about imagining a world in which there is only one object, because *object* is a nonrelational term, we cannot conceive of a world with only one thing. If there were a world with only a chair, but no humans, tables, or titles, would it really be a thing? To this we might add that, unlike many objects in the physical world, things are an encumbrance in that they do not merely occupy space, but are also in competition with us for it.[68] As we shall see at greater length in 3.1, knowledge is constitutive of social objects. Knowledge—or at least belief— that a certain pen belonged to Napoleon, that this chip of wood is a relic of the Holy Cross, or that a given painting is by Tintoretto changes our attitudes to it and makes us look at it "with different eyes."

Note that all the properties I have listed are relational in the sense that they have to do with the relation between a subject and an object. In my view, this is the feature that sets "things" apart from generic physical objects. These latter have a location in space and time, can enter into causal relations with other objects, but not with social objects, because they are not the sort of thing that is always in play when, for want of a better word, we say "pass me that thing there."

Instruments. At a higher epistemological level than things we find instruments, namely things for doing other things, things with a practical purpose. In order to distinguish things from instruments, Heidegger's distinction between *Vorhandenheit* and *Zuhandenheit* comes in handy.[69] *Vorhandenheit* is the being "to hand" of everyday objects, which are thus thought of as simple things. This is an important observation because it allows is to distinguish things from the much wider range of objects: the Moon is certainly a physical object, something that stands in front of us (as in the German word for "object," *Gegenstand*), but it is not a thing, and after all it makes little sense to wish for the Moon. *Zuhandenheit,* on the other hand, is what marks instruments such as wheels, clubs, pincers, knives, lighters, and kitchen shears. Instruments are "to hand," just like things, but they are also, so to speak, "for the hand"; they are made to be used precisely by the hand, which is in turn the instrument of instruments or that with which we handle them.

One advantage of the Heideggerian distinction is that it brings to the fore, as an essential characteristic of things and instruments, the fact that they have to do with the hand, and with being manipulable, as I said earlier. The philosophical tradition, from Anaxagoras[70] and Aristotle[71] down to Hegel,[72] has given due importance to the "instrument of instruments": the grasp allows us to use scissors and pens, doors, chairs, stools, and computers and to make agreements (one gives one's hand to seal a contract or to make a marriage). Long before language, these functions underlie the emergence of humanity and the construction of social reality, as I argue in 4.2.3.2.

Artworks. Artworks are instruments whose function is not practical but rather (according to the theory one subscribes to) expressive or emotional.[73] They have what Kant would call "purposiveness without a purpose," which may in turn be interpreted either as an internal purposiveness or as a lack of purposiveness. I return at length to artworks in 5.2 and briefly to art in 5.3.3.1. What I wish to emphasize for now is that there can coexist in the same object both the instrumental function and the artwork function. They cannot be enjoyed both at once; it is either one or the other, as in Jastrow's duck-rabbit. In short, artworks are artifacts whose potential for instrumental value is put in brackets, and in which there is a very high level of inscription. This is why artworks provide us with a bridge to those preeminently social objects, namely documents.

Documents. At the pinnacle of social objects we find documents, which, as we shall see in 5.1.4.1, can be subdivided into the strong (inscriptions of acts) and the weak (registrations of facts). At the pinnacle of strong documents we find the highest form of social objects, namely institutional objects. Thus, those social objects that are not mere applications of a rule but that impose a rule are institutional objects insofar as they are social rather than ideal.[74] The paradigm cases of institutional social objects are statute laws. Thus, the institution is the high point of the social, which in its turn is the highest level of the theory of objects. According to their normative force, social objects are classified into the regulative and the constitutive; and according to their form, they are classified into the implicit and the explicit.

Regulative social objects regulate social behaviors that are already in place, such as driving on the right or the rules of ball games. Here we have rules, whether they be written documents or merely informal agreements, for instance about whose turn it is to wash the dishes. *Constitutive* social objects bring into being objects that would not exist without them, as we find in the rules of chess or of card games.

Institutionalness is often manifested in specific forms of inscription. Think, for instance (I return to the distinction in 3.2.2), about the difference between a stroll and a procession. You can take a stroll when you want, in whatever direction you care to take. There is no ceremony to be observed, and there are no statues to be carried about or anything like that. When we have to do with institutional objects, inscriptions have a role as indicators (for instance, a mayor may wear a chain of office, military types wear certain uniforms, a married person has a band). Laws are a form of explicit codification where etiquette is a form of implicit codification, even though this latter may end up being written down. Indeed, if we think about "Miss Manners," it has precisely to do with written legislation for good manners.[75]

2

ONTOLOGY AND EPISTEMOLOGY

After listing the basic objects in my catalog, I propose in this chapter a distinction between epistemology (as the sphere of knowledge) and ontology (as the sphere of being), which is based in the first instance on the impermeability attributable to being relative to knowledge understood as socially justified (and perfectible) belief. The ultimate aim of the distinction is to take account of the novelty of the social world relative to the physical world or, crudely, of the novelty of fines relative to atoms.

The basic idea is very simple. It is obvious that, to say that water is H_2O, I have to have theories, conceptual schemes, and a language. I do not need any of that apparatus to quench my thirst with a glass of water, to notice that water is wet or that it is transparent. This second sort of experience seems much less conditioned by conceptual schemes than we find in the case of scientific research in such a way that the Kantian thesis that intuitions without concepts are blind is hardly applicable to everyday experience. More positively, if we look for the characteristic feature of ordinary experience's autonomy from scientific elaborations, we find it in an impermeability to conceptual schemes, which I tag with the technical term unemendability.[1] *For instance, we cannot correct optical illusions simply by appealing to conceptual schemes. In this way, we have some knowledge that has very little to do with ontology: I can be perfectly aware that I am faced with an optical illusion, but this does not allow me to emend what I see. It is precisely the notion of unemendability that underlies my defense of the real world's independence of conceptual schemes. While epistemology has an active, linguistic, and deliberative role and aims at the emendation and refinement of concepts, ontology presents itself as a theory of experience that, at its most basic level, can be applied without language or concepts, purely passively and without emendation. To reuse the earlier example, I can either know or not know that water is H_2O, but it will make me* wet all the same, and I cannot dry myself off simply by thinking that hydrogen and oxygen are not themselves wet.

Chapter 2.1 undertakes to expound the "transcendental fallacy," which is the collapse of experience into science that, if I am right, has its paradigmatic expression in Kant's transcendental philosophy.[2] The underlying assumption is that Kant shared with empiricism the idea that science is simply a specialized and codified form of experience; since the empiricists held that the certainty of science was threatened by the instability of experience, Kant aimed to overturn the perspective, founding experience on science, specifically mathematical physics. In this way, not only does scientific knowledge of the world depend on conceptual schemes, but so too does our everyday experience. Over the last two hundred years, Kant's formulation of the fallacy, which is summed up in the principle that intuitions without concepts are blind, has undergone further radicalizations. Nietzsche and the pragmatists read it as saying that there are no facts, but only interpretations; the version of Derrida and the postmodernists is that there is nothing outside the text. What these reductions of being to knowing have in common is the hypothesis that here is no ontological level outside and independent of conceptual schemes; and it is precisely this that I assert with what I call slippery experiment, which aims to show the independence of reality from conceptual schemes and perceptual apparatus.

Chapter 2.2 is dedicated to ontological distinctions and seeks to give a positive account of the critical results arising out of the treatment of the transcendental fallacy. Once we have found a solid level of reality—not so much a launching pad from which to raise up a world as something resistant and hardly penetrable—we can then bring into focus a range of ontological distinctions that mark the difference between truth and reality, between the world within conceptual schemes and the world outside them, and between science and experience.

Thus, in 2.1 I criticize the confusion between ontology and epistemology, and in the second I set out positive criteria for distinguishing the two levels. There remains a legitimate objection, according to which, even allowing that there is a level of being separate from knowledge, experience nevertheless constitutes knowledge, since every relation with ontology turns out to be necessarily mediated by epistemology—which means that there is no way of getting away from the upshot of the transcendental fallacy (which is not after all a fallacy). To this objection I reply in the 3.3, where I outline a theory of experience based on

three main arguments. The first starts from the grades of knowledge. It is com-
mon enough to encounter different levels of knowledge, and it would be absurd
to claim that all of them respond to what is required for science. The claim in
favor of the omnipresence of science, of concepts, and of conceptual schemes is
nourished in large part by an inflationary use of those words; if we operate a
reasonable deflation of them, we see that science is not so ubiquitous, as we can
see for instance by comparing what goes on in a restaurant and in a research
laboratory. My second argument is based on the variety of experience. The view
I defend is simply a recognition of what most philosophers concede in any case,
namely the fact that knowledge is just one of the activities (or games) that we
go in for in life. Other than the game of truth and falsity, or of what is and what
is not, we also have the game of the just and the unjust, of the beautiful and the
ugly, of the useful and the useless; in each of these cases it would be unfounded
to say that these experiences boil down to the games that find their ultimate
solution or explanation in science. My third argument depends on the classes
of object that were distinguished in Chapter 1. The physics game, which Kant
played in the Critique of Pure Reason, *supposed that there was only one type*
of object, namely physical ones. Granting for the sake of argument that physics
is the only way to interact with physical objects, there remain the vast realms
of ideal objects and above all—for the main purpose of this book—of social
objects. At this point, after presenting the classes of objects and the instruments
for handling them, I proceed to the core of my discussion regarding social objects
in Chapter 3.

2.1 THE TRANSCENDENTAL FALLACY

I imagine that many readers of the classification presented in the foregoing part will be asking themselves what right I have, I who am not versed
in any particular science, to make claims about how to divide the world up
into a catalog that may be reminiscent of Borges's Chinese encyclopedia. Do
librarians and archivists, those who set out goods on supermarket shelves
or in hardware stores, do anything very different? The problem is not that
of having inside knowledge (which in the cases of ideal and social objects
seems rather less problematic). What is really called for are principles of
classification, which can themselves be judged and criticized—but not on
the grounds that the archivist is not a physicist or a chemist. This is the basic

point, but to defend it, we have to establish the distinction between ontology and epistemology more clearly.

Justified beliefs. Roughly speaking, the distinction works as follows. On the one hand, we have ontology, which concerns what there is and does not depend on our conceptual schemes, such as the water in the sea, in the faucet and in my glass. On the other, we have epistemology, which concerns what we know about that there is and which depends on our conceptual schemes, such as talk about H_2O, a ruling of an administrative court, or nouvelle cuisine. Obviously, this distinction is rough and ready. In our experience, being and knowing are inextricably connected, and in any case, knowledge is related in many ways, referring as much to common sense as to history or tradition or the most advanced scientific research. Nevertheless, it is important to recognize how, in every experience we have, here is something that has to do with being and something that has to do with knowing (conceived as justified belief) and how the two spheres are not identical.

It might perhaps be objected that, insofar as it has to do with knowledge and acquaintance and hence with *true* belief (as well as justified, in line with the classic definition of knowledge), epistemology can never be in conflict with ontology. Indeed, there can never be conflict between what we know about what is and what is because if we know that there are certain entities, it follows that it is true that there are these entities and that these entities exist. If anything, the conflict will be between what we *believe* there to be and what there really is in the world. I would like to clarify from the outset that, in this section of the book, I use the word *epistemology* as a label for those theories of knowledge that aim to give an explanation that is unified and continuous both for ordinary knowledge and scientific theories. In particular, epistemology gives pride of place to the beliefs that are formed within the practices of science, which we take to be true and justified (and hence knowledge), but that are always open to improvement. These beliefs can be formulated only within a conceptual scheme that is itself, at least in part, a historical inheritance and in large measure open to modification. In this sense, insofar as they call for a conceptual and linguistic apparatus, knowledge and truth are opposed to being and ontology. In their turn, these articulate distinctions that do not derive from modifiable conceptual schemes, but from cognitive mechanisms that have been inherited and are thus more rigid. On these grounds, the beliefs that ontology handles (and which we discuss more at length in 2.3.1.1) can be improved on only with great difficulty.

Theory of knowledge and ontology. One unhappy consequence of systems like Kant's is that they confuse ontology and epistemology. The confusion arises quite naturally from the choice of beginning with the subject. If, as Kant says, the "I think" must be capable of accompanying all my representations, it follows fairly naturally that being and knowing should collapse into each other. This is because "being" is no longer a property of an independent object, but rather a characteristic of something that is represented by a subject. This operation is obviously not a free lunch, and it renders an altered image of reality, on which the conceptual schemes constituted the world. But, after all, this is no different from claiming that rheumatism—the thing, not the name—exists only because there are doctors to diagnose it. This confusion then gives rise not only to an exaltation of science as the only custodian of reality but also to a critique of science for the very same reason. Both those philosophers who are friends of science and those who are its enemies have shared the presupposition that there is no relation with the object that is unmediated by conceptual schemes and, in particular, by conceptual schemes that subserve knowledge (rather than, as happens in the overwhelming majority of cases, as we see in 2.3 and 3.2, social action). The only question left open and the only point that remains to be debated, was that of whether the best conceptual schemes were, as Quine claimed, those of physics or, as Heidegger claimed, those of philosophy.

At the risk of repeating myself: There is nothing more natural than to confuse things being as they are in the world with the knowledge that we may have of it. Indeed, it is common enough to say that there are men in the street, when all we see are hats and coats. It is even more common to make the stimulus error that comes about when, for instance, we have our eyes closed and we respond to the question "What can you see?" with the reply "Nothing" or "Blackness" (which is not the same as saying that there are flashes or motes), because we have taken on board a prototheory of vision on which the absence of light means falling into total darkness.

The skeptical claim that being is not, that, if it were, it would not be knowable, and that, if it were knowable, it would not be communicable is a negative version of the claim that knowledge and its socialization are not secondary but rather constitutive features of our relation to being (or, as I prefer to put it, to objects). It was this that Plato sought to present in a positive light: Things call out to be perceived, perception needs to be saved as memory, and memory has to be fixed as concept. This was how things stood until modern times. Rather, this is how things have stood until today, given that, if we describe our access to knowledge of objects, we cannot do without some such formulation. All of which is unexceptionable, so long as we bear in mind that this is *theory of knowledge* and not *ontology*.

Indeed, we are considering how we know the world and not what there is in the world; and we should not confuse the two issues. I anticipated earlier in this chapter that there is nothing to fear from the objection that, to say what there is in the world and hence to do ontology, it is necessary *to know* what there is in the world and hence to do epistemology. In 2.3, I explain a theory of experience as very different from science. What I wish to draw attention to at this point is that a confusion between ontology and theory of knowledge carries with it a very high cost. This is paid in the first instance by annulling ontology. One might ask oneself how so bizarre and incredible a doctrine as nihilism could have been accepted if it means that both in perfectly furnished rooms and in garbage dumps that it is hard to get rid of, we can imperturbably say that there is nothing. On the other hand, in evacuating epistemology, it is a given that knowledge is nothing if is not knowledge of something that transcends it. Otherwise, what difference would there be between knowledge (justified true belief) and belief that one knows—in other words, between knowing and not knowing?

From Descartes to the postmodernists. Who started all this? It is a long story, but it really takes off with the moderns, in the first place Descartes, who radicalized suspicion toward sensible experience in favor of intellectual knowledge as the sole source of certainty. Its most influential formulation is due to Kant, who underwrote the old confusion and turned it into a discovery and a philosophical verity. As I have already said, I call this confusion the "transcendental fallacy," because from it derives the transcendental philosophy that fuels an epistemologically justified constructivism or, in simple terms, the idea that reality, including physical objects, depend on our conceptual schemes.[3]

Elsewhere I have argued in favor of thinking of "logocentrism" not so much as the subordination of writing to the spoken word, as Derrida (the term's inventor) proposed, but rather the alleged determination of experience by conceptual schemes.[4] I have distinguished three sizes of logocentrism. Size M is that of David Hume, according to which our present perception is determined by our past perceptions. Size L is that of Kant, according to which intuitions without concepts are blind. Size XL is that of

Nietzsche, according to which there are no facts, but only interpretations. It is easy to see that nevertheless logocentrism is in every case a tightfitting garment and, paradoxically tighter-fitting the larger the size. This is because it is at least plausible to suppose that (apart from the inevitable surprises) experience determines our expectations, and that conceptual schemes can condition our conception (but not our perceptions) of the world, while the claim that there are no facts but only interpretations holds good neither in heaven nor on earth. For present purposes—for brevity and the general aims of the book—I leave to one side the M-size of logocentrism, because it is only a minor nuisance, and I concentrate on the transcendental fallacy not so much in its three sizes, as in three of its phases: (1) transcendentalism: that we determine what is by what we know about it: "intuitions without concepts are blind"; (2) pragmatism: nothing transcends the conceptual schemes, which are in turn identified with our forms of life: "there are no facts, but only interpretations"; (3) postmodernism: these schemes are themselves determined by other schemes (traditions, texts, usages and customs) in an infinite regress: "there is nothing outside the text."

2.1.1 *Transcendentalism*

2.1.1.1 INTUITIONS WITHOUT CONCEPTS ARE BLIND I was suggesting that the Kantian fallacy has a Cartesian prologue: "It is a rule of prudence not to repose full trust in those who have betrayed us even on a single occasion." Thus, in the opening page of the *Meditations*, Descartes proposes to teach us not to trust the senses, those unworthy servants that, in his view, have misled us and that we would therefore do well to distrust systematically.[5] Consistently with his starting point, Descartes maintains that certainty is not to be sought outside, in a world full of sensible errors, but within, in the *cogito*, the seat of clear and distinct ideas. This choice depends on the fact that, in general, Descartes demands too much, namely 100 percent certainty: "All science is a certain and evident cognition, and he who doubts of many things is no more learned than he who has never thought of them," asserts the second of the *Rules for the Direction of the Mind*.[6] It is still to be argued that demanding so much is the right move, given that, in the place of certainty, what we get is an incurable doubt: if we require experience to meet the same standard as science, we will end up not being certain of anything. The proof of this is to be found in Hume, who became a skeptic, just like Descartes, considering that inductive arguments based on experience can never be 100 percent certain. Given that for Hume all knowledge comes from experience, the real abyss is not between 100 percent and 1 percent probability, but rather between 100 percent and 99 percent. It follows that all our knowledge is founded on slippery terrain that offers no guarantee of safety.

The reasoning that underlies the transcendental fallacy is thus:

1. The senses deceive (they are not 100 percent certain);
2. Induction is uncertain (less than 100 percent)
3. Science is more secure than experience;
4. Therefore, experience must be resolved into science (it must be founded on science or, in the worst case, be shown up by it as the "manifest image" and a snare).

Now, what is wrong with the fallacy? My hypothesis is that we are dealing with a confused knot of elements that do not have much to do with each other. In particular:

1. The fact that I sometimes mistake a firefly for a lantern (occasional sensory error);
2. The unjustified conclusion that, in that case, I ought systematically to doubt all my experiences, including the fact that I have two hands (methodical doubt: I might be dreaming, I might be mad, I might be the victim of a deceiving demon);
3. The fact that sooner or later bulbs blow (the empirical nature of objects: it may be that there is an eternal bulb, but I act as if there is none);
4. The unjustified conclusion that the principle of causality, empirically founded on the law "if I switch the switch the light goes on," should be regarded as a mere datum of habit, because soon or later the bulb will blow.

In this way, the fallacy weakens the primitive and unreflective certainty with which we interact with the world (for instance, I am sure that the world goes on behind my back—but I might at this point begin to doubt it) without offering in return a different certainty. It seems to be no use to make a fresh appeal to the senses, which is where Kant comes in: rather than found the sciences on experience, the idea is to turn the point of view upside down and to found experience on science and, specifically, on physics. This is the point of the Copernican Revolution, which is a matter not of asking how things are in themselves, but rather how they must be if they are to be known by us.

Kant's argument is roughly as follows: Metaphysics is an arena of endless debate, and in particular of battles between specters, where every philosopher says the opposite of his colleagues and his predecessors; physics, by contrast, has reached indubitable results by mixing the a priori certainties of mathematics with empirical analysis, and has thus obtained agreed and rich laws of nature. As a result, metaphysics has only to naturalize physics, by which is meant that it must explain its laws not only as the upshot of the speculations of a certain group of scientists, but as the way in which our minds and our senses work. In this way, it is not so much a question of how things are in themselves, but of how they must be constituted in order to be known by us.

What does this naturalization amount to?[7] Nothing more than the claim that the laws that the mind gives to the world are those of physics. In turn, these give certain access to notions that are as secure as those of mathematical operations and as informative and full of content as those that we draw from experience. It is at this point that we see the fallacy. Science presents itself as a more sophisticated sort of experience, and experience as a sort of well-behaved science; in the middle, we are all playing with junior physics or junior chemistry sets.

This fallacy presented itself as the royal road down which went most of the philosophers of the nineteenth and twentieth centuries.[8] By giving the name "Copernican" to his revolution, Kant succeeded in associating the idea that, being taught that the sun does not really set, means also we should prefer as a privileged observation point what we know relative to what we see and, hence should conclude that encountering a thing and knowing it are ultimately the same. The results are as I have already indicated: What we see is made to depend on what we know; there is the idea that conceptual schemes are everywhere at work; and it is claimed that we are never in contact with the thing in itself, but always and only with phenomena. On this view of things, it is clear that it is senseless to talk of ontology or of experience distinct from science.

My aim is to show that this upshot is anything but obvious.

2.1.1.2 THE THESIS OF PHENOMENA   Let us take the first point, namely, the dependence of the world on the ways we know it. Here *knowledge* means having an experience that is more or less science, even if it is nothing of the sort, given that we can easily *encounter* an object without knowing it, which is to say without having the slightest idea of its internal properties and even without identifying it. When the citizens of Metropolis look up and shout, "It's a bird! It's a plane! It's Superman!" it is clear that they see *something*, but they do not know exactly *what it is*. They fix a reference,[9] which is a procedure that precedes both identification, which will come about only in a subsequent moment, and definition, which will happen only very much later, if at all (which it does not in the overwhelming majority of cases). If we did not take this into account, we would be forced to claim that we see something only when we know it. This is obviously false, though Kant seems to think on the whole that this is how things stand.

We ought to remember the following. The sentence that sums up the Copernican Revolution, that asks us to ask "not how things are in themselves, but how they have to be in order to be known by us," involves an ambiguity that depends on the meaning of *know*. This can mean (a) the operations carried out by our senses and our categories, whether we follow them or not, in knowing the external world, or (b) what we, as experts, know about things. Furthermore, given that in order to investigate (a) and (b), it seems that we also need (c) to know how things stand as regards our cognitive architecture, our senses and our nervous system, the three levels begin to interfere with each other in ways that cannot be easily unraveled.

Quite apart from the epistemological problems that these overlappings carry with them, at the ontological level, objects are reduced to the subjects that know them. According to how we think about how subjectivity intervenes, this reduction can come in various guises, but will in every case end up with the idea that *esse est concipi*: Things exist only insofar as there is conscious representation of them, with a consciousness that also constitutes the ultimate foundation of science. Let us call this assumption *the thesis of phenomena*, because it proposes that there are no things in themselves, but only for us, as phenomena.

2.1.1.3 THE THESIS OF CONCEPTUAL SCHEMES   We come now to the question of conceptual schemes. Kant's basic idea is that absent the sort of spectacles that are concepts, our intuitions would not be orderly, and that the intuitions that we get through the lenses of concepts are obviously not things in themselves, but rather phenomena, which is to say the things that *appear* to us in a certain way, namely the way that is determined by the cooperation of our sensory makeup and the conceptual instruments that we possess. From this there follows what I propose to call the *thesis of conceptual schemes*, which lies at the root of the transcendental fallacy and of the logocentrism that follows from it: "intuitions without concepts are blind." Now, there is no doubt that, in order to do science, we need concepts, but the idea that they are strictly necessary for experience raises a variety of questions.

The first is point of fact. Is it really so? Are intuitions without concepts really blind? Here I do not mean merely to claim that I can bump into something without foreseeing it or without having a concept of it, but rather that I can have visual experiences that are very complex without being able to recognize exactly what I am seeing. In which case, such as that in which I see a part of a vacuum cleaner without knowing what it is, I have the intuition without the concept. Or conversely, I can have the concept, for instance that the two lines in the following figure are of the same length, even without an intuition that they are so, because I continue to *see* them as different:

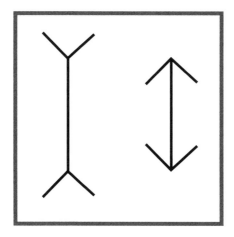

The Müller-Lyer illusion

It would be pure question begging to object that, in order to grasp the apparent difference in length as between the lines, I in any case need to have the concepts of equality and inequality. Or, rather, it would be a covert absurdity that would become apparent if it were claimed, for instance, that in order to see color I need the concept of color (or even the concept of *that very* color).

Behind the point of fact, there this a theoretical and terminological problem hidden. This concerns exactly what is meant by "concept" and, hence, by "conceptual scheme." A clear and distinct idea? A word? A physiological system, perhaps made up of neurons? A conscious scheme? Kant probably meant the last, even though the others also crop up in various measure and in various combinations; and the relative meaningfulness at first glance of the claim that intuitions without concepts are blind derives precisely from the fact that "concept" is used in highly ambiguous ways.

Behind the terminological point, there is an even broader problem hidden. This concerns the whole issue of the thesis of conceptual schemes. It is thought that we cannot access the external world without recourse to schemes. This remains to be shown, though, because to show that it is so, we would have to have recourse to an impossible experiment, namely seeing what happens to a subject who had no conceptual schemes. What we can nevertheless demonstrate is that in very many cases we are able to explain our behavior in the world without appeal to schemes, and how much, in many other cases—such as that of the two lines—what we see is in conflict with what we think. To the question about the need for categories of experience, and to that about how many and which categories we have, there are too many answers and we could equally well reply that we need 12, 120, 1200, just one (that of causality, as Schopenhauer suggested) or, indeed, none.

According to the thesis of conceptual schemes, in addition to the dependence of objects on subjects, we also have the determination of objects by scientific theories, which thus take on a role that is no longer merely explanatory but becomes constitutive. Suppose, indeed, that a metaphysician who was well inclined toward the neurosciences decided that the world depends essentially on our brain states; in that case, he would have to conclude, for a subject who had suffered a right parietal lesion, and who as a result no longer *perceived* half the visual field, that half of space does not really *exist.*[10]

2.1.1.4 *The Eye Has Its Own Ways of Reasoning*

Nevertheless, the claim that intuitions without concepts are blind, which is the main plank on which rests the centrality of conceptual schemes, can be defended in many ways.

The first and most obvious concerns cultural constructs. Take a piece of writing like the following:

SHADOW

It would be easy to argue that an illiterate (and perhaps someone who does not know English) would not be able to decipher the writing, and, as a result would not recognize the shadows of which it is made up. But it is fairly clear that to call on reading as a sort of operation in which concepts intervene on intuitions is a pretty weak argument. It is obvious that reading is a conceptual achievement, in which seeing is subservient. The same thing holds even more for all the consideration that historians of art and iconologists adduce regarding the role of culture in the redescription of the world.[11] That, however, is entirely beside the point and has nothing to do with the proper and austere meaning of "intuitions without concepts are blind," or with the claim that concepts *can intervene* in intuitions. For Kant, it is not a matter of drawing attention to how concepts guide intuitions—especially when we are dealing with recognition or drawing—but rather one of claiming that without concepts we are blind and, moreover, that the sphere of vision (and of perception in general) turns out to be wholly determined by the conceptual. Which obviously does not hold of physical objects; as we see in 3.1.2.1, things are very different again as regards social objects. Faced with such a lapidary affirmation as that intuitions without concepts are blind, we can do nothing other than to reply as follows.

1. *We can see even without concepts.* The spots that follow are not very conceptualizable, and calling them spots is not to gather them under a concept, but we have no trouble in seeing their positions and relations.

Random shapes can be seen

2. *We can have concepts and yet not see.* The groups of triangles drawn below all have the same shape, direction, and disposition, but that does not mean that we do not see them differently

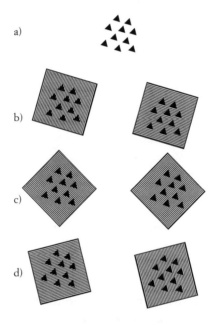

Relative orientations

3. *Intuitions without concepts can see perfectly well.* The possibility of having complex visual states without being able to understand exactly the nature of what is being perceived is precisely what happens to congenitally blind people who are operated on as adults at the end of the process of visual rehabilitation. From the viewpoint of physiology, we are certain that they see distinctly what they have in front of them, but they are undoubtedly unable to understand what they are seeing, as we see from the fact that they need to touch.[12]

4. *Seeing the duck-rabbit*. A final point: There is a sense in which the thesis of conceptual schemes can be upheld, which is not just the obvious and legitimate one of epistemology. But Kant never thought of it. It concerns the language that we use to *describe* our experiences.

Joseph Jastrow's duck-rabbit

It certainly may be thought that my not being able to see both the rabbit and the duck at the same time (though I know they are both there) depends on what I am like rather than on what the duck-rabbit is like. But this concerns above all what is meant by *seeing*, and it is this sense, which is not a matter of the physiology of perception as Kant thought, but rather of the semantics of the words and sentences we use, which can be used to defend the thesis that "intuitions without concepts are blind." If indeed someone were to see both the duck and the rabbit at once, then *seeing* would probably acquire a meaning different from the one we usually give it. The moral of this tale seems to me to be splendidly summed up in the principle adopted by Gaetano Kanizsa: "if we must say that the eyes reasons, it reasons in its own way," which is to say that it sees what it wants to see and not what we think or want.[13]

In other words, it is highly risky to collapse ontology and epistemology, because it betrays the nature of ontology and the structures that we meet in the world, as well as the nature of epistemology, which essentially concerns true opinion accompanied by a reason but then spreads out and descends, betraying its own nature, into the opinions and the arguments, both complete or just sketched in, that accompany our experience. It is important to grasp that, in order to see the sun, we do not have to have a true opinion accompanied by a reason, for otherwise we would have to say that Ptolemy had never seen the sun or set foot on the earth.

Another pair of pictures to clarify this point:[14]

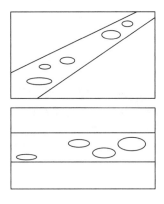

Giraffe necks

The first picture does not tell us much. Someone might point out that it is the neck of a giraffe passing by the window. We might say, without too much bad faith, "Yes, it's a giraffe!" Now look at the second picture. Would we believe it if someone said it is the neck of a giraffe? No, because we just cannot see it. For sure, if we were Polonius, we might reply that we had seen the neck of a giraffe, or, if it pleases, a giraffe's tail or the Mona Lisa.[15] We would have made the person happy, but making people happy is not the only thing in life (think about Polonius's sticky end). What does this little experiment prove? That it is not true that there are no facts, but only interpretations; with a bit of imagination I can see a giraffe in the first picture, but with all the imagination in the world, I cannot see it in the second any more than I can manage to see both the rabbit an the duck at once (and not one after the other) in Jastrow's figure.

2.1.2 Pragmatism

2.1.2.1 THERE ARE NO FACTS, ONLY INTERPRETATIONS   As I have already said several times, the natural radicalization of "intuitions without concepts are blind" is the claim that "there are no facts, only interpretations."[16] This claim is its hyperepistemological form and is a prelude to postmodernity. The first thing to note is that, as "intuitions without concepts are blind" took advantage of the ambiguity of the word *concept*, so "there are no facts, only interpretations" plays on the ambiguity of the word *interpretation*, which means many, or rather, too many things. As I have suggested elsewhere,[17] there are at least seven meanings: 1. *expression*: "The prime minister interpreted the will of the nation"; 2. *execution*: "a splendid interpretation"; 3. *translation*: "'Chien' means 'dog'"; 4. *clarification*: "'Hot dog' doesn't mean a dog that is hot"; 5. *understanding*: "Here, despite appearances, Socrates is being ironic"; 6. *demystification*: "He thinks he is hungry for knowledge, but he is really after the money"; and 7. *totalization*: "There are no facts, but only interpretations."

We may use an example to show how little these linguistic uses have in common a single meaning. Suppose Angela Merkel and Nicolas Sarkozy meet. They are asked (she in German and he in French) if they need an interpreter. In sense 1 (expression), they should say that they do not need one because the mere fact of speaking shows that they know how to interpret. The misunderstanding would be removed by an interpretation in sense 4 (clarification), and an interpreter in sense 3 (translation) would be called. If this person took himself to be interpreting also in sense 2 (execution), he might call for a round of applause at the end of his performance, and perhaps in doing his job he might also add some interpretation in sense 5 (understanding), if he said to Sarkozy, "I know that you don't particularly like this woman, but you should understand her because she is only doing her job, which is not so different from you," or indeed in sense 6 (demystification) if we suppose he said to Merkel, "Don't believe a word of what he is saying to you, and in the long run it's your business and I don't care." If we had to deal with interpretation in sense 7 (totalization), we could not see why the pair met or what they were talking about.

Quite apart from the ambiguity of "interpretation," there is something strange about the sentence, "There are no facts, only interpretations." On the one hand, it looks plausible enough; if we don't think too hard about it, it might seem that there are no facts, but only interpretations: things can be evaluated and described in many ways, everyone has his own point of view, the sciences progress by means of conjectures, the meanings of some novels seem to be inexhaustible and so on ever more weakly. But now let us see what happens if we make just very slight adjustments to our sentence[18]:

1. "There are no madmen, only interpretations."
2. "There are no pacts, only interpretations."
3. "There are no cats, only interpretations."

Sentence (1) looks like a slogan for the sort of postmodern antipsychiatry that exemplifies all the defects of the strong textualism to be discussed in 3.2.2; (2) is a deplorably cynical declaration; and (3) is a perfect absurdity. If we now reread "There are no facts, only interpretations," the sentence that seemed profound now appears false,[19] a sign of deplorable dishonesty; and, with hindsight, we are induced to ask why such a sentence could, in certain lighting conditions so to say, have seemed profound.

2.1.2.2 INFINITY IN EXPERIENCE   The answer is fairly simple. Nietzsche's sentence recalls Walter Benjamin's equally extremist (though less morally serious) claim that translation is impossible or Paul Valéry's denial that there is such a thing as the true meaning of a text. There is a respect in which these expressions are equivalent insofar as they *introduce infinity into experience.* By asserting that there are no facts, but only interpretations, that translation is impossible or that there is no true meaning in a text, a practical activity of interpretation is made endless, when it is anything but. In fact, if we observe what actually happens in life, we see that we interpret *a great deal,* but not *always* and certainly not *infinitely.* At most, we interpret indefinitely, by which we mean that we cannot decide a priori how many interpretations a given text (especially an unclear one) can bear.

But it is a long step from there to saying, for instance, that there are *infinitely many* ways to use a screwdriver. I can easily imagine that, in addition to its proper use, a screwdriver can be used as a weapon, as a lever or (as we mentioned at the beginning of the book) as a very hazardous bathroom accessory. But, beyond a certain point, we end up with the comic if not the absurd. Things are rather different as regards the structure of matter, the working of the brain, or the explanation of the mind-body relation. I have no difficulty imagining (if for no other reason than that it is what has historically been the case) that we should investigate the question for thousands of years and come up with very many explanations, which are also interpretations. It must be admitted that the issue is subtler than that of how to use a screwdriver, and the questions are theoretical rather than practical. All the same, the number of speculations is not infinite; it would be potentially infinite only in the trivial sense that we could always *add* more details; but in this sense even a shopping list is potentially infinite.

Moral: In practice, interpretation necessarily comes to an end, just as Wittgenstein suggested with the image of a spade that sooner or later is bent and can dig no further.[20] This feature of practical affairs derives from the fact that sooner or later we need to make *a* decision, not two and certainly not infinitely many. In the "sooner or later" it is always the "sooner" that has the upper hand over the "later" given that the practical subject is finite, does not have time to waste, is not concerned with centuries, but rather with years, days and minutes. This seems to me the really decisive point. It is perfectly legitimate, from the scientific point of view, to say that the ultimate truth has not been found and that every gain in knowledge is partial and amounts to no more than a step along the way toward the truth. In this sense, "a step along the way toward the truth" is another way of saying, "There are no facts, only interpretations," given that there is no difficulty about understanding that what was once explained by phlogiston is now explained by oxygen, or about imagining that it will be explained in yet another way in ten thousand years if it is explained at all.

This does not remotely allow us to say that, in that case, every part of our existence is just another step along the path toward the truth. "The mail is delivered at 9:00" is not a step along the path toward the truth; it is a notice that tells me about a timetable, in which the only room for interpretation derives from the only ambiguity in the text, namely whether the 9:00 in question is morning or evening. "The mail is delivered at 21.00 hours" removes this ambiguity without itself being a further step along the path toward the truth. These points help us to see the underlying problem. If someone asks me what time it is and I reply, "It's 9:00," there is nothing to interpret, except the usual ambiguity of morning or evening, which removes itself at some latitudes. Nevertheless, supposing I am talking to my psychoanalyst, "It's 9:00" might give rise to a variety of interpretations. If the analysis is unending, if my analyst and I have lots of time to waste, and if I have enormous sums of money, then hermeneutics is free to run wild. We might go on for years interpreting that "It's 9:00." But even in that case, we cannot go on forever, given that sooner or later one of us will die.

The disparity between the situations brings out the difference between the sphere of the sciences—the search for absolute truth—in which the claim that there are no facts, but only interpretations might make some sense, and the sphere of life and experience, where such a thing makes no sense whatever. Thus, there is an essential difference between science and life. In science, things are subject to doubt until we have absolute certainty about them, which means that the overwhelming majority of our knowledge is doubtful, even if this does not license us to say there are no facts, but only interpretations. In experience, things are true until the opposite is shown, which means that we live in a world of certainties, which make up the pretheoretical background to our agency, and only occasionally, when there is misunderstanding or perceptual mistake, are we pushed to review our beliefs. Thus, in claiming that there are no facts, but only interpretations, Nietzsche confused science with experience and applied Murphy's law: If anything can go wrong it will, or, in our case: if there is even a remote chance of misunderstanding, then it will be misunderstood.

We found the beginning of this story in Descartes: the senses *sometimes* mislead us, so we must *never* trust their witness, and if we do not have a clear and distinct idea of something, we don't merely have little knowledge of it, we don't know it at all. Nevertheless, we should not forget that Descartes himself took his doubt as a sort of dietary or ascetic maxim (that we should doubt at least once in the course of our lives), and above all was clear that it was proper to practice doubt only in theoretical matters and never in practical ones. By contrast, in the two centuries that separate Descartes from Nietzsche, the upshot has been that doubt has been normalized, transferred from science to experience, from the exception to the rule, from theory to practice.

2.1.2.2 THE PRIMACY OF MISUNDERSTANDING The normalization of doubt has found fertile ground in hermeneutics. Down until the eighteenth century, the rule in interpretation was *in claris non fit interpretatio*, meaning that normally we read or look at, rather than interpret, the things that are there clearly to be seen. It can occasionally happen that there is something obscure or an obstacle to our understanding. It is then, and not before, that we need to interpret. Things begin to change at the start of the nineteenth century with romantic hermeneutics, according to which misunderstanding is the starting point and understanding is sought in the face of various difficulties. It was a complete reversal. The world became obscure and hard to decipher, or rather—specifically with Kant—it became a scientific laboratory full of unsolved puzzles and working hypotheses. At this point it became quite natural to think that the sentence "The mail is delivered at 9:00" or "It is 9:00" becomes enigmatic or worse, given that there is no true meaning in the text and there are no facts, only interpretations. But in the real world, things are not like this at all. Suppose a pact or contract admitted of infinite interpretations. If we follow a case in court (a place where, at least if you are innocent, slogans like "equality under the law" are more reassuring than would be "there are no facts, but only interpretations"), we see that the starting point is that interpretation is anything but infinite, and that the choice is faced between *two* interpretations of which only *one* will be found to be the true one. We might remark *en passant* that this is also the situation in science inasmuch as there are many erroneous interpretations and only one true one, except that in science, we can wait while in life we cannot because life is too short.

The effect of the normalization of doubt is that the world appears uncertain, vague and full of ambiguity, and that the interpreter becomes a creator charged with bringing light into the very shadows that he contributed to bringing into being. Nietzsche did nothing but take the next step after romantic hermeneutics: if everything is threatened by misunderstanding, why should any interpretation claim to be the true one? They are all true and none of them is, because there are no facts, but only interpretations. We shall see the final side effects of this assumption when we consider the postmodernist claim that "there is nothing outside the text."

2.1.2.4 *GAVAGAI*   There is a further point before concluding our consideration of "there are no facts, but only interpretations." In the twentieth century Quine offered partial justification of the primacy of misunderstanding with his argument for the impossibility of radical translation.[21] Quine's example is well known. We hear a native say "*gavagai*" when the leaves rustle and we see a rabbit go by, so we conclude that what he is saying means "rabbit." But perhaps the native meant an undetached rabbit part, the mereological sum of all rabbits, a temporal slice of a rabbit or rabbithood. Hence, radical translation is impossible, misunderstanding is the norm, and at the end of the day there are no facts, only interpretations.

This is not quite right, though. The argument for the impossibility of radical translation does not apply to material objects but to language, which is a social object. Quine does not throw doubt on whether we and the native see a rabbit (a material object); he doubts only that I am in a position to understand the word (a social object) that the native uses to refer to the rabbit. In fact, Quine goes no further than to claim that we never have a final guarantee for the passage between words and objects, and (unlike Nietzsche) he does not exclude the possibility of there being truth as coherence within our theories and conceptual schemes. Which is to say that truth as conformity between a proposition and a thing leaves the stage and is replaced by truth as coherence within a system of theories. In short, I can never be sure that the book I am pointing at is really blue (it could be that what I mean by blue is really red), but I will never have a reason for doubting that a molecule of water is made up of two atoms of hydrogen and one of oxygen, nor, all the more, that contract work attracts an emergency tax of 20 percent. Nevertheless, what Quine agrees with Nietzsche and the whole of post-Cartesian epistemology about is that a theoretical doubt (was it really a rabbit or the passage of a rabbit or a part of a rabbit?) is quite enough to motivate unlimited skepticism. This is a skepticism that does not upset the pragmatist Quine, who is solidly anchored in and protected by his practices, but that can be unleashed whenever one begins to suppose, as the phenomenological tradition does, that agency depends on knowledge. This is why skepticism generally has a more baleful influence on continental philosophy than it does in the analytic tradition.

To claim that one ought to have complete mastery of the context in order to be able to translate sensibly is to conjure up the ghosts of absolute knowledge: If you do not know everything, you do not know anything, and you cannot say anything even about the smallest and simplest things (indeed, because things are small and simple is a reason for doubt about them). In this direction, we are led to overlook the way that there are lots of people who do not know French, yet do know that *chien* means "dog." After all, it would be easy to show that natural objects and many artifacts call for very little knowledge of context (even a dog can use an armchair to sit on, without having to have a thought like "Here is an armchair"), and that the problems arise essentially with social objects: "Apply a 20 percent emergency tax" is wholly incomprehensible if one does not have a grasp of the context, and we can easily imagine a society in which it makes no sense while we can hardly imagine a society in which, once a chair has been sighted, it would not be sat on. In this sense, the fact that Averroes in Borges's story was unable to understand what Aristotle meant in talking about the theater does not mean that translation was impossible for him, as it would be if he had the same difficulty with activities like eating, relaxing, and sitting down.[22] It is rather a sign of the fact that often enough, without a prior understanding of the context, social objects appear incomprehensible. But even in these cases, we have to concern ourselves with fairly complex social objects that call for the interaction of many other elements of society. Thus, when in *Madame Bovary* the pharmacist Homais replies to Léon using the English "yes," both of them understand what he says, though neither of them knows English; or an Italian barman might happily say "*et voilà*," knowing what he is saying and making himself understood by his client, even though both are perfectly ignorant of French. In the same way, I understand that the lack of serotonin causes depression or that hemoglobin is important, even though my knowledge of medicine is incomplete. Translation is perfectly possible, and this constancy is much firmer than the counterexample of "*gavagai*" would suggest.

In short, the impossibility of radical translation points to a limiting case and seeks to make it into the rule.[23] In any case, it might be noted that even as regards ideal objects, those that lend themselves to a relaxed theoretical contemplation and hence to idle and unending interpretation, we come in the overwhelming majority of case to quite unmistakable conclusions. For instance, during the Cold War, Russian and American mathematicians demonstrated the very same theorems by different routes, given that there was no exchange between the two scientific communities. But this never meant that the theorems (I repeat: arrived at by different techniques) could not be translated, for it was immediately clear that they were the same theorems; but if the argument about translation held, this would have been impossible. It might be objected that ideal objects share a single language, but this is too vague; the Greeks and the Indians, for instance, developed very different mathematical systems, but that did not prevent them from arriving at the same results. It is true that translation is more complicated in the case of social objects, as any professor trying to validate exam credits in the Erasmus international exchange program well knows. If the discussion about Erasmus credits sooner or later comes to a close, years can be devoted to considering whether cargo cults count as genuine religious rites, but, except in a very few cases, this is not a big problem.

To sum up, as regards natural objects such as rabbits, the margin for interpretation is limited by what we have in front of us and is independent of our schemes and expectations. As regards ideal objects such as theorems, interpretation is stabilized by a common and shared content independent of how it is presented. As regards social objects such as Erasmus credits, the difficulties may be greater but are not in principle insurmountable, given that the social world is the realm of practice and so does not allow us to waste too much time. Quine's is a limiting case, more or less like Cartesian doubt, given that it aims to reconstruct an idealized situation or radical translation, when normally we have to deal with translation that is anything but radical: In the real world we learn quickly and easily that a bathtub is for having a bath and not for growing tomatoes (that might happen, but it is rare and surprising) and that money is for making payments and not for lighting a cigar (that too might happen, but mostly in films).

2.1.3 Postmodernism

2.1.3.1 THERE IS NOTHING OUTSIDE THE TEXT

We thus come to the final version of the transcendental fallacy, the postmodern saying "There is nothing outside the text."[24] Conceptual schemes, in other words, are measured only by themselves in the absence of any world that transcends them. The saying itself, however you take it, looks obscure and problematic. What does it mean to claim that there is nothing outside the text? That the sun and the earth do not exist outside the text? That the sun goes round the earth if it is written in a book that it does? That objectivity and the existence of an external world are just so much useless passion? That there are things more important for us than objectivity and the existence of the external world? The most important aspect of this proposition is the powerful practical effect it has.

To get a grip on this matter, we need to look at a polemic that has been going on over recent years, and not just in philosophy, namely the dispute between relativism and antirelativism. Relativism amounts to moral permissiveness and is the polytheism of values in the twentieth century; antirelativism is the reaction to this situation, the recovery of tradition, the respect for natural law and, if need be, for revelation. It is obvious that this is a question with immediate political impact, though it derives from theoretical questions. Let us try to get it in focus by looking at the events of the last thirty years, rather than the history of the last two hundred, and date its beginning with the publication in 1979 of two genuinely epoch-making books, one a thick tome by American philosopher Richard Rorty[25] and the other a slim volume by French philosopher Jean-François Lyotard.[26]

Rorty's book in particular gave voice and form to a widespread philosophical feeling that realism was past its sell-by date and that for centuries philosophy and science had had to deal with a confrontation between conceptual schemes and not with the verification of, say, words or concepts on the one hand and the world on the other. If this was how things stood, Rorty observed, the time had come to conclude that objectivity, and the assumption that the world was "out there," were obsolete fixations, obsessions, or transitory superstitions of philosophy from the seventeenth to the nineteenth century, and that they had to be replaced with more fertile and productive ideas, such as social solidarity, dialogue among persons and cultures, and tolerance. After all, Rorty observed, "truth" is something for which we have no use, it is a sort of slap on the back, a compliment we make to a proposition or a situation that serves our purposes or that we like for some other reason. In his turn, Lyotard was a pioneer in taking account of computing technology, which was just then beginning to make its mark on society, and claimed that we were moving toward a dematerialized world, one that would be more democratic and spiritual than modernity's centuries of iron and coal: reality would no longer be what it had once been, and perhaps it would not be at all.

2.1.3.2 THEORY AND PRACTICE   There is no harm in admitting that even good philosophers can make mistakes just like everyone else. We have seen that, far from disappearing, objects have multiplied. I am not referring just to dumps of old computers and other relics generated daily by the world that Lyotard called "immaterial," but above all of the proliferation of the Web-based objects we saw in 1.1. The job, as I said, is to organize them into an ontology and not to muddle them with a hermeneutics. If this is how things stand, it seems implausible to maintain that objectivity understood as correlation with reality (the old conformity of the proposition to the thing) is nothing but a passing fit, or that it is a useless ornament. After all, there are definitely many fields of life—from the choice of your doctor to the housing market—in which we prefer objectivity to solidarity. And it unlikely that dialogue can take the place of truth, though it might at most aspire to the status of a regulative ideal; if anything, as we see from the practice of out-of-court settlements, it is nothing but a second-best, for all that it might be unavoidable. But it is really not clear why we should transform a second-best into an ideal, which seems in any case often to be inapplicable, as we would soon find out if we wanted to fix the height of Mont Blanc by stipulation. As for the ideal of "ironic theory," of holding one's views and beliefs at arm's length, as Rorty recommended as a remedy for dogmatism, an encounter in court with, say, an "ironic postmodern witness" would make us rue the witnesses of yesteryear. It is worth recalling that the primacy of solidarity over objectivity was also given an outing by Roland Freiser, the chairman of the Nazi People's Court from 1942 to 1945.

All this leaves out the fact that hermeneutical and postmodern scorn of truth and objectivity has provided arguments and impetus to criticisms of relativism that are carried forward in the name of "greater reasonableness."[27] In fact, in the postmodern world, the argumentative structures employed by antirelativist popes and postmodern philosophers share a common robust element, namely the idea that conceptual schemes have a constitutive role over reality.[28] In particular, for the conceptual schemes of Cardinal Bellarmino, the earth is at the center of the universe, and this claim is corroborated by the Bible, Aristotle, and Ptolemy, eminent textual support. Once it is admitted that there is nothing outside the text, these elements cannot be seen off by mere recourse to the fact that out there, in the physical world, the earth is *not* at the center of the Universe, for the simple reason that no such "out there" exists. So far, so much in common. At this point the postmodernist and the antirelativist pontifex part company. The philosopher will conclude on these grounds that geocentrism is a culturally valid as heliocentrism, and will get himself caught up in the contradictions of relativism about reality (which is very different from relativism about morality), finding he has to face such questions as: If Ptolemy and Galileo are equally right, do we have to put Aesculapius on the same level as Pasteur? Evolution on the same level as intelligent design? Laws of nature on the same level as miracles? The pope, by contrast, finds himself with the advantage of being able to go beyond the either-or of Ptolemy and Galileo (as well as the others), by appealing to the greater reasonableness relative to which the century-long disputes over knowledge are reduced to regional conflicts.

2.1.3.3 FROM RELATIVISM TO REALISM

The dissolution of facts into interpretations and of the world into texts has not led to the emancipation that Nietzsche and the postmodernists talked about, but rather to populism and authoritarianism. That is the bad news. The good news, however, is that none of it is true. Reality stays where it is and where it has always been, perfectly indifferent to our theoretical wranglings, but sensitive to global warming. What I would like to contrast with these dispiriting results is that we have been making much ado about nothing, because reality has not disappeared, being has never been superseded by knowledge and knowledge has never been overcome by will. What I propose therefore is a passage from hermeneutic relativism to realist objectivism. While radical hermeneutics regarded them as principles of violence and subordination, objectivity and reality are in fact our only bulwark against arbitrariness. This principle applies in the first instance in moral-practical questions because it provides a theoretical foundation in the recognition of a sphere of reality independent of interpretations and of conceptual schemes, reformulations, and linguistic manipulations.

I hope that this has made clear the underlying motive for my contrasting ontology and epistemology as well as the practical motivations for it. In my view, the remedy for the transcendental fallacy is not at all a critique of relativism, which is a noble, perfectly respectable, and in many cases inevitable view. Relativism does not mean that everyone can do his or her own thing, but that everyone has trouble giving up the forms of life in which he or she was brought up. Rather, the point is to insist on the extremely broad spheres of reality that are independent of theories and of cultural conditioning, as much from East as from West, from above or below, by humans, animals, or male chauvinists; and to put the accent on the way that the real world's autonomy asserts its rights even in the social world. At the point at which there is the risk of falling from the frying pan of politically motivated subjectivism into the fire of equally politically motivated antirelativism, realism has an important part to play in a game that affects us all, and the distinction between ontology and epistemology is not of merely academic interest.

The main advantage of this distinction is, in my view, the way it points to the difference between the world and the conceptual schemes by which we refer to it, and thus suggests that in very many cases, the sharing of a world depends much more on the characteristics of the objects than on agreement of conceptual schemes. In a single field, a snail can wend its way, a dog can be taken for a walk, I, who know very little about plants, can look around me at the same time as a gardener, who has a practical interest in them, or a botanist, who has a theoretical interest in them. What I suggest is that the only one in this list who has science, who operates an epistemology and conceptual schemes in his relations with the field is the botanist. The gardener can get by with practical directions, and act without knowing (or even believing to know) the principles of what he is doing. The snail, the dog, and I pass through the field with experiences and perhaps with various reflections (the snail does not see, the dog sees in color, but differently from me, and I see more colors than he does and can even think to myself, "Look, a four-leafed clover!") but all without having science. The deliberate exercise of language and conceptual schemes, the sphere of activity, concerns only a fraction of those passing through the field. And it should be remembered that even the botanist, if he wants his conceptual schemes to be true, has to depend on something that is not itself conceptual, namely vision—at least if what we said in 2.1.1.4 about intuitions without concepts being able to see perfectly well is right—which he shares at least with me and with the gardener. For the rest, what holds is what I call the *slipper experiment*,[29] which aims to show the independence of the world both of our conceptual schemes and of our perceptual apparatus.

2.1.4 The Slipper Experiment

The experiment goes as follows.

1. *Men.* Let us take a man who is looking at a carpet on which there is a slipper; he asks someone else to pass him the slipper, and the other usually does so without particular difficulty. A banal interaction that shows nevertheless that, if the external world really depended even a little, not so much on interpretations and conceptual schemes as on neurons, the fact that the two men do not have *the same* neurons would make the sharing of the slipper impossible. It might be objected that the neurons do not have to be numerically identical nor even by way of the relative positions of the synapses; but this not only weakens the claim but also contradicts a obvious and hard to refute fact namely the banality that differences in past experiences, culture, and brain structure and power can make for significant differences at a certain level and lead to disputes about opinions. But the slipper on the floor is another thing. It is external to and separate from us and our opinions; and for this reason it has an existence qualitatively different from what we encounter when we reason about the standing of such questions as futile medical care or preventive declarations of war. In other words, the sphere of facts is not so very bound up with that of interpretations. It is only when an evaluative element is in play that

dialogue can be important; to establish that some behavior is legitimate or not, it is better to listen to a variety of opinions and talk the thing over; but to establish that the slipper is on the carpet, I look and I touch, and in any case discussion does not help much.

2. *Dogs.* Let us now take a dog that has been trained. It is told, "Bring me the slipper." Again, it does what it is told without difficulty, just like the man before, even though there are enormous differences between my brain and its, and its understanding of "Bring me the slipper" can hardly be compared with a man's; the dog would not wonder whether I was really asking it to bring me the slipper rather than quoting the sentence or being ironic, while at least some humans might do so.

3. *Worms.* Let us now take a worm. It has neither a brain nor ears. It is much smaller than the slipper. It has only the sense of touch, whatever that might mean exactly. Anyway, we can hardly ask the worm to bring the slipper. All the same, if in moving across the carpet the worm meets the slipper, it can choose between two strategies: either it goes round or it goes over. In either case, it meets the slipper, even if not in the way that I do.

4. *Ivy.* Then we take an ivy plant. It has no eyes or anything else, but it climbs (this is how we express it, treating the ivy as if it were an animal and attributing to it an intentional strategy) up the walls as if it saw them; or it slowly shifts if it encounters a heat source that does not suit it. The ivy either goes round the slipper or it goes over it, just like a man, even thought it has neither eyes nor conceptual schemes.

5. *The slipper.* Finally, let us take the slipper. It is even more insensitive that the ivy. But if we throw another slipper at it, it meets it just like the ivy, the worm, the dog, and the man. Thus, we cannot see in what sense we can accept even the most reasonable and minimalist version of the claim about the supposed ontological intervention of the perceiver on the perceived. After all, we could equally well not take the second slipper, but simply imagine that the first one is there in the absence of any animal observer, in the absence of any plant or other slipper interacting with it. Might there not be a slipper on the floor in that case? If the slipper is really there, then it must be so even if nobody sees it, as follows logically from the sentence, "There is a slipper"; otherwise we might say, "It seems to me that there is a slipper," or, more correctly, "I have in myself a representation of a slipper," or even

"I have the impression of having a representation of a slipper." Making the existence of things depend on the resources of the my sense organs is no different from making them depend on my imagination, and when I claim that a slipper exists *only* because I see it, I am really saying that what I am having is a hallucination.

This experiment may seem poor and obvious, but if the reader will have the patience to read on, I promise to show how many consequences we can draw out of it.

2.2 ONTOLOGICAL DIFFERENCES

Where, in the previous section, I pointed out the main forms of the confusions between ontology and epistemology, in this we pass to the constructive part of the discussion and aim to articulate the differences between ontology and epistemology. This will permit us to both to treat experience as distinct from science and the external world as distinct from conceptual schemes in which physical objects are to be found. The differences are between truth (considered as an epistemological factor, as a justified belief taken as true) and reality (as an ontological given); between the world internal to our conceptual schemes and the world external to and transcendent of them; between science, as a knowledge-gathering and deliberate function, and experience, as what, whether we want it or not, we always have so long as we are alive. These three differences can be spelled out as follows.

First, reality is not truth: reality is something that is, while truth is a property of a judgment about what there is. The fact that, for every truth there is something, its truth-maker, that makes it true shows that truth is founded on reality, against what the defenders of the collapse of ontology and epistemology claim, according to whom reality is founded on truth, namely from its insertion into the network of conceptual schemes.

Second, and in line with what we have just said, the external world does not depend on the inner world: physical reality transcends consciousness and the conceptual apparatus with which we understand the world (as we see in 3.1, things are slightly different as regards the social world).

Third, there is a difference between experience and science: the ways that we deal with reality in everyday life, in practical and esthetic experience, as well as in perceptual experience, are not degraded or primitive versions of science, but rather activities that are to a large degree extraneous to science.

The overall sense of these three distinctions is simply this. We are led for obvious reasons to confuse the things in the world with the way that we know them. And very often the former get taken for the latter, being for knowledge, as in the splendid opening lines of *The World as Will and Representation*: we believe that there is a world, but there is only a eye that sees and a hand that feels.[30] Schopenhauer seems not to have noticed that what he was describing was not a negation in the world, but rather the assertion that, so far as he could tell, there are in the external world at least two things, namely an eye and a hand. He did not see this, though, because, as a victim of the transcendental fallacy, he identified truth with reality, the inner world with the external world, and science with experience. Thus, it seems to me unavoidable to propose and articulate these distinctions in order to outline the genuine nature of an ontology.

We may summarize these in a table and proceed to expound them.[31]

Epistemology	Ontology
Truth Does not arise from experience, but is teleologically aimed at it. Emendable	Reality Not naturally aimed at science Unemendable
Inner world (= internal to conceptual schemes) Paradigm: *the conceptual scheme* In the head, refers to the world	Outer world (= external to conceptual schemes) Paradigm: *everything that is not emendable*
Science Linguistic Historical Free Infinite Teleological	Experience Not necessarily linguistic Nonhistorical Unemendable Finite Not necessarily teleological

2.2.1 First Difference: Truth ≠ Reality

Let us begin with the first difference. It is fairly obvious that truth has to do with science and vice versa: we would not know what to do with a science that did not promise the truth, or at least an approximation to it. It is equally obvious that reality (mountains, lakes, thunder, and squirrels) has nothing to do with truth. Reality itself is what it is; truth is a discourse that, in certain circumstances, we can put together about what is.[32] To claim that truth, or at least talk, is present in every encounter with reality is an extravagant request that depends precisely on the transcendental fallacy.

Material differential. Now, if we consider the slipper experiment, we notice that in all the interactions there was something left over that was independent of conceptual schemes. I propose to call this the *material differential*,[33] because it is what remains once we have taken away the conceptual schemes (and even the perceptual apparatus). Philosophers have often reflected on the material differential, for instance, in considering "substance" as what underlies change and attributes (which in turn, being secondary or tertiary qualities, are referred to the perceptual apparatus or to conceptual schemes).[34]

With the material differential, we have in the first instance to deal with a nontheoretical background to the theory. Whether it is the basis that is presupposed in our actions and in our judgments (for instance that the world continues even beyond the door of our house), or a "precategorial" world because it has not yet been cut up by the categories that we use to know it, we find ourselves in any case in front of (or rather surrounded by) an element that is omnipresent in our experience, and that presents itself also as the foundation for the theory and for science, which would make no sense if they could not refer to a stratum that was real and pretheoretic, I propose to characterize the material differential in the first instance in a negative way, through the idea of *unemendability.*

2.2.1.1 UNEMENDABILITY   Though the notion of a "background" has often been discussed by philosophers, I would like to draw attention to a feature of it that has been less often emphasized, namely the fact that *this background is often in conflict with our theories,* and in that sense it does not obviously appear as their presupposition, given that experience can be unruly and surprising. The point is more important than it might seem. In Aristotelian terms, science is the grasping of *regularities* and, in empiricist terms, the *repeatability* of experiments. Some of these features are to be found also in experience, which nevertheless has to come to terms with *surprise.* Something unforeseen can always happen to break the regularity. The empiricists saw how much this sort of case conflicts with the image of science as regularity, and, as hinted in 2.1, they found that surprises and unforeseen experiences constituted an insuperable obstacle for the reliability of induction. Nevertheless, unless every now and then something happened to break the series of our predictions, we would have no way of telling real experience from imagined. Schopenhauer's image of waking and dreams as pages of the same book, except that the first are read in order and coherently while the latter are read at random, is suggestive, but misses the point; for if waking life really were so smooth, we would not have grounds for calling it "waking."

A surprise would not amount to much if it could be immediately corrected. For one of the characteristics of experience is indeed the fact that it is there and it cannot be corrected, there is nothing to be done about it, and it does not go away or change. This feature is unemendability, and it is fundamental—being both enduring and not a matter of chance—to *reality*, rather than to *truth*. The basic idea is essentially this: If we agree that that it is a fundamental requisite of objectivity, including scientific objectivity, that there be invariance under transformation,[35] all the more should we suppose that the independence of objects from the subject's conceptual schemes (and from epistemology in general) is an even stronger criterion of objectivity. This is exactly what unemendability is: If I look at fire, I can think that it is process of oxidation or the action of phlogiston or of caloric, but I cannot (unless I have asbestos gloves on) not burn my hands if I put them in it, and this is one of the things of which we are as sure as we can be.

The sphere of what is unemendable is not limited to perception but is clearest and most impressive in the irrevocability of past events, which appears like a necessity that we recognize after the fact. Someone might not know that, during the battle of Leipzig in 1813 a part of the Saxon army abandoned Napoleon and sided with the Prussians, Russians, and Austrians. All the same, that is what happened, and the conceptual difficulties that are generated by imagining a time machine that takes us into the past follow from the fact that it is not possible to intervene in it. For instance, the idea of returning to the past to kill one's grandfather in the cradle so as to perform a sophisticated sort of suicide turns out to be quite implausible, given that if we are here now, then our grandfather must have been then. Now, if we are happy to accept the irrevocability of the past, why should we not think of present events as aleatory? They often present themselves to us in such a way as to crush our expectations or contradict our conceptual schemes (for sure, Napoleon did not expect the Saxons to be turncoats), because experience puts us in touch with what Wolfgang Metzger called "the encountered,"[36] which is to say, something that can oppose to our thought the same resistance that we encounter in the laws of logic: The whole is greater than the part; what is red is not green; if I have lost the key, I cannot open the door; and if the Saxons change sides, they change sides. In this sense, unemendability is the clearest and most powerful expression of a material necessity.[37]

2.2.1.2 NAÏVE PHYSICS   Having set out what I mean by unemendability, I would like to illustrate briefly the role it plays in my overall strategy regarding the distinction between ontology and epistemology. A first point is that my way of conceiving the relations between the two dimensions is obviously not the only one, and we may take note of at least seven main positions.[38]

1. Within the grouping that gives most weight to epistemology, we have the revisionary claim,[39] which proposes that we should adopt in our everyday practice and not just in research work, the kinds of decomposition and recomposition of reality that are used in science.

2. At the opposite end of the scale, there is the naïve view,[40] according to which prescientific perceptual experience captures a reality and, so, a truth. In these terms, the naïve position expresses a basically polemical, but very important, point that brings to the fore the way that our perception of the world is not conditioned by conceptual schemes. On this account, there is a deep difference between "naïve physics," which has this subversive intent, and other branches of naïve knowledge (naïve biology, naïve economics), which are simply inadequate forms of knowledge and only of psychological interest.

3. Then there are the *phenomenological* positions,[41] which, like the naïve theories, affirm the complete reality of phenomena as such (as appearances), but do not take a view on the truth of the phenomena but rather operate a programmatic bracketing or *epoché*.

4. The *ecological* approaches[42] describe experience, as much for humans, animals, and plants, in terms of the vital principles for survival in the environment. Relative to the foregoing versions, the ecological account takes very little interest in knowledge gathering, but comes in useful when we have to determine the scale of the phenomena implicated in experience, as I suggest in 2.2.3.3.

5. The *experiential* view,[43] on the other hand, combines the phenomenological and the ecological approaches and conducts its enquires

primarily in psychological terms; this is a phenomenology with a less radical *epoché*.

6. The *evolutionary* positions[44] pass from psychology to ontology (with a pinch of salt, not in every case and not from every point of view, as the naïve does) on the basis of an argument to the effect that, if we have evolved to represent the world in a certain way, and we have no independent reasons to think that this is just chance, then we have a reason to thing that the world is after all thus and so, containing the features that we attribute to it.

7. Finally, there are the *descriptive* positions,[45] which, unlike the revisionary approach, seek to capture experience on the basis of categories that they have to assume are well founded and not mere observation data.

What I am offering with the notion of *unemendability* is a vision that I would call (8) *antagonistic*, which shows how little epistemology figures as the natural destiny of ontology and thus offering an underlying justification for the descriptive positions. It will be noted that I make ample use of the analyses that derive from the experiential, the ecological and the descriptive versions, but the viewpoint I feel myself closest to is that of naïve physics. Paolo Bozzi used to point out the extent to which the world of everyday life is impervious to the most evolved conceptual schemes.[46] Without committing myself to his claim that the world of naïve physics is more real than that of expert physics, I do want to say that the conflict between naïve physics and expert physics, and the unemendability of the former, is enough to show that one sphere of experience is impervious to the conceptual schemes of science.

2.2.2 *Second Difference: Inner World ≠ External World*

We proceed now to the second essential difference. Unemendability shows us the existence of an external world, not relative to our bodies (which are part of the external world) but rather relative to our minds and more exactly relative to the conceptual schemes with which we try to explain and interpret the world. This external world is populated by natural objects and ideal objects (at least by their exemplars as we pointed out in 1.1.3 and 1.3.2.2), as well as by the physical part of social objects. I infer the autonomy of the external world by extending the argument from unemendability read in the key of the autonomy of esthetics from logic and the antinomy between esthetics and logic.[47] With these rather cryptic ways of talking, I mean, in the first instance, that perceptual experience (esthetics) is not subordinated to the action of conceptual schemes (logic) and, in the second, that this non-subordination shows itself, in line with the experience of unemendability, as insubordination, as the conflict between perceptual experience and conceptual schemes.

2.2.2.1 THE AUTONOMY OF ESTHETICS FROM LOGIC   Let us return once more to Descartes's condemnation of the senses: The senses fool us, and we should not trust those who have fooled us even once. Here, as I said in 2.1.1.1, the criterion of exactness has been set too high: The fact that we can mistake a firefly for a lantern is not a good reason for not trusting the senses, which after all remain the surest route to knowledge, not only because we use the senses to discover the mistake, but also because they are surer than other faculties such as memory, not to mention imagination. On the other hand, Descartes has pulled a fast one. He says that we should not trust *those who* have fooled us even once. In this way, he treats the senses as if they were persons, with their own intentions, inclinations, and characters. However, the senses are not persons; they do not have a character and do not do anything on purpose. Once they fool us, this does not mean that they are showing some perverse attitude toward us. If anyone fools me in a systematic way, it is not the senses, but rather mistaken theories or the media baron of the day. That is another story, not to mention the fact that, somewhat paradoxically, Descartes maintains that the senses are the servants of the spirit and they do what it wants, but then he puts the blame for mistakes on the servants and not on the master. In any case, the fact that a person can lie to us once, misleading us for instance about his knowledge or abilities, is a quite important signal, because it can reveal a disposition that he might act upon on other occasions. But the senses do not have intentions or characters; if anything, they show a firm tendency to disappoint, to not give us what we hoped; and this might be a sign of that very lack of character that is often described as a "bad character"; nevertheless, it is quite contrary to a will to mislead.[48] Even if the senses sometimes betray us, they remain our basic reference point when we sniff the milk to make sure it has not gone bad, we jump out of the way when we see a car coming, or we jump at a threatening sound.

Here we encounter the independence of perception from conceptual schemes or, to put it more positively, the existence of nonconceptual contents. These contents show up precisely in the traditional dissatisfaction with perception considered as a source both necessary and untrustworthy. How can it be that sensible experience should be *at one and the same time* necessary and untrustworthy? It is clear that something has gone awry, and it is precisely the demand to see sensible experience merely the precursor of science, as typically happens with induction (and its critique) as we discussing in connection with the transcendental fallacy. If I put the light on one hundred times, the one-hundred-and-first-time it might not light up because the bulb has blown, *as perception tells us*, which therefore is not guilty of anything if the law was mistaken and it has nothing to do with that law. Thus, the supposed contingency of perception is only the contingency of the laws that go beyond perception, that are based on such nonperceptual inferences as one might make. Relying on perception, I might formulate the law: "If I put the light on, I see colors, when I put if off, I do not," but not the law: "Whenever I press the switch, the light goes on."

2.2.2.2 THE ANTINOMY BETWEEN ESTHETICS AND LOGIC   The accusations leveled at perception are exaggerations of the assumption that perception is nothing but the obscure precursor of science as we can see from looking at how many and how various are the cases in which thinking differs from seeing. Thus, even if the appeal to antinomy might seem superfluous, it is in fact decisive. It is not enough to say that perceptual schemes are independent of conceptual schemes, because that would leave it open whether the former as the forerunner of the latter, while the asymmetry between seeing and thinking take on importance precisely to call into doubt the legitimacy of the idea that experience exists only to be adopted into science. In addition to not being conceptual, reality often turns out not even to be conceptualizable, demanding the recognition of a different ontological status. Things that are perceived do not become real thanks to thought (which is indeed capable of correcting and interpreting perceptions, but on another level and for different purposes), inasmuch as thought cannot change either perceptual content or the perceived object, but at best can sometimes explain, once the nature of the object has been understood, why the perceptual content could mislead. In other words, perception is not an imperfect and emendable forerunner of thought, just as experience is not of science.

Here then, we have a plain refutation of the claim that the (active) intellect plays a constitutive role relative to (passive) sensible experience. I suggested in the previous chapter that by *logocentrism* I mean the claims for the constitutive intervention of thought in vision and in sensible perception in general. If thought really were constitutive of sensibility, why do we say, "Please pass the salt," rather than just modify the flavor of our food by the power of the mind? Why do we want the wine to be tasted at the restaurant? Why do we complain at the travel agency? For sure, it is not forbidden to claim that the mind always looks beyond what is effectively perceived; nevertheless, we often notice when we do supply an integration—which is not exactly perceptual—and when we hold off from doing so. Here is the central point: apart from the successful integrations, there are cases in which what we see does not coincide with what we think, or it goes beyond our current knowledge.

As I said in discussing unemendability, if it were true that thought constitutes reality, then, unless we were masochists, we would only see what we like and we would never be surprised. Whatever we do, we cannot help seeing things that we do not want to see or that we cannot help seeing or even things that we have reason to think could be or that are not as they seem, as in the case of optical illusions (they are called *illusions* only because it is supposed that the eye is a medium for science and the truth). I can have all the contrary philosophical opinions in the world (or, and the point is telling, no philosophical opinions at all), but the senses will go on doing their own thing. I know perfectly well that the earth is not flat but round; all the same, I continue to see it as flat. I *understand* that I should read "ontol.gy" as "ontology," but there is no way of convincing the eye to *see* "ontology"—indeed, the only way this can be made to come about is, as when one is correcting galley proofs, not to pay attention to what is written.

What really counts in this hymn to *aisthesis* in its obstinate resistance to concepts is exactly disappointment, namely the contrast between what we expect in thought and what we encounter with the senses.[49] In disappointing our expectations, the senses might fool us, but what matters is that they do not supinely confirm our expectations, thus displaying what we might call *passive resistance*. Through the phenomenon of disappointing our expectations, the world displays its autonomy from our schemes and thoughts. Just as I notice the role of the eyes in reading only when I have forgotten my glasses, so in general I notice that I have a body especially when I am ill and I come up against the autonomy of the world only when it disappoints me. My appeal to sensibility is thus the reverse of sensism, where the sensist is someone who overestimates the epistemological value of the senses and regards them as knowledge-gathering instruments; I, on the other hand, praise them from the ontological point of view, for the resistance they oppose to our conceptual schemes. It is from this antinomy that we derive the autonomy of the world and its transcendence of thought.

2.2.2.3 THE AUTONOMY OF THE WORLD RELATIVE TO CONCEPTUAL AND PERCEPTUAL SCHEMES   I now come to the point of what I have been saying in this chapter and of what underlies the slipper experiment with which I closed the previous one. Reality possesses a structural and structured relation that not only resists our conceptual and perceptual schemes but also actually precedes them. If for just this reason that "external world" should be understood as "external to our conceptual schemes and perceptual organs." Unless such a world existed, all of our knowledge would be indistinguishable from dreaming.[50] I can (and in certain circumstances, I ought to) doubt the *truth* even of all of my experiences, without for that reason doubting that there is something in general. This is quite the reverse of "There is nothing outside the text," as we can see by looking at the third of our differences.

2.2.3 Third Difference: Science ≠ Experience

2.2.3.1 SCIENCE AND DOCUMENTALITY   The basic idea that I want to support is essentially that there is a crucial distinction between having an experience on the one hand and talking about experiences or doing science on the other, between having a headache and describing it to someone or formulating a diagnosis. In the case of *talking* about experiences, and all the more so in the case of doing science, we are dealing with an activity that is linguistic (scientists talk), historical (the activity is cumulative), infinite (there is no end to science), and teleological (it has a purpose). Let us unpack these features.

1. As I suggested in 1.3.2.3, it is hard to contest the importance of *language* and of writing in science as an intrinsically social activity. There is no doubt that scientificity deals with documentality, with a system of communication, inscription, codification, registration,

and patents. While we can easily imagine experiences taking place without language and without writing, the communication and registration or discoveries is indispensable for science: "publish or perish" may be an academic aberration for the individual researcher, but it is a categorical imperative for science, which, considered as a collective and progressive enterprise, necessarily requires communicative exchange, both oral and written, and the depositing and the institutionalizing of discoveries. None of this holds for experience, which can take place without any communication, registrations, or linguistic expression.

2. The intrinsic *historicity* of science is just one consequence of this fact. We have to deal with science to the degree that each generation can take advantage of the discoveries of all the earlier generations. For this reason we can speak of sciences that are younger or older, thus hinting at the idea of a biography, growth and development that derive precisely from the possibility of inscription and documentation. By contrast, it is meaningless or purely metaphorical to speak of a "young experience"; at most there are "youthful" experiences, which are things that happen in youth.

3. As regards *freedom*, it seems obvious that science is a deliberate activity. At a certain point in the intellectual history of the European peoples (if, at least we assume the prevailing view, which sees science as a form of life that is not universal, even if it is universalizable), scientific activities began to be undertaken and evolved freely even though they often responded to practical needs. This genesis could have not happened, and that this is so can be seen from the fact that other civilizations have not undergone scientific development, and that others again have developed a science that is noticeably different from ours. Here again, the contrast with experience is telling, given that experiences display an intercultural constancy and do not appear to be the result of any deliberate choice. I am referring not only to perception but, once we have abandoned the legends that say that the Inuit see more shades of white than we do, also highly structured features, such as myths and basic family relations. The fact that these modes of organization and motivation of experience can be found in radically different civilizations, which is not what occurs to science, speaks volumes for what Vico pointed to in referring to "universals of

the imaginary": What is universal to mankind is not science (which is merely universalizable), but experience.

4. Coming, then, to the point about *infinity*, the most prestigious sciences are those that can boast a long past and have a very long future ahead of them, those that most closely respond to the idea of knowledge and unending development. None of this can be said of experience, which not only is not projected into an unlimited future (in any case, its duration can never be greater than that of a human life), but is also not even conceived as progressive. By this I mean not merely that the idea of honing the senses does not seem very plausible (at best one can use glasses and hearing aids to remedy their weaknesses),[51] but even in the practices and techniques that are most widespread in the world progress is not necessary an ideal. While everyone would prefer to be treated by a doctor from 2212, rather than by one of 2012, and would quake at the idea of being cured (and especially operated on) by one of 1812, the thought of eating the bread of yesteryear or of finding a fabric made before globalization can be very attractive. Furthermore, while the idea of endless progress in the sciences is pretty straightforward, the idea of an infinite improvement in the knack of doing up your laces, tying your tie or making your bed is hardly more than a joke.

5. As regards *teleology*, the point is very simple. Science is a deliberate activity, as is much technique, which from this point of view falls between science and experience: Making the bed does not seem to be subject to improvement (at best, they invented elasticated sheets), but it calls for some deliberation. And this holds in spades for science. If someone went into a laboratory without any purpose, he would have serious difficulties in doing science, while someone who, for no reason, felt hot, saw a color, or had a toothache would have no reason in the world for excluding the having of that experience. Even though the history of science loves tales of serendipity, of fundamental intuitions had in the bath or under an apple tree, when we move from folklore to evaluation, the question of intentions counts heavily. Typically, Fleming's discovery of penicillin, in which chance played a large role (it was a mold that had grown accidentally in a fridge that had been left open), the discovery seems less meritorious that others, because less deliberate.

To make the distinction between science and experience clearer,[52] it is useful to propose a differentiation among instruments into those that are empirical, those that are technical and those that are epistemic, and then between objects that are epistemic and objects that are ecological. The point of these two distinctions is to make manifest the gulf between what we have experience of and what we have science of (holding firm to the fact that the things we have experience of we can also have science of, for instance if we are medical doctors as well as sufferers from gout or depression).

2.2.3.2 EMPIRICAL, TECHNICAL, AND EPISTEMIC INSTRUMENTS

Let us start with a simple consideration. There is a crucial difference between putting on glasses or contact lenses and setting up a telescope or a microscope. The glasses, including sunglasses when used on a bright day or under a spotlight, and the contact lenses reestablish a necessary function for a human being in the world. The others serve the purposes of scientists and are harmful outside the library or the laboratory: just try driving with a telescope or a microscope to your eye; moreover, just try behaving so as to identify the world in accordance with the conceptual schemes you have of it. In this sense, there are empirical instruments, which can be used for looking at the world around us, technical ones, that serve some specific purpose, and epistemic ones, that are of use only in science not to show what there is in our ecological sphere, but rather to visualize things that fall outside it. In my view, this is a perfect case of how the quantitative tends to overflow into the qualitative.

Experience	Eyes Eyeglasses Sunglasses	They do not increase a function but correct a dysfunction relative to an environmental or ecological setting.
Technique	Spyglass Binoculars Opera glasses Magnifying glass Jeweler's eyepiece	They do not restore a natural function (except perhaps the opera glasses) but do not promise infinite progress, given that science is done with telescopes and microscopes. They help us to see what would be accessible from a different point of view. Hence they do not make visible anything that is extraneous to our ecological sphere, but they help us to see better something that is already in it.

Science	Microscopes Telescopes	They have no use in the environment and so do not restore a function. They serve the potentially infinite development of knowledge. They make visible rather than help to see.

With this table, I do not mean to deny the existence of things outside our ecological sphere,[53] but rather to differentiate between *simple seeing* and *epistemic seeing*,[54] between *visualizing* and *seeing*.[55] Simple seeing is always presupposed, both logically and ontologically, in epistemic seeing. We can doubtless say that in the social world and in epistemology—with the clarification that I will suggest in 3.1.2.2—we never have simple seeing that does not also carry with it the intervention of epistemic seeing, because it is only if one knows what the procession of the Madonna dell'Arco is or what a *Cattleya labiata* is that one can be said to have seen the procession of the Madonna dell'Arco or a *Cattleya labiata*; but it remains the case that the epistemic seeing feeds on a simple seeing. To return to the point made in 2.1.1.1, the principle according to which intuitions without concepts are blind is applicable to visualizing and to epistemic seeing, but not to simple seeing. Better still, the principle applies to reading,[56] so much so that some sorts of epistemic seeing can be nothing other than a form of reading, as in the case of the readout of a particle accelerator or other instruments for physical and chemical analysis.

2.2.3.3 ECOLOGICAL OBJECTS AND EPISTEMIC OBJECTS The question of the difference between seeing and visualizing brings us fairly naturally to discussing the ecological dimensions characteristic of the human world. As I noted in 2.2.1.2, an ecological ontology turns out to be pretty poor; but ecology is important for ontology insofar as it contributes to fixing the size of what figures in our sphere of experience. There are some things that we have direct experience of, and others that fall outside it because too big, too small, or too far away. My claim is that that the sphere of experience applies to things of mesoscopic size, while science deals also with the microscopic and the macroscopic, leaving it open of course for science to concern itself with the mesoscopic. I illustrate this point with the following table, exemplifying some epistemic objects and some ecological objects.

Below ecological size	Epistemology	Quarks, atoms, molecules, C-fibers, and enzyme reactions
Borderline	?	Viruses, mites
Ecological size	Ontology	Tables, chairs, mountains, having the blues or being nervous, burning oneself, meters, kilometers, sounds between 20 and 16,000 Hz, social objects in general
Borderline	?	Venus
Above ecological size	Epistemology	Galaxies

As I have said, the ecological sphere embraces objects that are neither too big nor too small and that are suited to our senses in ecological conditions and to the average length of a human life. I would like to stress that this is not a marginal domain or a banal zone as much negatively as positively. Negatively: Every critique of eliminativism and of reductionism makes at least implicit reference to the ecological dimension. Positively: As we saw in 1.3.3, everything to do with social objects necessarily falls within the ecological scope. Checks and birthday parties, promises and pensions can never exceed this sphere, and, as we shall see in 5.2.1.3, artworks turn out to be eloquent witnesses to this necessity.

2.2.3.4 EXPERIENCE, SCIENCE, TECHNIQUE   In what we have been saying about instruments and sizes, we have encountered a dimension intermediate between science and experience, namely that of technique. I would like to deal briefly with this matter, about which there appears to be some confusion, for instance when people talk about "technoscience," assuming either that science and technology are the same thing or that the former is the foundation of the latter. It does not seem to me that this is how things stand, if for no other reason that the banal observation that there are civilizations without science, while we cannot find any group of humans entirely short of technology, which is to say, in the account I propose, deprived of the capacity to register and to iterate.

This definition may appear rather surprising, given that when we talk about "technology," what we have in mind are things like automobiles, screwdrivers, radios, and perhaps particle accelerators. My hypothesis—which I defend at length in 4.1.1 and I have suggested in talking about "writing" in 1.3.2.3—is nothing less than that the paradigm of technology is iterability, which in turn presupposes registration. From this point of view, technology in its fullest sense is language, writing, and calculation, which are poured into the paradigmatic instrument that is the computer, and the real factories are banks and libraries. Nevertheless, the very instruments, like screwdrivers, that seem not to embody any principle of iteration in effect serve to facilitate iterative activities: it is hard to imagine a world with just a screwdriver in it or an absolute hammer. And a screwdriver or a hammer that served to make only one turn of the screw or to make just one blow would be bizarre objects suited to an art gallery on the Lower East Side, but they not be technical instruments.[57]

If this is how things stand, technology is more basic and transcendental than science. It is inconceivable that science could arise without the presupposition of a technology in the sense just specified, but this does not mean that science and technology should be confused, any more than ideal objects should be confused with the forms of their socialization. And, if the sphere of experience affected by science is modest even by a scientist's reckoning, the range of applicability of technology is extremely wide, to the point that what ordinary language understands by "having experience," means simply the possession of techniques for dominating known situations. If we think of this aspect of things, we become aware that the sphere of experience does not constitute that semi-wild state that we usually imagine when we think of a world without technology. Furthermore, we understand that the admission of the massive presence of technique in experience does not in any way lead us to suppose that experience depends on science, since *science depends on technology, which in turn grows out of experience.*

2.2.4 *Anticipations of Experience*

At this point, we have a world of experience that is not reducible to that of science, and that can be described in terms of three principles,[58] to which I give the vaguely Kantian-sounding names of "anticipations of experience," to mean that they are what—not a priori, but simply in the light of good sense—we can say in general before having any experience whatever.

The first principle is that *the world is full of things that do not change,* and, even at the height of a hypertechnological world, where generations of objects destined to rapid obsolescence follow one after the other, there are some objects that remain the same, such as combs, buckles, buttons, bags, and knives, not to mention earrings and necklaces, for even the superfluous is tenacious and lasting. This world of objects that resist evolution correspond to those invariances in human thought that are unmodifiable and that recur even in the most sophisticated thought—a world on which we could found the idea of a descriptive metaphysics that makes up the underlying framework of the ontology proposed in this book.

The second principle is that *the world is full of medium-sized things*, which are neither too big nor too small and make up the furniture of our existence. As we have seen, what is neither microscopic nor macroscopic but "mesoscopic" has a great deal to do with our notion of a *thing*.

The third principle is that *the world is full of things that cannot be corrected*, which are the things that I have suggested calling *unemendable*. It is precisely the unemendability—the stubbornness and solidity—that of things that makes me prefer them to subjects as the key to understanding everyday life. By this I do not mean that the world is incorrigible, but only that the objects of experience do not display that sweet plasticity of the thoughts that go round in our heads, of the hypotheses that we formulate and then discard, of the firm intentions that we promptly forget.

2.2.5 Another World?

It might well be asked whether what we have been describing is a world different from that of science. I am inclined to deny that it is. In 1716, Leibniz put forward a hypothesis: If we took the world and put it before a mirror, with left in the place of right (and thus with Trieste to the west of Turin), nothing would be different given that left and right, like all spatial relations, are nothing in themselves. The western Trieste and the eastern would not be two very similar cities with different geographical coordinates: they would be the same city. In 1768, Kant would object to this; space is absolute, and within it, we demarcate the shape of the left hand and of the right, so that if God had created just one hand, it would have been either left or right. Who is right? Now we know, at least for our world and other possible worlds with laws similar to ours. Physics now has an absolute method for distinguishing left from right defining one of them (the left) as the one in which the decay of a neutron *always* "twists." This means that on earth, or in any other point in the universe, the left (and hence the right) can always be defined in a certain way. Have we always been so lucky?

Sadly not, and not merely as a point of fact. To establish, for instance, whether the attack on the Twin Towers was one event or two is a rather different sort of issue: there is no lack of witnesses (the scene has been viewed over and again by billions of spectators) nor are we short of experts, yet no one is in a position to decide. This is by no means a limiting case, and if the social world needs newspapers, law courts, parliaments, and even talk shows, it is in large measure for this reason. Science is a marvelous thing and it would be absurd to want to do without it; and, as I have noted, when we talk about *science*, we have in the first instance in mind physics, which studies natural objects. But, as we have just seen, even relative to natural objects, there are levels of granularity that are not interesting for physics, even though they are very important for our everyday life. Moreover, natural objects do not exhaust the list of what is: the world contains also social objects and ideal objects, about which physics cannot have the last word. We can take three things as certain, though. First, no adult of our times would deny the existence, for instance, of electromagnetic fields, which are part of our cultural baggage, but not part of our experience. Second, ordinary and ecological experience, just like ordinary language, is not sacrosanct; nevertheless, it is a starting point that we cannot duck out of because the manifest image of the world is not a veil of *maya* that systematically misleads. Third, a pure ontology, like a pure epistemology, is inconceivable. A much better solution is to try to keep things under control with a lot of good sense and on a case-by-case basis; to classify kryptonite among nonexistent things, we need in the first place to know what it is and that it is not in the world investigated by physicists, but in that of DC Comics.

So much as regards the *empirical* relations between ontology and epistemology, where the latter is systematically presupposed by the former. It is therefore fine to make use of all the notions we have available to clarify our ontology (or to prefer to go to a medical doctor rather than to a shaman declaring that *all* disease is psychosomatic). All the same, we should not forget a crucial point, namely that ontology, what there is, is—at least as regards physical objects—*logically* independent of what we know, which is shown by the working of ordinary language. For instance, we distinguish in ordinary use between *happy* and *euphoric* just as we do between *unhappy* and *depressed*. The assumption of an external world independent of our conceptual schemes is already present in this distinction. When we are happy or unhappy, we suppose that there is some external cause, an object out there;

conversely, we may be euphoric or depressed simply because of some chemical dysfunction, so much so that in the contraindications for psychotropic medicines, the warning is that they can cause *euphoria* and not *happiness*.[59] In fact, without the assumption of an external world, there would not even be the distinction between *knowing* and *not knowing*, which is what we might pompously call the *ontological rootedness of science*. This is undoubtedly part of the manifest image of the world, but it would be hard to treat it as an illusion that could be corrected by scientific inquiry.

Given that these last considerations point to an empirical dependence of ontology on epistemology (indeed, it is very hard to do without what we have of science, and we might only manage it if we took precautions like that of the phenomenologist's *epoché*), and to a logical dependence of epistemology on ontology (as a point of right, if there were not this distinction, it would be impossible to distinguish knowing from not knowing), I do not see what grounds there are for conflict between the two dimension, unless in border disputes that can be amicably negotiated. The point is simply that if we do not pay attention to the distinction between what is and what we know (epistemology as justified belief, as set out in 2.1) we collapse ontology into theory of knowledge. If, as I hope, in this chapter, I have been able to set out some arguments for distinguishing ontology and epistemology, our next job is to illustrate the salient features of experience that are not reducible to science. This move is of particular importance in the overall strategy of the book, because it allows us a new perspective on the age-old problem of the relations between the natural sciences and the sciences of the spirit, which I take up in a rather untraditional way in 3.1. To do so, we must first take a more detailed look at the world of experience, considered as the habitat of social objects.

2.3 THEORY OF EXPERIENCE

If one proposes a theory of the logical independence of experience from science, one generally runs into the Kantian counterargument, which I shall call the *critique of pure content*, which runs roughly as follows: One cannot speak of unstructured content, because the mere fact of speaking of it introduces structure and conceptualization.[60]

This argument aims to be a variant on the self-refutation or liar paradox, as are arguments against relativism or in defense of the principle of noncontradiction. Someone who says everything is relative either admits that his own claim is relative, and hence that not everything is relative, or takes his own claim as not relative, and hence again not everything is relative. Likewise, someone who criticizes the principle of noncontradiction must submit to the law, otherwise his words would be meaningless; but if his words are meaningful, they cannot be used in a critique of the law. The critique of pure content, however, is not in the same league as the refutation of relativism or the defense of the law of noncontradiction. Rather, it appears as an exaggeration of the Aristotelian principle (itself purely rhetorical) that anyone who criticizes philosophy is doing philosophy. This goes something as follows: even someone who does not criticize philosophy, for instance by sleeping, eating, cutting down a tree, tying a can to a cat's tail is doing philosophy. This is obviously not so. Likewise, even if we cannot speak of or think about nonconceptual content without using concepts, that does not mean that our experiences are necessarily mediated by conceptual schemes. Three points need to be made.

In the first place, we have a sphere of experience—typically, perceptual experience—that does not seem in the least undermined by science insofar as it has no need of being verbalized or conceptualized (even if it is often enough verbalized or conceptualized). And this sphere is what is normally presupposed even by the theories that deny the possibility of pure content; if you do not assume pure content, you cannot even deny its existence, simply because if you do not think of a notion of pure content, you cannot think of a notion of content in general.

In the second place, the critique of pure content assumes that our fundamental functions are connected with knowing and not, for instance, with doing, and that therefore science is the omnipresent dimension in life. To be sure, there are those who add art to science, but even they think that art is somehow connected to knowledge, a sort of vicarious or integrational science that may be in some way alternative to it.[61] But bearing in mind the variety of language games—which I propose to call *games* tout court for reasons given in 3.3.2.4—does not imply extending knowledge-gathering functions to art; it means rather the recognition that there are prescriptive games, performative games, prayers, and so on, all of which fall outside science and are expressed in linguistic form. Which means that we can stand outside science not only by being silent, but also when we speak in the non-denotational sphere.

In the third place, there are many features of common sense and pre-science that are not necessarily resolved when we cross the threshold into science.[62] This is not just a matter of false ideas, of superstitions and mythologies, for they include, for instance, the knowledge that scientists have outside their own particular disciplines, that pharmaceutical salesmen have, that the ministries of health and of scientific research have, that librarians have, and that nontheological popes have.

To organize and set out the arguments and counterarguments on the basis of these observations, I propose to examine three ways in which a theory of experience differs from science, in terms of grades of knowledge, types of experience, and classes of objects.

2.3.1 Grades of Knowledge

Many philosophers (agreeing on the point with the rest of the world) have quite reasonably recognized that there are grades of knowledge, just as there are junior schools, high schools, and universities and just as there are various levels of degrees, from bachelor's and master's to doctoral and postdoctoral posts. All I want to point out is that we have perfectly sound reasons for thinking that the passage from obligatory education to the higher reaches of research work is by no means necessary. Unless we are going to allow a world full of ignoramuses, we should take on board the idea that the elementary grades of knowledge, which is what we have to do with in the overwhelming number of cases in life (when we have a pain in the foot, we know only what it feels like and leave the diagnosis up to the doctor, without this meaning that the pain was a mere appearance), are not merely stages on the road to knowledge, but are incontestable elements of experience.

Thus, we all admit that knowledge comes by degrees, and it is senseless to suppose that in the earliest (and most widespread) stages in the process we have science; furthermore, as I labored in 2.2, the natural destiny of experience is not to lead to science any more than the natural destiny of a potato is to end up as fries.

2.3.1.1 COMMON SENSE AND BELIEF   If this is how things stand, we can get clear about the underlying confusion in Russell's claim that if common sense is sufficiently developed, it teaches us to believe in physics, but physics teaches us to that common sense is false.[63] This is one of those sentences that inspires us to immediate agreement: It is clearly right. If you do not believe in witches, if you doubt that red wine thickens the blood, and if you are skeptical about the wisdom of buying lottery tickets, then we can say that you are in possession of a reflective common sense and you needs must follow what science says.

But it isn't like that at all—suffice it to think of how belief (in the narrow sense, not just that of an unverified opinion) is ubiquitous in everyday life.[64] The overwhelming majority of our actions, from taking the bus to going to the doctor, from putting our money in the bank to putting on a sweater when it is cold, are all guided not by scientific knowledge but simply by habits and precautions that have very little to do with science. These habits and precautions, however, do not put us in the hands of superstition. It is not as if putting on a sweater when it is cold, thus following the advice mother gave us so long ago (and that we have verified as useful and wise, unlike some maternal advice), is the first step on a slippery slope that will lead us to believe in the vampires of Transylvania. It is misleading to think that this kind of trusting to common sense is a defect; the idea of a life guided only by science, like that of one guided only by reason, would be subject to such a mass of evolutionary disadvantages (complexity, obscurity, slow decision making, and so on) that it would kill anyone who *really* tried to live in accordance with science and reason. After all, the only case of someone who blindly followed the reasons of science in life was Manzoni's Don Ferrante, who, having established that the plague was neither a substance nor an accident, took no precautions and died cursing the stars like a hero in Metastasio.

Indeed, the first level of a theory of experience is a theory of *belief*. As we have seen, one of the major problems with the collapse of ontology into epistemology is the implicit assumption that knowledge is the unavoidable condition of our relation with the world, when it is clearly not so, if for no other reason than that, if our behavior in the world really were determined by what we know—and not for instance by our habits, our beliefs, and our desires—we would do virtually nothing. The reason for the ubiquity of belief is very simple: Our lives are not permeated with knowledge, which we have not yet reached in many areas. In those areas where it has been reached, it is the province of a few specialists. Moreover, these specialists are, in 99 percent of cases, perfect laymen in sectors other than their specialism, where therefore they allow themselves to be guided by beliefs, habits, and authority.

Believing, then, is a relation of what Leibniz called "the analog of reason,"[65] namely the fact that, just like animals, humans generally act on a "shadow of reasoning" enriched by a mix of habits, hopes, and fears, and not by certain science. It is impossible to have true opinion accompanied by a reason (Plato's and many philosophers' standard for knowledge) about everything, so much so that those who believe themselves to have formed for themselves and on good grounds opinions on every subject are paranoid personalities.[66] It is for this reason that belief comes into play, to fill the gaps in our knowledge and to allow us to get on with things, generally to complete satisfaction of ourselves and others. Believing thus comes to seem like a sort of quasi-knowing, superficial but useful. It also has this feature: It has its value only up to a certain point and, sooner or later—at least in principle—we must take account of genuine knowledge, otherwise every belief would appear justified and would in its turn justify anything. By noting this about belief, we have implicitly assumed that there are grades of knowledge. At this point it is worthwhile to give an account of the rising levels, which I present as three *epistemological differences* parallel to the ontological differences set out in 2.2: the difference between encountering and seeing; that between seeing and thinking; and that between having knowledge and having science.

2.3.1.2 ENCOUNTERING AND SEEING Let us take this first picture.

A man in jacket and tie

I come across it; I encounter it. For sure, I can say that I see it, even if I cannot see much, but it is true that I encounter it with my eyes rather than with my nose or my ears. My manner of interaction with this image is little more than what happens when I run into a stool: I come across a picture, and that is all. I see something, I recognize a person, but there is nothing I can do about it, I see it there much as would my cat if I had one. It is a very minor matter, but if we think about it a moment, we see that the overwhelming majority of our experiences (what we catch in the corner of the eye, mild itches and even the thoughts and feeling that we are not fully aware of) seem to fall into the same sphere as the picture, which is that of the realities we *encounter* rather than that of those that we *represent*, of which we have taken the measure, on which we can gloat, to which we can make corrections and subtractions. The former is unemendable and is a matter of ontology. The latter is, in various degrees, emendable and is a point for epistemology.

2.3.1.3 THINKING AND SEEING   Let us now enlarge the picture.

A man who looks like Piero Angela

It will be admitted that here things are a bit different and we might even say in a certain sense "better." I can pick out a man, I can tell roughly how old he is, the context he is in (I see a table set for dinner behind him) and his state of mind (he seems cheerful). If I live in Italy and watch television, I can even say that it is the science show presenter Piero Angela. Here my intuitions do need concepts and my ontology is not enough on its own and needs to call on a bit of epistemology. It is at this level that the process of emendation begins to take place, at which we can begin to discuss, for instance, the age of the person in the picture (is he a well-preserved seventy or a rundown fifty?), his mood (is his smile spontaneous or forced?), even his character, his aptitudes, and his morals (is he a great science journalist, or did he get where he is by politicking?), or obviously his identity (is it really Piero Angela or a double? Or is it just any gentleman with a cordial air?).

Here experience counts crucially because someone who has never seen him will be hardly likely to say, "There's Piero Angela." The image is no longer something external and encountered but rather, as I was just suggesting, something that is represented: we have at least to some degree interiorized it, we have refer it to the entries in our personal encyclopedia, and we can, if we like, play a game of eidetic variations on it, which may be amusing (by adding a beard and darkening the hair do we get his son Alberto Angela?) but which are certainly culturally conditioned (it would never have occurred to Schopenhauer to say, "There's Piero Angela").

This does not alter the fact that we saw something in the first picture, where the principle that intuitions without concepts are blind did not apply. Even there we saw something: not really an image, but certainly something. All these second-level constructs are, so to speak, objects of a higher level, whose lower level—that of "simple seeing," as discussed in 2.2.3.2—is as unemendable as the smaller picture itself is. It is the fact that it presents itself as more manipulable by our reasoning does not in its turn alter the fact that the substance of which the larger picture is made is just the same and possesses the same tenacity and autonomy: All the efforts in the world straining our concepts and our imagination will not help us to see an elephant in place of Piero Angela's tie, and even to "see" a striped fish there would call for a stretch of the imagination.

2.3.1.4 KNOWING AND HAVING SCIENCE   Let us proceed to the last distinction, that between having even very broad and detailed knowledge and being effectively involved in a scientific enterprise.

Piero Angela

The enlarged picture does not give me much more than the preceding one (indeed, it is out of focus, as we see from the lines on the shirt), even though it allows me to make more sophisticated inferences. For instance, if in the earlier size, the image was of a banquet, which could have been a lunch or a dinner, private or public, now it seems more likely that it is a lunch (it looks like natural light), and not an official function but perhaps a wedding breakfast.

I do not want to bore you with the phenomenology of Piero Angela, but rather to suggest another level. Let us stop looking at Piero Angela and think about what might be going on in his mind, not in this instant or rather in the instant that he was photographed, but rather "in general." What is Piero Angela thinking about? Well, probably projects, memories, emotions, perhaps even his tax return, but then also much more precise notions connected with his professional life, notions about the structure of the atom, DNA, the Sumerians, dinosaurs, and three-toed sloths. Perhaps he knows a lot about the duck-billed platypus. It is quite plausible that—on the same principle by which a modern newsstand contains more information than the Library of Alexandria in the time of the Ptolemies, for history is getting fuller—in Piero Angela's head there is more true knowledge than Pierre Bayle possessed. Yet, is Piero Angela a scientist? Certainly not. Over the years, and as a result of presenting items on the most varied scientific subjects, he will know more about science as a whole than the average scientist, who normally knows a great deal about his own field and much less about other sectors. But by far the greater part of what Piero Angela knows he knows on the authority of others, by way of a relationship of faith. There is nothing wrong in this. It would be great to know all the things Piero Angela knows. I do not know more than a tenth of what he does, and I am not a scientist. Yet, if he had to teach at a university (and I am sure that he would do it splendidly), it would be a graduate course on the popularization of science rather than a course in physics or biology.

Now, what does this case show us? Exactly that it is one thing to know many things as Piero Angela does, and it is quite another to be a scientist, and yet another to be socially recognized as such (if Piero Angela had a brother who was a doctor, he would be the scientist). In the end, it is the old story of Plato's *Theaetetus*: knowledge is not sensation (as in the case of the smallest picture of Angela), nor is it opinion (as in the medium-sized picture), but it is *true opinion accompanied by reason*—and, we might add, underwritten by an institution. The last is what is suggested, but no more than suggested, by the last picture. The point is not too hard to grasp, but if we maintain that intuitions without concepts are blind, then we have to claim that even our most distracted perceptual operations amount to true opinion accompanied by reason.[67]

2.3.2 *Types of Experience*

With the argument about grades of knowledge, I hope to have established two things: first, that the passage from the lower grades to the higher is not to be taken for granted; and second, that in the overwhelming majority of cases, it is not necessary nor even desirable. With the argument about types of experience, I aim to introduce a second consideration in favor of the autonomy of experience relative to science. There are many experiences that lend themselves to being redescribed in terms of knowledge, but many others do not: playing football, eating a sandwich, looking at a sunset, undergoing harm, challenging to a duel, leaving a watch as an heirloom, or giving a dog a name. Are any of these forms of knowledge? Obviously not, unless we follow the logic that led to the creation of degree courses in communication science.[68] In some cases, there is knowledge presupposed, such as the rules of football, but it is trivially true that *knowing how football is played* is not the same thing as *knowing how to play football.*

The theory of science assumes that the only game humans play is that of knowledge. But, if we simply compare a will with an inventory of goods drawn up by the person making the will, we will see that these are two entirely different operations: the first is an act that disposes of something; the latter is a record or register that simply takes account of what is. As we will see in 5.1.4.1, this distinction underlies that between a strong document, which is performative and brings a social object into being, and a weak document, which is the mere registration of a fact, whose function may (but need not) be epistemological. Obviously, for a future historian, the difference between the will and the inventory may be minimal if his aim is to know about the testator's goods, but there is no doubt that they are still texts of a profoundly different nature. If this is not obvious, it is because of a sort of blindness to questions of the functions that, in our lives, have to do with things other than knowing and judging, such as asking, praying, ordering, cursing, and doing things (social objects) with words, gestures, or inscriptions, to such an extent that, as we will see in 3.1.1.3, we can reconstruct the phases of the discovery of social objects by noticing that, by comparison with logic and mathematics, this is a shorter and more recent history.

In my view, this is a particularly important point. The various grades of knowledge presuppose that, in the end, knowledge is unified, given that at the highpoint of knowledge, we cannot arrive at two alternative results, except perhaps for the case of the wave-and-particle nature of light—which is nevertheless not important for our lives, but perhaps becomes so when it is appealed to as a surreptitious support for a theory of double truth or, worse, a theory of half-truths.[69] Nevertheless, we have no difficulty admitting that experiences, even when they are highly codified, are very different and are not all governed by the rules of the knowledge game. It is one thing to follow a university lecture and quite another to find oneself in hospital, in court, at the restaurant, at the match, in a museum or the rock concert.

Trying to keep a little order, I propose articulating the argument about types of experience into three phases. The first is the classic argument, which I call the *argument from faculties*, which concerns the differences among knowing, desiring, pleasure, and displeasure. The second is what I call the *argument from stating and performing*, which is a matter of the difference between constative and performative utterances. And third, there is a variant on the argument from the plurality of language games, which I prefer to call the *argument from times and places*, on two grounds: first because, as we saw in 2.1.2, the argument from the plurality of language games was used in the last century as a support for a sort of hyperrelativistic anything-goes approach to knowledge when, for our purposes, it helps to take account of experience according to its own principles; in the second place, and more to the point, because I believe that it has less to do with language games than with different times and places, which set different rules, as is in any case implicit in phrases such as "in its time," "in its place," "in due course," and "in the proper setting."

2.3.2.1 ARGUMENT FROM FACULTIES   Let us begin with something obvious. There are propositions that hold good independently of what physics says because they capture something phenomenologically obvious, such as "the sun sets" or "I have the intention to go to the seaside"; others, on the other hand, cannot be reduced to physics, such as "*The Magic Mountain* is a masterpiece," "it is wrong to beat up on the elderly," "this pen is mine," "I promise to give you €10 tomorrow" and "the Battle of the Nations began on October 14, 1813." Others again can be resolved quite independently of physics, such as "5 is an odd number," "Emma Bovary never met Count Mosca," "Pimpa is a white dog with red polka-dots." Let us put things in Kantian terms and talk of "faculties." There is not only the faculty of knowledge, but also that of desiring and that of pleasure and displeasure. In these cases, and Kant programmatically admits as much, we have to do with areas that have little to do with knowledge, and in which therefore the equation ontology = epistemology does not hold.

Let us take *morals* and *action*. Here knowledge is undoubtedly an advantage, but there are situations, which are far from infrequent, in which we have to act with partial, gappy, or virtually nonexistent knowledge. Yet we continue to act, because life requires it of us. In certain cases ignorance is even a good: not knowing when we are going to die or whether God exists or not or whether or not we are free, is no harm at all. In the first case, if we knew, we would be paralyzed. In the other two, moral action would have no sense, because behaving properly in the eyes of the almighty (or even in front of police officers) is not meritorious but cowardly; and acting from necessity, like a rolling stone, is mere physics. It might even be argued that a moral decision that was based on pure knowledge would not be a decision. Typically, the priority lists in a hospital emergency room (a sophisticated case of "women and children first") are not made to corroborate decisions, but simply—and quite reasonably, though it has nothing to do with morality—to eliminate them. As such, they are no different from the advice, which is not moral but procedural, given at the beginning of an airplane flight, to put on one's own oxygen mask before helping those nearby.

This holds also in the case of pleasure and displeasure. When I say that a thing or a person is handsome or ugly, I am making a very clear judgment (which may have consequences, if I am on the jury of a literary prize, a song festival, or a beauty contest), yet the assertion is made without sufficient reason, since, if I explain to others, for instance why I like or dislike the Brillo box, the explanation will make virtually no difference. If then others explain to me why I ought to like or dislike the Brillo box—especially if I am sure of myself, of my taste and of my culture, and I am little inclined to allow myself to be bullied by pointy-headed experts—that will make no difference whatever. Beauty pleases even in the absence concepts and, without taking anything away from the importance of esthetic education, can please even in the absence of knowledge, to such an extent that, in esthetics, the unknown "*je ne sais quoi*" and vagueness are positive attributes.[70] Thus far, I will be told, there is nothing new: in the classic phrase *de gustibus et coloribus non est disputandum* ("there's no arguing about tastes and colors"). Now, apart from the fact that there is endless argument about tastes and people say all sorts of things about them, it does not follow from this that they are unimportant or nonexistent. As in the case of morals, we find a large and important ontology about which science has little or nothing to say. I would add two less Kantian considerations.

First, judging and referring are not by any means the only activities in which our spirit engages. As we will see in the next section, showing and exemplifying, which, in line with what we said about the exemplarity of the exemplar, exhibit an object as a member of a class, without on those grounds seeking to give any epistemological definition. Moreover, we should not forget that *judging* means at least two things, according to whether we mean judgment as assertion (S is red) or judgment as evaluation (S is beautiful, S is just). Typically, esthetic judgments can always be taken back; they do not follow a logical progression and are not binding on anyone.[71] I can say that the Parthenon is ugly or that the *Book of Kells* is simply grotesque, and no one can tell me I am wrong, unlike the case in which I claim that stones fall to Earth in order to reach their natural place.[72] Furthermore, what we formulate about works considered as works are not so much judgments as *evaluations* or *appreciations*. The language (or other) game of evaluating the beautiful and the ugly has little to do with the language (or other) game of judging true or false, while it has a great deal to do with the ontological game of the present and the absent (we cannot give a genuine esthetic evaluation of a work that does not exist). Of course, one might claim that esthetic judgments are not so different from factual ones, and that therefore one can be right or wrong, but it seems hard to maintain the position to the bitter end, if at least we agree that denying that Mont Blanc is beautiful is much easier than denying Mont Blanc is 4,810.9 meters high or that thirty-nine people died in the fire in the tunnel under Mont Blanc on March 24, 1999.

Second, as we see in the next section, Austin proposed not just the distinction between constative and performative utterances, but noted also that if the constative are subject to the rule of conformity to the pair true-false, the performative respond to the distinction between the felicitous and the infelicitous,[73] but they do so in a way that is much less direct. Saying that a party was successful or failed, fine or grim, fun or boring is generally more relevant than saying that the party was true or false. This last intuition may have been what Heidegger had in mind when he spoke of "placing oneself in the work of truth"; except that Heidegger seems never to have considered the distinction between the constative and the performative, and it might seem that he was treating the constative as performative. This is in general typical of historicism, which starts from the premise that history, regarded as a set of facts, is a source of truth: but what truth can there be in the French Revolution or in the Revocation of the Edict of Nantes? We have to be careful here, because what is at stake is not a proposition such as, "The French Revolution began in 1789," which is precisely the sort of thing that can be true or false. We are asking rather what the French Revolution corresponds to or is true of. But this question is senseless because, unlike propositions, historical events are neither true nor false.

To claim that the revocation of the Edict of Nantes is in itself true is no less senseless than to claim that the force of gravity is in itself true. Nevertheless, it makes perfect sense to ask whether it was a good thing or a bad thing, just as one can ask about the felicity or infelicity conditions of performatives. We may think—rather than about art as a placing of oneself in the work of truth—about more prosaic things like jokes, where being true or false is beside the point, and what really matters is whether they are told well and are fitting to the context; if there is a mistake in the *performance* or inappropriate to the setting, then the joke, for all that it was meant to make us happy is infelicitous, a failure, a misfire. But if the joke—or the tragedy—is recited in the proper way and in the proper context, then it is felicitous in Austin's sense, and really makes us laugh, just as a successful tragedy really makes us cry.

2.3.2.2 ARGUMENT FROM STATING AND PERFORMING

Let us try to get to the bottom of this last point.[74] However opinionated we are, we do not spend our whole lives passing judgments. Viewed aright, there are many other things we do: we give and take orders, we offer and accept excuses, we give names and titles, we formulate prayers and greetings, we hurl insults, we make promises and sign contracts, we read books and listen to concerts. In the midst of all of these activities, the referring game, that of indicating something and deciding whether it exists or not and whether or not the words we use to define it are right, turns out to be pretty marginal relative to the thousands of other more common practices. Despite this, and perhaps because it is professors who invent theories, we think that our fundamental game is that of making judgments, preferably true and well-founded ones. As I said in 2.2.3, this is a very important activity, but much rarer than is commonly thought and even scientists do it only in certain rather sporadic moments. What is so rightly called "the moment of truth" is certainly an experience freighted with practical consequences and is not limited to the sphere of science[75]—think how crucial the question "is she betraying me?" is, or what it is to bear witness under oath—but it is hardly an everyday thing. In short, judgment is not the warp and woof of our experience, but a rather rare yet decisive moment, and the saying "judge not lest you be judged" is not so much a moral precept as a description of what normally happens.

Not only is judging a rare activity, an island in the archipelago of practices distinct from those of science, but referring, indicating something and accompanying this activity with a judgment is a very occasional practice, which lies beyond important aspects of our experience, such as the needs and interests that lead us to watch a film, look at a picture, listen to music, or read a novel. In these sorts of activities, what has the upper hand is something more like a *simple showing*. In the beginning, we have situations like that in which two people are taking a walk and come upon a lizard on their path. One says to the other, "Look." The other looks and need not say anything. The same thing happens with sunsets and many other circumstances; sometimes (and it is a great moment) it can even happen with a picture in a gallery, so long as our companion does not feel the need to respond to a "Look" with some comment or other. Corresponding to showing there is looking, which does not need to be accompanied by a judgment whatever. A case might be the Bergotte's death scene in Proust. The writer goes to see a Vermeer exhibition to find the picture he loves best, the one in which the background is a broad yellow wall, and he formulates a judgment that has nothing to either with the painting or with his state of happiness: "There, now I can die."

Another activity that fills our lives is—as I noted in the last section—exemplifying, and this is the reason why this book puts exemplarity in pride of place. Yet philosophers often criticize exemplifications. When Socrates asked about the essence of the musical and was given examples of musicians, he grew angry because what he wanted was the essence: "I asked you what is the musical, and you reply by naming musicians! That is not right, we cannot do it this way!" But is it so obvious that we cannot do it this way? After all, exemplifying is one of the most common things in life, and the proof of that is that Socrates's interlocutors found it perfectly natural to respond to him as they did with examples. The reason is very simple: we do not have access to essences (or at least we only very rarely do). What we have are rather analogies, likenesses, and approximations, which can all be gotten across with examples. For this reason it is not so very wrong, when we do not have an essence (and I repeat that it is very hard to have one) to respond to someone who asks what is the musical by saying "it is someone like Mozart, like Jovanotti, like Bob Dylan." We may note that exemplification is one of the major activities in art.[76] For instance, it is what Tolstoy wanted to tell us with the death of Anna Karenina, which is not simply the content of a judgment such as, "If you set yourself against the conventions, whether right or wrong, of your times, you will end up in trouble." It would have been enough to write two lines to make the point. If he wrote so much more at length, it was to exemplify, and the great success of the exemplification can be seen from the fact that the death of Anna Karenina really does make people cry.

2.3.2.3 ARGUMENT FROM TIMES AND PLACES

This argument goes no further than to note that what might seem appropriate in a lecture may not be so in polite company (indeed, Proust's Professor Brichot is intolerable). And this is not a mere matter of taste, but with the variety of forms of experience: I recall the observation made earlier about the varieties of experience with which we have to deal at a rock concert or in a museum, in a law court or at the tax office, at a wedding or at mass. If someone thought to behave at mass with the same attitude as in a trial, or regarded a wedding with the same standards as he applied in the tax office, it would be right to call him to order. But what order? Reductively, we might say it was a lack of tact. But it is not often thought that such a person is lacking an understanding of the difference between utterances that state something, those that merely ask for something (prayers, for instance) and that are neither true nor false, and those utterances that do something producing social objects.

Let us take the case of justifications. It has been rightly noted that the system of excuses is a powerful arsenal of assumptions to which, rightly or wrongly, we allow an underlying plausibility, and the same argument can be extended to the whole sphere of what is "plausible."[77] In excusing oneself, we allow sentences like "I did it without thinking," "I was upset," "I didn't know," "I thought that . . ." Here we have a sphere of common sense that has virtually no reference to science (to that sphere that in court is left up to the expert witnesses). For sure, the world of experience is a bric-a-brac crammed with all sorts of objects: expressions that cannot be reduced to a scientific translation (as in the case of "upset"); common sense theories about how we reason and how we should reason; modes of perceiving the world that resist everything we know about the matter in hand; and also some scientific notions that have found their way into common usage (as when we refer to "Alzheimer's" instead of "gaga"). These are not the same thing. For we can certainly emend parts of common sense, perhaps not "upset" or "the blues," but at least "gaga," in the same way that we can correct beliefs about spontaneous generation or about the fall of massive objects, but we cannot see the earth as round, nor, in everyday reasoning can we bring it about that *modus tollens* appears as cogent as *modus ponens.*

A further point: In the world of experience we are not called on to capture essences, but to describe phenomena,[78] and it is a very curious demand to replace descriptions with explanations, which is just a systematic application of the stimulus error pointed out in 2.1.0. A headache can be explained in various ways and it would be very embarrassing if I were not allowed to say, "I have a headache" but were required to formulate a diagnosis. If, giving rein to my most pessimistic hypothesis, I declared, "I have a brain tumor," someone might respond, "No, you do not have a brain tumor," and someone else would formulate other hypotheses; in the worst case, someone might say that I am right. After all, it seems much more sensible to say, "I have a headache," given that no one, not even the greatest doctor in the world, could object that it is not true, unlike what happens when someone says they have arthritis in the thigh, if it is possible to have arthritis in the thigh. The point is that, where in the case of "I have a brain tumor" my assertion has at least sense, the patient who complains of arthritis in the thigh would have done vastly better to have said that he has a pain in the thigh. His way of putting it raises the questions of whether he is referring to anything, and if so, what, granting that arthritis cannot affect the thigh. The patient does even better to indicate the part that hurts and say, "It hurts here."

In saying this I do not mean that we should just give the doctor our name and then go by pointing; all I mean is that, in describing our complaints to the doctor, it is better to use ordinary and not at all scientific language and without hazarding diagnoses that might turn out to be incomprehensible or misleading. And, in my view, this is a luminous example of how little science is necessarily interwoven with experience, for it makes a rigorous division of labor, where experience is all on the patient's side and science is all on the doctor's. Science, unlike experience, is a game that not all of us can really play. Socrates got at least this right: Someone who claims to be a doctor on the basis of reading some medical books is an impostor.[79] In a time when we use Google to explain our symptoms, and to die of fright, this observation is as fresh as ever.

2.3.2.4 FROM THE PLURALITY OF EXPERIENCES TO THE PLURALITY OF OB-JECTS The moral to be drawn from all this is simple: The game of knowledge and of referring is just one of many. As we have seen, there are prayers, orders, and genuinely performative acts. In all of these cases, we really cannot see what role epistemology could have in referring physical objects to a conceptual scheme, while there is undoubtedly and powerfully present an epistemology in the sense of a constructive action of conceptual schemes. Except that these schemes do not apply to physical reality, nor do they modify it (for all that they refer to it), but rather they construct objects of quite another kind, namely social objects, of which the simple Kantian has no intuition whatever.

2.3.3 Classes of Objects

We come then to the classes of objects, which is a matter that I hold most dear precisely because it is thanks to these differentiations that I can obtain justification for the treatment of social objects that lies at the heart of this book. As we saw in 1.3, there are not only natural objects in the world, and the treatment of them is not the sole prerogative of physics, unless we want to cancel biology and regard the art of gardening, winemaking, and beekeeping as ultimately reducible to physics. There are also ideal objects, which are the prerogative of mathematics and logic, neither of which is natural science and, as such may not even be forms of knowledge. And last, there are social objects, which lie entirely outside the sphere of natural science, though they are omnipresent in our experience. With all this, I certainly do not wish to deny the possibility of one or more sciences of social objects; indeed, I shall shortly propose a social epistemology. What I want to draw attention to nevertheless is the way that all of us, few of whom are social scientists, have available to us some experience of the world which it would be absurd to attribute to science.

The point I want to stress (and to the best of my knowledge it is a matter that is rarely taken sufficiently seriously) is that the variety of games corresponds to a mass of classes of objects: natural and ideal objects, which are not created by games, and social objects that are created by games. On this view, the most interesting thing is probably the fact that, in the specific case of social objects, ontology is more closely interwoven with epistemology, for social objects concern what we know, and sometimes only with what we believe about them. What we chased, so to speak, out of the window—with a fairly brutal defenestration—can now make an honorable entry through the main door, now that we have found its proper place.

3

SOCIAL OBJECTS

In this chapter we enter the heart of the project. In Chapter 1, I set out the general features of the sui generis epistemology that deals with social objects; in Chapter 2, I expounded the principal theories that have been proposed on the matter; and finally I illustrate my own theory.

Once we have recognized and motivated the distinction between ontology and epistemology, and once the specific features of experience have been defined, the way is open for rehabilitating the transcendental philosophy in a realm wholly different from the one for which it was first proposed, namely not the realm of natural objects, but that of social objects. The basic idea is that a thesis like "intuitions without concepts are blind," which is hard to apply to the natural world, explains splendidly our relation with the social world, which is made up of objects such as money, roles, and institutions, which in turn exist only because we believe that they do.

To get to this conclusion, we have had to distinguish among classes of objects, and between ontology and epistemology. In particular, we have had to assume (a) that natural objects exist independently of our conceptual schemes, while social objects require such schemes essentially; and (b) that the schemes that are at work in the experience of social objects are different from those that apply to the science of natural objects. At this point, it is no longer possible to maintain that natural reality is constructed like scientists' theories, as the postmodernists claim. And it is even harder to maintain that, in the absence of conceptual schemes, we have no relation to the physical world, as some less extreme philosophers have thought though they had not taken into account the way that, unlike social objects, natural objects exist independently of subjects and hence of conceptual schemes.

As we have seen, social objects depend necessarily on subjects and in this framework, we elaborate the constitutive law: Object = Inscribed Act, which implies of necessity the intervention of subjects, of acts, and of intuitions endowed with concepts. The theory I propose is thus a weak textualism, insofar as it assumes that inscriptions are decisive in the construction of social reality but—unlike what, in 3.2, I call strong textualism—*it does not entail that inscriptions are constitutive of reality in general. Weak textualism is therefore a weakening of Derrida's thesis that "there is nothing outside the text," which is transformed into "there is nothing* social *outside the text."*

3.1 SOCIAL EPISTEMOLOGY

The theory of experience adumbrated in 2.3 aimed to provide the framework within which a social ontology makes sense.[1] Now, this ontology is also, and quite legitimately, an epistemology, since, as we have clarified at length, Kantian transcendentalism can be applied to its legitimate sphere, where the overlap between ontology and epistemology is not mere permitted, it is indispensable. In this chapter, I want to take account of that special class of entities, social objects, which emerge as the objects of a theory of experience and could be the subject matter of a hypothetical fourth Kantian critique, a critique of social reason finally applied to its proper sphere. In 3.2, I proceed to discuss the alternative theories that have been proposed about social objects and I apply to them what we might call, in Kantian fashion, a dialectic of social objects. In 3.3, I set out my own proposal, which is based on the law Object = Inscribed Act, and which, if we want to continue the Kantian analogy, represents the analytic of social objects. After articulating the main features of social objects in the chapter on ichnology (the doctrine of traces), I aim to furnish the equivalent of Kant's deduction, which is the justification of the possibility of social objects, which consists in the potentiality, common to men and animals, to leave traces that can evolve into ever more complex structures to the point of constructing the world of values, aims and meanings.

As I have already said, the ultimate aim of the theory of experience is to justify a taxonomy of objects, which is to say the foundation of the typology of objects (natural, ideal, and social) that I set out in Chapter 1. The most important feature of the taxonomy is the possibility of founding a theory of society. In effect, once we know that ontology is distinct from epistemology, we arrive at two important results. One is that we know which spheres of being are intrinsically dependent on epistemology—and these are social objects, not natural ones, even though here epistemology is not a matter of the justified beliefs that feed into science, but rather those that are generated within social and institutional interactions. As regards social objects, ontology is systematically subordinated to epistemology, but not to complete knowledge, in line with the grades of knowledge distinguished in 2.3.1. The underlying assumption is that social objects exist because we think they exist without being, on that ground, merely subjective, as I pointed out in 1.1 and 1.3. The other main result is that we show how, insofar as they intrinsically independent of epistemology, social objects are nevertheless not dependent on physics, but on social practices (redescribed by the social sciences) that can quite happily do without the physicalistic model.

A simple experiment will show the limits of trying to reduce social objects to subjective entities. I might decide to go the movies; if at the last minute I change my mind, the original decision is not binding on me. There is nothing there to bind me, but only an expression of my will, which, not having been expressed on the outside, remains purely psychological. Things are rather different if I invite someone to go to the movies with me; if I change my mind, I have to inform the other and perhaps give some justification. What I constructed with my invitation was thus an object that is not annulled by a mere change in my will. Suppose, then, that I issue the invitation in the form of a promise, perhaps telling my son, "I promise I'll take you to the movies this evening." Now if I had said only, "I promise that," I would not have made any promise at all. As we have seen, a promise comes into being only when there is some object to which it refers and some time frame, however vague ("I promise to give up smoking sooner or later"). If, on the other hand, social objects were purely relative constructs and depended wholly and solely on single subjects, they would not carry with them any obligatoriness, and it would be possible to decide that "I promise" is a promise, though it is merely the first person singular present indicative of the verb "to promise."

This provides a clue to the debates in course on the topic. Often what gets called *relativism* might be better called *conventionalism*, by which I mean that social objects are subject to canons and are regulated by norms.[2] Conversely, relativism does not at all mean *subjectivism*; we can imagine indefinitely many social objects that have not been realized, such as civil partnerships in Italy, but which would nevertheless be governed by rules, themselves established by the legislature in nonarbitrary ways. In this framework, what

I am proposing is both a step backward and a step forward relative to Kant. The step backward is a reproposal of realism against transcendentalism, which is a return to before Kant. The step forward is the recognition of the world of social objects, which brings into focus an ontological territory that Kant never considered. The result I am hoping for is an advantage both for philosophy and for everyday life: *to give to transcendentalism its own field of application in the social world and its objects.*

3.1.1 *From the Spirit to the Letter*

3.1.1.1 SPIRIT AND OBJECT   Let us begin with the step backward. The great thing about objects, starting with natural objects and artifacts, is that they push us in the direction of a realist philosophy, given that natural objects have their laws and make sure that those laws are respected and that artifacts, if they are well made, incorporate their functions: When I see a chair, I do not have to activate a category; it is the chair that tells me—just as it tells a cat—that I can sit there.

This simple fact is in direct opposition to idealism and to the transcendentalism that has guided most efforts to elaborate a theory of experience since Kant. What sort of theory did the nineteenth century propose? To describe the world of experience, the category of the "science of the spirit" was thought up, beginning with the hypothesis that there are large structures, such as history or language, that determine human behavior. This move is at least in part just giving a name to the problem to which we do not have a solution, as we can see from the difficulties Wilhelm Dilthey ran into more than a century ago.[3]

Dilthey agreed with the positivism of the time, according to which we try to isolate a sphere of the sciences of the spirit, but he did not share the project of a unified science because the sciences of the spirit had to have different objects from those of the sciences of nature. This seems a relatively easy proposal to put into practice, when it is a matter of distinguishing philology from physics or historiography from chemistry. It is already a bit more difficult when we start talking about biology or economics, and it runs into an insurmountable obstacle when faced with psychology. Here we have a discipline that treats the spirit, recognizing such phenomena as language, memory, habit, imagination, and intention, but that at the same time is undoubtedly rooted in an irreducibly naturalistic format: if one part of the brain is damaged, it produces aphasia, if another then amnesia; wine and coffee change our mood; and in general psychic phenomena are in one way or another connected to electrochemical reactions in the nervous system.

Wilhelm Windelband pointed this difficulty out with polemical intent.[4] If the distinction is based on the objects involved, we should rather differentiate the sciences in the light of their different methods. In this direction Windelband proposed to distinguish the *nomothetic* sciences (those that aim to discover laws that hold good in every case, from the Greek *nomos*, law) from the *idiographic* (those sciences that concern the individual, *idios* in Greek). Trying to reply to Windelband, Dilthey observed that the instrument of the sciences of the spirit was hermeneutics, which could be clarified by distinguishing between *understanding* (sciences of the spirit) and *explanation* (sciences of nature). Obviously, it might be objected—appealing to the skeptical tools as exhibited in 2.1.2.1—that it is not at all clear what *understanding* means, and it is even more obscure when we can be sure of having understood: Are we sure of having understood the words said to us, a book we have read, the problems of a relation of ours. All the more so, how can we know that we have understood Caesar crossing the Rubicon? Dilthey's strategy in the face of this objection is twofold. On the one hand, he admits that we can never claim to have penetrated in full the depths of an individual's intentions (even if they were clear to him, which is itself not obvious); but, on the other hand, he notes that when we are doing history, our primary relation is not so much with the intimate life of an individual, as it is with public and visible institutions, what Hegel called the "objective spirit," meaning such things as the family, civil society, and the state, to which Dilthey added the forms that, for Hegel, fell under absolute spirit, such as art, religion, and philosophy.

At least as regards the definition of the sphere of applicability of the sciences of the spirit, the answer seems intuitively adequate: The sciences of the spirit are concerned neither with the deep and subjective levels of the spirit, because in that case they would cease to be sciences, given that their object would not be public and interobservable, nor with the material basis of the spirit, because in the case, they would obviously be sciences of nature. In the perspective that is our present concern, the limitation of this sort of approach is, nevertheless, that, in Kantian vein, the sciences of the spirit postulate the priority of the knowing subject relative to the known object, which is thus deprived of its autonomy. In other words, the theoreticians of the sciences of the spirit saw the difficulty—the unacceptable claim to make physics dominate everywhere—but were too cautious in their response to it. The idea here, then, is that the key to ordinary life is something that more or less recalls the transcendental categories that help us to organize experience. That much is clear. Given that these categories are very abstract while the things encountered in experience are very concrete, however, how is the passage from the former to the latter to be secured?[5]

The answer is simpler and much less pompous than one might think. Let us leave to one side the debate between Dilthey and Windelband and look at things closer to home. The Romans used to say, "*si vis pacem, para bellum*"—if you want peace, prepare for war, for if you are armed, no one will want to attack you. But experience and history teach a different lesson. Once someone has weapons, he is dying to use them, not least because the arms industry pushes to produce more. The ironic and absolutely logical result is that "Parabellum" was the name given to the German Luger P08 pistol, to the famous Soviet machine gun with the circular magazine, and to a 9mm bullet. This slightly sinister anecdote can be read as an indicator of the projectual power that finds its way into objects that incorporate functions and tasks. The chair is for sitting on, the glass is for drinking, and the pistol is for shooting, alas. It is true that in some cases the object allows promiscuous uses, as when a coffee mug is used as a penholder or a recycled CD is used as a mat under the mug-penholder. The room to maneuver, though, is less than it might seem, and this gives rise to the thought that even an omnipotent designer is more often than not guided by the objects around him. Furniture is the prime case of this. A piece of furniture prefigures a slice of life. An entire decor is the novel of a whole life, including that of the interior designer, which is why we can read in the eyes of the couples proceeding around the Ikea the disquieting question, "Is this all of life?" I am certain that this is why furniture superstores that look at us from the side of the highway seems to be taunting us sarcastically, "Who do you think you are? Don't kid yourself that you're that much better than me."[6]

3.1.1.2 REIFICATION These are my grounds for the realistic reversal on the basis of the methodological indications proposed in 1.1.2. The idea is to import into the realm of social objects the experience of the socialized objects discussed in 1.3.1. The reason for this is that objects are meanings incorporated into things, and thus present the great alternative to transcendentalism: There is no need to write reams of instructions on how to use the world inside our heads, because when we see a screwdriver, we always know what to do with it, and if, to recycle the earlier example, we decide to use it to clean our teeth, so much the worse for us. Things possess an *affordance*, they seem to lend themselves to this or that, unless they are so badly designed as to be quite misleading or are part of a practice that we do not know about; for someone who does not know what a bottle is, a corkscrew is as mysterious as the Odradek is for someone who has never read Kafka.[7] It is especially true that the information is in the environment when we have to deal with artifacts whose instructions are useless. For the objects themselves contain information, which was put there by the manufacturer, and if it is hard to decipher, the object itself will correct it or end up in the attic.

If so, then the idea of looking for the categories in things instead of in our heads is not such a bad idea as Kant supposed in criticizing Aristotle for his "rhapsodic" organization of the categories.[8] After all, rhapsodies can be very fine: When Wittgenstein described the *Philosophical Investigations* as "leaves from an album," was he not aiming at rhapsody? In any case, they have the advantage that, if they are objects' rhapsodies, they never lose sight of reality. It is not for nothing, if we go back to the origins, that there is so much talk of objects in that great realistic treatise that is Aristotle's *Metaphysics*.[9] A natural outcome of this objectivism is the recognition of a high level of autonomy to social objects, which are indeed dependent on subjects—more so than they are on natural or ideal objects—but that possess an autonomy and a hard, obtrusive, cutting and sometimes even dramatic consistency, which makes them very different from shadows or dreams. This is obvious and what is surprising is the amount of time that has been called for before philosophers recognized them as objects.

3.1.1.3 THE DISCOVERY OF SOCIAL OBJECTS

This is not the place to embark on a historiography of how social objects were discovered, which is bound up with the creation of the sciences of the spirit and of the historical and social sciences.[10] What I would like to note very briskly are five of the ingredients that underlie the present theoretical discussion of social objects.

History. The first ingredient is the recognition of the specifically historical character of social objects. And the merit for this can be given to Giambattista Vico,[11] who, in dispute with Cartesian rationalism and naturalism, made the case for the original features of the historical sphere, which concerns human interactions. Vico was moreover convinced of something else that is less than certain, namely that, unlike the study of nature, which is God's work, in history we can have a knowledge that is peculiarly certain, which is an idea denied by the fact of controversy among historians and by the general lack of transparency in the social world.[12] By way of example of the passage from the animal to the human and from the natural to the cultural (understood as essentially a social process), Vico singles out marriages, law courts, and burial practices. These are social acts that do not describe anything and do not add anything new either to the physical world or to the ideal world. Relative to what we will soon be saying, it is worth noting now the relation between institution and inscription. There is, for instance, no sacrament without a sign or a form of inscription, whether it be the water in the baptismal font or the oil of extreme unction, for already at this level there emerges the law Object = Inscribed Act.

Society. The second element is due to Thomas Reid,[13] who stressed the autonomy of social objects and distinguished them from the merely psychological productions or manifestations of the will. Reid's underlying idea was that philosophers had given too much attention to the solitary operations of the soul, for instance in judgments, which do not change their nature by being expressed or not; the proposition "this chair is red" remains the same whether it is merely thought or spoken out loud, and it makes no difference to the nature of the chair. Alongside these, there are social acts that involve at least two persons (a miniature society), and are things like orders, promises, and questions. The propositions in play completely change their status according to whether they are uttered or not: "What is the time?" and "Open the door" are not a question and an order if they are merely thought. Thus, if Vico had directed our attention to inscription, Reid brings to light the feature of social acts that distinguishes them from simple thoughts.

Performatives. The third stage was secured in the middle of the twentieth century with J. L. Austin's theorization of linguistic acts,[14] which to some extent render explicit the specific characteristic of social acts, namely their performativity. To the extent that social acts need an expression, they are linguistic, even though we have seen that this is a little misleading and we discuss the point more at length in 3.3.2.5. But, because they are not mere descriptions of something (the typical case being "I do" in a marriage ceremony), but rather produce something, they present novel features relative to other parts of language. While saying "This is a chair" does not act on the chair in any way, saying "The meeting is open" or "I declare you doctor of philosophy" produces an object that was not there before. If suitably fixed, the expression is a *poiesis* and constitutes an object.

Objects. The fourth stage is relatively eccentric relative to the others and is represented by the philosopher of law Adolf Reinach,[15] who proposed a typology of social objects, which he took to be "juridical objects" and which he thought could be deduced a priori insofar as characterizable in terms of logical form, which is much what I had in mind when I pointed out that the sentence "I promise" is not a promise. Reinach insisted that what is produced by social acts is not a *praxis* that is limited to itself, but a *poiesis*, the construction of a durable object. Thus, unlike some other social events, such a birthday parties and funerals, a degree ceremony or a wedding are not exhausted by their stating something about an event and they have consequences that continue well after the event.

Inscriptions. The last ingredient is broadly reconstructive and is the contribution of Jacques Derrida, who suggested reinterpreting Austin's linguistic acts in terms of inscriptions,[16] thus introducing (albeit in too strong a form) the thesis that there is nothing social outside the text. Vico's intuition about the necessity for inscription in the construction of social objects thus receives a new lease of life. Now inscription is recognized as what fixes performatives, transforming *praxis* into *poiesis* and thus bringing into being an object in the full and rigorous sense set by the law Object = Inscribed Act.

3.1.2 Social and Textual

At this point, we have at our disposal all the elements needed to define social objects in terms of textualism: the recognition of a social realm distinct from the natural (Vico), of an intersubjective sphere distinguished from the objective (Reid), of performative acts as against constative ones (Austin), of social objects parallel to physical and ideal objects (Reinach) and inscribed acts as opposed to linguistic acts (Derrida). From the swift historical reconstruction, we turn to the theoretical proposal.

3.1.2.1 THE TRANSFORMATION OF THE TRANSCENDENTAL The core of my step back relative to the transcendental, as will have been noticed, consists simply in trying to speak about objects without making them mere projections of subjects, which was the outcome of Kantian transcendentalism and its variants throughout the nineteenth and twentieth centuries. A step forward, if I may be so bold, consists in transforming the sciences of the spirit into a social ontology and in introducing social objects understood as a realm in which transcendentalism really does apply. Let us call this transformation of transcendentalism *textualism*,[17] a name that will keep us busy and that underlies the definition of a *social object* that we will analyze in the next chapter. The idea to show how transcendentalism is perfectly right and useful though, as we have seen, it does not work for physical objects.

Let me explain with an anecdote. Some years ago, I had to take a Eurostar train. As often happens, something went awry; in this case, the doors would not open. Lots of railway workers, ticket collectors, and other personnel battled with the things, but it seemed there was no remedy. After half an hour it seemed that a solution had been found, and one of the ticket collectors solemnly announced, "Now the doors can be opened." I tried to do so by pushing the button, but the door did *not* open. In my disappointment, I felt like giving the ticket collector a little oration of the following sort: "In the mid-twentieth century, the English philosopher J. L. Austin brought to our attention some singular features of certain utterances, which he baptized 'performatives,' that do not describe states of affairs, but produce them, such as the utterance 'I do' at a wedding or 'I bet five shillings it will rain tomorrow.' Supposing the utterance 'Now the doors can be opened' would have brought about the opening of the doors, you have confused two kinds of utterance and have treated as constative as a performative. But—apart from the fact that the constative is false, as well you perceive—it is clearly not so. A door is not a meeting, which can be opened by the chairperson's saying 'The meeting is open.' The door opens if and only if its material makeup is such as to allow us to open it. Otherwise, you might as well say 'Open Sesame!' and good luck to you." Obviously, I did not allow myself this rant and get myself thoroughly hated, but all the same the doors would not have opened.

I have the feeling that, in confusing science and experience, the regulative with the constitutive, Kant was making the same mistake as the railway employee. It is one thing to define the conditions of possibility that are the coherent conditions of knowability and plausibility; it is quite another to think that these conditions determine our experience of physical objects.

Someone might say that Kant never claimed anything of the sort, though I doubt it if for no other reason than that, if that were so, he would have had no need for the deduction or the schematism, he would not have needed to claim that the "I think" must accompany my representations or that the conditions of the possibility of experience are the conditions of the possibility of the objects of experience. If anything, the problem is another. Between the regulative and the constitutive, as between science and experience, it is easy to get confused, as I have to have shown to the point of boredom in 2. On the level of functions and faculties it is thus always difficult to avoid fallacies and confusions, and here Kant is quite right: we are dealing with a spontaneous tendency of human nature. Nevertheless, I wonder why we cannot recognize the difference between these two claims:

1. Mountains, lakes, beavers, and asteroids depend on our conceptual schemes; and
2. Banknotes, diplomas, debts, prizes, and punishments depend on our conceptual schemes.

To claim that mountains and rivers are thus and so because there are humans that have sense organs made in a certain way and categories of a certain sort calls for a certain courage. In fact, mountains and rivers are what they are all on their own, and, if anything, are *known* by us through the specific forms of our senses and our intellect.[18]

Let us now put the matter in terms of social objects. Someone might surely say that marriages and divorces, mortgages and chess games, debts and seats in parliament are thus and so because our (human) senses and our intellect are made in a certain way. This would not be a surprising thing to say. We can be reasonably sure that for a beaver there are no mortgages or divorces, though there are mountains and lakes. It is worth noting that the compresence of empirical realism and transcendental idealism, which applies so ill to natural objects, fits the case of social objects perfectly. I encounter a debt much as I encounter a mountain (empirical realism), except that I know that that, unlike the mountain, the debt would not exist if there were no humans like me with senses and intellects like mine (transcendental idealism) And a mountain is a certain number of meters high or has existed for a certain number of years quite independently of our conventions (even if with the change of conventions we can obviously change the units of measurement), whereas a mortgage lasts a certain number of years and involves a certain sum of money only because it has been agreed on.

3.1.2.2 THERE IS NOTHING SOCIAL OUTSIDE THE TEXT   Thus, many of Kant's claims, which are unacceptable as regards physical objects, are perfectly acceptable as regards social objects. One could almost try rewriting the *Critique of Pure Reason* referring to social objects rather than to physical objects, and one would discover that the wild and indemonstrable assertions such as the "The I Think must be able to accompany my representations" are perfectly in line with juridical and social codes, for instance when involuntary actions (such as manslaughter) are regarded as attenuating circumstances, and obviously in excuses: "I'm sorry, I did it without thinking" means "excuse me because, while performing action *x,* the I Think did not accompany my representations."

The same holds for such complex and implausible claims regarding the physical world as "intuitions without concepts are blind." If it is perfectly possible to knock into a stool and feel pain without concepts, there is no doubt that we could never understand that we are in a lecture, at an execution or witnessing a coronation without concepts. In effect, Kant's claim, which is so hard to apply to the natural world, can be illustrated very clearly by thinking of a beaver that finds itself at a concert, an eighteenth-century gentleman with a subway ticket in his hand, or most of us when we find ourselves at a fancy banquet faced with a mysterious piece of cutlery. (Is it a mullet mallet? A lobster chopper? Or a special tool for peeling mangoes?) The thesis "intuitions without concepts are blind" explains perfectly well our relation with the social world, where, if we do not have the right categories and concepts, we do not get very far; try taking a stroll in the streets of Tokyo, and you will understand the role that familiar writings and signs play in our getting about in the world, and the disquieting sense of estrangement we feel when faced with ideograms we cannot decipher.

This applies not only to Kant. We might say that many philosophical claims that are false or surprising when applied to the world of natural objects turn out to be true and banal in the world of social objects. To take a typical case, Berkeley's thesis that a tree that falls without observers makes no sound is only partly true, given that the tree in any case produces the vibrations that, if there were an observer (specifically, a hearer), would be translated into sound. The thesis that a social object of which all memory or registration had been lost does not exist shows itself to be fully true; and in turn proves how much the ontology of social objects depends on epistemology.[19]

Starting from the properties of objects, from their solidity, but recognizing the specific role of subjects, we thus have social objects, which are objects of a higher order than natural objects and endowed with properties that are irreducible to those of natural objects. The position that I propose is an alternative both to postmodernism (social objects do not exist and physical objects are social constructs) and to uncritical realism (social objects are reducible to the physical objects underlying them). I set it out more fully in 3.2, presenting the varieties of realism and textualism and the dialectic between them. What I want to stress at this point are some of the specific characteristics of social reality (considered as the sum of social objects) relative to natural reality (considered as the sum of natural objects).[20]

3.1.3 A Sui Generis Epistemology

As I have said, in the social world, epistemology is constitutive of ontology. This obviously does not mean that the social world is only accessible to scientists, who, after all, can often show (in the guise of the idiot savant, the limited specialist) a peculiar incompetence in dealing with people and their behavior in society. The epistemology of social reality excludes social omniscience and presupposes an adequate endowment with certain social concepts, but its primary feature above all is as an epistemology (and for this reason sui generis) more of *believing* and *doing* rather than of knowing and contemplating.

As regards believing (of which enough said in 2.3.1.1), the paradigm case is the stock exchange, where values are fixed not by an objective enquiry, as in chemistry of physics, but rather by the sum of the beliefs of the players. Furthermore, it is not enough just to know what a certain social objects is (a party), but one needs to believe that the social object exists (*this* party) for it really to be a social object. As regards doing, the knowledge that is acquired with reference to social objects is practical in nature and concerns action and behavior. In this respect, it has no theoretical ambitions: even when we go in for moral evaluations of our fellow man, we are not proposing novel theories of action or of society, but simply passing judgment (often enough of blame or derision) on others' actions.

The peculiarity of the competences called for by social epistemology can be seen precisely in moral judgments, which have rightly attracted the attention of philosophers. Rousseau defined morality as "the sublime science of simple souls,"[21] picking out by means of this oxymoron (the knowledge of the ignorant) the fact that the type of competence put in play is certainly a set of rules, norms, and values, but these are not acquired through study. Even uneducated people have a highly developed ability and a dialectical thrust in judging their fellows, in that sort of popular eristic that makes the cap fit the person they want to make wear it, even though they are quite indifferent to other fields of knowledge,[22] which may explain why scandal sheets sell much better than science journalism.

This fact has received a wide range of explanations in the philosophical tradition: anamnesis, the voice of the heart, the law of nature. In line with what I will say in 4.1.2, we may more simply have to deal with behaviors and evaluations that are acquired, whether formally or informally, through education and imitation. This knowledge can be further specialized in practice in such directions as etiquette, jurisprudence, and politics. But the origin of it is in imitation, which explains why this sort of knowledge can be found also in individuals who have no scientific education. Two important consequences for the status of social epistemology follow from the role of mimesis in the constitution of social reality.

The first is the importance attributable to literature, film, and history (and their antecedents in myth and tragedy), and the developments, parallel or alternative to humanistic culture, in religions. All these provide models of behavior and evaluation, from which follows the importance of examples and narrative in morals.[23] This is confirmed by the fact that the core of humanistic culture is literary knowledge and that religions include rites and myths. It is in this sense that Homer and Hesiod were regarded as the educators of Greece, even though (as Plato polemically noted) what they transmitted was not knowledge, strictly speaking. In the same way, the description of the social world that Proust's *Recherche* offers is not a treatise of sociology, even though it can serve as a model for some people, as it did for me.[24]

The second consequence is that, given that mimesis does not provide knowledge but at the most a practical competence, we can explain why social reality appears so opaque to the actors in it. This is why there are economic think tanks and courses in social sciences and why so much importance is given to historical understanding, which throws light retrospectively on a reality that was not at all transparent to the players in it. In general, we might think of the epistemology of the social world as like the kind of situation that is created in a battle. All the participants have local and specific competences that are clear and codified; orders are transmitted and executed following protocols and chains of command; the soldiers are required to perform actions for which they have been trained; the officers and generals draw up plans based on precedents and sometimes the historical models they learnt about at the military academy; the reconnaissance details seek to give a picture of the situation, and the spies seek to understand the enemies' intentions. But, as in the examples of Pierre Bezukhov at Borodino or Fabrizio del Dongo at Waterloo, nobody knows what is really going on as the battle unfolds, sometimes the outcome is unclear even after the firing has stopped, and no one knows who has won and who has lost. It will only be later that this is known, and sometimes only after a board of inquiry has thrown light on what happened, even though the witnesses called were present and indeed were agents on the scene.

3.1.3.1 AGAINST HUME'S LAW   This is not the sole peculiarity of social epistemology. A significant difference between social objects and natural objects is that Hume's law, according to which you cannot derive an "ought" from an "is," does not apply to the former. Hume's law is a warning against natural law theories: from certain dispositions of things in nature, we cannot draw moral laws; in any case, for Hume, nature is anything but absolute and certain, so that we would be committing the fallacy of *metabasis eis allo genos* (taking a thing of one kind, nature, for one of another kind, culture), without even gaining in certainty what we lose in freedom, given that nature is not the sphere of absolute regularity but rather that of probability and contingency.

This is obviously not the situation with regard to objects that come into being already within culture, as social objects do. Here getting "ought" from "is" is par for the course. All normative institutions, such as laws, permits and permissions, prohibitions, and so forth derive "ought" from "is," from the specific beings that they are as social objects, in flagrant and absolutely legitimate contravention of Hume's law. It would be very odd indeed if there were a law from whose being we could not derive an obligation. If it were objected that it is circular to cite the case of the law, we might find a more abstract case, such as that of a promise; in the very being of a promise its being maintained is implicit, and so it is intimately connected (indeed, identical) with the "ought," given that someone who makes a promise on the presupposition that from "is" no "ought" follows would not be making a promise, but lying to or tricking his interlocutor.

3.1.3.2 AGAINST OCKHAM'S RAZOR

As already hinted in 1.1.3, in the social world, the principle of parsimony in the multiplication of entities turns out to be wholly inadequate. The fact that we run into redundant classification, or that in Italy there are too many laws, should not be taken to be an argument in favor of the indiscriminate use of Ockham's razor, but should rather be considered as a reason for proposing better designed and more rational classifications that are better able to place and handle varieties of entities. The reason for this is fairly intuitive: A classification that regarded only natural objects as existent would have problems finding room for the artificial borders between states, and a classification that envisaged only the distinction between the true and the false would not know what to do with fiction, with art, with irony, which we run into daily in the human world. The positive alternative to Ockham's razor can be found in my view precisely in privileging exemplification as suggested in 1.1.3; it is not a matter of cutting and reducing, but rather of forming in a reflective way, new categories and new catalogs. This holds even if we do not bear in mind that—as we saw in 3.1.1.2—in the social world, reification is an indispensable way of giving consistency to acts and intentions on which the effective functioning of our world of relations depends. Banally, if we did not reify a promise, but considered it as just another thing we add to the world, and not simply as a manifestation of the will, then we would not be able to explain why not keeping a promise is a much more serious matter than deciding not to take a solitary walk because it has just begun to rain.

3.1.3.3 SOCIETIES AND PERSONS

In this anti-Ockhamist spirit, we may say that both societies and persons exist, against what is claimed by social atomists (only persons exist) and by social holists (only societies exist). In effect, the Latin tag according to which the senators are good men but the Senate is an evil beast makes a point of which we have continual and direct experience and also reveals the coexistence of both individuals and societies, just as there is no harm in saying that there exist atoms, molecules and promises. I believe it is possible to describe the relation between individuals and the societies to which they belong as that between *inferiora* and *superiora*, when the society is an object of higher order relative to the individuals and is endowed with its own features, just as a melody conserves its own characteristics even if all the notes that compose it are transposed by an octave.

In the social world, the relation between *inferiora* and *superiora* has two peculiar characteristics. First, not only are the individuals *inferiora* relative to the society, but society is also an *inferius* relative to the individuals when they are considered as social beings. In other words, the society is the fruit of the individuals, but the individuals are in many decisive ways fruit of the society in which they were brought up. This is consistent with the fact that, without individuals, the society would not exist at all, while individuals without society would exist but would be different from what they are. In the second place, why the transposition of a melody does not compromise its identity, a large change in the individuals that make up a society may alter the society as a whole.[25] In all likelihood, the Breslau/Bratislava of 1840 was socially much more like that of 1940 than it was like that of 1950, when most of the Germans had left and the city had been repopulated with Poles. In some cases, such as the intervention of a single factor—for example, a charismatic leader—it is possible to change the identity of a group.

3.1.3.4 POSSIBILITIES AND NEGATIVE ENTITIES   A further feature of social epistemology is that if we take *possibility* to mean not merely logical or metaphysical possibility, but rather an eventuality expressed by way of inscribed acts, such as declarations, articles or the like, then the possibility of a run on the stock exchange can effectively bring about a run on the stock exchange, the possibility of a nuclear attack can provoke a nuclear attack, and, when we talk of "preventive war," what we are faced with are things that exist because subjects believe that they exist.

In this framework, there also exist negative facts or absences, as is typically the case of debts; as we will see in 3.2, debts provide a very strong argument in favor of the weak textualism that I defend. For there to be a debt, it is necessary that somewhere (in the heads of the debtor and creditor, on a piece of paper, in a computer file) there be some registration of the debt and credit. If all the social actors were to forget the debt, then it would disappear; and this, as we have already seen a number of times, is the crucial difference between social objects and physical ones: if everyone forgot about Mont Blanc, it would still be there. Conversely, for a debt as a negative fact to subsist, there must be something positive that exists, namely the registration. In this case, I also believe that the law Object = Inscribed Act allows us to take account of negative facts, as we see in 4.3.3.3.

3.1.3.5 VALUES AND EVALUATIONS   In social epistemology, behaviors and persons are exemplifications of values, and theories of social objects are themselves intrinsically evaluative, unlike theories of natural objects. This evaluativeness[26] can be summed up in three theses.

The first thesis regards *individual actions*. Social reality is the fruit of human actions and of their consequences, including the undesired ones. This point is connected to the fact that social objects exist *as social objects* (it is clear that the Parthenon would exist as a physical object even after the extermination of humankind) only because there are subjects who believe that they exist. Now it would be a form of blindness, or, as Nietzsche would have put it, *niaiserie*, to hold that Hitler had nothing to do with the invasion of the Soviet Union in 1941, and that this attack was the upshot of superindividual laws that would have produced their effect even without him. There is therefore no difficulty about maintaining that Germany would never have invaded the Soviet Union without Hitler, that France would never that invaded the Russian Empire without Napoleon, and that the Macedonians would never have got as far as Afghanistan without Alexander the Great. To the objection that these are all cases of figures of extraordinary charisma, we might reply recalling a simple under secretary who, in Bulgaria in World War II, by refusing to sign an agreement with the Germans, held up the deportation of all the Jews then in the country—and this, it may be said in passing, is a witness to the power of documents. Notions like that of "responsibility" and "choice" that run through our moral vocabulary and everyday life make sense only if we assume that individual action makes a difference to social life. Institutions like elections would be merely bizarre if we did not recognize the influence of the individual on the social world.

The second thesis is that of *structural mechanisms*. Social reality contains structural mechanisms connected to the interactions between humans and their material environment, which are not susceptible to being changed by simple fiat. I have already appealed to the case of the economy; in the same way, there is no doubt that canons of beauty are dependent on subjects and change over time, but this does not mean that someone who has been educated in a certain society and in accordance with certain canons can recondition his own tastes by purely subjective actions.

The third thesis concerns *mindful transformation*. The structures may be changed, normally by means of collective action that is mindful or reflective. I am not certain that a *mindful* collective project can guarantee a transformation better than an unreflective one. What is nevertheless clear is that transformation is possible and that we have very many examples of such transformations in history. What I would like to stress is the connection between ontological realism and *social transformation*; an understanding of a structure makes the transformation possible, and often suggests how to go about it. This is the Marxian thesis (which returns in Derrida's idea of "deconstruction") that understanding and analyzing reality for what it is necessarily incorporates a judgment and a critique.[27] And in any case, if we suppose that it is not realism but—what should we call it?—irrealism that undertakes to change how things are, the question remains of how irrealism can understand that there is a difference between changing the world and believing you have changed it, pretending you have changed it, and dreaming of changing it.

3.2 REALISM AND TEXTUALISM

In 3.1, I described my position on social objects as *weak textualism*, and I explained that it is a variant of transcendentalism, which in the twentieth century was defined as the claim that "there is nothing outside the text." I apply this, not indiscriminately to all objects, but only to social objects, taking the formula, "There is nothing *social* outside the text."

The task I now undertake is that of presenting the main positions that have been adopted regarding social objects,[28] so as to bring to light the difficulties they face and thus motivate my opting for weak textualism. As I have said, what I aim at is a sort of transcendental dialectic to show the unsustainability of the alternative positions. But here I do not propose a critique of psychology, of cosmology, and of rational theology, but rather of three positions that I call *strong realism, strong textualism,* and "weak realism." We may set them out in a table:

Strong realism	Strong textualism
Social objects are not socially constructed	All objects are socially constructed
Weak realism	Weak textualism
Social objects are socially constructed on the basis of physical objects	Social objects are socially constructed from physical objects

In the following pages I shall try to show how strong realism tends to assimilate social objects to the domain of ideal objects, while strong textualism tends to assimilate natural objects to social objects, which in turn are reduced to mental objects. The remaining options are weak realism and weak textualism and I shall conclude in favor of the latter, given that it is the theory I defend. Let us begin then with strong realism, whose rule is that social objects are not socially constructed.

3.2.1 *Strong Realism*

3.2.1.1 CRYPTOTYPES A chimpanzee uses a stick to get ants out of an anthill and eat them. Then it puts the stick down. Another chimpanzee comes along and uses it in just the same way. When the first chimpanzee comes back, the second one gives him the stick back. I do not know whether it always happens like this, but it does happen sometimes. Moral: Property exists even when there is no explicit codification of it.

Rodolfo Sacco, who has emphasized and theorized this example, suggests that we are dealing here with "cryptotypes,"[29] which fall into objective but hidden typologies. It is hard to imagine that any positive right whatever could have informed the chimpanzees about property and the norms applying to it. Here we see very deep-rooted intuitions; there is a sense in which running into a social object is like discovering a continent or a theorem. We did not create the laws, and even the legislator in formulating them has to observe material and formal constraints, which might lead us into the misleading supposition that there is a law of nature. Indeed, these laws present immanent features that seem hard to get around; just as it is impossible that there should be color without extension, so it is impossible that there should be a promise without a promiser. Nevertheless, from the fact that property seems (at least in some circumstances) to be endowed with some lawlikeness that is prior to any positive codification, it does not follow that the norms that regulate it, or even the concept of what may be considered property, arise from nothing without the intervention of history or society. Property exists, more or less, as do progress, technology, and many other things. Among the things that do exist, however—and we would do well not to forget the point, because we see its consequences for weak textualism— there is also a very simple form of writing, namely memory. If the second chimpanzee had not remembered that the stick had been used by the first, then we would have had a fight on our hands—unless, of course, the first had also forgotten, and had no inscription of having had the stick.

Here we can make out the resources for a stronger claim than Sacco's, namely the theory of Reinach who, as we saw in 3.1.1.3, precisely because of his realistic position as one of the first to discover social objects, considered essentially as juridical entities and distinct both from physical and from ideal objects.[30] Reinach illustrates the prenormative a priori nature of juridical entities by means of a comparison with physical entities. A rose, which is a physical object, is the basis for objects of higher order, which are founded on the rose and which Reinach calls "states of affairs" (*Sachverhalten*): the existence of the rose, its being a flower, its being red, its being perfumed, and its being in the garden. These states of affairs depend on the rose but are not identified with it, since the "being perfumed" of a rose, the state of affairs corresponding to a propositional content, is not itself perfumed and its "being in the garden" is not in the garden.

As the rose supports the state of affairs of being red or of being in the garden, so, every time I make a promise, such as "I'll give you 10 euros tomorrow," there are activated, on the one hand, a claim and, on the other, an obligation.[31] In order to make the promise disappear from the world, there has to be a revocation, a renunciation or its fulfillment; the claim and the obligation thus cannot be considered nothing or merely arbitrary, but must be granted an objective existence distinct from that of the other objects that Reinach lists—physical, psychic (simply thoughts in someone's head), and ideal. Unlike physical objects, juridical entities cannot be seen or heard; at most, the things to which they refer can be perceived: I see a stick or a house and not my property in them. For this reason, Reinach's theory should not be confused with natural law theories: the mere fact of distinguishing juridical objects from physical, psychic, and ideal objects excludes the legitimation of natural right. There is nothing like a "natural right," because in the thing that we call *nature* there is no "right," any more than in colors there is the *Mona Lisa*.

Furthermore, unlike mere thoughts, juridical entities persist even when no one is thinking about them: I have a mortgage even when I manage not to think about it. And, unlike ideal objects, they have determinate existence in time; in a certain sense, their ambition is the opposite of that of ideal entities: if these latter aim to exist forever, promises and bets want to come to an end sooner or later. A slightly anomalous case is that of institutions, which want to live in eternity, as individuals do, and perhaps plan thousand-year Reichs. But these aspirations are doomed to the same end as individuals' dreams of immortality.

3.2.1.2 **THE MATERIAL A PRIORI**   The notion that social objects are to be met with in the world and possess a peculiar normativity derives directly from Husserl's idea that the world is not made up of a disorderly mass of sense data, but rather of objects that are already endowed with their own lawlikeness and that display the same bindingness as the laws of logic. It is possible to find in every object an essence that is not relative and not transitory, an a priori necessary archetype, even if discovering it (the first formulation of an ectype) can come about contingently and a posteriori. Emboldened by this principle, Reinach mounts a frontal attack on the presuppositions of juridical positivism, according to which the law produces its own concepts autonomously. In reality, positive law creates its entities by means of acts of disposition, but in doing so, it encounters this kind of a priori law, which is not a natural law, and which embraces principles that are not purely formal or arbitrary and that exist independently of any juridical doctrine. The discovery and formalization of these a priori laws thus becomes the task of ontology, which Reinach understands as the a priori doctrine of the objects and which he pursues in a manner that is essentially Platonic: there is a pure science of law just as there is pure mathematics, and this science constitutes the foundation of the a posteriori disciplines, which in turn are free to accept or refuse the pure principles. With this last consideration Reinach wants to take account of the fact that, unlike mathematics, in the realm of law we encounter very different jurisdictions conditioned by history and geography in such a way that while it makes no sense to speak of *Albanian mathematics* it makes perfect sense to speak of "Albanian law."

There are three main points to realism. The first is that *reality* incorporates within it not only physical objects but also higher-order objects. The second is that these entities, which are discovered exactly as one discovers a continent or a molecule, constitute a material a priori, possessing the same powers of necessitation that the tradition attributes to logic. And, the third, and certainly the most audacious, is that in these entities are included *values*, which are in the objects before they are in the minds of those who contemplate them; that is to say that not only am I able to recognize the essence of a chair on the basis of a chair and not on that of an idea of a chair, but I am also able to recognize the good or evil of an action or line of behavior irrespective of the dispositions of my subjectivity.

Against the idea that a person can do what he wants with himself, and that society and its objects are the infinitely malleable product of this omnipotence, realism catches a very solid consideration: wherever we are in the world, we find objective connections that are not products of chance. These structures are not merely in the heads of the persons who make up a community or, worse still in the heads of interpreters, but are endowed with properties that belong to objects. Strong realism thus suggests an important point: it is not the structures of human thought that are necessary, but rather the states of affairs and this applies even in the realm of law. In an obligation or a property right, the element that is juridical is closely connected to how, in the actual world, the promise, the cattle, and the appreciation of land values *are*. Social objects are states of affairs that can be encountered in the world; someone affected by amnesia "encounters" a promise made as something new, but if he remembers what a promise is, he cannot help feeling obliged to the other party. In their turn, states of affairs are determined by the objects that make them up.

3.2.1.3 SOCIAL PLATONISM   So far, so good. All the same, if we descend into the details and want to assign a necessity to social objects not as archetypes but as ectypes, we find ourselves having to regard the tax rates for fiscal 2008 as necessary, when on the contrary it is obvious that the laws are enacted on the basis of contingent principles. Now it is precisely contingency that is determining for the concrete occurrence of social objects. This can easily be seen by considering the variety of states of affairs that, in different juridical traditions, fall under the notion of a "contract," and even more significantly, by bearing in mind the deliberate use in law of vague notions that allow a high level of flexibility in handling relatively homogeneous states of affairs.

Most likely, the conclusion to be drawn is this: we (in this case, Italians in 2009) possess determinate social objects that we have *discovered* in the course of our history. These objects are carriers of laws of essence that are configured in a certain way. That does not mean that we have discovered *the only* possible social objects either in space or in time. As regards space, because of their history, the Chinese, for instance, have discovered some social objects that are different from those we have discovered, and many that are identical, each of which is endowed with its own necessities; thus we avoid inferring that the *variety* of objects implies that they are *random*. As regards time, we might notice that even an institution like the family, which is often cited as a paradigm of immutable naturalness, has undergone huge changes in many societies within living memory. Nevertheless, these transformations are never presented as the upshot of simple decisions, but they have always had to negotiate with states of affairs and laws of essence.

Put this way, Reinach's proposal seems in the first instance to be a maxim ("Do not think that the laws are mere fruit of subjectivity") rather than a positive instrument for the construction of a theory of social objects. Moreover, Reinach maintains that juridical objects possess their own "independent being," but there arises a problem about this. We may agree with Reinach that it is immanent to their nature that social objects have a beginning and an end in time, as we can see from the a priori falsity of sentences like "Aristotle wanted to play ace-high poker," "Plotinus thought he had scored a goal," "Proclus supported Panathinaikos," and "Antisthenes took out a mortgage." In the end, realism finds itself caught up in an irresolvable contradiction, conceiving of social objects as having all the characteristics of ideal objects, in particular eternity and independence of subjects. In doing so, it overlooks a fundamental feature of social objects, which I tried to illustrate in 3.1 in introducing the theme of textualism. Even though Platonic idealism may be appropriate for ideal objects, for objects that are so intimately dependent on subjects as social objects are, it must make room for a transcendental idealism of a Kantian sort.

3.2.2 *Strong Textualism*

The transcendental idealism in question appears to be well represented by strong textualism, whose rule is: All objects are socially constructed. But here the transcendentalism is really too strong. If the limitation of strong realism is that it leads to a Platonism that elides the difference between social objects and ideal objects, its opposite, strong textualism, which has been much practiced by the postmodernists, is based on an unbounded transcendentalism that draws no distinction between natural objects and social objects, nor between ontology and epistemology. The result is an absolute constructionism according to which the whole world is the product of conceptual schemes.

Given that this position was discussed at length in 2.1.3.1, a few observations will suffice. For strong textualists, there are natural objects (illnesses, for instance) that are treated as social objects (literary criticism), and there is in general no difference between something that is independent of our conceptual schemes (again, illness) and the fact that there are things whose existence is closely tied to our conceptual schemes (literary criticism or the development of a new treatment whose success will depend in any case on how effective it really is). In this way, we find a world that wavers between solid banalities (literary criticism is socially constructed) and complete absurdities (illness is socially constructed).

In general, these extremes are reached by a systematic conversion into another genus (*metabasis eis allo genos*): we begin with a claim that has very restricted application and then it is generalized and applied to fields where it becomes meaningless. Consider the position of Foucault, when he claims that perhaps when the human sciences disappear humans will disappear.[32] What has gone wrong here is the generalizing of the particular case from which his inquiry started, which was the assumption that madness is a result of psychiatry.[33] In one sense, this is banal. Our specific way of dealing with behaviors that we call *mad* is psychiatry, which tells about things like schizophrenia and paranoia, where once the vocabulary was that of possession, demons, or gods. Furthermore, madness is certainly an epistemological object, since to call something "madness" instead of "divine possession" is certainly a choice that has to do with what we know.

If we think more about it, even at this level, the theory does not work and the supposed causal nexus is nothing but a semantic confusion, in which madness$_1$ as an ontological datum (= a certain symptomatic behavior) is muddled with madness$_2$ as an epistemological datum (= medical explanation). This is no different from confusing measles$_1$, the illness, with measles$_2$, the diagnosis. Now we can hardly say that without medicine madness$_1$ would disappear any more than measles$_1$ would. All that disappear are madness$_2$ and measles$_2$, which is not much of a consolation, given that this would rob us of remedies and knowledge that could be useful. This absurdity becomes quite plain when it is applied to humanity, as a natural kind, whose disappearance is prophesied. That featherless biped existed before and will presumably exist after the human sciences will, if ever, have ceased to exist. And to think—or at least to write—the contrary is simply to mistake ontology for epistemology, the social for the individual, and to consider the individual as the realm of an absolute subjectivism that, on the kindest reading, can be ascribed to solipsism. In this framework, the most serious problem with strong textualism is that, by excluding from the start the possibility of an *adaequatio* between intellect and thing (given that there is nothing outside the text), it turns out to be *ex hypothesi* immune to all possibility of falsification. The situation is literally psychoanalytic; if the analyst asks you whether you have ever felt homicidal urges toward members of your family, you can answer "yes" and confirm his hypothesis, but this is not falsified even if you answer "no," given that in that case the analyst would argue that it is a case of resistance.

Someone might object that there is nothing wrong with claiming that social objects are socially dependent, but in that case we would not really have a theory, but a solid tautology. The claim would become interesting again, or at least not tautological, if it were suggested that "socially constructed" meant "subjectively constructed," except that, in that case, we would be faced with a clear falsehood, as we can see if someone decided subjectively that theft is no longer a crime or that money has no value. If the thesis of strong textualism seeks to be less than a tautology (social reality is social), then it must be a claim that social reality is subjectively constructed (to say that it is "intersubjectively" is simply a way to cover up the problem), which is tantamount to a psychologization of the whole of the social world. It is even more unpleasant to think that the sun, the moon, the rain, and the muggy atmosphere are simply figments in our imagination. The question then arises, if this is how things stand, of why we are so interested in the weather forecast.

3.2.3 Weak Realism

Let us proceed to the weak realism proposed by Searle, which at present is the standard view about the nature of social objects. His rule is that social objects are constructed on the basis of physical objects. Let us proceed to illustrate Searle's rule for the construction of social objects.

3.2.3.1 X COUNTS AS Y IN C

Searle's view is realist because it implies that things like promises and symphonies have their own peculiar reality. They are not figments or motions of consciousness or of the will, and they can be defined as being of a higher order than physical objects because social objects rest upon a *res*. Searle motivates the constitution of social reality with the rule "*X counts as Y in C*," meaning that a physical object X, such as a piece of colored paper counts as the social object Y, a €10 banknote, in context C, the Europe of 2010. This is the reason why, unlike Reinach, I prefer to think that this is *weak* realism. Searle is realist in claiming that social reality cannot do without physical objects, but it is reductionist in claiming that there are no properly "social objects" but only physical objects (pieces of paper, pieces of land, human bodies, and so forth) that are employed for social function by means of what Searle calls "imposition of function," which amounts to the same thing as "counting as."

3.2.3.2 FROM LINGUISTIC ACTS TO SOCIAL OBJECTS

The formation of weak realism can be described as a strategy in four moves, which exemplify a tradition very different both from that underlying strong realism and from that which generated strong textualism.

The first move can be located in Oxford in the 1950s in the teaching of, among others, J. L. Austin, and in Berkeley in the 1960s and 1970s, with emphasis on the especially delicate part of language that is made up linguistic acts. The open-order analyses of Austin take on systematic shape in Searle's work, which offers a complete taxonomy of them,[34] and more besides. Searle does not restrict himself to classifying speech acts but also—and this is the first bud of social ontology—recognizes the presence of objects that arise, for instance, out of the peculiar acts that are performative: as we have seen, a wedding or a judge's sentence, which may last only a few minutes in their culmination as rituals. Yet the social objects that correspond to these acts may last for years, and the philosopher is called on to provide an adequate ontology for them. To do so, however, he must furnish a theory of mind, given that the characteristic of objects such as the prime minister or a search warrant is that, unlike cows and mountains, they only exist if there are minds ready to believe that they do.

This is Searle's second move, located in Berkeley in the 1980s. Austin restricted himself to talking about language (and perception); Searle set himself to looking for a theory of mind.[35] Could a machine that passed the

Turing test get married? Does a computer used by a turf accountant really bet? Could it launch a ship? Could it make a will in favor of another computer? Obviously not. And this is because the human mind is endowed with something that computers are not, namely intentionality, which is the capacity to refer to something in the world, making use of the representations that we have, roughly speaking, in our heads. This intentionality, however, is not a sprit or a little cloud that comes down to earth; it is something real, like photosynthesis or digestion. This is very delicate point because to claim that the individual "I" is in many cases the result of collective intentionality does not mean that reality is constituted intersubjectively. Rather, there are pieces of reality that exist perfectly well on their own, and that do not depend on language or consciousness. Others, to be sure, do so depend. We should not muddle the cases, though, lest we fall into strong textualism.

The third move in Searle's strategy is scattered here and there, but still in the 1980s.[36] Searle observed the spread of strong textualism. In the end, the moral seemed to be that, paradoxically enough, there are words but not things, concepts but no objects for them to refer to. It would be a mistake to see in the reaction to this unlimited textualism just a polemical moment, given that it is in this framework that Searle built the theory of reality as a "background,"[37] as something that does not need to be demonstrated because it is the basis of all our demonstration, that is one of the basic elements of his general ontology, and that gives us both the deep meaning of this realism as well as a sense of the profound unrealism of a strong textualist who uses his laptop on the airplane to his next speaking appointment to make up arguments for the nonexistence of the external world.

The fourth move is located in Paris in the 1990s. Searle enters a cafe and pronounces a sentence in French, "*Un demi, Munich, à pression s'il vous plaît.*" This very simple sentence activates an immense invisible ontology: the social exchange between Searle and the waiter, a network of norms, prices, tariffs, rules, passports and nationalities, a whole universe, Searle observes, of a complexity that would have dismayed Kant if only he had taken the trouble to think about it. Here we are at the opposite pole from strong textualism. If that doctrine dissolved tables and chairs into mere interpretations, the weak realism of Searle affirms that social objects too have their own existence.

It is not hard to see how here we are coming to close the system. The philosopher of language who had studied speech acts had encountered performatives that are able to construct social objects; the philosopher of mind who had studied intentionality had seen its role in the construction of social reality; the polemicist against postmodernism had elaborated a realist ontology that helped us understand why, even against our aims and hopes, it is useless to try not to pay for one's beer at the bar by claiming that social (and perhaps also physical) reality is socially constructed. All that remained for the social ontologist to do was discover this new realm of objects that, for all they require the minds of persons, cannot be in any way defined as "mental."

3.2.3.3 PROBLEMS WITH ACTS

So far so good, as regards the cultural politics and the coherence of the philosophical quest. But we also know, and Searle himself is aware of the fact, that there are counterexamples to this theory, and above all, there is a serious problem with clarifying a key notion for Searle, which is that of "collective intentionality."[38] Collective intentionality is the central span in the bridge leading from X to Y, from physical reality to social reality, given that it underlies the assigning of functions that are not individual—as, for instance, might be deciding that a horse is a senator or believing oneself to be Napoleon—but are shared, as in the case of attributing value to money. Searle is rather evasive about explaining a function that is so important for the working of the whole of his theory. In effect, he could not be too explicit, because it is not clear where such functions as regarding *The Virgin of the Rocks* as a work of art are to be found—perhaps somewhere halfway between believing oneself to be Napoleon and believing that this piece of paper is worth €50.

Nevertheless, the idea is that social activities in the strict sense do not arise from the meeting of two individual intentionalities, but rather from a collective intentionality, which is what makes the violinist's execution make sense only when he plays in an orchestra or the footballer's movements only when playing in a team, and so on with other examples. It is clearly only thanks to collective intentionality that the assignment of function can really work as Searle requires it to. Here we need to know more, but this is a point on which Searle is rather evasive. He tells us, in the first place, that there is a formal difference between individual and collective intentionality: While individual intentionality is "in the singular" (we express it with sentences like "I intend to go to the cinema"), collective intentionality is "in the plural" (we express in it sentences like "we intend to build a boat"). Next, he says that collective intentionality is no less "in the heads of individuals" than individual intentionality is, and on this basis, he offers a rather impoverished scheme, in which the first figure is wrong and the second right, without its really being clear why.

Collective intention

Not everything that is simple is also true. In fact, the scheme seems much more complex. It presents itself as a phenomenology of the spirit, which we might illustrate with this slightly arcane diagram:

$$IC_1 \rightarrow II \rightarrow IC_2$$

In the first instance we have immediate collective intentionality (IC_1): the baby that has not yet distinguished itself from the mother, that cries if another baby cries, and that has not individuated itself in the mirror stage. Then we have individual intentionality (II): the Cartesian subject that fashions itself and distinguishes itself from the world in a very mediated way. Finally, we have collective intentionality as the mediation of individual intentionalities (IC_2): group rules, democratic procedures, and the like. This last takes shape only much later and in certain people, such as those who are unwilling to participate in waste separation and do not see anything wrong in parking in the third row, it never takes shape at all.

Searle's reasoning trades on the confusion of IC_1 and IC_2 and does not take account of II. Indeed, when, in line with his general theory of intentionality, Searle says that collective intentionality is a biological primitive, a faculty that we inherit evolutionarily, he is formulating an empirical hypothesis about IC_1, which explains nothing about the passage to IC_2. And, as regards the passage from IC_1 to II, the only thing he says is that individual intentionality is "derived" from collective. Which is just to say that there is a passage from IC_1 to II. Furthermore, assuming that collective intentionality is a biological primitive does less than justice to obvious cultural variations: the extreme collectivism of the Chinese (in which something like collective intentionality is comprehensible, but in that case not as a biological given) as against the extreme individualism of the Neapolitans. Again, IC_2 is nothing but a reproposal of the social contract, which in any case admits of alternatives, such as the state of exception theorized by Carl Schmitt,[39] and widely practiced both before and after him.

It is hard to get away from the feeling that we are dealing with a deus ex machina. We can fully understand the need to hypothesize a faculty of this sort to make Searle's theory work. We can also recognize that neurons have been identified that would at least explain empathy,[40] even if, as we see in 4.1.2, these neurons seem better adapted to explaining mimesis. However, a theoretical need and an empirical discovery do not add up to a philosophical justification. The problems get harder if we go further and ask (1) what exactly is collective intentionality; (2) whether it is able to explain *all* of social reality; (3) whether it is able to explain *part* of social reality; and (4) *where* we are to locate this intentionality.

The nature of intentionality. As to the first question, it is not hard to see in Searle's hypothesis a sort of reproposal of Hegel's objective spirit. Human will, thoughts, intentions, desires, and hopes are solidified in institutions: families, societies, states, railway stations, post offices, outings to the country, university departments. In my view, this is idea is splendid, but only if we see that the condition of possibility of this spirit is the existence of letters and of inscriptions, as I argue in 5.3.2. Conversely, following Searle, if we replace "collective intentionality" with "supersoul," the problem, from being occult, immediately becomes plain.[41]

An explanation of all social reality. As to the second point, are we sure that it works in all cases rather than just for, let us say, soccer, American football and basketball, but not for other less amusing games such as "driving in traffic" or "paying the taxes"? It would be even worse if we were to read the behavior of firms in terms of intentionality. We would have a description of an irresponsible, egoistic, highly competitive psychopath with delusions of grandeur, as we learn from reading a company's self-presentation as if it depicted an individual (it is clear that, in a firm, the understatement required by the fact that self-praise is no recommendation does not apply).

It is worth noting that in everyday life, we are used to being more precise than Searle. After all, we distinguish at least three types of situations. (1) The *mass* in which collective intentionality determines individual intentionality. This model certainly captures a real experience, such as exaltation before a dictator or a rock star or in a voodoo rite. But it doubtful whether it offers a reliable guide to social ontology. After all, these cases have less to do with the physiology of the social world than with its pathology, or at least exceptional cases. While one might say that a jazz jam session exemplifies collective intentionality,[42] it remains to be seen in what sense society as a whole is exemplified in a jam session. (2) *Guilt*, in which individual and collective intentionality determine each other, because it is a cause for guilt to have given in to collective intentionality if it was wrong. (3) The *trick*, in which an individual intentionality plays on collective intentionality (a case that Searle does not consider).

As we see in detail in 4.1.2, collective intentionality suffers from three main defects as an overall explanation of social reality. The first is that there are highly codified practices, such as military, sports, or dance training, that are explicitly aimed at promoting collective intentionality, which must therefore be anything but a natural *prius*. Second, collective intentionality is unable to explain change, whether at the collective level or at the individual level. And last, it does not explain choice or decision. If there were only collective intentionality, we could replace elections and opinion polls with the simple interrogation of a single individual, perhaps just by examining our own consciences.

An explanation of part of social reality. As to the third question about whether Searle's hypothesis explains al least *some* social objects, it is worth observing that collective intentionality, and indeed intentionality in general, does not explain even the paradigm case of social object that Searle himself privileges, namely money. There are two problems here.

Searle claims that "anything can count as money"; since monetization is in large measure due to convention, this claim—which we may translate "anything that collective intentionality decrees is money is money"—seems reasonable up to a point. In addition to pieces of metal and paper, bags of salt and shells are or have been currency, but never tables or cows, because they are not manageable enough. Likewise, we cannot use soap bubbles, carbonized paper, grains of sand, atoms, or fresh meat as coins. The sequences of ones and zeroes in a computer have certainly taken the place of cash in a very large number of transactions, but their physical representation is an object 8.5 by 5.5 centimeters, is thin enough to go in a wallet, is resistant enough not to break, and is made of plastic that does not melt or dissolve in water. Searle has replied to this objection,[43] noting that there are cases in which unwieldy currencies have been adopted. For instance, in ancient Sparta, because the ephors did not want large sums of money to be taken out of the city, they adopted heavy metal bars as currency. To this we may object (a) it is not by accident that this happened in a state whose economy tended to autarchy; and (b) this is not a counterexample to "not everything can be money," but if anything to "there can be no context which requires money not to be manageable" (a much stronger thesis that is not implied by the former). *Normally* we assume that money ought to be easy to transport, but in a context in which this requirement does not apply, it remains true that the physical features of money are relevant to the ends it serves—in Sparta, normal money would not have done its job precisely because too easy to export. In any case, a coin weighing two hundred tons would not have been currency even in Sparta. It is also worth noting that the ontological constraints turn out to be closely related to the ecological constraints noted in 2.2.3.3, given that at the North Pole even a pound of fresh meat might count as money, but there would remain restrictions on physical size—imagine a banknote that was a mile long.

In the second place, and more seriously, the intentionality of money is far from certain. As Carl Menger observes, money arose in a way that was itself unintentional though as a result of intentional actions.[44] No one ever decided to invent money; rather, as I explain in 3.2.4.3 and 4.2.1.3, in the course of accumulation and exchange, the use of markers evolved the form of coin giving rise in the end to the concept of money. To be sure, history provides examples of goods that have been declared tender by legislative act, but in most cases the law has simply recognized as money goods that had already taken on this role. It is economic convenience that calls on individuals, who are aware of their own advantage and irrespective of the public interest, to exchange their own goods with other that can be counted on in a wider market. They will prefer those goods that embody the features that make them fit to be means of exchange. In this connection, it may be helpful to note a pretty clear proof of the unintentional nature of money on the basis of my original readers' experience. About a decade ago, many national currencies were replaced by the euro. Clearly this process was fully and strongly intentional, given that it was preceded by popular referenda, parliamentary votes, and institutional acts of various sorts. Now, what is the psychological result of this noteworthy intentional ingredient? The fact is that those who had been brought up with their national currency initially viewed the euro as an abstract currency, which they tended to convert in the old currency, with unfortunate economic consequences. It will be different for children who have been brought up with the euro; for them, who have not seen it as the result of intentional deliberation, it will be a fully concrete currency.

Where is the intentionality? The last question outstanding is: Where is collective intentionality? The point is not secondary but turns out to be crucial, since, at least as regards the social world, not only is there no entity without identity, there is no identity without residence, even if it is a temporary abode. Now, there is a banal answer to the question of where individual intentionality, considered both as representation and as volition, is to be found: *in our heads*: roughly speaking, behind the eyes, under the hair and between the ears. We can grant Searle's claim that, considered as a biologically inherited faculty, collective intentionality (type IC_1) is likewise in the heads of individuals. It would be a much riskier proposition to answer the question of where to find the sort of collective intentionality that underlies the construction of social reality, which is to say IC_2: Is it scattered about in the air? We might try supposing that, for Searle, collective intentionality of type IC_2 is in the heads of individuals, just like individual intentionality, with the only difference that where the former takes the plural form "we intend," the latter takes the singular "I intend." This is not a very satisfying answer. How can collective intentionality, considered as an individual psychological phenomenon (it is a "we intend" that is nevertheless in the heads of *single* persons), build a bridge between the individual and the social? Does it not risk sounding like the royal "we" that the queen uses to address even those who are not her subjects? How on earth could a purely formal difference from individual intentionality perform the miracle of passing from the individual to the social? It is clear that, for the construction of social reality, we need some way to externalize intentionality, something that allows its content to be shared.

Little by little, if we try to answer these questions, we see that the intentionality that is so obscure and ungraspable is deposited not in heads, but in texts.[45] As I elaborate in detail in 4.1.2 and in 5.3, what for Searle is collective intentionality is in fact the upshot of education, imitation, and inscriptions that are deposited and manifested in rites, social conventions, family relations, power relations, laws, religions, and, most typically, documents from which arises our social life. Conversely, a good argument against collective intentionality might be: If the glue of society really were collective intentionality, what use would we have for documents? Must we regard them as mere records of the attribution of roles and function that we carry out collectively? This would not make sense, because if collective intentionality is created and uncreated at will, in a sort of permanent revolution, it is hard to see why we should fix certain moments that are destined to be overcome in any case—and I wonder what Searle would think if he learned of the Trotskyist upshot of his theory. If this is not how things are, if we do have a need of documents, how can it be claimed that everything depends on collective intentionality? After all, traditionalism had the advantage of evoking a mysterious, not to say occult, entity that could at least explain the overall stability of social habits, and also the role that written texts and documents played in this. We will return to the question of (nonoccult) tradition in 4.1.2.4. For the moment, I would like to invite the reader to reflect on a simple fact: It is not much of an explanation to say that people play *Risk* thanks to collective intentionality, while it is clearer and more comforting to suppose that before starting they read the rulebook.

3.2.3.4 PROBLEMS WITH THE OBJECT   If we consider the object involved, the problem is at least twofold: it is not at all clear how, from a physical object, we manage to get a social object; and it is not at all clear how, from the social object, we manage to identify regularly a physical object that corresponds to it.

From the physical to the social. To explain the passage from the physical to the social, Searle offers the example of the transformation of a wall into a border.[46] The idea is that first there is a physical object, a wall that separates the inside from the outside and defends the community. Then, little by little, the wall disintegrates, leaving nothing but a row of stones, which are useless as an obstacle but which have transmuted into a social object, a border; it is the same as the yellow line in a post office or an airport that indicates where to wait one's turn. Now, we can understand how, in disintegrating, a wall can in some circumstances become a border. But it is not at all clear how, on the basis of this simple analogy—a fortuitous situation that may have actually occurred, but how often we do not know—we got to the yellow line or the centerline on the highway. The question is complicated by a further consideration: If a physical object really could constitute the origin of a social object, every wall would constitute a prohibition. But it is clearly not so, as anyone who wants to knock a wall down in their house knows, so long as this operation does not contravene some norm, which is itself essentially a documental reality. Neither should we forget that one of the most famous walls in modern history, the Berlin Wall, arose out of a border that already existed and was converted by a letter signed by Erich Honecker dated August 12, 1961.[47] In short, the normal situation is that, first a document is signed, then a border is traced, and finally a wall is put up with lookout posts and guard dogs, while Searle's thought is, rather curiously, that the border is what is left when the walls, chain-link fences, lookout posts, and guard dogs have gone away.

Still on the question of the passage from the physical to the social, we may note a point that will become important as we proceed. Before adducing the case of the wall, Searle cites animals that mark their territory, but then he decided to abandon the example because it seemed inadequate.[48] Why inadequate? Not in an absolute sense, given that it is a good example; but it does not suit Searle's theory. In effect, there is no moment in which the trace constitutes a *physical* limit. The trace is a smell and an olfactory limit does not make for impenetrability, for all that it fulfills its performative (or, in the case in hand, perfumative) role. *Right from the start* it is something that does not begin as a physical obstacle and then become a social obstacle, but it arises as a trace, which in its essence is mildly physical and strongly social, otherwise we would have to find some material impediment on which to base the taboos on incest or cannibalism. The case of marking territory could have been a good example of how fiat borders[49]—those that are established by a decision—turn out to be quite indifferent to how they are embodied, so that, from this point of view, there is no difference between an olfactory trace and the Great Wall of China. And if Searle had followed it up, rather than privileging money and the wall, he would have saved himself a lot of trouble, in particular that of how to explain with his theory those social objects, such as debts, that do not have any physical counterpart. For, according to weak realism, there is a world of difference between a wall and a debt: The former is the presence of something; the latter is the absence of something. On the other hand, the trace that marks a territory establishes a means by which, being present as an olfactory given, it can refer to an absence, which is the animal that has marked the territory. In this sense—and this is one of the strong points in favor of weak textualism—it constitutes a superordinate structure as much to the wall as to the debt. All this suggests that the true dimension in which social objects find their raison d'être is the realm of inscriptions, which is to say a *special kind of physical object*, and not physical objects in general, as Searle supposes as a result of the excessive weight he puts on collective intentionality.

We may add to what we have been saying a consideration that I look at in detail in 4.3.3.3, and that concerns a social object such as the state, that cannot be seen with the naked eye and that does not receive its identity from the matter that it is made up of, but from traces and documents. This may not be evident if we think about nineteenth- and twentieth-century states, but the states of the ancien régime, like modern multinationals, did not derive their identity from being territorially contiguous, but from a network of documents in a process, as I analyze in 5.1.2, has come back on the scene in the formation of the European Union. It was only in the romantic period that appeal was made to territorial contiguity and the unity of a people: X (the hexagon, the pentagon, the boot) counts as Y (France, Spain, Italy) in C (in the context defined by the collective intentionality of the French, the Spanish, and the Italians).

To show the secondary role played by the material mass in determining a statelike entity, we may note that we measure the surface area of the state, which is surrounded by a border as a trace (think of the ancient rites of the foundation of a city in which it is the boundaries that are traced) and not either in depth or in height. We do not say that a state grows when a new volcano adds to its height, nor that the skyscrapers of Hong Kong or Dubai make those states larger; by contrast, when Dubai or Holland reclaim land from the sea, then that does constitute growth. Now, the surface counts precisely because it is what is bounded by a trace, and this is the closest thing to the representation of the state on a map. The value attributed to the surface is thus a fundamentally textual feature, which is to say determined by the possibility of representing the identity of the state on paper by means of inscriptions, in accordance with an intuition I set out in

5.1.3.1: marking the territory, marquisates, the Italian region of the Marche (or the Welsh Marches), marks of recognition or of infamy, trademarks and Deutschmarks all illustrate a deep interrelatedness, representing at various levels physico-documental unities.

All this points to an even more general consideration. The example of money, which Searle adduces as the normal case of a social object, constitutes—if we follow the constitutive rule that X counts as Y in C—an exception. It is relatively easy to transform a button into a coin to deceive a blind man, and then once again use it as a button. In the overwhelming majority of cases, the operation looks much more complex, if not impossible. This is a very serious limitation that compromises the paradigm status of the example adduced. Indeed, it is easy to claim that, simply by inscribing a piece of metal we get a social object, and that, once use has effaced the inscription, we have a physical object again. This is not at all the norm, but rather an exception.

From the social to the physical. We return at length to the example of money in 3.2.4.3. Let us look now at the second aspect of the problem, regarding the reversibility from the social to the physical. It is fairly intuitive to say that a banknote is also a piece of paper, or that a president is also a person. Just so, when Searle is alone in a hotel bedroom, there is only one physical object, but many social objects: there is a husband, an employee of the state of California, an American citizen, a driver's license holder and so on. It is not quite so easy in other cases that are a bit different but not wildly so. What are we going to say about debts? After all, debts undermine the rule X counts as Y in C: We have a social object Y, the debt, to which no X corresponds. The X cannot be either the creditor's money or the debtor's, which in any case are already social objects, as money, Ys. But it is no easier in the case where the debt is a physical object. The cock that Socrates owed to Aesculapius was not a physical object that counts as a debt in the Athens of 399 BCE: it is simply a physical object that Socrates owes to Aesculapius. As in the case of the state, so also in that of a debt, we see that the social object finds its manner of existence in the inscription of acts (that Socrates owes a cock to Aesculapius) and not in physical objects (the cock that Socrates owes to Aesculapius). Debts and negative entities in general are just one of the many possible cases. Consider the very banal matter in the real estate market of rights of way. Where is the X that counts as Y in C? It is not the road or the corridor, any more than the cock is the debt of Socrates.

Y-independent terms. Little by little, the social world that Searle describes with the austere simplicity of a shepherd king runs up against the complexity of modern life. As Barry Smith has pointed out,[50] we very often have to deal with Y entities that are independent of any X, that is to say, they do not coincide ontologically with any part of physical reality. In Smith's view, these are "representations." To get a better grasp on the notion of "representation," Smith describes them as "quasi-abstract entities," offering the case of blindfold chess. The idea is that chess can be played without any physical medium. It can be played on the Internet, where the board is not present in the way that the physical chessboard is: it has two localizations, corresponding to the two computers. What is more, two masters can play in their heads without even having a board represented on the screen. Smith applies this model to money; after a certain point and making use of evolved technology, we begin to do without the physical counterparts, which are replaced by traces in a computer. Here, too, we have a social object to which no physical object corresponds, only a representation. This is a relevant and acute observation, which nevertheless leaves two questions open.

First, if the representation came about without the inscription of an act, as when there is no registration in the memory bank—of which more in 4.2—there would be no game, just a series of unrelated flashes. There is a difference between imagining that one is playing chess (for instance, remembering a game and thinking about alternative moves) and playing chess mentally, as, according to Leibniz,[51] the Arabs play chess in the desert to ward off the boredom of caravan journeys. The former is a solipsistic exercise, where I can cheat by moving the knight diagonally and decide that the one who undergoes checkmate is the winner. The latter is already a social object precisely because, even with blindfold chess, there are moves declared, there are acts, just as in a game of battleships played without paper, and these declarations are inscribed in the memory, just as a record of a game can be written down in chess players' magazines.

Second, is it really true that the blips in a computer are not physical at all? Are they really *res cogitans* totally separate from *res extensa*? It is enough to visit a technological cemetery, whether it be a Chinese recycling plant or just a corridor in a university department cluttered with computers that are no longer in use, to see how much plastic and silicon are necessary to support the traces so central to information technology. Unless we say that a computer possesses a soul distinct from its body, we have to allow that the blips are material. In short, it is hard, if not impossible, to say that, even in the case of money that has been transformed into computer traces, there are only representations and nothing physical to support them, even if the body is not large. But suppose that it is so, that representations need nothing physical. In that case, there is no need to answer the question: what is the difference between a hundred real dollars and a hundred ideal dollars? And how do we distinguish the representation of one hundred real dollars from one hundred dollars merely imagined or dreamed? We have fallen out of the frying pan into the fire, from too much matter in Searle to too little in Smith. Are we sure that this is how things are in the real world?

3.2.4 *Weak Textualism*

3.2.4.1 OBJECT = INSCRIBED ACT At this precise moment, you are reading a book. You have your trusty Moleskine in your pocket, some tickets and receipts, your wallet. If you are in an office and you raise your eyes from the book, there will be mountains of pieces of paper, letters, faxes, packages, and packets, to say nothing of what you would see if you are in a library. What is there surrounding the computer screen? A frame made of Post-Its. And what is there inside the computer? An enormous mass of registrations and inscription, just as there is in your mobile phone and in so many other gadgets. I think it would be harder to find a stronger proof of weak textualism. The double phenomenon of the explosion of writing without paper (to which I will return in 4.1.1) and, at the same time, of the survival of paper in a society that in theory could do without it is the plainest proof of the rule Object = Inscribed Act. Social objects follow from the registration of acts that involve at least two persons and that are inscribed on any kind of physical medium, from marble to neurons, by way of paper and the world of the web. My claim is that, by means of this simple rule, we can make sense of the whole of the social world.[52] As can be easily seen, this viewpoint derives directly from Derrida's philosophy, which in my view offers the basis for a very powerful social ontology. Now, relative to the views of Derrida himself, there are three main points of divergence.

The first is a premise of the weak textualism and consists in limiting the constitutive role of inscription only to social objects, and not extending it to objects in general, which is the claim of strong textualism. My claim, then, is that "there is nothing *social* outside the text" and not "there is nothing outside the text," since the constitutive rule of social objects is Object = Inscribed Act.

The second variation is to attribute a systematic rather than deconstructive role to the notion of grammatology. This is what I aim to do in this book as a whole and, specifically in the analyses I offer in Chapter 4. On this view, the passage from grammatology to ichnology—the theory of traces that I set out in the next part of the book—is the transition from a critique of logocentrism to a phenomenology of how inscriptions can account for the construction of social reality.

The third point of difference, which occupies us in Chapters 5 and 6, is an unpacking of the notion of *documentality*, which I have used to sum up my theory. The true upshot of grammatology, in its complete and positive form, is a theory of documents, which explains both those documents that determine social reality and those that are useless but omnipresent and are works of art, as well as the role of signatures and, in general, idioms in the social world.

3.2.4.2 THE PRIORITY OF INSCRIPTION   Why do I take inscription to be so important? For many reasons, which I hope are becoming clear as the book proceeds. In the case in hand, in the comparison of the theories of social objects, because of the difficulties that weak realism runs into. Indeed, Searle does not deny the role of documents and inscriptions; though he does not stress the point, the paradigmatic value of money depends on the fact that money is essentially an inscription that is manifest in many ways, on metal, on paper or in the file of a computer. Searle has more recently been more explicit in recognizing the importance of inscriptions in his social ontology.[53] Yet, he still does not think that to recognize the role of writing is to pass from weak realism to weak textualism, where the latter is the solution to the problems of the former. Let us see how.

Smith's example of the chess played from memory and apparently reduced to a pure representation is in fact an illustration of the role of inscriptions in the social world, and applies splendidly to the case of money, as we see in the next section. Here, too, with the development of technology, the physical counterparts tend to be replaced by computer traces. And here, too, there is a social object that does not correspond to a physical object, but only to a representation. Yet, a representation is objective and does not reduce without remainder to the mental acts of the two players or to those of the many players on the stock exchange, or yet to the much larger horde of people, generally less well off than brokers, who work with money. Now, this representation is, strictly speaking, a piece of writing.[54]

The chess game does not require a particular board, or two particular computers, or particular neurons. If there is to be a game, though, there must be some medium, and so the game depends generically on something physical—and, more specifically, that medium must be describable as an inscription. If it is said to be false that some social object depends on a *particular* physical medium, but that it is true that every social object depends generically on *some* physical medium (an inscription of some sort), then we can persist in the criticism of Searle without falling into Smith's representationalism. The point is very simple: Searle did not take into account the way that the true physical media were the inscriptions on the coins and on the documents, rather than the metal of the coins, or the bodies of professors or of medieval knights. That is all. It applies to the social objects that I called institutions in Chapter 1. Artifacts like things, instruments, and works are generally more dependent on the inscription than on the type of medium, though you can open doors either with a key or with a magnetic card, according to the sort of lock, you can publish novels in many copies and on various types of media, such as a Kindle, just as we have seen with money.

The considerations applied to Smith go all the more for Searle. The difficulty with Searle's social ontology derives from his not having wanted to suppose that the physical correlate of a social object exists, but it is the trace as inscription in general—whether it be written on paper or embodied as a brain engram, as an inscription in memory that recalls a promise, a debt, an obligation, or an omission.

3.2.4.3 THE EXAMPLE OF MONEY   We can verify this point by looking precisely at the case of money. As we have seen, for Searle, money is the quintessence of a social object: the physical object X (metal, paper) counts as the social object Y (coin, banknote) in the context C (for instance the European Union in 2009). Everything seems to be explained, but in reality nothing is. In the first place, it is not clear what is supposed to have been explained, whether it is the origin of currency or the origin of money. In the *Construction of Social Reality*, Searle talks indifferently of "money," but seems to confuse the two things, given that he seems to be thinking of currency when he speaks of money as the physical X. To ask someone whether he has currency is very different from asking whether he has money and not in the least indiscreet or offensive. Currency is concrete, money an abstract buying power that, if need be, I can replace with a pistol to get the people in the bank to give me some of that good that is cash. In such a case, it would be bizarre to say that X (the pistol) counts as Y (money) in the context C (the bank); and it would be stranger still to say that the pistol counts as *currency*. We can thus see that (1) in the case of *money*, X counts as Y does not hold; (2) in the case of currency, X counts as Y holds only because we assume that X is already currency and Y is money. For this reason, it is helpful to adopt an account of money, in line with a recent proposal by Maria Grazia Turri,[55] that makes three main claims.

The first is the *distinction between money and currency*. Money is a concept that occupies time but not space and can be embodied in different materials including currency. Currency, on the other hand, is a social object whose essential feature is to be capable of bearing inscriptions, which explains very well why we could pass from currency made of metal (not necessarily precious metals) to banknotes and magnetic media. It would be a mistake to think, for instance, that when currency becomes electronic, it is turned into a concept and becomes money.

The second thesis follows from the first and we may call it the *thesis of the priority of currency over money*. As we have seen, currency is concrete while money is abstract, but the realm of currency is, as such, wider than that of money, given that it has at least four functions, not all recognized by all economists: as a measure of value, as means of payment, as means of exchange and as a value reserve. Only as a reserve of value is currency in the strict sense the physico-social realization of money.

The third thesis may be called the *thesis of the priority of currency over value*. Very often economists, like ordinary folk, tend to think of currency as something that derives from precious metals. Here we see the two earlier confusions joining forces. On the one hand, this confuses the object (currency) with the concept (money), and it proceeds to state that the only meaning of the object is realized out of the concept, or that the currency has value only as money, which is to say as a reserve of value. On the other hand, and starting from the same premises, one is tempted to perform a *hysteron proteron* and suppose, quite naturally, that money derives from precious metals.

The underlying argument here seems to be roughly as follows: Gold is valuable. Hence, first gold coins are issued, then silver ones, then paper, and finally computer traces, but the promise remains to return, at least in principle, to gold. But on August 15, 1971, President Richard Nixon abolished the full convertibility of the dollar without, by doing so, turning the dollar into waste paper (or metal or plastic). In any case, and above all, there have always been currencies entirely without intrinsic value: shells, inedible salt, formed bits of clay. But, most radically, it seems fairly obvious that, in order to say that gold is valuable, we have already to have some currencies, at least as measures of value and computation, that consider gold rare and for that reason valuable.

In light of these considerations, which I will expand in 4.2.1.4, let us return to Searle's rule. In general, Searle's mistake is to regard as *constitutive law* of the social world what is only a very common *social phenomenon*. A coffee mug counts as a penholder on the desk; a sarcophagus counts, quite independently of the original intentions, as an archeological find and as a work of art in an Egyptian museum; a broken comb counts as a piece of evidence in a police investigation; any object whatever counts as an example of the class to which it belongs. The principle of "counting as" is particularly important for those peculiarly prized social objects that are artworks. As I will argue at length in 5.2, Duchamp's ready-made does not break the rule for artworks or the Western esthetic canon, but rather the reverse: the physical object X counts as the social object Y in the context C (the gallery, the museum etc.). It may be this assumption that lies at the heart of Searle's view.[56] This fact explains how a physical object can count as a social object and also how, in certain circumstances, an ideal object can count as a social object, as when 666 is held to be the number of the Apocalypse or 911 is the number of emergency services.

Let us return now to the case of money. In this case, Searle's law looks like this:

1. X (gold) counts as Y (money) in C

    This holds for the economy based on the gold standard, whose justification was that gold was a good guarantee for registrations. Choosing a metal that is hard to find, that does into rust, and that is malleable provides an easily recognizable record for accounting purposes, which is not true for earth, air or water, which are too common and hard to handle and hence not good for recordkeeping (unless the earth bears inscription like Babylonian tablets, which themselves originated in money). This economy evolves quite naturally into the paper-based economy and its computer-based successor, taking the form:

2. X (paper) counts a Y (money) in C

Nevertheless, it is clear that in (2) gold has no role to play, and the law turns out to be just *a particular case of the law Object = Inscribed Act*. Social objects are the results of social acts that have been registered, even if only in the heads of individuals. Given that the heads of individuals are limited both as to their capacity and as to their shareability, especially as regards debts and credits, instruments for calculating began to be adopted, and in some cases became specialized in those inscriptions that are so important for society, namely money.[57] If this is right, the next move is to examine more closely the law Object = Inscribed Act, in which we find the keystone of social reality.

3.3 OBJECTS, ACTS, AND INSCRIPTIONS

3.3.1 *Objects*

Imagine a marriage in which all the participants suffer from Alzheimer's in a world where writing has not been invented.[58] The ritual goes ahead as laid down (assuming that these forgetful people manage to reproduce the ritual); at the end of the ceremony, there is an extra husband and an extra wife on the face of the earth; and they all go home happy, except that they wonder why on earth they are happy. The following morning, the forgetful spouses wake up and ask each other who they are and what they are doing. Nothing helps them in this, not their memory, obviously, nor the memos that other societies have invented to keep track of the social objects that they institute, whether they be marriages or funerals, noble titles, political posts, debts and credits, promises and punishments. Then we might note that if *only one* of the participants in the ritual, whether one of the spouses, the persona officiating, one of the witnesses, or just a guest, were to recall the ceremony, we still would not have a social object, but just an individual memory. It is for this reason that inscription, considered as a memory that is in principle accessible to more than one person, plays such an important role in my theory. Suppose, indeed, that there were a record somewhere, such as a marriage certificate. If it were to be discovered by chance, the object would be resuscitated. If the discovery took place after the death of the spouses, we would have a genuine marriage in which the couple did not know that they had been married.

Nevertheless, registration is a necessary but not a sufficient condition of the existence of social objects; without registrations, there are no social objects, but a registration (such as a memory in my mind) does not necessarily constitute a social object. This holds also for those publicly accessible registrations that are inscriptions. Fingerprints become a social object only when they are taken by forensics and used as evidence in a trial, and in such a case, they are media for an investigative procedure. Or when they are taken and transferred onto a passport and thus become part of a document with an even more explicit and, so to say, embodied social character. From this point of view, documents should be conceived of as something that is given once and for all, as the peak of the documental pyramid that I set out in 5.1.4.3: Not all inscriptions are documents, but there is no inscription that cannot become one in the right conditions for acquiring social power.

Thus, at the source of the construction of social objects there are social acts fixed by memory, *even more and even before they are expressed in language.* Indeed, we can imagine social objects that come into being even in the absence of language. For instance, an agreement sealed with a handshake, a tourist's haggling in a souk, or the system of exchange that the Portuguese used with the natives of West Africa in the fifteenth century; they left goods and returned to their ships while the natives took them and gave in return other goods, all without anyone saying, "This is an exchange." But we cannot imagine social objects in the absence of memory, and in the absence of writing, which is a codification of memory and, within social reality, tends to give rise to documents. The constitutive formula Object = Inscribed Act may be exemplified as follows:

Object	*Act*	*Inscription*
Promise	Promising	Memory
Banknote	Emission	Banknote
Marriage	Swearing	Registry and/or memory
Novel	Writing	Novel
Painting	Painting	Painting
Symphony	Composing	Score

The *Act* is what happens between at least two subjects, a miniature society. For instance, a promiser and a promisee: a man alone in the world would not be the master of it, he would not have any possessions; at most, he would have at his disposal most of the things that he finds, but obviously physico-ecological limitations would impose restriction even on this. The *Object* is the promise, the debt, a marriage or a war; an object that in its turn, such as in the case of a war, presupposes other objects such as the human groups that are in conflict. The *Inscription* is the idiomatic registration of the act, for instance on a piece of paper, with a handshake, or even with a look, which is to say on the tablet that is in the heads of the parties to the agreement.

3.3.2 Acts

Let us proceed to explaining the acts that underlie the objects. In Reinach's typology, which provides a basic guide, the fundamental social acts are promises, commands, communications, requests, questions, replies, prayers, thanks, warnings, offers, acceptances, agreements, renunciations, revocations, concessions, transfers, conveyances, and dispositions. My basic claim is that the common feature of all these acts is the presence of a performative element; even in communication there is more than mere statement insofar as it has to do with adopting a position or making a notification. I propose to classify these acts by their *functions*, where acts can be distinguished into doings (*praxis*) and makings (*poiesis*), into social and nonsocial and then, within the realm of the social, into institutional and noninstitutional; and by their *modalities of execution*, according to whether they are linguistic or nonlinguistic (or tacit), or they are spoken or written.[59]

Function	*Execution*
Doings and makings	Linguistic and nonlinguistic acts
Social and non-social acts	Spoken and written acts
Institutional and noninstitutional acts	

3.3.2.1 MAKINGS AND DOINGS Consider the sentence, "I take a walk."[60] Once I have taken the walk, there is nothing left of it. The walk—that individual, concrete walk, not the archetype "walk"—ceases to exist in the exact moment in which I stop walking and becomes at most an ex-existing object. Now let us consider, "I make a vow to the Virgin Mary." It takes just a few seconds to make a vow, but to maintain it may take an entire life. The difference between the two sentences is essentially in the fact that, in the case of the vow, unlike that of the walk, the act is not a mere utterance; in addition to that, it produces an object, it constitutes an entity that can survive after the act, exactly as a marriage survives after the nuptial ceremony. In the terminology promoted by Aristotle and discussed in 3.1.1.3, it is a *poiesis* or making. If I promise something, I perform an act that goes beyond mere description (which is a *praxis* or doing), and over and above that, I constitute an object, namely the promise (which is a *poiesis* or making). What assures us that we have a *poiesis* and not merely a *praxis* is the inscription and the survival of the act on some sort of medium.

3.2.2.2 SOCIAL AND NONSOCIAL ACTS I propose to call social any act occurring between at least two persons who are *formally* aware of the fact that this act is taking place; in this sense, someone who buys a newspaper distractedly and pays for it while thinking about something else, leaving the newspaper on the counter at the newsstand has performed a social act, even if his attention was elsewhere and his consciousness was directed at something else. Conversely, someone who intently and consciously desires to buy a newspaper, but who has only thought about it, has thereby limited himself to thinking about buying a newspaper and has not performed a social act.

In this framework, social acts are distinguished from other acts or the purely individual states that happen in the psychic lives of single people, even when they are turned towards others, as in the case of envy.[61] It is important to note that social and psychological acts often bear the same name, which is a source of confusion. Take the notion of *forgiveness*, which is a fully recognized social and public act (a formal indulgence, reconciliation, and so on). From all that, it does not follow that some psychological act must correspond to the social act: one might pardon an act of genocide but not a private offense. This is not a matter of applying different measures, but rather of two different acts, the one social, the other psychological.[62]

Unlike purely psychological acts discussed in considering subjects in 1.2, social acts are thus not inner experiences or expressions of such, though they do presuppose them. They are not inner experiences because they are social operations. And they are not expressions of inner experiences because there is an essential difference between displaying an intention to do something for someone and promising to do it (typically "I'd love to help" is not a promise to help), or between expressing one's desire to someone ("I'd like a cup of coffee") and asking for or ordering something ("Make me a coffee").

Obviously the fact that one can ask for something also by making an assertion, for instance about one's inner state, is a well-known phenomenon in the philosophy of language and is the object of study in conversational pragmatics.[63] For instance, someone might say, "I'm cold" and, in an appropriate context, by that means ask someone else to close a window; or he might answer, "What shall we do now?" by asserting, "I'd like a coffee," and so issue an invitation to go to the bar. This does not undermine my claim. Indeed, pragmatics presupposes a distinction among various speech acts, such as assertions (which can be expressions of experiences), questions, requests, and orders.

Making a small change to Reinach's classification,[64] I claim that the essential features of social acts are: (1) intention (spontaneity and punctuality); (2) expression (the requirement of being perceived and understood); and (3) inscription (the need to be registered).

Intention. As to spontaneity and punctuality, we have a distinction between, on the one hand, social acts and, on the other hand, intentional states such as sentiments, perceptions, and representations as well as conscious states such as convictions or doubts. On our account, the intention is the fact that in my mind I possess a representation of the object of my promise, bet, conferral of status, and so on; but, unlike intentional or conscious states, this intention requires an expression. A doubt or a sentiment is not weakened by being merely thought, while a social intention is weakened in such a case.

Expression. As we saw in Chapter 1, there is a fundamental difference between thoughts considered as psychological items that are (apparently) in our heads and stay there, and the expressions of these thoughts in acts that are displayed on the outside to others. We grasp this essential difference when we compare, on the one hand, thinking of declaring war, getting married, promising, or buying something and, on the other, saying, writing or acting in such a way as to signal to others that we are declaring war, getting married, promising, or buying something. In the second case, assuming that conditions are propitious, this "really is" declaring war, getting married, promising, or buying something.

As regards perception and understanding as constitutive of the expression, here we have the essential feature of the act that distinguishes it radically from judgment, namely the fact, already noted by Reid when he refers to "social operations," of being addressed to others. In Reinach, however, we have a further and subtler distinction than Reid's, between acts that are *directed* at others and acts that are *addressed* to others.[65] Acts such as expressions of esteem or insults are, in Reinach's view, directed at others, but not addressed to them and, unlike conferrals of honors or challenges to duels, are not social acts. I, on the other hand, would say that they are social acts and would not be acts only if I esteemed or loathed someone in the depths of my heart, but never expressed by sentiments or if there were no society to give them meaning; but they are not acts that give rise to social objects. On these grounds, I would suggest calling them *sterile acts*. Even when we have a sterile action, to make it a social act, it is necessary that my interlocutor understand or at least give some sign of having understood.

Inscription. As I have said several times, inscription is the characteristic feature of the weak textualism that I defend in this book. I do not mean merely that some type of manifestation is called for, which need not be linguistic and may be mute or negative, but I go further to assert that the inscription, at least in the heads of the participants, of some act is as necessary as are intention and expression. An act that had all the features outlined so far, but that was not inscribed, would not be able to produce a social object and would be a sterile act. It would be even more sterile than acts directed at but not addressed to someone because, without a memory that someone has attested his esteem, none of the things that, in normal contexts, follow from attestations of esteem, such as the increase in self-confidence, gratitude to the person who has expressed esteem, and even pride.

3.3.2.3 SOCIAL ACTS AND INSTITUTIONAL ACTS   A birthday party is a social act; a parliamentary decision is an institutional act. We might then say that institutional acts may have various levels of deliberateness and of rituality. We will put off detailed discussion until 5.1.3.2 and 5.1.3.3. For the time being, I would like to say something about social actors, meaning those who perform social and institutional acts. Without some institutional reality, we can make no sense of an *office*, which is conferred by assigning to a social actor an honorific role or full powers that remain such even when they are not exercised or when, for contingent reasons, they cannot be exercised. For instance, the full powers that that were conferred on Karl Dönitz as chancellor of the German Reich in May 1945 pertained to an office that

corresponded to very little by way of real power, but it was to all intents and purposes an office. We ought to distinguish that from a *role*, which may be a social prerogative that does not arise from a formalized institution. For instance, in the animal kingdom, we have the idea of the dominant male in a group. It is true that this role is generally acquired by means of a series of ritualized acts. But, unlike the conferral of an office, the acts of acquiring a role do not consist in mere fiat; there need be no third-party authority that confers the role of dominant male to a gorilla or to a wolf. In some cases, the role is not acquired even by a confrontation with its previous incumbent; for instance, in an emergency, such as a fire or an accident, someone may assume leadership, thus creating a wholly new role that did not preexist the emergency and that was not acquired through any ritual.

For the sake of completeness, however, we must allow that there are intermediate forms between roles and offices, which are taken on by consensus, for instance, in cases of election by acclamation. Here, the institution that confers the office in a second moment is merely rubber-stamping an investiture that has already taken place. Finally, it is worth noting that both offices and roles, considered as social functions, are distinct from personal identity and character insofar as they are psychological and individual functions. The charismatic leader is just one possible version of leadership, which can be exercised even without charisma as a result of the pure practicality of legitimately conferred power.[66]

3.3.2.4 LINGUISTIC AND NONLINGUISTIC ACTS

Social and institutional acts can be either linguistic, which is the normal—as well as more visible and more audible—condition, or tacit. By *tacit act* I mean a typology of acts that are very similar to each other but not entirely identical. In the first place, there are social and institutional acts that come about tacitly,[67] such as the abandonment of objects, with or without formal cession, as when one leaves the last slice of meat on the platter. Here we might also speak of implicit or mute acts. For instance, in Roman law, an obligation may arise out of *litteris contracta*, *verbis contracta*, *consensu contracta*, or *re contracta*. Each of these levels indicates an ever-higher grade of implicitness. In particular, in the case of *re contracta*, a real contract such as sitting down in a bar carries with it an intention to make an order so that, if we do not, the waiter gets angry and, if the waiter does not come, we get angry.

It makes sense, then, to distinguish within the realm of *tacit acts* two kinds of situation, which are not identical though they can occur together and are unified by the fact of not depending on linguistic formulation. On the one hand, we have *mute acts*, either positive or negative: occupations (or seizings), derelictions (or abandonments), and deliveries, which are not subject to codification. On the other hand, we have *traditional acts*, which are codified by unwritten laws—a point we will return to in 4.1.2.4—which go from the behaviors of Neolithic people, for instance mutual grooming to reinforce clan belonging, to the requirement to drink a glass of sherry before dinner in a London gentleman's club, or to codified gestures that can be inserted within functions and ceremonies that involve speaking or writing: handshakes, ribbon-cuttings, laying on of hands, and so on (we will return at length to the social value of gestures in 4.2.3.1).

Traditional acts occur in societies that regulate their behavior, or at least parts of it, not on the basis of written norms but on habits, which nevertheless have to be written, at least in memory, since, if one forgets or does not know the habit, the acts lose their social meaning and give rise to misunderstandings. This is certainly a different situation from that of mute acts. Traditional acts refer to a prejuridical state or one of primitive law, while mute acts are wholly normal even in hyperjuridical and hyperinstitutional settings. The protocols observed by ambassadors when they go to present their credentials can hardly be thought of as a hangover from archaic or prejuridical situations. There is no difficulty in imagining acts with a high institutional content that are nevertheless tacit: the number of steps the French president goes down in front of the Élysée Palace to receive a visiting dignitary is a strong indicator of status, but it is a wordless process.

3.3.2.5 SPOKEN AND WRITTEN ACTS   Austin was aware that we cannot maintain that "marrying is just saying a few words." Rather, *in some cases*, marrying is just saying a few words, given that in some cultures cohabitation is sufficient for marriage. After all, the speech act is not the *eidos*, but just a manifestation, and the necessary condition for the performative is that there be a registration,[68] which is to say an inscription, and that this be in conformity with a ritual. The role of the registration is confirmed by the fact that, in the Italian civil marriage, after the spouses have said "Yes," the person officiating asks, "Have the witnesses heard?," which is to say, "Have

they registered?," otherwise they would be "words in the wind" or "talking to the wall," which are the two features that Plato[69] attributes to the tabula rasa that is not of the right consistency, being either too soft and unable to keep traces, or too hard and unable to receive the inscription. After this, the parties proceed to the material writing of the act. The same thing happens with examinations in the Italian universities. They are not valid unless the speech act has been registered and signed, and the social object that is a "professor" is constructed by written acts: the notification of a vacant chair, the curriculum of the applicants, and the deliberations of the appointing committee. In this connection, it is interesting to note that "act" denotes the document that registers the act. Yet the inscribed act is not *identical* with the object, but rather *identifies* it and makes it reidentifiable. In some but not all cases, the act can coincide with the object, which explains the great prestige and practicality of banknotes, each of which is an act (its issue by the central bank) deposited in the object.

One might think that giving pride of place to marriage prejudiced Austin's analysis.[70] On the one hand, there are acts such as declarations of war that, because of the nature of the case, only rarely happen in the presence of all the social actors involved. It is implausible to think of the king of Spain going to the queen of England to tell her, "I declare war on you," because there is always the chance that the queen might respond, "I declare you under arrest" and thus put the business to an end. It is much better to have recourse to writing and to inscriptions that can do without words and restrict themselves (for instance in a preventive attack) to requesting a recognition of the state of things.[71] In other cases, it is not even necessary to address the adversary directly; it may be enough to address his parliament and the act will have the force of a declaration simply because one assumes, as is proper to the written form, that via the radio or the press, the message will reach its addressee, who was not present at the formulation of the act, *roughly* as happens when a politician on an official visit to Japan makes a statement about waste disposal in Naples.[72]

In other cases, which are even more interesting because they were considered by Austin, though he did not draw out all their consequences, an act which is such as a matter of law, rather than as a matter of mere fact can *only* present itself in written form. Take one of the performatives that Austin cites: "I leave my watch to my brother." Given that we are dealing with a will, the act will produce an object only once the person who wrote or dictated the will is no longer in a position to pronounce any words. On the other hand, it would be very bizarre to suppose that a speech act is necessary to make out a parking ticket; how long does the officer have to wait, and how many officers are called for? In some cases, such as that of a radar trap, the speeding fine can be generated without any human agent able to speak and endowed with *originary intention*. Even with human agents, a look of disapproval or approval can reinforce or compromise social objects such as prestige or authority.

Then we ought not to forget *apparent speech acts*, which are those acts that consist in the repetition of a formula, as in the majority of rituals, or that are performed orally and are immediately inscribed by means of a system of registration. It is possible to stipulate oral contracts by telephone, although, unfairly, it is not possible to undo a contract orally. The oral contract comes into force as soon as the registration begins. In this way, the registration is writing.[73] Hence, we are dealing with inscribed acts that are apparently no such thing except in their superficial presentation.

A final point about inscribed acts. Social acts always have propositional content in the sense that they concern the attribution of properties or relations to objects or other entities. This is not in conflict with the fact that not all social acts are linguistic or require a language to be performed. The examples I have adduced of social acts that are not linguistic—clicking a mouse or shaking a hand—are compatible with the propositional nature of the act: in fact, they are counterexamples to the claim that social acts are always linguistic, rather than to the claim that social acts always have propositional content. That said, I insist that what we use to express and inscribe propositional content in social reality are often nonlinguistic codes, and excessive emphasis on language risks underestimating the importance of inscription and memory.

3.3.3 *Inscriptions*

In certain cases, such as that of a marriage, the act constitutes an object, and in others, such as the name given in a baptism, it makes it reidentifiable. In both cases the act would be inefficacious without an inscription. Increasingly, baptism is replaced by or preceded by inscription in the civil register, but before this happened the registers of birth and funerals were the basic means for knowing the social and demographic facts that were otherwise inaccessible. This simple consideration, along with the monumental evidence of archives, should suffice to illustrate the social centrality of inscriptions. As I said in 1.3.3.3, inscriptions are the quintessence of social objects. An inscription is thus not a mere registration; it is always potentially directed to a form of public legibility.[74]

Since the various aspects of inscription will be examined in Chapters 4, 5, and 6, I restrict myself here to one concluding consideration about *context*. It is to Derrida's merit that he stressed its importance in his theory of linguistic acts.[75] This stress grew quite naturally from the recognition of the inscribed nature of the acts. If, in the case of oral expressions, it is quite easy to tell whether the context is appropriate or not, according to whether the wedding takes place in a registry office or in a theatre, writing makes matters more complex. On the one hand, documents should incorporate internal criteria of validation, such as filigrees and signatures (as we will see in Chapter 6). On the other, they remain open to problems in determining what a document proper is, whether a document is valid or an act is legitimate, especially at a moment in which there is an explosion of writing, which means a multiplication not only of inscriptions but also of contexts. As to how to determine contexts, there is no general rule to be observed: they are the object of pragmatic debates, for instance in political debates, or of empirical enquiries, as in the cases of historical research and literary hermeneutics, of which it is not possible to propose an ontology but rather a symptomatology of the sort I will set out in 5.1.1.2.

4

ICHNOLOGY

The thesis that I seek to defend in this chapter is that the law Object = Inscribed Act captures the essence of social reality, both structurally and genetically. Not only do social objects consist in inscriptions structurally, both in the narrow and in the broad sense of archiwriting as memory, rituality, and tradition, but the meanings and intentions that are present in the social world also draw their origin from the sedimentation and the reelaboration of traces.

The underlying idea is that, in line with the foregoing analyses, it is a mistake to suppose something like a spirit behind the letters that make up social reality, even more so institutional reality. These realities grow and feed themselves on the basis of a system of inscription that, by allowing the fixing of acts, contribute to creating meanings and social bonds. A human being who does not possess a language, habits, or memory and is thus deprived of inscriptions and documents in the sense I shall try to make clear would have trouble cultivating social intentions, sentiments, and aspirations. This priority of the letter relative to the spirit, just like that of technique relative to meaning, is particularly clear in the case of artworks, but it obviously applies to the constitution of social roles, family relations, affective schemes and self-consciousness. In this framework, I hold that the central notion of the formation of meanings within social reality is imitation.[1] The hypothesis supporting this is that the iteration of letters is the root of the spirit or, to put the point in less arcane terms, which I hope to clarify, that technique and mimesis oversee the formulation not only of the relations and the structures, but also of the meanings that these have from subjects. For this reason, I develop the notion of ichnology *considered as a* doctrine of traces. *Their articulation aims to set out the basic thesis, a theoretical distinction, and an ontology of inscribed things.*

The basic thesis is that communication is not the starting point in the construction of social reality; instead, it depends on registration considered as the possibility of the inscription of acts. In other words, we can imagine a society without spoken language but not without writing. This is already a lesson we have learned from animal societies, where there is no articulate speech, but where there reign precise rituals and systems of territorial demarcation. Moving to human societies, it is often supposed that they are founded on oral communication, which is subsequently aided by writing as a sort of telecommunication prior to the invention of the radio and the telephone. Conversely, the hypothesis that I wish to defend is that, even on the basis of simple historical evidence, writing does not have its origin in the transcription of spoken language or as a vehicle for telecommunication, but rather as a system of registration. We have a general function for "keeping trace" in which accountancy and the calendar precede (and produce) the elaboration of a writing system that can (but need not) evolve in the direction of alphabetic writing. Even without the genetic conjecture about the priority of registration relative to communication, there is a structural consideration. It is evident that a registration has to have a communicative value; otherwise it would be meaningless, for instance, to stake out a terrain if the stakes had no communicative force.[2] Nevertheless, if there were no way to register, the idea of communication, and the closely related one of a code, would be unthinkable. Thus, the prophecies of the twentieth century that foresaw the progressive disappearance of writing and its replacement with oral communication did not take account of at least two important points.

One is that a system of communication that was unable to keep traces and to register the communications would be ruinous, because it would lead to the dissolution of society; it would make no sense to telephone amnesiacs, and we would be very badly off indeed if the whole social world depended on the finite memories of individuals. Thus, the prophets of the disappearance of writing seem not to have noticed how frequently, when one is on the telephone, one needs a pen to write down what is being said, as well as the fact that the telephone companies printed (and still print) directories and still send out bills and stipulate contracts.

The other point is that even systems of oral communication, such as the radio or the mobile phone, are naturally disposed for writing and registering. The cinema, which is strangely opposed to the book, is a registered and repeatable object, essentially like writing, and these days is often recorded on the same media used for writing. The instrument that has made most of an impact on the world of today, the computer, was first thought of as a calculating apparatus *and then used for registering writing; only later did it evolve, just as happened to the ancient scripts, into a means of communication.*

In Chapter 2, dedicated to the theoretical distinction between writing *and* archiwriting, *I went into the issue of registration, aiming in the first instance to respond to a well-founded and natural objection: Many social objects are supported by purely oral, or even tacit, agreements, and history records great societies that have gotten by without writing. How, then, can we defend the law Object = Inscribed Act? Is there not a misfit between the extremely broad realm of registration and the much narrower one of inscription? It is precisely the distinction between archiwriting and writing that allows us, in my view, to overcome this difficulty. The way out is to recognize within the forms of registration and of keeping trace a sphere that surrounds writing (or writings) more or less properly called so. In this way, archiwriting represents the genus of which the various sorts of writing are the species. This provides the presupposition for an evolutionary path that can, but need not, evolve into writing* in the strict sense, *granting that it is possible to define something as the strict sense of writing (a sense that would be in the in-itself and of-itself of extremely varied practices) and that it is possible to fix where archiwriting ends and writing begins. Along the gradation from marking a territory and registering in memory to writing alphabetic letters, ideograms, numbers, symbols, and sequences of 0 and 1 in a computer, there is no point of rupture, but rather a continuous process. And even this does not have to read in evolutionary terms, given that I can put my computer on a desk and claim to have thereby marked my territory in the office; I can, with a nod of the head, indicate that I agree to an appointment, and at the same time note it down in my notebook or on my laptop. Furthermore, the presence of sophisticated systems of inscription does not exclude the use of memory techniques and arithmetic devices such as rosaries and abacuses, which in their own ways reach their objectives perfectly.*

Chapter 3 aimed to provide an ontology of all the things that fall within the sphere of archiwriting (and hence of writing). To account for inscriptions as a whole, we take an ascending hierarchy of three fundamental elements: traces, *registrations, and inscriptions in the technical sense. By* traces *I mean every sort of modification of a surface that recalls by recording something that is not present. In this sense, a figure is not a trace relative to its background, because the figure is present; were the figure the footprint of an animal, an organic exhibit in a forensic enquiry or a sign made with chalk, then we would have a* trace that recalls something absent. By registrations *I mean those traces that are laid down in our minds, which are represented, naïvely but inevitably, as a tabula rasa or blank slate, as an instrument on which to write. Relative to traces outside the mind, registrations have a double value. On the one hand, they are themselves traces, but on a very specific sort of medium; on the other hand, they constitute the condition of the possibility of recognizing external traces, since there are no traces as such, but only, as Hume might have put it, for a spirit that contemplates them. By "inscriptions in the technical sense" I mean every form of fixing that is accessible to at least two persons, from the restaurant bill to a passport.*

Inscriptions in the technical sense are the summit of the hierarchy, because they construct common objects. We cannot look into the mind of another, except in a very approximate way and without being able to have access to what meanings things have for another person; but we can rifle their papers, look into their computers, their mobile phones, and their wallets. Being open to access by more than one person is one of the preeminent features of inscription in the technical sense, and it is codified in objects that are essentially designed to be exhibited, as we find with identity cards, tax receipts, and money. As I said in 3.3.2.3, even social acts that are oral or tacit, without written annotations in the strict sense, can be considered as inscriptions because they are available to more than one person; it is for this reason that very early in the construction of the social world there emerges the figure of the witness as someone who, by being present at an act, has the role of third-party guarantor of the fact that has taken place. When inscription in the technical sense emerges, humankind makes a decisive step forward because it gives rise to the world of social objects, of shared intentions, and of the transmission of technology.

4.1 REGISTRATION AND IMITATION

4.1.1 Registration Science

In the coming pages, I propose the creation of a new degree course, or even better a new university faculty, with its own BAs, MAs, specializations, doctorates, faculty boards, freshmen, newspaper debates, ministerial commissions, grants, and evaluations. The name of the new faculty or degree course would be *Registration Science*, and it would offer solutions to the changing needs of a society that, at the beginning of the third millennium, finds itself facing the challenges of a world that believed it was dominated by communication (and alas by greater or lesser communicators) but suddenly finds itself at the mercy of registration.

4.1.1.1 FROM COMMUNICATION TO REGISTRATION

Of course, I am joking. I do not mean anything of the sort. What I propose, much more simply, is to justify my theory of social objects by illustrating the importance of writing and registration in our world and to show how this importance is sometimes ignored, thus giving rise to errors of perspective that, in my view, need to be corrected. There is no doubt that our society, and probably any society, is an information society: We cannot live without knowledge. If not even Robinson Crusoe can, it is even more necessary in a complex society.

Nevertheless, it is often thought that this means that we are in a society of communication, by which is meant as much the need for communication for society as (and probably especially) the fact that we find ourselves in a historical period characterized by an unprecedented increase in communication. Now, I am not convinced of either of these notions.[3] To be sure, in order to exist, a society must communicate. The act of communicating is not sufficient on its own but turns out to be a function subordinated to something more essential, namely registration. The thesis I would like to develop is that we are in a society of registration, and that this is the condition of the possibility of a society of communication and, obviously, of information. This may appear surprising, but if we look at the transformations of recent decades, we see that they are more in the direction of registration than in that of communication.

4.1.1.2 THE FUTURE IS NOT WHAT IT USED TO BE

Let us see how. In 1909 Filippo Tommaso Marinetti published in *Le Figaro* his "Futurist Manifesto." It was a hymn to speed, power, mechanics, and, alas, war as the only way of purifying the world. The least we can say is that a lot of water has passed under the bridge, which seems obvious enough. But the peculiar thing is that that water has flowed in the opposite direction from what was prophesied, perhaps because the future enjoys showing futurists and futurologists to be wrong. Let us take an object fashionable in 2009, a century after Marinetti's manifesto, such as the iPhone. What is futuristic about this? It looks like an inoffensive bar of soap, with its smoothed edges, and the person who designed it was surely not thinking about mechanical force or about the speed of an F1 car. Rather, everything is calm and silent—indeed, silenced—and the only speed that is used to measure its efficiency is that of its connection. Above all, and paradoxically for a telephone, if the iPhone has become a status symbol, it is because it has a bigger memory than an ordinary mobile phone and because it is more convenient for writing and registering. That is to say, it is an archive, just like a tablet for cuneiform writing, which functions also and accidentally as a telephone. It thus embodies the quintessence of the digital, whose very name evokes the *digitus*, the Latin for "finger," the omnipresent finger that plays all the keyboards that have invaded our lives.

So far as I can make out, the future belongs to scribes. This was not what the futurists imagined, and there is nothing to be done about that. But not even Kubrick imagined it on the eve of the revolution that has turned our working lives, and even our emotions, upside down. On the spaceship in *2001: A Space Odyssey*, ordinary typewriters are used for writing, while the computer Hal 9000 is a superbrain that speaks. The personal computer would begin appearing in our homes just a few years later, but there is no hint of it because no one thought that the important part would not be the "electronic brain" (as was the expression then, though it is worth noting that it is no longer used) but more powerful instruments for writing and for storing, not that this—rather than spaceships—would be the real fuel for delocalization and globalization.

The future is not what it used to be, and there is one common element in so many of the failed prophecies: it was said that writing would disappear in favor of the radio, the television and the telephone; yet here we are writing and reading all day long, tapping away on the keys of computers and mobile phones. From this failed prophecy, many others have followed as a matter of course—for instance, that the television would eat up the computer (do you recall when the idea was to use the TV screen as a monitor?), when exactly the opposite has happened. Or again that paper would disappear from our desks, while it has been precisely the ability for the first time in centuries to write without using paper that has led to the avalanche of paper that hits us every day: the mountains of unrequested advertising, but also so many things that were undreamed of when paper held the monopoly, such as free newspapers and cut-price books.[4] And then there was the postmodern expectation of the computer-based world as immaterial, while the masses of obsolete plastic and silicon make a substantial contribution to problems of waste disposal and old computers take up office space before they fill up recycling plants (when they are available).

No one had predicted what has been an explosion in writing that was quite unimaginable in science fiction novels of only fifty years ago. "What? Writing will be so important in fifty years' time? More important than speaking and traveling at the speed of light? Is this what the future holds?" Yes, this is what the future has held, and it takes delight in surprising us. Though it was expected to be all speed, noise, power, and the dominance of the image over the word, the future has turned out to be all silence, writing, and archive; it looks more like a pyramid than a spaceship. How can this have come to pass? How can it be that all of today's technology aims essentially at writing and registration? How can it have come about that (another prophecy that was not too hard) the control of energy is, at least from the political viewpoint, less important that the control of memory? To answer these questions, I do not think it is adequate to appeal to the power of technology. For, while it is also true that technology arouses new needs, it surely responds to often unexpressed requirements, as has happened with the explosion of writing. No one, not even the people producing the computers and the mobile phones, could have imagined what has happened. Which means that what has come about, taking us in part by surprise, is nothing less than the revelation of the essence of the social world, as we will see in 5.3.1.

4.1.1.3 COMMUNICATION   If this is how things stand, the question arises of whether there is not something wrong, or at least exaggerated, in two of the most widespread assumptions that have guided reflection about our society over the last century, namely (1) that ours (in particular, more than others) is a society of communication; and (2) that communication is more efficacious the more synchronous it is (I speak, you listen, you reply), or that perfection in communication can be reached only, as Plato (the first philosopher to condemn writing) said, in oral discussion.

What then is the premise for the conviction—which has spawned studies, disciplines, and faculties dedication to communication, themselves unheard of before the twentieth century—that modern times are, more than any other period, characterized by an explosion of communication? I hazard a hypothesis. The idea that underlies the creation of communication science and theories of information is probably an effect of the introduction and impact of instruments like the radio (and of its role in the dictatorships of the 1930s and in World War II), early (unrecorded) television,[5] and the telephone in every house. This system of communication is the ultimate sign of modernity. Very well, then. If this is how things are, why do we find ourselves in a massive return to writing?

Alongside the reflections about the communication sciences, the last century was dominated by the idea of dialogue and communicative transparency.[6] The basic idea was that philosophy's job was to analyze language and to establish the conditions for a dialogue that would be humankind's ultimate aim. But things went differently. On the one hand, with the decline of the postmodern to which we referred in 2.1.3.1, the linguistic turn ceased to be the crucial subject of philosophy (whether analytical or continental), while on the other no one talks any more about communicative transparency, not out of spite, but simply because nothing of the sort was possible. Information does not aspire to transparency, it does not want it; and dialogue is a utopia that is not practiced even by those who preach it. What has happened instead is the triumph of control and the tracing of everything that, from the supermarket to the mobile phone, email, and online purchases, increases the possibility of control.

4.1.1.4 NOISE To say that ours is, more than others, a society of communication and information is thus a double mistake. The first is a failure to consider that there cannot, in the strict sense, be a society without information: even the ancient Egyptians knew how to bring each other up to date about important matters. Hence, it is not a peculiar feature of our society. The second is that we are informed not just about important matters, but also about facts and factoids that inflate and ultimately annul information.[7] In other words, information is annulled by "noise," understood in the first instance in the sense of information theory, that is to say, as what interferes with a signal and compromises its communicative quality. But we may take it also in the other senses of this pregnant word: as the ring of a mobile phone and the subsequent conversation on the train; the Windows startup logo, which interrupts the meditation of a group of Trappist monks; gossip of all sorts: "Bob was caught sneaking off to the seaside with Carol," and everyone is asking "Who is Bob?" and "Who is Carol?" and "Why is everyone talking about them?"

Sometimes it turns out that everyone is talking about them because they are government ministers; but normally the question goes unanswered because Bob and Carol work in the mass media and so, as is right, most people do not know who they are. Relative to the traditional society of communication, the messages we receive do not merely tell us things we are not interested in. They very often demand that we give our view and that we reply in a hurry by computer, BlackBerry, or iPhone. To be sure, we can respond with the first thought that crosses our minds, which is what generally happens, but even in that case, we do not win the battle against the "white noise" which is not (in the urban legend cited in the title of Don DeLillo's fine novel) the voices of the dead speaking to us through radio frequencies or a badly tuned television, but rather the masses of inscriptions, messages, and registrations that are deposited on the Web and will never go away

4.1.1.5 REGISTRATION   What has the upper hand, evidently, is not communication but, so to speak, one of its conditions of possibility, namely registration. As I said above, not only is a society without registration inconceivable, but without registration communication itself is also held in check. An unregistered communication binds no one, but is a mere physical signal, a pseudo-communication: it is one thing to taunt a bull with a red cloth, but it is quite another to use a red traffic light to say that one should stop unless one wants to risk a sanction of some sort—and here registrability and registration are constitutively in play. In this preeminence of registration there is a return to the origin, and, as I have said, a revelation of the essence. The first writings, as we will see at length in 4.2, were not used to communicate, but to register debts and credits, to make up for the finitude of individual memories.

   Now, is this not precisely what has happened anew in the explosion of writing in the last thirty years? It has been an explosion much more of registrations than of communication, and it has permitted globalization, overcoming the limits of synchronous communication and allowing the transportation of packets of registrations, from accountancy to the registry of births to services, and most of all on the stock exchange and the movement of money from one part of the universe to another. It could never have worked with the telephone. This transformation affects the world of social objects as a whole; even the possibility of drawing up agreements and signing contracts irrespective of the parties' physical copresence in space and time is directly dependent on this increased writing power. Paradoxically, this transformation affects also communication. Television stations have set up websites from which we get programs with a time delay, and we can read the newspaper on our computers or look at a site written by a radio station and listen to a recording, taking advantage of the film library of Babel that is YouTube.[8]

Here is the datum that we do well to start with. Human beings are animals that communicate. But no communication is possible without registration: Would communication among amnesiacs make any sense at all? Our task at this point is, so to speak, to make registration less obvious, not to take it for granted lest we fail to see its true character. This is not such an easy undertaking, given that communication is so overwhelming a phenomenon as to make the condition of its possibility fade into the background. All the same, without registrations in our heads, we would have nothing to communicate; neither would it make sense to do so because, as I have said, without a registration of what is communicated, without its being fixed, communication would be literally talking into the wind.[9] From the conceptual point of view, there are three basic reasons for regarding registration as prior to communication.

In the first place, registration has a role in *fixing the object* to be communicated. There are two good reasons for not communicating. One is not having anything to say, and the other is not remembering what one wanted to say. In practical terms, the two come to much the same and this is why, from Plato to Husserl, philosophers have always drawn attention to the need to fix content as the basis of knowledge. In fact, even leaving aside the hyperbolic case of the amnesiac speaker, it is enough to think of the incompetent speaker who is unable to fix the content of what he wants to say and who gets in a muddle, confuses himself, and then forgets what he was trying to get across. Even if his failure is regarded as defective communication, at their source is defective registration.

In the second place, registration is necessary for *codification* (as we will see analytically in 4.2.3.3). Imagine someone who tried to communicate using a code that was not fixed, for instance, mixing up a variety of languages without rhyme of reason; we would not understand much of what he says. Now imagine someone who sought to communicate with us in his private language, a language for which we do not have the code. We would not understand anything, just as in the case of the communicator with unclear ideas. In this case, too, we would be dealing with something that superficially seems like defective communication, when it is really defective registration and in particular a defect in codification.

The third key role of registration in communication is *reception.* Suppose we are addressing some clear and distinct idea to someone in a code that is perfectly fixed. He, however, has taken a drug that makes him unable to remember more than a few words at a time; halfway through a sentence, he has forgotten the beginning, and when the sentence is finished, he can remember only the last two words, and then only for a very short time. Supposing that he does not know that he has been given the drug (and even if he were told, he would soon forget), it would seem to him that we are expressing ourselves in an incomprehensible way and that we are suffering from serious communication problems, even though in reality, it is he who is afflicted with a radical registration defect.

4.1.1.6 Differing   Now I should explain why registration has all the powers I attribute to it. The basic idea is that mere communication has no social value unless it is accompanied by registration. If someone communicates something to me and I immediately forget what I have been told, all I can do is ask for it to be repeated and to pay more attention, or, if the object of the communication is not easy to remember, like a telephone number or an address, then I need paper and pen. On its own, communication is worth very little, and what holds for a piece of information applies all the more to an order or a promise, not to mention a performative act that would have no sense at all if the communication lacked a registration.

To clarify this point, I want to return to the example of globalization. I long wondered what was meant by the coupling of writing and difference of a sort suggested by Derrida,[10] just as I long found his reflections on *différance* decidedly cryptic.[11] Now I think that the example of globalization, and everything it entails, can make the slightly disturbing coupling evident, and even banal, and can give a concrete case of the notion of *différance.* I propose to call this *differing,* to hang on to the verbal, participial aspect, where it indicates not just diversity but also, with a slight effort,[12] the act of deferring or putting off. The power of registration lies precisely in deferring or putting off to later, in fixing and postponing and hence in deferral, in transforming the volatility of words and processes into the solidity and permanence of social objects. Only with powerful instruments for registration and hence for deferral is it possible to control a globalized world, and it is not by chance that it is exactly writing—the world of the Web—much more than the spoken word—the world of the radio, of television, and of the telephone—that has contributed to the growth of globalization.[13]

4.1.1.7 INSCRIPTION The role of writing now appears in all its force. In effect, it might be legitimately objected to what I have said about registration that, however important that may be, what really counts is that what is registered can be made manifest. In other words, what can be done with registrations that are enclosed in our heads? Very well, but it is easy to see that this is not how things stand. My shopping list is undoubtedly a registration (I had no intention of telling anyone else what I had written, and it is doubtful that it wanted to "communicate " it to me), but is certainly not enclosed in my head. After all, the list can indeed be read by someone else, but it would be bizarre or incongruous to think that it was a form of communication, unless we are suffering from one of those conditions that makes us think that everything in the world is talking to or addressing us, including other people's laundry bills and shopping lists.

What I called in 4.3.3 an "inscription in the technical sense" is a sort of registration that is in principle accessible by others, and that may, but need not necessarily, be transformed into communication. In effect, here we have registrations that are accessible to others but are not *required* to change into communications. If I ask someone the time and he tells me, then we have established communication. But if I read the time of a transaction on an ATM receipt, can we really say that this is communication? It seems to me that there is an essential difference.

Thus, not only in what we call *communication* is the contribution of registration dominant, but also, contrary to appearances, most of our social life is carried out under the aegis of registration, in line with the law Object = Inscribed Act. This is why even in the most extraordinary predictions, our future will not be able to get away from writing and will not be able to do without it. For there are so many actions that we perform in a day and, insofar as they are social acts, they will always leave a trace. Whether it is the printout of the phone company, the receipt from the bar or the restaurant, the bus or train ticket, the taxi receipt, the email sent or received.[14] The social world gives us such a wealth of evidence of this fact that it is almost not worth recalling them, but they go from the awkwardness of losing one's wallet to the social exclusion of clandestine immigrants and, quite simply, to those who have little money. All these lacks and difficulties derive from a defect in registration and not in communication. Not to mention the nightmare of senile dementia, which expels us from the social world: to anticipate a theme I will return to in 5.3, the connection between spirit and memory is anything but accidental, but rather marks their consubstantiality (in his poem on the death of Napoleon, "The Fifth of May," the Italian poet Alessandro Manzoni describes his body as "bereft of all spirit" primarily because it is "oblivious").[15]

4.1.2 Imitation

Registration's role is not limited to checking; rather, it lies at the base of the construction of social conventions and behaviors. No habit is inevitable, except for the habit of forming habits. All conventions are a bit like this. All conventions are conventional, but the fact that conventions are created is not conventional at all, but is rather the one of the most fixed constants in the social world. How this happens has stimulated very various responses. I would like to defend a rather banal claim: When we have to deal with social conventions understood as rules of behavior, they are formed by imitation, which turns out to be an essential ingredient in the construction of social reality. This banal claim, which is itself copied to the point of parroting, runs the risk of seeming original to the point of eccentricity when I claim that imitation is transmitting through inscription; but I hope to be able to defend also the less mimetic part of my view.

Let us begin with a typical social act, even if it is not a very frequent occurrence: the surrender of a military unit. In the 2004 film *Downfall*, we have this scene: In the last throes of the battle for Berlin in April 1945, some German units are holed up in a fortified area; they are determined to resist, and theirs seems to be as clear a case as there could be of collective intentionality "to sell their skins at a high price." The Russians arrive, and there is moment of hesitation—which is itself collective—then one German soldier throws down his machine gun, followed by another and another. In the end, they all surrender, except for some officers who prefer to commit suicide. At least this time, there will be no battle. How can we explain this scene, which has so many, less dramatic, counterparts in civilian life?

Let us return to the question of collective intentionality examined in 3.2.3.3: The soldiers surrender because together they decide that it makes no sense to fight, they form a "we" intention that can be expressed as "we surrender," and that puts an end to it. But, if we look more closely, we see that this does not add up. They all surrender, and, given that we have a group, there will be a point at which they will have thought, "We surrender." But it is certain that the first to do so thought only, "I surrender." Furthermore, was not the fact that many, but not all, of them surrendered in the end, with an undoubted shared action, the end of the war? Certainly not. The war was over only when the surrender was signed, first in that Berlin square and, some days later, by the rest of the German forces in Holland, Denmark, Norway, northern Germany, and Bohemia. Hence, it was not at all a collective intentionality that brought about the peace, but *individual* intentionality, that of the individual signatories of documents.

It should be borne in mind that an apparently collective action, such as a secession from a state, in which by definition there does not yet exist a final decision maker, there is nothing but the sum of single votes, if it is carried out by referendum, or an act with some signatures, as in the case of the Declaration of Independence of the United States. It would be misleading to think of this as the expression of collective intentionality, if for no other reason than that many colonists remained loyal to England; yet it is certainly a document accompanied by many signatures. In short, even if we say that intentionality is always individual, we may still say that individual intentionalities can be expressed in collective documents. Apart from being rather evanescent, as we saw in 3.2, collective intentionality does not even explain a behavior like that of the surrender scene, which would seem to speak in its favor. As I have said, probably no one thought, "We surrender." More simply, the first soldier surrendered, quite plausibly without even thinking, "I surrender," and the others saw what he was doing and *imitated* him.

4.1.2.1 MIMESIS AND MIRRORING   Setting collective intentionality aside, we find ourselves faced with one of the oldest intuitions about human nature—and indeed about animal nature if parrots and monkey are, in the popular imagination, the paradigms of imitation.[16] Man grows up imitating and continues to imitate as an adult. Very early on, this intuition was taken over by a philosopher; for Plato, imitation explains almost everything, including the relation between the sensible world and the world of the Ideas.[17] And if Aristotle (quite rightly) denies that tables and chairs imitate Ideas, he allows (equally naturally) that children tend to imitate their parents; this is one subject on which psychologists agree even today.[18] Even without appealing to philosophical authorities, it seems obvious that we are born to copy; as Tarde puts it, the fundamental feature of every social fact is the fact of being imitative,[19] and it is hard not to agree with him at least about this.[20] Here there is no need to invoke an occult faculty but rather only to recognize an obvious and banal behavior as much on the stock exchange[21] as in class struggle, as much in advertising as in fashion.

This is not just a question of acts, but also of knowledge. Mimesis underwrites what is known as *social cognition*, which involves both the understanding of other people's behavior on the basis of attributions of mental states such as beliefs, desires, emotions, and intentions ("mindreading"), but also the sharing of such states ("empathy").[22] The identification of certain areas of the brain, known as *mirror neurons*,[23] which are activated not only when we perform certain movements or have certain emotions but also when we see others performing those movements or expressing those emotions, has been regarded as evidence that our understanding of others' behavior comes about by a mental imitation of it. In the light of the relationship between mimesis and mirroring, it is worth noting that the mirror neurons are especially sensitive to gestures, which are themselves the point of origin of mimesis. For the Greeks, *mimesis* initially meant a set of gesture techniques meant, so to speak, to make the invisible visible: the Bacchic exaltation, sorrow in funerary rites, and even the movements of the heavens reproduced in dance.[24] This is just the beginning of the long road[25] that would lead to devotional literature, such as the *Imitatio Christi*, or to sophisticated artworks that, at least for a long period in the Western tradition,[26] have presented themselves as imitations either of nature or of other works of art, and that in very many cases have produced mimetic attitudes in their readers, sometimes with extreme outcomes, as with the suicides induced by reading *Werther*.

So far, so good. Indeed, *too* good. One problem with the claim being made is that it appears, so to say, inflationary: mimesis is everywhere. Do we have to conclude that everyone is imitating, and hence that everyone is doing the same thing, except perhaps one who is at the origin of the imitative chain?[27] Thank goodness it is clearly not like that, and when it is, it is in situations that are strongly conditioning, such as collective psychoses, Nuremberg rallies, and voodoo rites. Morals, law, and common sense rightly suppose that we— and not some inscrutable First Imitated—are responsible for our actions. Thus, when he was blamed for the suicides on account of *Werther*, Goethe quite reasonably replied not only that more people died in the English mines, but also that the suicides from mimesis fell on the perhaps weak but wholly individual shoulders of those who had taken their own lives.

This consideration is reflected also in our negative attitude toward conformism. Even if imitation is the rule of the social bond, conformism is blamed, plagiarism is punished by law, and it is regarded as rude to imitate someone else's speech and gestures (at least to their face). At the opposite extreme, creativity may even be overvalued and very often the tension between imitation and originality develops a sort of double bind: we need to imitate, to have models, but at the same time we ought not to imitate because it is a limited and servile attitude. How do we get out of it? In one of the recurring polemics about the imitation of the classics, Paolo Cortese, an early fifteenth-century humanist, said that he would like to resemble the ancients in the way that a son resembles the father, not in the way that a monkey resembles a man. The point seems to be that, where the son puts in something of his own (even an Oedipal hatred), the monkey does not.

If imitation is at the root of the social bond, it is also on this basis that a subjectivity forms with a high (if not very high) level of autonomy: there are originals and conformists, creatives and noncreatives, strong characters and weak characters. These categories of folk psychology are based on common observation, and even in cases of pervasive mimesis, there will be phenomena of originality: the class struggle has charismatic leaders, fashion rewards (at least the appearance of) originality and even on the stock exchange there are individuals who make a profit out of general panic.[28] If, then, as I have said, collective intentionality can be replaced by the more ordinary and less esoteric notion of mimesis, we might ask how mimetic acts are the constructors of social reality. And here conventions come into play.

It has been rightly observed that there is a difference between imitation and convention.[29] Convention is, at least to some extent, a chosen and aware imitation, even though there are persons who are so conventional that they do not even understand that their actions are guided by convention. My claim is that convention is not just imitation. Convention is just one of the passages in the process of articulation and complication that leads from mimesis to the construction of social reality. In other words, and the point is fundamental, imitation is the cause of convention because it is the origin of the whole of social reality.

4.1.2.2 TRANSFORMATION   To explain how we get from imitation to originality and to transformation, I propose a just-so story.[30] We start with a generalized mimetic condition, one that concerns the low and elementary level that is at work in earliest childhood. Then symbolic structures are formed, generated out of imitation but taking on original forms, in which the self is constructed always providing that some people will be more influenced than others. The direct and unreflective imitations can certainly return as pathologies, weakness, and atavism, as when we find ourselves reproducing unawares a tic of someone we are talking to. The other is right to be indignant given that direct imitation is regarded as unbecoming, if we think of imitators as satirical actors. Mimetic archaisms can be manifested in such things as folding the hands, scratching the nose, winking, coughing (at concerts and conferences) when someone else does, falling into hysterical laughter, and salivating at the sight of someone eating.[31] But above all, remaining in a territory that makes up our remote past, or the ultimate end in the case of the *Werther* suicides, pornography and voyeurism as sources of excitement would be quite inexplicable for a *cogito* that was impermeable to mimesis, whose natural reaction would be envy.

Then there are educational and professional environments in which individual mimetic acts are regulated and codified. In the arts, the ideas of a *canon* or of a *masterpiece* have developed to provide models or objects of imitation; likewise in the trades, in etiquette, in technical instructions, sports and so on. In this last case, the illusion can arise of collective intentionality, where the intentionality has been specifically produced by training in the selection of imitation: soldiers doing the goosestep, a well-trained and cohesive football team, an orchestra that can play even when the conductor is distracted. Moreover, while the conscious self can imitate at will or try to resist the impulse to do so, the unconscious cannot manage this so that it can imitate without knowing or understanding, or can fall victim to atavisms, as when, with the passing years, we realize that we are replicating our parents. This might encourage us to think that, while it is doubtful that the unconscious is structured like a language,[32] it is entirely plausible that it is structured like a recording apparatus.

It might nevertheless be wondered how imitation is transmitted. Since the mid-1970s,[33] the social sciences have taken up the idea of a *meme*, understood as a unit of information reproducible by a mind or some other medium that corresponds to the gene of genetics. According to meme theories, the meme encapsulates information that is transmitted by imitation. For our purposes, this seems like an excellent solution, except that it is not entirely clear what a meme is, given that it seems rather like a deus ex machina. It has been pointed out polemically that one of the few cases in which we can point to the transmission of a meme is that of a chain of Saint Anthony's letters,[34] which is extraordinarily true but does not constitute an ironic argument in favor of memes, but rather a serious argument in favor of something else, namely inscriptions. Habits, the models of accepted or rejected behavior, are transmitted by way of rites, etiquette, films, newspapers, family lore, libraries, which is to say by means of inscriptions that can be writing in the normal sense (books and newspapers), registrations, such as DVDs or CDs, and codified behaviors inscribed in the minds of people, as I will show in 4.2. From this point of view, the appeal to inscription, which is connected to the daily experience of reading and writing, gives the same explanatory advantage of memes without having to take the direction of something vaguely science-fictional. The world is full of inscriptions. That is all there is to it, but it is already a great deal, given that these inscriptions constitute the whole world of society, culture, and the spirit.

4.1.2.3 INSCRIPTION AND INTERPRETATION

The link between inscription and imitation is crucial for my purposes. On the view I defend, inscription, whether in the proper or the metaphorical sense, is everything that is transmitted by imitation: A behavior is visible and transmissible insofar as it is registered. It seems to me that, with the system of inscription-imitation, we satisfy and intuition shared both by common sense and by philosophical and sociological reflection, and we do not say anything that is incompatible with mirror neurons, nor with reading neurons,[35] nor yet with the evolution of forms of inscription in bureaucratic apparatuses and in cultural systems, which is to say with the usual instruments with which we not only explain the social world but also act within it.

In outline, we have to consider a process that works on four basic levels. The first is that of the mind considered as a deposit of inscriptions. It is this table, covered with registrations, that is the condition of the possibility of mimesis. From here we pass to the more complex levels of the person, society, and culture, where imitation is ever more explicitly manifested by way of inscription and interpretation. This appeal to interpretation is not in conflict with the criticisms made earlier. Indeed, if it makes little sense to talk of "interpreting" the natural world, as we saw in 2.1, there is no doubt that in the social world interpretation has a central role (3.1), and it is precisely its action that explains the process that leads from mimesis to originality. However wide a range of meanings we give to "interpretation" (2.1.2.1) their characteristic feature is their relation to some kind of inscription. The interpreter confronts a text, either in the narrow sense or in the broad sense of rites and traditions, and, in reproducing it introduces transformations. In this way we have, at one and the same time, a mimetic transmission and an individual variation. In this framework, inscription, imitation, and interpretation are the fundamental ingredients of the social world, as is particularly evident today when, as we have seen, the explosion of writing and registration is making an explanation in terms of communication inadequate.

I would now like to explain briefly how the perspective I am proposing can give an account not only of the construction of social reality, but also and more specifically, of the genesis of institutional reality, which is to say, power. How, in other words, is it possible that my receiving a document from the ministry makes me a professor, allows me to assign marks for exams that are part of the degree course, which in turn has legal consequences for graduates? How can it be that another document authorizes the Bank of Italy to issue banknotes that can be used everywhere in Europe and that can, if need be, be used to generate other documents, for instance by paying a stamp duty? I would like to respond to these questions by introducing two elements, *tradition* and *securitization*.

4.1.2.4 TRADITION AND SECURITIZATION   Let us begin with tradition. From time immemorial, both philosophy[36] and common sense have recognized the value of tradition, which orients our judgments through prejudices, confers authority on practices that have the agreement of generations on their side. Now, no tradition would be possible if there were no possibility of registration, performed orally, as with the poems and rites in the case of preliterate societies, or written down in laws and documents, which often transfer a sacred power to the tradition (the "unwritten law") within the secularized space of bureaucracy that is no less potent that that of the traditional space (as Kafka teaches), given that the official who has to give us a form to fill in exercises with his disobligingness a power that is at least the equal of a soothsaying king.[37]

In any case, as we noted in 1.3.3.3, even in bureaucratized societies we witness a survival of traditional authorities, for instance in good manners. If etiquette *need* not be written down, secret societies *ought not* to write down their rules, but if they could they would, albeit with the same care that the mafia uses to communicate (using slips of paper to avoid computer interception). Typically, these associations elaborate complex rituals, such as the initiation to the Masons, which take the place of writing. Etiquette and secret associations, all the same, are exceptions to the rule of bureaucratization, but they demonstrate that the normal upshot of the evolution of tradition is toward written rules for the construction and distribution of power in modern societies.[38]

Let us proceed to the role of securitization, which I here take in a larger sense than the narrowly economic meaning of the exchange of real property or credit in return for scrip. Rather, the notion is that of the possibility of fixing in writing values, activities, titles, offices, and goods. What I am suggesting here[39] is that the possibility of writing is at the heart not only of the construction of capital—as well as of the crises that it periodically undergoes[40]—but also of every form of power that unfailingly depends on systems of distinction, classification, hierarchy, and archiving.[41] This is no more than a logical extension of the idea that a society without memory is inconceivable, but it carries with it a further point, namely the link between registration and power. On the one hand, there is no power that is not underwritten by some form of inscription, whether it be a document carried in one's pocket, an academic mortarboard, a military rank, a chief's headdress, or even a submission ritual within an animal society. On the other hand, registration in the social world is an obvious source of authority; indeed, one acquires power simply by having control over registrations, by a telephone company's possession of the records of traffic, by registering customer's purchases at the supermarket or by merely buying a mailing list. The fact that such registrations are, at least in theory, regulated by privacy laws is a sure sign of the power held by those who have them. It is likewise eloquent that almost all free services, such as the use of email addresses and chat rooms or access to computer sites and functions, are conceded in return for personal data. Nor is it by chance that traditionally this information was the prerogative of the state, which is to say the entity that, in modern societies, embodies legitimate power, just as, in postmodern societies, the handling of information and registrations itself confers sovereign authority.

In 5.3.2.4, we look at the characteristics of the postmodern computer-based bureaucracy and its predominance over the state. For the present, I want to use the extreme opposite to point up the role of inscription in the constitution of power. This is the case of what some philosophers have called "bare life,"[42] meaning a life deprived of all rights, reduced to its mere biological sense. It is not by chance that this is called "bare," shorn of inscriptions, whether they be clothes or documents, cell phone numbers, or credit cards. This life is described as completely without power, at everyone's mercy, and it is not hard to see what is meant when one thinks about the destitute, the *sans papiers*,[43] or concentration camp inmates. It seems clear that the level of impotence is inversely proportional to the number of inscriptions the subject has at his disposal. The poor man does not have money, but he does have an identity and, at least in theory, rights; the *sans papiers* does not have documents, but he may well have a cell phone and documents whose validity is contested; and at the bottom of the pile, totally without rights and powers, there is the inmate in the concentration camp. If there is any need to illustrate the connection between power and inscription, I think that example is quite sufficient.[44]

4.1.2.5 POWER   Let us look more closely at the question of power. The fact that *secretary* does not necessarily denote a subordinate position is illuminating about the relations between inscription, imitation, and power. We do not have to go back to the myth of Thoth, the pharaoh's secretary and inventor of writing, who, according to one legend accreted to his name, overthrew the king.[45] Suffice it to think, in a quite humdrum way, about the power of the person who keeps the minutes of a meeting, or who keeps the cash of a holiday outing. Conversely, the first thing an American firm does when it fires a manager is to cancel his email account while the decision is being communicated to him, so that he cannot even minutes later avenge himself in any of the thousand ways that have already been put into effect. Registering the incoming and outgoings, transforming flyaway words into permanent writing, fixing events to make them into objects (contracts, titles and so on), and then, on the level of social imitation, codifying behaviors, rules of elegance and style, hierarchies of values and aspirations, marking in visible ways conditions and status—all of these are the traditional prerogatives of inscriptions. In the same way, on the level of political management and justification, it is once more registration and inscription that have the upper hand; the juridical fiction of the will of the nation or of the social contract rest upon the principle, set out in 3.2.3.3, that individual intentionality is in the head while collective intentionality is in the text,[46] and the practice of voting would have no sense if there were no way to count the votes cast. Contrary to what is depicted in the frontispiece of Hobbes's *Leviathan*, the body of society is not made up of the so many individual bodies, but of inscriptions and documents.

But inscriptions out there on paper are not enough. There need to be also internal inscriptions in our minds, which relate to one another by means of imitation. The power of conventions, then, is in effect the power of inscriptions, of written and unwritten laws or, more exactly, written elsewhere, in the heads of persons.[47] Obviously, all this runs up against very precise limits. Proust noted that, outside the Faubourg Saint Germain, where the ruling conventions established his elegance, a duke might easily pass for a pickpocket or a madman. And what goes for the social world applies even more to institutional reality, which is the chosen home of documents. The power of documents is real and important, but only within an institutional reality that recognizes its legitimacy, and in a society where institutions competing with the dominant one are nonexistent or politically irrelevant. Conversely, in a situation of conflict, when the king has been found naked or inflation has turned money into wastepaper, documents display all their weakness and social reality betrays its fragility, that of a constructed reality, which can always be deconstructed.[48]

I imagine that some readers at this point will be disappointed not to find in power, the object of so much desire, nothing that is substantial, nothing like an autonomous force, a Nietzschean or Leibnizian potency. How can it be? Is power nothing but a matter of secrets, secretaries, and paper shuffling? No: power is also other things, and in the first instance the use of force and, even more powerful, the *threat* of the use of force. But it is nothing in itself. Lucretius got the point when he saw that the life of the politician is the realization of the myth of Sisyphus:

> For to seek after power—an empty name,
> Nor given at all—and ever in the search
> To endure a world of toil, O this it is
> To shove with shoulder up the hill a stone
> Which yet comes rolling back from off the top,
> And headlong makes for levels of the plain.[49]

4.2 WRITING, ARCHIWRITING, THOUGHT

I think that, by proposing imitation as a valid alternative, I have answered the question: What do you put in the place of collective intentionality? In line with the hypothesis that inspires the metaphysics of this book, this is an alternative that makes powerful use of inscriptions, registrations, and traces. But at least two issues are left open. The first is that not all social acts take place on paper or in computer files. For instance, there are sometimes verbal agreements; you say that in these cases we have inscriptions in the heads of persons, but how do you show that this is not a mere metaphor? The second is that a treaty or a check has never come into being on its own. Behind the paper there is always something, such as an intentionality (not collective, but individual) of which you do not seem to take account because of your exclusive concentration on inscription.

These are threatening challenges. After all, the whole social system of acts and inscriptions presupposes that behind those acts there are intentions, which in turn have to do with memories and thoughts and not with writing. And, weakening the claim, were I to allow that it is not necessary to conceive of the mind as a system of inscriptions, there would still be an enormous problem, namely the fact that the inscribed acts that are "in the minds of persons," which are a central and constitutive part of social reality, would be reduced to a simple metaphor. And, at this point, the whole theory would at best boil down to a theory of bureaucracy (in a complex society there are many documents), which is to say a special case of weak realism: there are certain Xs (pieces of paper) that count as Ys (documents) in a society C; and they count as documents because there is a collective intentionality that makes them count as documents.

To avoid this upshot, I set myself three goals. The first is to illustrate the whole sphere of the application of writing, which is much wider than is generally thought for instance when the oral and the written are opposed to each other. The second is to show that, around that sphere there is another even wider which is that of archiwriting and which embraces both the forms of inscription that are present out there in the world (but that are hard to regard as writing by current definitions) and, above all, those that are in the mind. Relative to these last, writing is not a mere metaphor, but rather the best approximation to what really happens when we perceive, imagine, recall, and, in short, *think*. The third is to show the deep and not casual connection between thought and writing, thus furnishing an answer to the age-old question, "What does thinking mean?"

At this point, the next thing to be done will be to illustrate the genesis and the structure of inscription, namely the element that bears the load of all the argumentation offered so far. This is what I shall attempt in 4.3.

4.2.1 Writing

When we visit a museum of ancient art—and even more so, when we visit an archaeological site—we seem to be surrounded by old things. They say that those stones are charged with history. This does not happen on the beach. There everything seems modern and indeed it is, if we think about the Coca-Cola, the swimsuits, and the umbrellas. But when we look at the sand, the rocks, and the sea, we do not seem to be faced with depths and temporal abysses. Is this not strange? The stones of the ruins at Paestum are old, but those over there on the beach are not. How can we explain this? It can hardly depend on the internal composition of the minerals in each case because they may well be just the same. The stone in the amphitheater may be exactly the same as that of the coast nearby, where people go bathing and take the sun. So what does the difference in attitude derive from?

The answer is very simple. The "old" rocks, the ruins, have been subject to inscription. They are fragments of something that once was social, and in just this sense historical. The other stones, those on the beach, are no more modern, but they do not seem to have a history. You may say that this is no great discovery: nature is distinct from history. But, if you pay attention, there is a way to make the extrahistorical or ahistorical stones ancient, and that is to treat them from the point of view of geology and specifically of ichnology, which reads and deciphers them, recognizing them as inscriptions. In this way, the stones will receive an age and a history. The passage from nature to history is thus nothing but the recognition of an inscription and the request to know what it means. Conversely, *traces make up the central span of the bridge that leads from natural objects to social objects.*

Let me explain. The metaphor of the world as a book written by God in mathematical language is as old as the world, and turns up every time in a detective story missing persons are identified thanks to the traces that new technology can decipher. As such, it is above all a metaphor[50]—but the social world is constructed from writing in a way that is neither metaphorical nor science-fictional. It is the world of maps or of the tattoos with which bodies are covered in inscriptions, which serve functions that may be esthetic, of group belonging or ritual, but it is above all the world in which agreements are made, documents are drawn up, certificates are delivered, and money is used.[51] Let us take the scene in which Hamlet makes his vow. The ghost of the king has appeared on the battlements and demanded that his son do justice for him, and then he has left asking him, so to speak, to keep a trace of what has happened: "Adieu, adieu, adieu. Remember me." At that point, Hamlet swears, which is to say, produces a social object:

> Remember thee?
> Yea, from the table of my memory
> I'll wipe away all trivial fond records,
> All saws of books, all forms, all pressures past,
> That youth and observation copied there;
> And thy commandment all alone shall live
> Within the book and volume of my brain,
> Unmix'd with baser matter: yes, by heaven!
> O most pernicious woman!
> O villain, villain, smiling, damned villain!
> My tables—meet it is I set it down,
> That one may smile, and smile, and be a villain;
> At least I'm sure it may be so in Denmark. [*Writes*][52]

Object = Inscribed Act holds even at Elsinore. And Hamlet inscribes his oath using both the "table" that he has in his head and the paper in his notebook. Of the table in his head, he will make a tabula rasa, canceling all the "trivial fond" memories, all the impressions and images that had been registered up until then, and will leave only his father's order, his call for revenge and justice. Then, just to be sure, he takes his notebook and write. You never know: *verba volant, scripta manent*. The point is that the object must be fixed and registered somewhere, leaving traces; otherwise it is just *flatus vocis* that evanesces like the ghost. Thus in the scene with Hamlet we have been witnesses to the creation of a social object. But how did we get by before writing was invented? A good question, but we must ask whether we can really talk about a "before" relative to writing.

4.2.1.1 READING Let us begin with an observation. Reading is not in the first instance a cultural activity, but a natural one. Otherwise writing would never have come about, and we would never have learned to read. Let us take a sequence of signs at random, from those that a computer puts at our disposal:

!”#$%&’霹靂 뾺 삯 솃 ☁ ♪ ☂ ∀Ǝℵ ℑℜℇγγ℃Ω❧☞❖✪✛✔☞

Keyboard resources

Is there really a great difference among these signs? And then between these signs and those that make up the sentence you are now reading? Or do we not rather find here family resemblances? It is a mistake to think of writing as a transcription of the spoken word or as an imitation of things, which are the two naive paradigms for explaining the invention of writing. It is also a mistake to think that it was a witting or conscious project, something like a social contract. The fact is that reading is so complicated an operation that it would be absurd to suppose that human beings could, in the space of a few thousand years, adapt their brains to it; making a Copernican revolution,[53] however, we should think that writing is nothing other than a response to features that are already present in the brain of humans and some primates.

There are neurons that already respond, automatically, to shapes like those of T, of Y, and of L, to two circles one on top of the other like 8, to characters that recall Chinese ideograms. Which is to say that our brains are already predisposed to recognize written traces. It is not so much that our cerebral cortex has evolved to recognize letters, as that letters and traces have been selected to adapt themselves to the features of our brains. And they in turn, thanks to their plasticity, have developed a peculiar sensibility to the sorts of traces that are the signs of writing. Which means that the traces respond to deep needs of our minds, as we shall see at length in considering archiwriting and thought, but that for the moment I would like to stress by drawing attention to an important notion. Histories of writing agree in insisting on the fact that very similar symbols recur in different alphabets,[54] even though they have different functions and, in any case the fact that the Semitic alphabets were taken and transformed into the Greek and Latin scripts cannot be explained merely by a miserable lack of imagination; there was a certain functionality in those letters—or, as Hamlet might have said, there's method in the graphics. But, if this is how things stand, it seems clear that writing has a natural root, in the sense that our minds not only represent themselves as writing but are also predisposed to select writing systems. In that case it is no surprise that inscriptions are omnipresent in psychic and social life.

4.2.1.2 KEEPING TRACK   At the beginning, the essential function is to keep a trace: at one and the same time to keep track and to register. These are two operations that are carried out with a single gesture and that make up a single act in the brain, activated by sodium and fixed by potassium. The first painted caves of which there is still evidence contain pictures that show from the outset a capacity peculiar to our species, namely that of recognizing shapes only by their outline. In short, just a few strokes are necessary to get a picture of Tintin or of Mickey Mouse, and even few lines are necessary to pick out expressions, as we see in emoticons: ☺ ; -) ☹ : -l :-/ :-(:-P. The third dimension is not needed to get the shape, nor are full details called for precisely because the expressions are summed up in just a few lines. This explains why writing is so natural to us: as we have said, we just have neurons that are particularly given to recognizing these simple shapes. When one comes to think of it, this requires us to review the naive traditions about the origins of writing, which suppose that first we have things and then their images in hieroglyphics and then traces that are transformations of the hieroglyphics. This, for instance, was the view of William Warburton in the eighteenth century,[55] according to whom the characters of the alphabet are nothing but Egyptian hieroglyphics distorted by Moses so as to observe the prohibition on graven images. But this must be wrong; what happens is that the traces come first, even before figuration,[56] and they give rise to it. In other words, pictography is not the origin of writing. In the beginning there is the trace. Then, for the sake of simplicity and primitiveness sake, for ease of communication in certain contexts, one might have recourse to pictograms, though these remain highly stylized, as with the symbols on restroom doors.

It is not an accident that, in Italian, the word for a "tally" (*taglia*) can also be used for the bounty price put on an outlaw's head and for the size of a garment. The reference is to a system of accounting that goes back to the Neolithic, that was employed by the English exchequer until the early nineteenth century, and that was still in use in the French countryside even more recently. The idea is to take two sticks and to mark a credit with an incision; the creditor takes one stick and the debtor the other; the debtor cannot cancel the mark and the creditor cannot add one because the interference would be revealed by comparing the two sticks.[57] On this scheme, it is not by chance that letters and numbers are continually changing their roles, that both derive from traces and not from words, and that the same systems, for instance those of the South American knots, can be used equally well as alphabets, for calculation and as calendars. They are forms of registration exactly like the letters, notches, and incisions whose archaic forms, perhaps as old as the Paleolithic, remain in the I, V, and X of the Roman numerals that are still used to number the pages of prefaces in modern books. From Cro-Magnon people onward, the score, which is the accountancy of the illiterate in all times, and the cross in the place of the signature are all referred the sphere of traces rather than to the sphere of numbers as ideal objects. These calculations are anything but abstract; indeed, they are as concrete as the *calculi*, the little stones—cones, spheres, marbles, disks, rods, tetrahedra, cylinders—used for calculating. But even the electronic calculator holds on to a link with those stones, which have evolved not only arithmetically but also in their functions that have little to do with calculation, as ornaments, amulets, and chess pieces.

4.2.1.3 COUNTING   In this way, tracing underlies a range of functions that are foundational for a society: arithmetic, money, and the calendar. In the economic sphere, writing comes into being as an indicator of property and arises from the seal or the mark; ever since the Neolithic, marks impressed in clay tokens were used as the *calculi* we have just mentioned, and functioned as units for counting goods (cattle, sacks of corn) and subsequently as a kind of money; the coins were collected in boxes on which conventional signs denoted the quantity and the contents. It is from this function that cuneiform writing arises, where the tablets are an evolved version of the boxes.

Let us look more closely at the history of the *calculi*, because it contains almost everything that is needed for the genesis and the evolution of a society. About ten thousand years ago in Mesopotamia, we find symbols already in use for counting: cones, cylinders, spheres, hemispheres, and tetrahedra. Some of these represent units and others the multiplier of the arithmetic bases: 10 and 60 (10, 60, 600). After nearly five thousand years of uninterrupted use, a novelty was introduced: About 3300 BCE, in the Elamite city of Susa, the *calculi* were put inside containers on the outside of which impressed signs that are the forerunners of the cuneiform script to indicate the quantity. We should note that we have here two processes of symbolization here and not a passage from the thing to the sign. For the signs contained in the box were nothing more concrete or figurative than the signs written on the container.

About 2000 BCE something similar happened in South America, though not with arithmetic but with the calendar. The Olmecs made use of incisions or glyphs to indicate units of time such as days, years, and cycles. In 600 BCE the Zapotecs added signs for dates and for the personalities associated with them. Here, the construction of social reality by means of inscription is even more evident; in the final analysis, unless time is kept track of—psychologically, socially, and even by way of the elaboration of scientific theories—it would contract, and we would have no idea of what we have left behind. As Rousseau observed, before the invention of writing time passed and humanity remained young. It is quite simply so as not to lose consciousness of time that Robinson Crusoe keeps track of it with his notches.

4.2.1.4 PAYING   We can see that in keeping traces, the birth of writing, the development of mathematics and of chronology go hand in hand with the creation of money, as a confirmation of the link between writing and social objects that is picked out by the law Object = Inscribed Act. As we saw in 3.2.4.3, the social object par excellence, money, is from the outset an inscription contrary to what one might infer from the fact that, at least in theory and until 1971, a banknote could be presented at Fort Knox and exchanged for a quantity of gold.

If we go back to what we said above about the calculation that precedes money and that constitutes the condition of its possibility, we thus have (1) the *trace* as pure inscription; (2) the *computation* as the teleological use of the trace; (3) the *currency* as the use of computing instruments to determine value; and (4) the *money* as the financial use of the currency. It is precisely in this function that writing can contribute to the valorization and the mobilization of capital, with is to say the alienation of land-based property so as to transform it into something else: in a certain sense, inscribed clay is the basis on which the land can be mobilized. The emergence of a mercantile economy, and all the more of an economy of shareholders, would not be possible without writing, but in its turn writing derives its own existence from the sphere of the production of documents, such as documentation of transfers and of property titles. In other words, we misunderstand the meaning of currency if we assume that its primary, if not exclusive, function is to overcome barter. And not that alone: as such, barter (I give you some sacks of corn and you give me a cow) has no need to be replaced by money. Money does not come in to explain an improvement of barter, but the *creation of credit*. Peter receives three sacks of corn from Paul and promises to John that he will give him a cow tomorrow, though he does not have it with him; this formula is then fixed in writing, as has been happening since the late Neolithic: "pay to the order of."[58] It is a protocheck, which in its turn is the forerunner of the banknote. From this follows a little-noticed fact: the sequence metal coin → paper money is no more fictional than the sequence gold → money or word → writing. Just as it is a mistake to think of the arising of writing as a discovery that came in useful for communicating over distances, so it is a mistake to see the genesis of money as if it were the surrogate of value rather than the creation of value. In effect, we have here a sequence that implies from the outset a writing that is not guaranteed by any gold-value: the promise (the act inscribed in the minds of the contracting parties) → I pay → check → banknote (form of inscription). That the gold value does not go at the beginning of the chain is proved by the fact that this is also how a bill of exchange works, as the written counterpart of the debt.

In other words, the central element is not the possibility of using materials that are easier to handle and less perishable than the goods that are exchanged in barter, but rather the necessity of having systems of inscription that are ever more powerful to create a memory that is ever more extensive and capable of improving the mechanisms of credit. It might be said that this is the origin of finance rather than of money, but I cannot see any deep difference between the two. And the cause for this reflection is precisely the fact that, before gold coins were made, shells were in use: gold is rare while shells are much less so: the gold was brought in to replace the shells as a manageable and small object that allows, as I recalled before, *enumeration*. If the tokens could not be counted, the fact of having to hand a material that takes the place of barter would be totally irrelevant. Writing, the keeping track and keeping traces, the contract and the treaty precede exchange and make it possible; and this fact is made plain in the extreme case in which the treaty itself is used as a banknote. When the Ashanti subjected a neighboring territory,[59] they took the "books" of the sovereign of that territory, such as the treaties the sovereign had signed with other potentates, and demanded that those treaties should hold good also for them. What we have here, in a way that is not altogether surprising, is a sort of "bearer treaty," not so very different from our banknotes.

We must overturn the idea that in social reality we are simply dealing with physical objects, whether they are pieces of metal or persons, which a wave of a magic wand turns into money or archdukes; in reality, inscription precedes this. The metal is not precious in itself, but is so only because a value has been attributed to it socially, which is to say on the basis of a system of inscriptions and registration, just as it would be bizarre to confer on someone the title of archduke, inspector, professor, or police officer outside a network of inscriptions that makes these offices make sense. Try imagining what it would be to be an archduke or a police officer in another solar system or, more simply, ask yourself whether an archduke or a police officer would really be an archduke or a police officer if they were alone in the world absent the system of inscriptions and recognitions that makes up the social world. After all, it is true that the queen of England really is a queen while the queen bee is a queen only as a manner of speaking; but it also true that, if there were no humans ready and able to give recognition, and to give it in virtue of a capacity to keep traces, then the distance between the queen of England and the queen bee would be much reduced.

4.2.2 Archiwriting

I would like to draw a first theoretical conclusion from this phenomenology of keeping track in writing, in arithmetic, in chronology and in the economy—which is to say in the essential elements of any social reality. The law Object = Inscribed Act is omnipresent in social reality, and can be articulated in two ways, one strong and the other weak. The strong or literal version has to do with the construction of documents within an institutional reality. Here we have genuine writing at work, even if within the documents there can be idiomatic elements (such as curlicues or signatures) that are merely related to the traces. Then there is a broader and weaker understanding that concerns the construction of social objects; in this zone, we take in forms of inscription that are not identified with writing in the full sense—from marking a territory to making a mental note to performing a ritual—but that in point of fact fall within the sphere of what Derrida called "archiwriting,"[60] and whose full sense becomes clear when applied to the constitution of social objects.

Now, I think it is hard to deny two solid banalities. One is that humans share with other animals a capacity for keeping traces, in such a way that one might say that while animals presumably do not talk, they do write.[61] Presumably because of the expansion of their cerebral cortex, this capacity has reached a level of sophistication in humans that is unknown among other animals. The second is that it is this hypertrophy in keeping traces that underlies the passage from the state of nature, in which animals still find themselves for the most part, to what we call culture, which is exclusive to humans. Now, if we give credit to these two obvious facts and consider how early on in the history of mankind there shows the tendency to rites, to inscriptions, to incisions, to ornaments, and if we bear in mind that what we call history is closely wedded to the possession of inscriptions (to such an extent that the passage from prehistory to history is fixed by the quantity and quality of the inscriptions at our disposal), then the notion of archiwriting appears unavoidable if we are to describe the construction of social reality. The spectrum that takes us from nature and animality to culture and humanity is offered to us by the fact of keeping traces, which is at once a solid proof and an explanation of what would otherwise be mysterious: the fact that, at a certain point in the story of mankind, there appear writings, documents and institutions, which would not be possible without the notion of archiwriting. Archiwriting, then, comes before writing.[62] Nevertheless we must conceive of the sphere of archiwriting as not only preceding but also *following* writing, for the simple reason that it surrounds it: Writing is a highly codified mode of archiwriting.

It is not uncommon to find that archiwritings form on top of a piece of writing, for instance when what is written is interpreted: between the fourth or third century BCE and the second century CE, Judaism formed an oral tradition that may be compared with the Catholic notion of the *verba divina non scripta* (the unwritten word of God), or the jurisprudential concept of the *jus non scriptum* (the unwritten law), and this calls for the ancient tradition to be made to fit with the modern, to which latter then is given the status of revealed truth. In general, Catholicism tends to replace writing with archiwriting and the book with the ritual. On the other hand, when people talk about the "material constitution" of the Italian Republic, they are referring to the unwritten practices established in the second half of the twentieth century in a Western nation in possession of a written constitution. The relation between archiwriting and writing may thus be represented as follows:

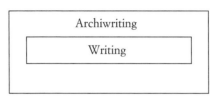

The sphere of archiwriting includes rituality,[63] memory, animal traces, technologically recognizable traces (DNA, etc.), biometric devices, and the idioms to be discussed in Chapter 6. We have to do here with a set whose role is to guarantee a cultural identity and to construct social objects, and which includes myths, rites, laws, proverbs, texts, images, ornaments, and even whole landscapes, as we find among Australian aboriginal nations.[64] In certain circumstances, within this context there arise writings in the full sense, which in turn give rise to other writings. In our history this seems to have happened at least three times independently of each other: in the Middle East, in China, and in Mesoamerica.

But for these writings to have been possible, they needed archiwriting, which can as well be registrations in the minds of persons who are stipulating a verbal contract as external traces, such as an animal's track, or a noncodified registration such as a knot in one's handkerchief. But above all, archiwriting embraces the thousand ways we keep track of everyday experiences and the world around us, ways that are so consubstantial with our very selves that, as I noted in 4.1.1.6, the loss of memory is something very different from any physical damage we might undergo, and comes to be identified with the substantial loss of identity.[65]

4.2.2.1 TABULA RASA   Despite the omnipresence of archiwriting in social reality, the place that is most densely packed with archiwritings is our minds, the seat of our memories. After explaining how writing in the narrow or, so to say, "literal" sense is not necessary for the possession of inscriptions, I would like now to introduce a second element. Contrary to what one might think, to have inscriptions in one brain, as Hamlet did, is not just a way of talking or a metaphor.[66] From Descartes to the contemporary analyses of neural nets, memory is explained as the inscribing of traces on the brain,[67] and if we may speak of writing as an extension of the mind, it is essentially because the mind is writing understood, held inside, and concentrated.[68] In fact, we may find earlier instances of this. Long before Descartes, there is a very ancient convergence between the mind and the trace, which could not be better attested than by the recurrent, almost obsessive, image of the mind as a blank table or tabula rasa, a medium able to retain traces. This is an image that we find in the Greek tragedians[69] and has come down to us having been reiterated all along the history of thought.[70]

In appealing to this figure, I do not by any means want to consider the tabula as an empiricist metaphor,[71] as supporting the claim that there is nothing innate in man. This is because, even if it were thus and everything were written on a completely virgin surface, there would in any case be the tablet itself and its capacity to receive inscription that was innate. Rather, what interests me is to concentrate on the tablet, irrespective of whether it is blank or not. For this metaphor interprets all the mind's activities—perception, memory, and thought—as forms of writing. In short, everything has already been written,[72] in the first instance by the ancients and, with only minor variation, by the moderns.

Thus, for Plato,[73] our souls resemble a book; it seems that memory writes speeches on souls; the possibility of error follows from the fact that the scribe can write badly. After inscription, a second workman intervenes, "a painter who, after the scribe, draws on the soul representations of the things said."[74] Aristotle adds a further thing: The soul is the place of the forms[75] and is in some sense identical with the entities it knows. These writing analogies are evident manifestations of the hypothesis of archiwriting. Or at least I hope this is so; the manner in which the mind represents itself to itself and understands itself is that of a writing device, and to think of a form of writing that is not preceded, followed, and surrounded by an archiwriting that governs the construction of social reality amounts to the claim that this mode of self-representation is merely casual.

In the printing era, Locke added a further specification.[76] We confront a white sheet shorn of typographical characters, which is to say, he explained, without any ideas of its own. Which amounts to saying that ideas are things like printed letters. Obviously, in this case, we have a strongly empiricist formulation. But it is not necessary to follow this line. Leibniz corrects the metaphor by saying that impressions are like the light that is projected on the backdrop of a theater stage, on a folded surface, not one that is neutral but more like the roughness of paper, thus returning to the image of writing. Leibniz comments that there is nothing in the intellect that was not previously in the senses, except the intellect, itself which is the faculty to receive traces and to adapt them to one's own forms.[77] It is an interesting point. An idea (for the empiricists, a representation) shows itself as writing, and it does so for the simple reason that, without the ability to keep traces, we would not have representations and hence we would have no psychic life.

Even forgetting is conceived of in terms of writing and the tablet. In particular, Freud wondered from the outset not so much how traces could be inscribed on the mind (after all, this is banal), as how it could be that the sheet was not filled up in a short time, reducing us all to the condition of Funes the Memorious in Borges's short story, who is able to recall every instant of the previous day and has to take a whole day to do so.[78] In short, Freud observed[79] that we are faced with two obvious facts, that we remember a great deal and that we repress even more, which is to say that we record it in another way, putting it to one side: How can the mirror in a telescope be at the same time also a photographic plate? To begin with, Freud hypothesized two types of neurons, one that allows impressions to pass and another that keeps them back.[80] But thirty years later, he found an answer that again makes use of a writing metaphor.[81] The mind is a "magic notebook" of the sort in use before the invention of computers: resin, a translucent sheet, and an inkless pen. The pressure of the pen on the sheet makes it stick to the resin and the letters can be seen; but if you take the sheet from the notebook, the letters disappear and the sheet is ready to accept new inscriptions, while the traces of the inscription remain on the resin, which thus presents itself as a sort of secret or unconscious memory of the notes taken. When today we ask our computers to look for the modifications we have introduced into a given document, we feel how the enormous power of this technical instrument resides in the grand style of its ability to be, at one and the same time, a total archive and an ever-virgin page.

4.2.2.2 TECHNOLOGY AND MEANING

There is a third and last, and the most important, element to be taken into consideration. We begin with an old intuition of Freud's,[82] which is connected with what we have just said about forgetting and repressing: Consciousness arises at the site of a memory trace, which is to say that the higher forms of the psychic life are reelaborations of phenomena linked to the keeping of traces and to memory just as we find in the comparison between the soul and a book. In Freud's view, the conscious mind is thus a superficial formation, localized in the cerebral cortex and corresponding to the outer membrane of single-celled organisms.[83] Now, what does this mean? Consciousness arises out of the inscription of a trace on the tablet, and is thus at once a physical event and the birth of something psychic in its highest form, namely consciousness. The heart of what we have been saying so far is thus that here we have a convergence between technology and meaning.

Let me explain. There are many ways to talk about technology and technique. There is of course a difference between a technical apparatus such as a radio or a chainsaw, a technique for transplanting hair, a technique for carrying out coups d'état or for formulating a law. *What unifies all these senses is the existence of a system regulated by iteration:* The radio is set up for certain functions, as is the chainsaw. Following a predetermined—indeed prescribed—plan, the colonels carry out their coup; following another, we transplant hair or formulate a law. When order is lacking, then we have improvisation, which is short of technique because the iterations are poor or approximate. It thus seems almost too obvious to say that inscription is the fundamental condition of technique and that keeping traces is, so to say, the mother of all technology. For all that it may seem rash, what I would now like to suggest is that, just as, for Freud, consciousness arises at the site of a memory trace, so also meanings, contents, values, and everything that is more or less confusedly thought of as "spirit" arises out of the technical iteration and the archiwriting that makes it possible. Typically, something like sainthood, which is undoubtedly a matter of the spirit, depends on ascetic behaviors of the body, on cultural codes that define a certain deportment as "saintly," on sacred scriptures and rites in which saintliness is invoked. Without these techniques of inscription we would not even have the notion of sainthood, not to mention more down-to-earth meanings. The double meaning of the word *sense*, as a particular and tangible element and as meaning and thought,[84] seems to confirm this intuition. By means of iteration, registration, inscription, and communication, which are all functions that are made possible by traces, we arrive at the construction of the social world, and it is within this world that meanings have their being. This is why it is important and natural to leave traces.

A final point: Everything that seems conjectural and undemonstrated, at least to the best of current knowledge, in Freud's metapsychology and in the philosophers' speculative hypotheses,[85] takes on the look of something simple and ordinary if we shift the focus from the origin of consciousness to the construction of social reality. As I have sought to show so far, this undoubtedly comes about through inscriptions and is also fed by inscriptions growing and being implemented by the passage from trace to the meaning. How? Precisely by way of registration and what follows from that, namely the possibility of iteration. Through iteration and by means of technique in general, we get something else, namely meaning. But, precisely because it arises in this way, meaning is always ready to withdraw, as when, as children, we make a word lose its meaning by repeating it, or when, in depression, life takes on the appearance of being nothing but iteration.[86]

4.2.3 Thought

In 1866, the French society for linguistics banned any research into the origin of language as futile. But perhaps the ban did not extend to philosophical speculations. So I throw down the gauntlet and turn to consider also the origin of writing and thought, so as to show that the tablet is not just a metaphor but also an inevitable and workable representation of the mind. Common sense and the philosophers are used to seeing a close relationship between thought and language, and it is a theme that has called forth thousands of pages; rather fewer have been written on the relation between thought and writing; historians, philosophers, and psychologists will have said to themselves, "If I have talked about the relation between language and thought, then I have already dealt with writing, which is a way of transcribing language." I have already said that I am not at all convinced that this is how things stand; and now I will try to demonstrate why.

Obviously, if we think of writing in the ordinary way that has been handed down to us, it will seem that there was a long period in which there was virtually no writing. There were masses of illiterates and, before computers and cell phones invaded our lives, even literate people, not to mention cultured ones, really wrote very little. In the end, there were only very specific professional categories who really wrote and wrote all the time: scribes and the authors of *feuilletons*. Now, things have changed massively: We all write, and the risk of falling back into illiteracy after leaving school, which was common enough before, now seems to be a remote possibility. But what does it mean to be literate? Taken literally, it means knowing how to use an alphabetic script. This meaning is not random, given that all histories and theories of writing assume that alphabetic writing is the most perfect form of it given that it reproduces the voice. Derrida has correctly shown that this assumption is anything but neutral.[87] Rather, it reflects the prejudice that there should be some impalpable element, thought, that is manifested through the voice. Here we find a particularly close link between thought and language, according to which the latter depends on the former, and that was taken for granted by philosophy until very recently and is still a commonplace.

The progression Thought → Language → Writing is already to be found in Aristotle: the ideas present in the soul are expressed by way of symbols, words, which in their turn are symbolized through writing.[88] On such presuppositions, it is not surprising that that alphabetic writing seems the most natural kind. More than two thousand years after Aristotle, Hegel defines it "the most intelligent" kind, and observes that ideographic writing seems closer to thought, but alphabetic writing is more manageable because it does not compel the creation of ever new ideograms.[89] The same presupposition underlies histories of writing, which recount its evolution with the constant scheme Pictograph → Ideogram → Alphabet. It is a progression that presupposes the philosophers' dogma, that the alphabet is the essence of writing because language is the essence of thought. With the aggravating circumstance, given that we are talking about historians, that this assumption does not even have empirical support, given that graphisms and traces can in many cases precede figuration.

The system Thought → Language → Writing seems to have an essentially ideological function. One begins by imagining that there is a *res cogitans* that is independent of any *res extensa* and that manifests itself in the first instance in a medium that is regarded as immaterial (the voice), and that only later is deposited or materialized as writing. In other words, this interpretation of the relations between thought and writing would be another installment of the mind-body debate. Furthermore, as regards the historians' description of the development of writing—presented as progress toward the alphabet—it is surely conditioned by the idea that the primary function of writing is communication rather than registration, which is far from certain, as I have tried to argue in the previous chapter.

Even leaving aside the narrowly historiographical question, those who place the alphabet at the highpoint of writings seem not to have taken account of the fact that the practicality (and essentiality) of the alphabet is contradicted by the fact that our writing system is awash in ideograms, which are not syntactic elements, but, for instance, numbers, with which we get on as well as the Romans, who used alphabetic elements, got on badly. In any case, suffice it to look at the keyboard of a computer, which is a machine for writing in a system that is supposed to be alphabetic, to see how many ideograms it possesses: I\!"£$%&/()=?^1234567890[+*]@°#§><;:_-. These are forty ideograms. And I have spared you the symbols on the buttons to get a DVD to go forward and backward or to raise the volume (which do not help writing), the emoticons that can be made out of combinations of stops, commas, brackets (which do help writing), plus all the things that we can find by opening the Symbol menu. If the alphabet really were so unconditionally superior to ideograms, we might ask why, after all this time, it has not won out, just as *Homo sapiens* did over Neanderthals.

In the end, the theoreticians of the priority of the alphabet do not explain why, if the alphabet is so practical, we got there so late. Normally, the reply is that a very high level of abstraction is called for in order to isolate vowels and consonants in the flow of the voice, to such an extent that, in many cases, before we arrive at alphabetic writing syllabic systems were elaborated. But this is not a convincing reply, not only because we might ask why, if syllabic writing is, so to say, the best surrogate for an alphabet, did we get there so late. It is also not convincing because picking out a vowel or a consonant is no more complex than picking out a number, and in any case, we have cases of writings, such as hieroglyphics, that had both a phonetic and an ideographic value. Since, at least in the periodization of the friends of the alphabet, these writings precede phonetic airing, it is very difficult indeed to accept the argument from the lack of abstraction or the difficulty of isolating pure vowels and pure consonants.

This is the ground of my doubt and of my hypothesis: are we sure that the sequence Thought → Word → Writing is right? Are we sure that writing comes last, and necessarily follows the word? I do not believe that this is so, but rather that writing is not at the end of the sequence but at the beginning. I am aware that, put this way, it seems that we talk and we write before we think, which is sometimes tragically true. Nevertheless, what I am proposing is simply a less Cartesian view of the nature of thought, one guided by the hypothesis that archiwriting is the condition of the possibility of thought, of the word and of writing in the common understanding.[90] My argument is in three phases. In the first place, I stress that spoken language is not at all the first and most natural form of expression, given that the first expression came about by means of gestures. In the second place, I show that writing is independent of language, not only because it precedes it, as in the hypothesis of the priority of gestures, but also because, unlike spoken language, it is able to register as well as and prior to communicating. And in the third place, I argue that it is precisely the capacity for registration, together with communicating, characteristic of writing, is what determines the representation of thought as writing.

4.2.3.1 GESTICULATING   Here then is the first step, or hand-wave, of my argument: Spoken language is not the first expression of thought. At best, it is the second, given that before that we expressed ourselves with gestures. This hypothesis has a highly respectable pedigree. It was proposed in the eighteenth century by philosophers,[91] in the nineteenth century supported by biologists and psychologists of the front rank[92], and in the twentieth taken up by anthropologists. Now it is being reproposed by cognitive scientists.[93] There are above all evolutionary reasons why, long before we expressed ourselves in words, we used gestures. The primates from whom we descend are very skilled with their hands, but much less so in the articulation of sounds. Confirming what we said in 4.2.2, the unadapted larynx of the primates means that they are unable to speak, but they are able to write, inasmuch as they can oppose their thumbs.

Returning to ourselves, the priority of the gesture explains many things. It explains why we are so given to expressing ourselves with gestures even when it is perfectly useless to do so, for instance, when talking on the telephone. It tells us why the television has so much more hypnotic power than the radio and why we often prefer to talk "face to face," which, if it were a matter just of verbal communication, would make no sense. Again, it explains why handshakes and other such acts are so important in expressing attitudes, such as the raised hand in swearing an oath, and why different human cultures have developed so many gestures to express forms of greeting, submission, benediction and execration. The discovery of the mirror neurons, and in general the phenomenon of mirroring referred to in 4.1.2.1, are further grounds to regarding gestures as prior to language.[94] As we saw, mirroring has its site in gestures; if someone makes a gesture, the mirror neurons in my brain fire as if I had made the gesture. Now, as I have argued at length, imitation is central to the constitution of human behavior and sociality and so there is a deep link between gesturality, rituality, and sociality.

Indeed, social reality, in its religious, juridical, political, and esthetic manifestations, necessarily depends on gestures, so much so that it can be enacted solely through gestures, as we saw in 3.3.2.4 discussing nonlinguistic acts. And we should not forget that the gestural is the essence of ritual.[95] Priests perform certain actions, and the fact that the word *pontifex* in the Latin title of the pope means "constructor of bridges" is an eloquent testimony of this. Rituals are performed with the feet, with bodily movements, and very often, as in sacrifices, with the hand. Suffice it to think that even today in the Christian rite, the sacrifice on the cross is expressed by gestures, with the sign of the cross and the exaltation of the host. The social importance of gestures consists in an action that is carried out externally, but that has an inner reflection, as dictated by the model of rites as external behaviors with inner effects. What philosophers have said about embodiment,[96] the nexus between bodiliness and thought, holds also for the centrality of the gesture, and this allows us to circumscribe Cartesian dualism which, in the specific case we are considering takes on the form Thought → Word → Writing. Here we have a set of sign and gesture behaviors deeply involved with the senses that determine thought in a way that I make clearer in a moment, and that can be summed up as the action determining the letter over the spirit, to which we will return systematically in 5.3.

But it is not just a matter of sociality. Pointing the finger is certainly a form of social blame, but pointing with the finger is an essential part of mobilizing objectivity and is very useful both as a substitute for words and as a way of teaching many—but certainly not all—words. After all, Saint Augustine was not so very wrong, in the *De Magistro*, to suggest that adults teach children to speak by pointing objects out to them: this is just how in works in may cases. Conversely, Wittgenstein was not so very right, at the beginning of the *Philosophical Investigations*, to criticize Augustine's theory of language. But

Wittgenstein was much nearer the mark when he described language as a toolbox and thereby recognized its essentially technical function.

The language of gestures can be a language in the full sense, so much so that the sign languages used by the deaf and dumb observe the same generative grammatical rules as spoken languages.[97] The disadvantage of gesture, however, is that we cannot do two things at once, such as talk and peel a potato: with a gestural language, either we peel the potatoes or we talk. Activities such as driving while listening to the radio are highly unlikely with a sign language; at most, we could watch television, but that is not to be recommended. This explains an interesting chronological gap: 170,000 years ago, *Homo sapiens* comes on the scene, and 50,000 years ago the technological turn begins. Why so late? The suggestion has been made that men kept their hands too busy talking.[98] Hence, contrary to what many philosophers think, language is not a biological gift that is innate in men. For all its age, it is an *invention*, just like writing.[99]

I would like to try out an alternative hypothesis: Language did not necessarily arise to liberate the hands. In any case, the history of technology teaches that the invention of a new tool does not necessarily cancel the old one. Instead, from an integrative, rather than from an alternative, viewpoint, we can see that language and technique both develop on the basis of the mobility of the hands. This development carries with it the greater sophistication of the techniques among which we find both spoken and written language, which share the same history and the same geography. In particular, I am much taken with the claim that the birth of language has a precise beginning with the adoption of agriculture and the need to pass techniques and timings from one generation to the next.[100] Thus, language arises as registration and writing. The evidence we have tells us that in the Lower Paleolithic (the interminable antiquity that runs from two and a half million years ago down to a hundred and twenty thousand years ago, with the emergence of *Homo sapiens*), we have stones that are unworked but gathered and arranged in significant ways; in the Middle Paleolithic (down to 36,000 years ago), we have traces and incisions; and in the Upper Paleolithic we have samples of geometric graphisms. All of which attests that writing began at the same time as language.

4.2.3.2 WRITING   If the hypothesis of an originally gestural language holds, then *writing precedes the spoken word*. Discussing Chinese writing, Leibniz observed that it resembles our alphabet, except that it seems to have been invented by a deaf man.[101] Or by a mute one: indeed, Hegel for his part defines an ideogram as "deaf reading, mute writing." There is nothing against thinking of prelinguistic humankind, so long as we allow for gestures and writing. Indeed, we have all seen mimes, dances, and silent movies (where the action is sometimes commented on in writing). Is this really such a strange situation? Is it so inconceivable? Especially if we consider that, unlike in silent movies, in our hypothesis we do not have alphabetic writing but rather graffiti that fix for instance rituals or instructions for the hunt. Gestures fly away no less than spoken words do and only writing remains; if, then, Bacon was so exact in defining a gesture as a fleeting hieroglyphic,[102] we might think of the hieroglyphic, the graffito on the wall as a gesture that has been made lasting, fixed, and registered.

The hypothesis that writing comes first is not so preposterous; all we need to do is not give in to logocentrism, which is a fairly natural temptation. In one chapter of his *Tristes Tropiques*,[103] Claude Lévi-Strauss tells the following story. The ethnologist on fieldwork is studying an Amazonian people we have remained in the Neolithic, the Nambikwara. He registers their ways and customs in notebooks, and this stimulates the curiosity of the natives, who at a certain point try to write for themselves, except—the ethnocentric ethnologist observes—because they are primitives, they do not understand that the essence of writing is to communicate. They get no further than tracing lines (which is their name for writing), and only the chief, who is a bit more intelligent than the others, shows that he has an inkling about the communicative role of writing. But is it really true that those who just traced lines did not understand what writing is? Perhaps they had captured its essence better than their chief and that the ethnologist because tracing lines is already writing, is already registering; registration precedes communication, which is by no means the sole and primary need of humankind, given that the need to register is at least as powerful for the purposes of mimesis and construction set out in 4.1.

The hypothesis of originary gesturality suggests a further consideration. It is not true that first we have an oral and participative culture linked to experience, and then we have an abstract written culture and that maybe the times of oral culture will return. Against this claim of primary orality and of the return to orality after the time of alphabetic writing,[104] I would like instead to set up the idea of a primary writing (specifically archiwriting), preceding the spoken word, and a secondary writing which, after being shut up in the limited sphere of paper books, is now exploding in the new informational world brought about by the Internet, email, texting, and unlimited opportunities for registration. This is a world that many have tenaciously tried to interpret as if it were characterized by a writing that is "more like" the spoken word, which is an untenable account, given that it is full of linear messages, full of formulae and even ideograms. Rather, the writing that is exploding today is not at all "more like" the spoken word than was book writing. Once we free ourselves from this conviction or fixation, we can look at a fact that, in light of what we have been saying so far, is of palmary importance: with the explosion of writings, we have returned to communicating intensely and continuously with our hands—albeit that in the first case the communication took place in a nonverbal language, while in the second it is in a language that is *predominantly* verbal. Look at an office, or people in the street bent over to write on their cell phones. This, by the way, has led to a reduction in sign languages, given that the deaf and dumb can communicate with their cell phones, which would have been very odd not so long ago.

4.2.3.3 THINKING   We have seen that gestures precede language, and writing preceded the spoken word. Thus, the technological explosion that freed the hand as a medium for communication about fifty thousand years ago allowed a first explosion in the use of writing as a means of registration. I hope that by now, the hypothesis that the Thought → Word → Writing system is the only plausible one has lost its air of obviousness. There remains then the third and last step, which is to show the constitutive role of writing in thought and language, which I would represent as the sequence Archiwriting → Thought → Language → Writing. In other words, archiwriting is the starting point and writing is the end point, and it depends on language. External writing appears as a more or less defective copy of thought; but when we come to wonder what thought is, we find, just as Plato did, more writing, the *logos* written on the soul instead of on the wax.[105] The idea of the dependence of thought on writing may seem science-fictional or pseudo-scientific, but I would invite the reader to consider that, if I had said, for instance, that thought finds the condition of its possibility in language, that claim would have seemed banal—when, come to think of it, it is either an absurdity or a tautology: it is absurd to claim that every thought requires a linguistic formulation; and it is a tautology to say that thoughts that depend on language, such as "today is January 12, 2009," depend on language.

My basic assumption is the following. Technique is a system of interaction that finds the condition of its possibility in registration. Hence, there is a general dependence of language, writing, and thought on techniques such as registration and inscription, which is to say what I have called *archiwriting*.

Archiwriting	Thought
	Language
	Writing

The functions that archiwriting guarantees turn out to be much broader than those that language can assure and this, I repeat, is a very surprising result, if we recall that the dependence of thought of language was a banality accepted as evident until very recently. Indeed, the very idea of "language" as a recognizable entity depends on writing,[106] to fix it, to regulate it (grammatical norms are literally norms of writing) and even to allow it to be transformed.[107] As regards thought, what I mean to uphold is not that *all* its functions depend on writing. Indeed, *thought* means many things, and some of these do not have to do with writing; but *some* of the most visible and important ones seem to depend on writing or, rather, seem to describe the parallelism between the inner *logos* and the outer *logos* that Plato outlined. Let us try to list them.

Visualizing.[108] If there are many good reasons for criticizing the principle that intuitions without concepts are blind, there as many excellent reasons in favor of what, for Kant, was its converse: that concepts without intuitions are empty. Thought is very often characterized as *vision*, and this characterization is testified to by linguistic usage: in Greek "idea" and "knowing" have the same root in "seeing," and in many languages "I see" and "I understand" mean the same. It is widely accepted that there are intuitive functions in reasoning that it would be hard to spell out in linguistic terms; when we mentally manipulate simple geometrical shapes, we are dealing with ideograms or pictograms rather than with alphabets. And the whole debate on the role of vision and imagination in thought, from the Greek philosophers to contemporary neuroscience, is based on the opposition between linguistic or discursive thought functions and those that are nonlinguistic, intuitive, imaginative, or graphic.

None of this is contested. The only thing I would like to add is to see the role of vision in thought as an action of archiwriting. Aristotle is right to say that the soul never thinks without images, and that thinking is like drawing a shape,[109] which is to say registering and inscribing in line with what both the ancients and the moderns have thought.[110] Indeed, it is not just a matter of thinking through images, but of using images and schemes in a conscious way to facilitate thought.[111] On this account, the neurons dedicated to reading are neurons of thought, not in the sense that only the literate think, but because those neurons are predisposed to recognize written marks. It is a commonplace in studies of writing that the linearization of writing influenced the formation of linear thought. I am not sure that this is how things happened, and it seems more plausible to suppose that thinking is in *many* cases the following of a line and the comparing of images, which is to say the manipulation of ideograms, pictograms, and alphabets more or less as we find in the traditional memory techniques. What is certain, however, is that in *all* cases, there cannot be thought without registration, without a deposit on the tablet of memory.

Registering. Here, then, is the feature that thought and writing have in common: They are two sorts of registration, the one inner and the other outer. It might indeed be asked what difference there is between registration and thought tout court, and my answer is, quite simply, that, while we do not understand what thought is (we have the phenomenon of thought, not its noumenon), registration is an evident element and writings are things that we have under our eyes every day. To think is to register; it is like writing on the mind. It is for this reason that when we stop registering, we stop thinking. And it is for this reason that society has come up with so many tricks to make up for the limits of the individual and of the collective memory—where the latter is what Frege tellingly called "thought,"[112] but that is essentially registration. This applies to individual thought, too; without registration there is no possibility of judgment, reasoning, formation of performatives, determination of objectives, or, obviously, the verbalization of thoughts. All of which is to say that what was traditionally attributed to language should instead by conferred on registration, which is at work even where there is no language.[113]

Codifying. In short, it is easy to turn the omnipresence of language in thought into a different claim, which takes language and thought as two outcomes of archiwriting. Let us take the case of language, examining it on the basis of the argument for the impossibility of a private language.[114] Let us suppose that someone decided to form a secret language, spoken only by him. To do so, he would need to proceed to a codification, which assigned a constant value to the terms he uses; otherwise not even he could use the language. This goes to show that the creation of a language cannot do without a codification or fixing of meaning that depends entirely on registration, which is one of the functions of archiwriting. This feature of the situation seems less than evident because language seems misleadingly immediate, immaterial, and spiritual, as if it were thought a medium of physicality, which is plainly not the case, given that acoustics is a part of physics.

Nevertheless, it might be objected that the private language argument holds for language but not for thought. Nothing seems to stop my thinking things independently of forms of inscription. Yet, as we have seen, some form of registration turns out to be indispensable even for thought, which is *logos* or a relation between at least two terms, such as the subject and the predicate in a judgment; but, for the sake of argument, we may imagine someone who is not convinced. After all, I myself stressed in 1.2 that the thoughts passing through a person's mind can turn out to be without any substance or fixed identity. That is fair enough, but access to these thoughts, as I pointed out at the beginning of the book, must pass through an expression or an inscription; thoughts must have an identity, a way of being fixed, to be regarded as thoughts within the perimeter of the individual's psychic life.

Let us try a thought experiment. Let us imagine a world in which there is no speech and no gesture and the only communication there is comes about by telepathy. It is easy to imagine that, if there were no way to codify meanings within the single minds, communication would be impossible. In other words, we cannot conceive of two minds transmitting pure meanings both because there are meanings that are not pure (we cannot understand what it would be to transmit "commodore" or "withholding tax" telepathically) and because even pure meanings need to be fixed. Characteristically, telepathic experiences are manifested (for those who claim to have had them) as the transmission of sentiments, which can be sharp and not codified, rather than of thoughts, which require codification and registration.[115]

Self-understanding. In connection with the question of the blank tablet, I have already said a good deal about the role of writing in cognition. But I still have to face a central point, namely the fact that the tablet is not just an image of knowledge, but also an image of the mind, which is to say that archiwriting is the essential form of the self-understanding of the mental. Certainly, we do not know that thought would have been if it were not writing any more than we know what thought would have been without language. There is no doubt that there technical inventions have affected our evident history, just as it is clear that (1) our evident history has affected that second nature that is thought and the various other functions of second nature—speaking, writing once we have learned to write, reading; and (2) the choice of the tablet as an image of the mind seemed obligatory, so much so that we do not know of alternative versions: at best we find the idea of the soul as *anemos*, as breath, which nevertheless presents virtually none of the features of a mind.

It is no surprise then that even Descartes, the modern thinker most closely associated with the *res cogitans* as a sort of breath separated from matter, describes the functioning of the mind in terms of the action of traces.[116] This inevitability recalls by analogy the linearization of time that Kant refers to.[117] We represent time to ourselves as a line, whatever time is in itself. The same could be said of thought, a temporal function that represents itself in a linear way, and that reflects itself and solidifies not by chance in inscribed productions within the social world. In short, we have no idea what *thinking* really is; but every time we raise the question, images of writing present themselves: wax tablets, inner desks, and libraries.

The time has thus come to respond to a very natural and justified objection: is the image of writing a metaphor or a true and literal definition? My view is that it is not a metaphor because *we do not have other words* for describing the functioning of the mind. It may be an extended meaning that is extroflected when we speak of the *memory* of a computer, ascribing to a medium for inscriptions the salient feature of our own psyches, namely the ability to remember. What is *mnemonic* about the memory of a computer? After all, memory is an essentially human phenomenon. If it is objected that it is memory because it conserves traces or inscriptions, then it is already admitted that it makes sense to claim that human memory is a form of inscription.[118] After all, as Kant would have said, we know ourselves only as phenomenon and never as noumenon. And that phenomenon that is the representation of the mind as writing is a transcendental from which we cannot escape, at least given our culture and the deep and ancient needs to which it responds, for that image is the representation of what thought is for us and not a representation of neurons and what they are in themselves.

Above all, these metaphors, if that is what they are, pass from being literary to being literal in the social world that is the object of our inquiry.

4.2.4 *Monism*

If it is allowed that the image of the mind as a tablet is not a mere metaphor, then we reach the same goal that Searle sought by collective intentionality, but with greater heuristic power. Indeed, it becomes possible to furnish a monistic vision of the laws of nature and of the spirit in terms of a genuine evolutionary development, namely that of inscription, rather than in those of a deus ex machina like collective intentionality. Furthermore, collective intentionality hides a deep dualism, given that it is the connection between nature and society, rather like the pineal gland that, for Descartes, was the bridge between *res cogitans* and *res extensa*. On the other hand, traces are first and foremost material things that are inscribed; but, as I have tried to show, by way of a process of enrichment and complication, they reach the state of thoughts. As we saw in 4.1, registration is invested in my theory with fundamental philosophical significance because it allows me to offer a coherent monistic interpretation of social reality, and allows us to give a materialistic reading of Bergson's idea that the past is repeated by matter and remembered by memory.[119] Thus, we have a pyramid of inscription, where everything is nature, but at whose vertex there is spirit and thought, and grasp of social, natural, and ideal objects.

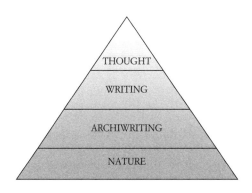

From nature to thought

Our next task, then, is to describe how inscription arises and is structured.

4.3 GENESIS AND STRUCTURE OF INSCRIPTIONS

I tried in 4.1 to argue in favor of the priority of registration relative to communication, and I set out in 4.2 the ubiquity of archiwriting, its relations to writing, and its role in the constitution as much of social reality as of individual consciousness, which is to say the whole of the world of meaning. Thus, I present archiwriting as a candidate to offer an alternative not only to collective intentionality, but also to individual intentionality. To complete the tasks of my ichnology, I still have to illustrate the progression that leads from inscriptions to documents, which is the passage from archiwriting to writing and from the social to the institutional. This is therefore a genetic inquiry and a structural exposition in which I am indebted, especially for the considerations about dependence relations and formal ontology, to the contribution of my friend Giuliano Torrengo.

4.3.1 Traces

A *trace* is any sort of modification of a surface that works as a sign or as a reminder for a mind that is capable of apprehending it as such.[120] It is the first, archaeological, level of the ontology of documents: if there were no traces or if there were no way to make inscriptions, there would not be—many levels higher up—any documents, nor even any traces such as musical rhythms, social rites, or individual rituals.

The trace functions both as a sign, something that stands for something else, as in the expression "traces of civilization," and as a scheme, as when we speak of the "trace of a speech." From this point of view, ichnology is superordinate to semiology and to the schematism, which are fancy ways of saying the doctrine of signs and the technique for the practical application of concepts, which latter, as we have seen, is particularly efficacious in the world of social objects and of documents. As we have already said and will say again in regard to registrations, the mind itself, considered as a function capable of recognizing signs, is made up of traces; this being so, ichnology constitutes the genetic condition of the possibility of *psychology*.

There are three axioms of the trace.

1. In the first place, nothing is a trace as such, but only for minds, including animal minds, which are capable of recognizing them. For a stone, there are no animal prints; for an animal or a hunter there are animal prints; but the animal, unlike the hunter, is unable to recognize a gun license as a document.

2. The second axiom is that traces are always smaller than their supports: the print is smaller than the soil, the signature than the sheet of paper, the neuron than the brain, the knot than the handkerchief or than the Peruvian calendar—and the emission of a sound is a sort of folding of the air. This axiom obviously concerns the way inscriptions appear. To be sure, one might object that the mass of inscriptions on a hard disk or in a brain is greater than the medium, but the way in which the inscription presents itself, for instance on the computer screen, is in line with the axiom that the inscription is smaller than the medium.

3. The fact that traces are always smaller than their media, and a medium is obviously material, points to the way that, in the end, also the trace is material; there are no spiritual traces or, rather, what people call *spiritual traces* are material, even if in many cases, the matter in question is not very visible or bulky.

A clarification of this last point is in order. There is a distinction to be drawn between traces that involve the personal level and that we recognize consciously, such as writing or signs left on the ground, and traces that involve the subpersonal level and that are not accessible to consciousness, such as those configurations of neurons that are known as *memory traces*. To some degree, this distinction is analogous to that between writing and archiwriting. The personal-level traces are material elements that can be accessed by the sensory channels (sight, hearing, and so on) and recognized by the mind as the trace of something else (the imprint of a cat as a trace of its passage). The subpersonal traces are modifications internal to the mind (the brain) that are caused by outer events. Can we say that these subpersonal modifications are traces of the events that caused them? What makes a positive reply problematic is that neural configurations are *not* accessible to the senses in the way that external traces are. Yet they make possible explicit memories of the events that caused them. The presence of this connection, which was a realistic hypothesis since antiquity, allows us to extend the notion of *trace* from the external environment accessible to the senses to the modifications internal to the mind and not accessible to the senses. For these latter, the first and second axioms need to be refined in the direction here indicated. It may be noted that the blips in computer have an analogous function to subpersonal traces: they make possible the images on the screen.

4.3.1.2 ONTOLOGY   From this there follow three ontological conse-quences, which derive from the fact that traces ensure the material basis of all social objects.

In the first place, as we have seen, there is no such thing as a "trace in itself" or the "in itself of the trace," because it is such only in reference to a mind that contemplates it. To put it in the terms of a negative ontology, it follows that the essence of a trace is not to have one; more positively, its ontologically important attribute is the function of reference to something else, namely its value as a sign. In this framework, the not having an essence can be explained by the analyzability of the notion of a trace into two in-gredients (1) a physical object; and (2) an intentional mental mechanism (of a more or less high level); it is for this reason that the ontology of the trace refers us to the higher level of the ontology of registrations.

I have just said that traces constitute the material underpinning of the ontology of documents; but this should not lead us to think that traces are mere physical objects. Relative to physical objects, traces show a peculiarity. The former are just what they are and it is only within the limited range of the object's physical resources that it can become something else, as in the case of the screwdriver that is used as a punch or the coffee mug as a pen-holder. A chair can serve as a clothes stand, but not as a canoe; a canoe can protect us from the rain, but it cannot become food. It is rather different with traces, because I can, perfectly indifferently, make use of a chair, a canoe or a banana to indicate a limit beyond which one may not go, a commitment for tomorrow or a role in an ecclesiastical, military or academic hierarchy. Once again, if we remove from the context the mind that has imposed the role of the trace (that has made that X count as Y), we are left with just a mute physical object. But given that the mind is composed of traces, here we have everything we need. The trace is at the beginning of the process that culminates in the conferring of the function of status, such as that of money or of a document, to a great extent irrespective of the physical features of the object that is its bearer, for an object of the size and solidity of a credit card can equally well be a driving license, an identity card, or a library card. If a physical object has an "in-itself" or essence independently of how we view it, this does not apply to the traces, which exist as such only because someone considers them so. The distinctive feature of social objects, over against physical ones, should be sought in their not existing independent of minds. In other words, *to be a trace* is a relational feature of a natural entity. As we will see, this peculiarity is inherited by the two forms that evolve out of the traces, namely the registration and the inscription, and sets up complex relations of dependence among traces, subjects, and social objects.

At this point it is worth clearing away the doubt that my theory of inscription could be reabsorbed into a weak realism that envisages (1) physical objects and (2) minds capable of recognizing/imposing functions on physical objects. As I have argued at length, ichnology is as superordinate to semiology as it is to psychology. This being so, it is ichnology that accounts for the sign function, which is to say for the fact that a stone can count as an ornament or a man as a president, as well as explaining the many other things that weak realism cannot explain, specifically (1) the reason why writing and documents are so important in the constitution of social reality, which is to say the sociopolitical importance of semiology; and (2) how inscriptions make possible the functioning of the mind and, within it, the sign function, of which the imposition of the function X counts as Y in C is a particular case.

There is a second point to be made about dependence on minds. As we have said, the mind is not determinately conditioned by the physical limits of objects and can make free use of them. This feature is evident enough, as can be seen from the artifices of memory-palace techniques (I can use a mountain to remind me of Muhammad, and I can equally well use Muhammad to remind me of a mountain); but another feature of traces is less evident but is decisive for the constitution of social objects. This is the way that, even in ordinary language, *trace* refers as much to the past (the trace as a sign: the pyramids are a trace of Egyptian civilization) as to the future (the trace as a scheme for a speech I shall give tomorrow and the memory neurons that are in many cases the same as those that are used for imagining the future. Just like the earlier point, this too signals the dependence of the trace on the mind, which is what philosophers call its *intentional character,* namely the fact that the trace is constitutively something that has value insofar as it is represented (or can be represented) in somebody's mind. When a trace is available to a mind, everything changes: the concrete can symbolize the abstract, the past can be addressed to the future, and the freedom of the spirit makes its appearance. This nevertheless does not mean a despotism of intentionality or a monarchy of the spirit given that, as we saw in 4.2.2.2, discussing technique and meaning, and as we will see better in the phenomenology of the letter in 5.3, spirit itself draws its being from traces. For the purposes of the construction of social reality, what is nevertheless important is that those minds are not in thrall to merely individual fantasies but rather have available to them representations that are shared by means of traces. If I am alone in the universe in thinking that I am the president of the republic, it certainly does not make me a president. It would be different if everyone thought I was the president—even though it could still be the case that everyone but me thought that, as in the case of Kurtz in *Heart of Darkness.* Social reality depends on a collectivity of persons—at least two and never a single individual—that have the powers of memory and intentionality, and on their interaction.

It should be stressed here that the dependence of traces on subjects is *generic.* In formal ontology,[121] we talk about generic dependence when a given type of entity cannot exist unless another type of entity exists, even when no specific individual of the latter type is required for the existence of the entities of the former. For instance, a school requires the existence of students, but there is no particular student whose existence is necessary for the existence of the school. Generic dependence may be contrasted with *specific* dependence. My experiences and acts of will depend specifically on me, in the sense that if I did not exist, none of my experiences and volitions would exist. The fact that social reality depends generically on the existence of a collectivity of individuals explains why no individual whatever has the power to alter the social objects in which he is involved. For instance, if it is decreed in some legitimate context that I have some right or duty, then I cannot shrug off the right or duty by simply ignoring the decree. More generally, social statuses and the rights and duties that attach to them cannot be acquired or lost merely by individual decisions. It is necessary that all or nearly all the individuals belonging to a certain community believe that I am the president of the republic for me really to be so. A collective and shared belief, however, is still not sufficient to make me president, not least because the object *president* is highly complex and calls for a range of other social objects and annexed validations, which are solidified in traces and documents, in inscriptions of acts. As we see shortly, shared belief is never a sufficient condition for the existence of a social object, and this is a corollary of the fact that social objects, as well as depending generically on individuals, also depend specifically on certain traces and, more precisely, on inscriptions.

The two facts I have drawn attention to here seem to suggest that traces are highly adaptable for minds. But there is a third sense in which traces appear to be unique and irreplaceable and this is when they are *imprints*. If I can use a canoe to remind myself of the doctrine of the trinity, it remains the case that the footprints of a partridge are not those of a pheasant, that my fingerprint is not my cousin's, and that this third valence of traces can be extended to signatures, which is to say, as I will discuss in Chapter 6, an artificial imprint (after all, we could sign using our fingerprints). This brings to the fore how, when we talk about "traces," we are referring to two distinct phenomena—the trace and the imprint—that are unified by the fact that the axioms outlined above hold for them, with the proviso that imprints have a greater ontological autonomy and identity than traces. Put simply, there are traces that can be used conventionally, or that slowly drift away from their origins, as with asterisks, which hardly remind anyone of the little stars that are hidden in their name (*astericolum*, "starlet") but that adorn our keyboards. And there are also traces that cannot be unstuck from their origin, that in ancient semiotic theories were regarded as "natural signs" as opposed to artificial ones, and that I am inclined to think of as imprints, not just the murderer's fingerprint, the footprint of the partridge, but also ashes as a trace of fire.

4.3.1.3 PRAGMATICS   Traces offer the material base for all social objects. They have three functions.

1. The passage from nature to culture. It is not by chance that, even among animals, entry into the sphere of culture passes through forms of inscription and marking about which we have already spoken:

marking territory, tattooing, circumcising, and so on. Culture is memory, and traces are the condition of the possibility of memory.

2. The passage from the concrete to the abstract. Objects are what they are and cannot be otherwise; traces (as well as, obviously, the objects used as traces, such as a pebble used to count) are liberated from that ontological fixity and become signs and schemes.

3. The construction of social reality. At this point it is not surprising that traces are the material foundation of the law Object = Inscribed Act and, more generally, of the whole of social reality, as I argued in 3.3.

4.3.2 Registration

A registration is as much the external traces (recognized by the mind) as it is the inner trace, deposited on the mind (the memory trace, which is a trace at the subpersonal level). The difference between a trace and a registration lies in the fact that registration is always very closely connected with a representation in a subject; if I see a trace outside me, I recognize it as a trace and I have a representation that is stored by means of a second trace (at the subpersonal level); at this point, I can recall the registered trace, as when I try to remember something and obtain a further representation with is the memory. As I have argued at length elsewhere,[122] registration can be defined as the tablet (*tabula*, writing medium) on which is laid down the table, namely the world, which should be understood primarily as the social world.

TABLE: TRACES

The mind recognizes traces as traces

External traces are laid down on the inside

TABULA: REGISTRATIONS

Table and tabula

There are three axioms of registration.

1. Registration is always connected to a meaning. A trace in the mind that is without meaning is just a trace and not a registration. This does not exclude the possibility that, with the passage of time, the inert trace written on the tablet can become a meaning, just as happens to traces left on the table. As external traces, which are in the first instance meaningless, they can be interpreted with more advanced instruments, so that the moment can come in which an inner trace, in contact with other inner traces, can receive a meaning and thus become a registration; the passage from the unconscious to the pre-conscious and to the conscious mind in Freudian theory would be a good way of describing this process.

2. Registration is a necessary but not sufficient condition of documents and of society. From this point of view, there is not a great difference between traces and registrations, or between external and internal traces. Without a mind endowed with registrations, a society is not possible, but with only one mind so endowed, we still do not have a society. We have already seen that the shared belief that I am the president of the republic is not a sufficient condition for my having that social status—I would not be president in any case if I were not voted for by parliament. But, as noted, the generic dependence of social reality on the subjects in a community is accompanied by a specific dependence of the single social entities on particular registrations. Let us consider a more elaborate case than that of the Alzheimer wedding already examined.[123] Let us imagine a wedding in which, just after the registers have been signed, all the memories about what has just happened of those present are canceled (think of the "neuralyzers" in *Men in Black*). Outside the town hall, no one, not even the partners, would think that the fiancés have finally got married. Yet if a trustworthy person were to show a video registration of the ceremony, explaining that someone (the aliens?) had canceled everybody's memories, and then exhibited the documents that are generated in the ceremony, the couple would *discover* that they are *already* married. In such a situation, it seems legitimate to hold that the two *believed* that they were not married, when *in fact* they were. It would seem bizarre to hold that they were not married before they discovered what had happened, and

that they became man and wife only with the discovery of the documents that attested that fact; rather, the fiancés were married even though no one, not even themselves, knew that they were. Their status as spouses thus depends on the presence of registrations (documents or memories) of a certain event, whose validity is collectively recognized. And this seems to hold of everything in social reality, because every social entity depends *specifically* on particular registrations or, more precisely, on inscribed acts.

3. Last, registration is the necessary and sufficient condition of belief, and a necessary condition for knowledge. If, in order to construct a social object, I need an actual or possible interlocutor, in order to have a belief, all I need is a mind capable of registering traces. Aristotle very neatly illustrated this process, which is in line with the hypothesis of the mind as a tablet.[124] In the flow of experience, the flight of sensation, like an army in rout, at a certain point stops, as when a soldier stops running away and gives his fellows courage so that the phalanx can form up again. In this way, belief forms out of experience, and it becomes knowledge when we are able to transmit to others the beliefs we are justified in holding as true. Here we find once more the need for a possible interlocutor, and this is why registration is the necessary but not sufficient condition for knowledge.

4.3.2.2 ONTOLOGY   We often use the verb "to trace" to mean the process of reconstructing someone's movements by his or cell-phone use; in this sense, "to trace" means "to register." Such traces are essentially external. Notches, marks, fissures in a wall, a snail's slime, a partridge's footprint in the snow, or the yellow of nicotine on the smoker's fingers are all out there. But when a trace is taken up in light of its meaning, because it possesses an intentional value for the mind that is contemplating it, it is a *registration*. Even inner traces are registrations when they manifest meaning, even though in the passage from considering the personal level (accessible to the senses) of the external traces to the subpersonal level (inaccessible to the senses), we have to take the precautions pointed out in 4.3.1.1. If, then, a trace is something typically ontological, a registration has a more markedly epistemological side to it. Let us clarify this point. Traces that are originally inexpressive (such as organic remains before the invention of forensic science) become registrations at the moment at which their sense becomes technically accessible. Conversely, registrations on vinyl disks revert to the status of mere traces as soon as there are no longer any record players capable of playing them. This will probably be the fate of a great deal of our computer archives, perhaps of all of them in due course, unless we construct trace transformers to bring our programs up-to-date and translate them all.

Regarded as a conscious representation, a registration is a trace insofar as it is picked up by a mind. Of itself, it is without social value because we can easily have many private memories. Here, too, we have to consider a necessary condition: There is no society without registrations, just as there is no society without traces. But this is not sufficient: Registrations and traces are not enough to construct a society. Traces and inner registrations stand to each other in a relation of reciprocal dependence. Traces exist only for minds capable of registering them, but these inner registrations in their turn need traces, not only in the empirical sense that the mind can be represented as a writing apparatus, but also in the transcendental sense that *the only things that can be registered are traces*. There is no circularity in this. A trace *within* the mind can reveal itself to be a trace *for* the mind even though it need not be so; for instance, we can imagine memories to which we attach no meaning but that recur in our dreams. These are the general ontological features. The characteristic aspect of the era *sans papier* that we are living in is, rather, that not only have the opportunities for "passive" registration and for noting traces increased immensely, but the means for "actively" transforming traces into meaningful registrations have also become exponentially more powerful.

The "passive" side is represented by the explosion in the possibility of archiving.[125] Both the data that lend themselves to being registered and the sites where they can be stored have grown. A cell phone is, to all intents and purposes, an archive, and the calls or purchases made, which once flew away as spoken words, are now registered in the archives of the telephone companies, in those of the banks and who knows how many other places. The fact that so many purchases are made with credit cards, that our passages on the turnpikes are stored away in the toll records, that our movements are traceable, that our correspondence is conserved on our computers and on others that we do not know about, that everything we have written in a whole life can be kept on a flash drive that is smaller than a lighter—all this indicates a power of registration of which even a decade ago we did not have the vaguest inkling, even though this mass of registrations is far from making up a true and organic archive, and it does not partake of that sort of reinforced and conscious registration that is tradition.

We move then to the "active" side of traces, which arises out of the growing sophistication of our instrumentation, which has induced a sort of long-sightedness about registration.[126] Nowadays we count among registrations endowed with meaning also DNA, carbon-14 readings, blood groups, and levels of radioactivity, which are all things that, until just a few years ago, were illegible and so were not recognized as traces. Obviously, there is a price to be paid. If we can now, using carbon-14, read prehistoric registrations, the files on which we record the results may themselves become illegible in a few years. It should not be forgotten that the process was already under way and, in general, that the progress of mankind goes hand in hand with the growth of registrations. This is the direction from "cold" societies without writing to "hot" societies that keep a count of the passing years and note the generations; and from there to the invention of borders, land registries, registers of births, death and marriages, censuses, and finally newspapers. The last serve not only the obvious purpose of communication, but, when they are amassed first in periodical rooms and then on websites, they also allow us to know what the temperature was in Bergamo on May 17, 1907, where we could not answer the same question for the year 907. It might be legitimately asked what sort of progress it is that springs out of knowing the temperature in Bergamo a hundred years ago, but progress seems to love waste, given that it surrounds itself with redundant information, for all that its first beginnings were in thriftiness if not in avarice, as we saw in 4.2.1, in the accountancy of goods and possessions.

4.3.2.3 PRAGMATICS Registrations form the mental base of individual consciousness and social reality. From the point of view of individual psychology, the inner traces that make up registrations are what is known as *memory*. If I prefer to talk about *registration*, it is to emphasize that I am not referring to a psychological phenomenon, the remembering of something, but rather to a substantial process, the fact that a trace is deposited on the tablet of someone's mind. This registration is not yet a social object and can become such only when it is made accessible to others, and this happens when the registration is presented as an inscription in the technical sense.

4.3.3 Inscription in the Technical Sense

An inscription in the technical sense is a registration endowed with social value, and, as we have seen, the possibility of sharing registrations that would otherwise remain purely individual depends on this value. Thus, even a natural event such a hurricane takes on social importance when it is shared, for instance (and preferably for the observers), on television. Here we have a registration in the weak sense, which is to say the registration of a fact, which brought to be shared by means of inscription. This is distinct from the more important notion of inscription in the strong sense, which is the inscription of an act, which, as we will see in 5.1.4.1, is the highest expression of the documental function.

4.3.3.1 AXIOMS There are four axioms of inscription in the technical sense.

1. Like traces and like registrations, inscriptions are the necessary but not sufficient condition of social objects. Without inscriptions, there are no social objects in the banal sense that unless a social act is inscribed in the sense we have been outlining, it boils down to mere *flatus vocis*, irrespective of the fact that in very many cases—recalling what we said about expression and in our considerations in 1.2.4 and 3.3—it is precisely the written fixing that determines the intentions and defines the object. Granted that, inscriptions can obviously be simulated either openly, as in a marriage in the theatre, on film, or in a novel, with all the intrinsic differences of the different cases, or covertly, as in frauds or with a rubber check.
2. An inscription is smaller than its medium. In this respect, an inscription resembles a trace and it does not call for further explanation; even in the case of computer media, it is still the case that the rendering visible of the inscription, for instance what we read on a computer screen, is smaller than the visible medium which is the screen.
3. The size of an inscription does not stand in any relation to the dimensions of the social object to which it corresponds. A click on a website can equally well buy a hairdryer as move a fortune in real estate.
4. An inscription is valid if and only if it is idiomatic in the sense I will set out at length in Chapter 6, or if it is recognized. I can recognize a signature made by another person as mine, but to do so I must

recognize it by word of mouth in the presence of its recipient or by way of a signed letter. If I do no more than recognize it in thought, that will have no value. Thus intentionality does not count at all in such a case, what counts is the inscription. We will examine the problem of idioms in Chapter 6, but for the moment it is enough to consider the pair form/signature. A preprinted form is validated by a signature, and without it the form is incomplete; if the signature is counterfeit, the document is false. What validates a formula, which is itself valid insofar as it is general, is an idiom, which is valid precisely because it is individual.

4.3.3.2 ONTOLOGY   By *inscription* I mean a registration endowed with social significance, which is to say accessible to at least one other person. We cannot see inside other people's heads, but we can look at their papers, especially if they are willing—or required by judicial injunction—to show them to us. This visibility is itself significant because the fact of being written, and hence shared or shareable, allows the registration to fix values, to integrate different values in a single system, to mobilize resources, to put people into relations with each other, to protect transactions as well as to certify identity, and to confer or safeguard determinate statuses. Inscriptions are not omnipotent: they need a society, a community of persons ready to recognize them as valid and binding, and to act accordingly. It is within a society that a few words, heard by the parties and by witnesses or in a piece of writing (a check, a contract, a supermarket receipt), become something significant and construct a social object (a marriage, a purchase, a fine, and so on). But for there to be a society, inscriptions are necessary in the sense that in a universe with no persons and no memories, which is to say without the possibility of inscriptions, we would certainly have physical and ideal objects, but we would have no social objects, in line with the constitutive law Object = Inscribed Act.

As we have seen, social objects depend specifically on registrations, which are inscriptions of social acts, such as written declarations or inscribed acts. Social acts are always addressed to someone and have *content*, which can involve other entities such as persons, objects, or events. The persons involved in the content of a social act do not have to be the same as those to whom the act is addressed. For instance, if I promise you that I will give Gino ten euros tomorrow, you are the person to whom I address the act, while Gino is the person involved in the content of my act. Inscriptions in the strong sense are registrations of the contents of social acts, along with the idiomatic elements such as signatures, and the persons involved in the content are required for the existence of the corresponding social objects. For instance, the marriage between Gino and Gina requires that both Gino and Gina exist. But social objects also require there to be a collectivity of persons who regard the content of certain acts as binding in certain ways and hence as *valid*. This is a generic sort of dependence in two respects. On the one hand, social institutions are binding insofar as a collectivity regards certain documents as valid; though an adequately numerous group of people are required, no particular individual is called on. On the other hand, the persons in a certain collectivity must regard as valid the documents that have been *produced in accordance with certain procedures*, even though the validity of single documents can always be disputed by individuals or groups.[127]

It should be borne in mind that in this section I am considering *inscriptions* in the technical sense, in light of what we said about archiwriting in 4.2.2. In this specific understanding, inscriptions in the technical sense are not just writing, but extend to a fingerprint on a passport or the hole punched in a railroad ticket, even though the model of writing as a technique for fixing memory and communicating a thought or an act is paradigmatic of inscription. Even more telling is the value of the inscription as an exteriorization and a fixing of those inner and volatile entities that are individual intentions. Recall what I have said about expressions: It is only when I say "I promise you x or y" that I promise x or y; and this, in the technical sense I am proposing, is already an inscription given that, still in line with the law Object = Inscribed Act, if the inscription does not follow the expression, then the object does not come into being. Thus, in the sense I am proposing here (and coherently with the analyses offered in 1.2.4, 3.3 and 4.2.2) we use *inscription* for every sort of registration of a social act that concerns at least two people. Thus, a promise made on television, a handshake, and a wink are inscriptions, at least in this technical sense. In short I am not saying that the world is made of writing; rather the idea is that whatever fixes a social act and brings social objects into being should be called an inscription to signal that it is not a private registration. From the substantial point of view, there are three considerations to be made about the peculiarity of the inscriptions in the sense here proposed.

In the first place, and unlike a registration, an inscription necessarily has *potentially public value*, which is to say that it must concern at least two persons. A memory in someone's mind may disappear with him. Given that no one can go and read his head, it is surely a registration rather than an inscription. Conversely, if this very same memory is noted down on a piece of paper it takes on at least potentially the status of a document. It may be hidden out of sight, and it may be of no interest whatever. But, unlike what is in a person's head, this type of registration is at least in principle accessible to others and thus constitutes a potential inscription. As in the case of registrations, this is an epistemological condition since, as pointed out in 3.1.2, as regards social objects, whose existence requires the practical and cognitive intervention of subjects, the dividing line between ontology (what there is) and epistemology (what is known) is less clear than in the case of physical objects.

An inscription does not just exteriorize a thought but also serves to fix it. It is worth developing a little what was said in 1.2 about the relation between intention and inscription. So long as something remains a representation or an intention in the mind, its status is fragile and debatable. We often and rightly doubt our own memories ("Did I really want this?")[128] as well as our intentions ("Do I really want this?"). This is not just a matter of the weakness of memory or of the inconstancy of our characters, but rather that representations and intentions have no exact limits of the sort that follow naturally from an inscription, which is a stable and shareable exteriorization. The writer who discovers that he has nothing to say, the person who finds at the last minute that he does not want to marry are fairly obvious examples of the fact that inscription gives form to interiority. All the more so in the public realm, a law that is just in the legislator's head is not binding on anyone, not even on himself, and will not be so until it is approved in the form of a written text. Quite rightly, a maniac for paperwork like the Emperor Franz Josef claimed that nothing really exists until it takes on written form, a claim that seems to anticipate Derrida's "there is nothing outside the text," applying it to its proper sphere, namely the social world.

There is a second sense that alerts us to the intrinsically social and institutional nature of inscriptions relative to solitary registrations. On the theory I am proposing, we have an inscription not only when an individual registration is written somewhere, potentially entering public space, but also when a *social act* takes place. This happens when, within a society, which normally involves no fewer than two physical or juridical persons (or their representatives[129]) words are pronounced or rites are performed that bring a social object into being: a promise, a bet, an oath, joining a secret society, and so on. In such a case, it is enough if the words are registered in the minds of those present, even only in those of the promisor and the promisee, with the precaution that, in such a case, it is may turn out to be "my word against yours." Thus, it is not strictly necessary that there be writing on paper or some other medium for there to be an inscription. It is easy to think of times when there were only acts, inscribed with easily remembered formulas on the minds of persons, presumably endowed with better memories than ours. When, as now happens, most operations can be performed with a click on a site, it seems as if the opposite is going on and the linguistic acts are becoming more tenuous. What the archaic situation of the speech act, the classical one of the linguistic act accompanied by inscription on paper and the present one of the click as purely written have in common is, at least as a rule, the simultaneity of the act with the inscription, as we see with the minutes of a meeting, which may be written up days later but, by a juridical fiction, are counted as contemporary ("read, approved, and signed") with the acts they recount.

In an inscription the word *spoken* (written, clicked, indicated) is essentially a word *given* to someone, precisely because it is a social act between two parties who are exchanging something. Now, the word given, because it has meaning only if it is conserved and registered, is already in principle an inscription. Let us return to the scene from *Hamlet* discussed in 4.2.1: the king asks his son to swear. And Hamlet swears. How? With the speech act of swearing: "I swear" and the swearing is done. In saying "I swear," Hamlet is not describing a swearing, but he is actively producing one: He is doing or making things with words, given that the swearing is an object that is not just a manifestation of his will and would continue in being even if Hamlet changed his mind. Thus the act is not just the *speaking* of words, it is the *giving* of words to someone, and for this reason becomes irrevocable. With this observation and recalling the analysis offered in 3.2.3, I would like to direct attention to two respects in which the theory of inscriptions differs from that of speech acts. In the first place, the linguistic quality of the acts is accidental; as we have seen, acts can be tacit and I can give my word merely with a nod of the head, as the Commendatore does when he accepts Don Giovanni's invitation to dinner,[130] or with a click of the mouse,[131] where it is their inscribability that is necessary and necessitating.[132] In the second place, the indispensability of the inscription explains why the acts are transformed into objects that endure after the act for hours, days, years, or even centuries.

It should be stressed in this connection that existence in time is a feature of concrete social objects, which are those that involve persons and things, and that are, in philosophical jargon, instances or *tokens* (what in 1.3.3.1 I called *ectypes*). Every token, which exists in time and space, is always the exemplification of some *type*, which is an ideal object without position in space and time. Articulating the type-token distinction[133] as regards the social world requires us to distinguish two categories of types. *Eternal types*, which correspond to my archetypes$_1$, are abstract possibilities, possibilities that a certain social object should exist. Eternal types are thus "social" only in the sense that they have exemplifications in social reality; but they belong in the category of ideal objects because they do not exist in time and space, and in this sense we find a limited validity for the social objects conceived of by Reinach. The exemplifications of abstract social possibilities can concern both specific social entities, such as the marriage between Gino and Gina or the University of Turin, and less specific entities, such as the laws that regulate the institution of marriage in a certain community. These last entities are social objects, insofar as they exist in space and time and require for their existence both inscriptions and persons, but they stand for more specific social entities, such as the concrete marriages between persons, in a relation that is more reminiscent of exemplification, and that I illustrated in talking about the relations between archetypes and ectypes. *Temporal types*, which exist in time and are subject to change (the Archetypes$_2$ of my scheme), are the parts of concrete social reality that make possible the existence of specific tokens, such as a particular marriage or a certain university. For a token to exist, there must be a temporal type, such as a law or a custom, that permits its institution. Every token of a social object is thus correlated both with a temporal type and with an eternal type. For instance, the marriage between Gino and Gina is a social object whose existence begins with a ceremony, but without an abstract possibility and without a law that permits its institution, it would not exist. To fix the terminology, we might say that the individual and concrete marriage is an *exemplification* of an abstract possibility and is also the *concretization* of a certain law, a declaration that is recognized as valid in virtue of which two persons become spouses.

In connection with the temporal type of marriage and the concrete marriage, there are two *instituting acts*. In the first place, there is the declaration that the citizens of a certain nation can get married by performing certain acts; in the second place there is the ceremony by which the two persons get married. The two acts are in their turn connected to two inscriptions in the strong sense, which are the inscriptions of the correlated acts. In connection with the temporal type of marriage there is an *instituting inscription of type*, namely the law that regulates marriages in a certain country. Finally, in connection with the token of each marriage, there is an *instituting inscription of token*, namely the certificate signed by the spouses and countersigned by the witnesses and by the person officiating.

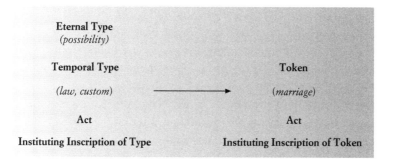

Even though these considerations are rather complicated, they aim to respond to a very simple objection: "Do you mean that, if nothing is written, there is no social object? That there cannot be an agreement sealed by a handshake? Or do you take these all to be inscriptions? Is this not stretching the word 'inscription' to apply it both to a book and to someone who promises to slash the other's tires tomorrow?" I would say not, both in light of what I have been saying here and what I argued at length in 4.2 about writing and archiwriting. After which, I repeat, everyone is free to think of archiwriting as nothing but a metaphor, so long as he is ready to redescribe in literal terms what he takes to be metaphorical.

4.3.3.3 PRAGMATICS   An inscription fixes a social object and constitutes it. I have argued at length that social objects do not necessarily require linguistic acts, but they do have imperative need of inscriptions in the sense of writing or archiwriting. In this connection, I would like to add four concluding considerations: (1) the identity of a social object depends on the few molecules that make up the inscription; (2) the determining inscription need not be a legal document; (3) the counterpart of an inscription can even be a negative entity; (4) once it is inscribed a social object with such force that it cannot be annihilated but only revoked unless there is some supernatural intervention.

Identity and inscription. The first observation, then: the identity of a social object depends on the few molecules that make up the inscription and not on the molecules, whether they be many, few or none, of the physical object to which the inscription may refer. Let us see how starting with an object made up of very many molecules: Poland.

Let us consider Poland today, with Warsaw fairly far to the east as a result of territorial gains after World War II, mostly at the expense of Germany. Then, there is Poland in 1941 under German control, where we find Warsaw at the extreme west, almost on the border. Again, there is Poland in the 1920s, when it was territorially very large because its two neighbors, Germany and the Soviet Union, had had problems (a lost war and a revolution respectively). Warsaw is at the center of a vast territory pushed slightly toward the west. If, instead, we look at Poland in the time of Napoleon, Warsaw is at the eastern border. In 1772 on the other hand, Warsaw was near the northern border. By now nothing will surprise us, not even the fact that in 1300 we cannot find Warsaw within Poland because there is Poland, which we have seen whirling round Warsaw, but there is no Warsaw. It may not be much, but it is certain: The identity of Poland does not derive from the molecules that make up its territory, but rather from the treaties, written registrations and agreements, all of which have the interesting feature of being signed at the bottom.

Let us move now to a social object whose physical medium, for all its size, does not consist in as many molecules as a state, such as a heavy industry firm like Fiat. Let us take Fiat in the 1930s. Its physical being consisted in a plant at the Lingotto in Turin; in its workers, employees, and directors; in the person of Giovanni Agnelli the elder; and in the cars. But is that how it now is? Obviously not. The Lingotto might become a museum, a hotel, or a conference center that no longer belongs to Fiat; the workers have (almost) been done away with; property relations have become more complex and ramified; and yet Fiat continues to exist, and its problems are not matters of identity. We may also note this: The cars that have always been and still are there constitute the being of Fiat only until they are sold: after that, they become part of the purchaser's property. The magic by which a car is no longer part of Fiat but becomes mine is a *contract*, which is a form of registration that features two signatures, that of the buyer and that of the seller. And contracts of this sort, along with the accounts books, packets of shares, communications and letterhead, faxes, wage packets, and so on (that is, *inscriptions*), underlie the identity of Fiat. We might say that it has a *characteristic activity* but, just like Poland, it does not depend on its physical molecules: in the end, the signatures that define Fiat will turn out to be only a little less than those that define Poland.

Now we may leave heavy industry behind and consider a service company, such as the Italian telephone provider Telecom. Thirty years ago, it was known as Sip (and before that, Siptel). Which physical molecules define its identity? Here, too, we have a certain number of operators and office buildings, and also, bizarrely, the handsets that the firm inventoried along with its landlines. Now that anyone can buy the telephone he wants, the Telecom set is no longer the only phone in the home, and today they are in a minority in houses from which the fixed phone is, in any case, disappearing. Moreover Telecom has gradually lost its monopoly on landlines. Should we conclude that it has become a different thing? In one sense yes: it is no longer the company with the Italian monopoly that it once was. But, just as its identity through the passage from Siptel to Sip to Telecom did not depend on handsets and wires, so now—as ever—its identity consists in signatures and documents, which is to say in inscribed acts. In short, the handsets and the wires can disappear or change hands without this necessarily bringing about the disappearance of Telecom. It is enough that the inscriptions do not disappear. There would be big trouble if they did.

Now let us ask, where is the being of Vodafone? This way of putting the question has the advantage of taking lots of molecules out of the picture. For, Vodafone has never owned telephones or lines, given that it specializes in mobile phones. So where is the being of Vodafone? What are the molecules that it consists in? Easy: in the SIM card, quite apart from its medium; in acts deposited in court, quite apart from their medium; and in shares, quite apart from their medium. All these are so many kinds of inscription and signature. The code deposited on the SIM card is in essence a signature, which establishes a conceptual unity between a bit in a bank's computer, a genetic code, and a trace of ink on paper.

Laws and traditions. A second observation: a determinative inscription need not be a legal document.

Let us take the social object that is the Florence soccer team Fiorentina.[134] AC Fiorentina was founded on August 26, 1926, and went bankrupt in July 2002, thus officially ceasing to exist. A new association, Florentia Viola, was founded on August 3, 2002, following the failure of AC Fiorentina 1926 to sign up to the B Division of the Italian League, and Florentia Viola takes the place of the old club in the hearts (and memories) of its fans. The new club uses the old stadium and the old ground, but it is a new social object, with new players in a different league (C2). Not having anything in common with the registration of Fiorentina, Florentia is, to all intents and purposes, a new social object, a new team with new players in a new championship. But the fans and the public at large continued to view it as the old Fiorentina and attributed to it the identity and the victories that Fiorentina had won in the past, even though that club is legally dead. On August 20, 2003, there took place an ontologically paradoxical event: With the expansion of the B Division from twenty to twenty-four teams, three of the teams that had been relegated the year before were saved and, given the failure of Cosenza to sign up, Fiorentina was promoted for sporting merit. This event was decreed by the Regional Administrative Tribunal (TAR) and the Italian Federation for Association Football (FIGC), which are official juridical and federal organs. But it is a mystery what sporting merit they could find in a club that had been founded barely a year before. Florentia was probably the only professional side not to have won even a junior title! What had happened? Quite simply, the titles won by the old Fiorentina were attributed to Florentia, forgetting that they were distinction objects from the juridical point of view inasmuch as they referred to different registrations.

How are we to deal with this? We seem to have a situation converse to that of the Ship of Theseus, the metaphysical puzzle that, in Hobbes's version,[135] presents us with two ships, one of which has had all its parts replaced one by one and the other that has been built using just the parts that were replaced: which of the two is the true Ship of Theseus? In the case of Fiorentina, we are dealing with entities that keep some of the physical components but that, in the space of a few years, give rise to two distinct social objects. How can we justify the continuity? Not on a physical base, because only one player survived; nor yet on a legal base, given that the two firms are distinct. Following what we said in 4.1.2.4, the continuity is rather a matter of tradition: it was

Florence's team, it had its own fans and it was perceived as the continuation of the old team. Moral: *The being of the social object "Fiorentina" is in the registrations*, which are not, however, those of the notary public, but rather in the memories of the fans, of the newspapers, and of the television. Let us move on to the case of Israel. Is its identity given by the fact that, nearly two thousand years after the destruction of the Temple of Jerusalem, a state was set up that occupied in part the same physical land, or by the fact that that is the land that the Bible talks about? It is hard to decide which, because the two issues are closely intertwined. Nevertheless, if one of Theodore Herzl's projects had been realized by the reconstruction of Israel in Argentina, the state of Israel would have been right there, with its continuity guaranteed by the written tradition and not by the molecules of a wholly different territory (and, as we will see in 5.1.2, the European Union itself has an essentially documental origin).

In some cases, the inscriptions can be not only extralegal but also actually misleading and can nevertheless impose themselves relative to appeals to physical objects. Madagascar was another place suggested at the beginning of the 1940s as a destination for the state of Israel. The result would have been the same as that of Herzl's Argentine project. But there would have been the added complication that what we today call Madagascar, the large island in the Pacific Ocean, designated a territory on the African continent and came to be used for the island only as a result of repeated errors.[136] Now, no one today is in doubt that Madagascar is that island, and it would be eccentric to try to return to the old denomination by way of an appeal to the identity of physical objects, *whose writ no longer runs.*

Negative entities. A third observation: The counterpart of an inscription can also be a negative entity, as in the case of a debt, which is not in either the debtor's or the creditor's pocket. So where is the social object? Once more, it is an inscription that helps us out.

In the Italian newspaper *La Repubblica* for January 4, 2004, we read, "According to the original plans, they should have been hidden, like an embarrassing corpse, in a hole dug in the night in the middle of the Po Plain, right behind the headquarters of Parmalat. But instead they ended up in the wrong hands, those of the Milan magistrates, and set on foot a round dance of handcuffs. They are three sheets of paper on which, a few hours before the case exploded, the Parmalat accountants had summarized the balance-sheet of the shell company of the group, which was designated to receive all the debts (along with a deal of the secrets) of Tanzi and his partners: Bonlat. Three sheets of paper, whose contents *Repubblica* now reveals."

As we see, the question concerned a shell company, but it was a very original idea to dig a hole to bury three sheets of paper. Wouldn't burning them, swallowing them, tearing them up into tiny little bits, or even flushing them down the toilet, as we learn from the movies, have been more practical ways of making the three sheets disappear? And yet that is not what they did. The head honchos at Parmalat wanted to go the whole hog; another hole in the ground behind the firm, which calls for time on a moonless night and can, in the end, be discovered. The result is that the three sheets were found, first by the magistrates and then by *La Repubblica*. Why? Because they continued to be *inscriptions*.[137]

Miracles. The fourth and last observation is that that once it is inscribed, a social act constructs so robust an object that it calls for a supernatural intervention to make it disappear. Let us take the annulment of a marriage. Canon 1142 of the Code of Canon Law establishes that the pope, for the good of souls, may dissolve a marriage and specifies, "'May be dissolved' means 'by grace' and with a dispensation, inasmuch as it is an administrative provision and not a sentence." Which is tantamount to saying that there was nothing anywhere ever; where there is a sentence, as happens in the case of divorce, we have to recognize the existence of an object. To the best of my knowledge, it is the only case that contradicts the formula Object = Inscribed Act, inasmuch as it is undoubtedly an inscribed act, but it possesses the marvelous power of annihilating a preceding inscribed act.

5

DOCUMENTALITY

We are heading toward the book's conclusion and toward its key notion, namely that of documentality, *which, on the hypothesis I am suggesting, is the form that social objects take, in line with the law Object = Inscribed Act. If a nine-teenth-century poet could adopt the saying that the world is made to bring a book to a close, and if the idea that the world is a book written in mathematical characters is a metaphor, it turns out to be literally true that the social world is constituted of documents, of those inscriptions that, according to the hypothesis presented in terms of an* ichnology, *precede and produce spirit. It is here that the notions of* social object, ichnology, *and* documentality *that I have sought to elaborate can help us to resolve a hoary problem.*

The terrain of social ontology is, after all, that of the sciences of the spirit. Nevertheless, as I recalled in 3.1.1.1, the sciences of the spirit had trouble in lo-calizing their objects. What is spirit? Where is it? If we understand it in terms of psyche, *does it not interfere with psychology, which is also a natural sci-ence? On the other hand, social ontology recognizes as its own terrain that of inscribed acts and of the social acts that arise from them. The intuition that inscription was central to the sciences of the spirit can be seen in the fields that they regarded as paradigmatic: the arts, history, and language. In all this, insufficient attention was given to the fact that the underlying model of all these expressions was that of the document. There are, as it were, only so many ways that we can deal with a purloined letter. Faced with the omnipresence of inscriptions and documents in their field of study, philosophers have set themselves to discover a spirit, when after all it was those letters themselves— perhaps because they were too blatantly on view, as in Poe's story—that could give a response to the question about the nature of social and cultural reality. For this consists precisely in the inscriptions of acts and the registration of facts, in the production of expressions.*

The reference to letters and to documents, to Buchstabenwissenschaften, or sciences of the letter, as the positive outcome of Geisteswissenschaften, or the sciences of the spirit that emerged in the nineteenth century, is not meant to be restricted to a methodological indication and perhaps to the solution of an old problem that is not very interesting for most people, but, in my view, contains within itself an important moral and political message. To maintain that science does not think or that the experience of truth is essentially extramethodical is, in the final analysis, a claim to occupy a position above all rules, which ends up with a dogmatic attitude when it does not lead to totalitarianism. From such a position, the notion of a dialog understood as the fusion of points of view seems to be close to useless or, more seriously, is tantamount to a contradiction: What sort of dialogue can there be if there are no rules? Will it not rather be a fiction of dialogue, an appearance that hides a monologue, and, indeed, a sort of bullying? Contrasting spirit and letter thus brings to the fore moral and political implications; sometimes philosophers, like ordinary folk, despise the letter (norms, limits) relative to the spirit, regarding the former as a mere formality, where the latter is a vital and authentic force. But it is precisely in the letter—in inscriptions, in documents, and in laws—that limits are fixed to tyranny and to the will to power. These are limits that the laws provide in civil life and that correspond to rules and methodical procedures in the sciences in such a way that to say that science does not think is not so very different from asserting that the political leader is above the law.

Proceeding, then, to the concrete presentation of this last part, in 5.1, I discuss documents in the narrow sense, which is to say those inscriptions that acquire power in such a way as to establish a link between documentality and governability, between the emission of documents and the whole range of the practices of governing. Because this claim may seem abstract, I undertake to exemplify it with the concrete example of the European Union. This is a case in which a political unit and unity has been constructed entirely out of documents; it is a unification that follows the letter and that is all the more significant because it came about after the bloody failure of the ambition to impose unity through the spirit. Here 5.2 is given over to works of art, those anomalous documents that are without practical utility even though they are carriers of high social prestige. Art and history were the basic themes of the sciences of the spirit; now we can see that what this strange couple had in common was the reference to documentality. Finally, 5.3, which is called "The Phenomenol-

ogy of the Letter," seeks to show how letters make up social reality taking over the three levels of spirit that Hegel acknowledged, namely the subjective, the objective, and the absolute. The basic idea is that, while the theory of the spirit (and its new version in the idea of collective intentionality) supposes that there must be something broader, indeterminate and collective that is solidified in institutions, the theory of social objects as inscribed acts proposes that, starting from inscriptions and institutions, there emerge individual intentions and psychological and spiritual acts by way of imitation, education and culture. Which is to say that we have not done away with spirit (and such an idea would be as implausible as it is undesirable) but now we know what it is made of, namely, letters.

5.1 DOCUMENTS

5.1.1 What Is a Document?

Perhaps contrary to what Saint Augustine said about time, if you (for instance as a traffic police officer) ask me for a document, I know what it is, but if you do not ask me, I do not know. More plausibly, the document that the officer asks me for is something that is highly stereotyped ("driver's license and logbook"), while we can imagine a long debate in a law court about whether or not a certain inscription should be deemed a *document*. Bearing this in mind, I suggest that we should regard as a document any inscription with institutional value. This definition seems to summarize the philosophical core of current juridical thinking, according to which "a document is a physical thing, simple or complex, able to receive, conserve, and transmit the descriptive, figurative or phonetic description of a juridically recognized entity."[2] This, however, is not a proper definition, because it furnishes the necessary but not the sufficient conditions; rather, I would say that it is a description. As I have sought to make clear, establishing whether an inscription in the technical sense is a document in the narrow sense is not a task for ontology, but rather for historical and institutional acts, given that we can produce a phenomenology of documents rather than an ontology of them.

Let us then unpack the description. "Document" derives from the Latin *documentum*, from *doceo*, and means "what shows or represents some fact." This characterization seems to fit the three spheres in which we generally speak about documents: the *historical*, where "document" means everything that seems useful for the reconstruction of the past; the *informative*, which takes in all the things that are bearers of information, in much the way that ".doc" is the file format for writings in Word; and the *juridical*, where "document" stands for anything with legal standing. Intuitively, it is this third sense, which is also the oldest and most traditional, that seems to be the most specific and the other two senses—so the historians tells us[3]—derive from it. Here, at least on my theory, as we see in considering the *phenomenology of letters*, "juridical" should be understood in a broad sense, having to do with the overall process of inscription of anything that appears socially important, from the economy to religion, in line with the analyses offered of writing and archiwriting.

If this meaning is dominant in the definition of *document*, whether it be public or private, a disposition (such as a law) or a testimonial (such as a passport, a license, or a diploma), then we ought to integrate, and make in some degree more precise, the description of a document as a *representation of some fact* with the account of a document as the *inscription of an act*. As we saw in 3.3.2, acts are such things as orderings, promisings, and bettings. In many cases, they are speech acts, but this is not necessary, as I can order something with a wave of the hand or a click of the mouse, or greet someone with a nod of the head. Documents register such acts and it is in this that their importance lies; my identity card proves who I am, my grandfather's will justifies the validity of an inheritance, the credit card receipt certifies that I have made a payment.

In the framework I am proposing, a document should be understood rather as something that is given once and for all and as making up a class of stable objects, as the reification of social acts which, in turn, change over time and space. What is constant here is not the kind of act in question nor the documents that follow from them, but rather the fact that without acts and without inscriptions, no society is conceivable. For not all inscriptions are documents, but there is no inscription that cannot become one in certain conditions by taking on a given social power.

Language reveals the link between documents and inscriptions. Once upon a time, a degree was called *a piece of paper*, and in technical contexts, *document* and *writing* (or *writ*) are often equivalent, in such a way that "my papers" means "my documents," which are the things that were once kept in the drawers of a desk. Thus, a document is of necessity a material *res*, even if the realm of documents is not restricted to paper, given that biometrical data and photographs can count as documents in the narrow sense, and sound recordings, films, and videos as well as DNA can count as documents in the broad sense.[4] In the overwhelming majority of these realizations, we can pick out the structure of documentality; first, there is the physical medium; then there is the inscription, which is by its nature smaller than the medium and defines its social value; and last there is something idiomatic, such as a signature or one of its variants, such as a coded digital signature, an electronic signature, the code for the ATM, or a PIN for the cell phone, each of which, in descending order, guarantees authenticity.

The variety and variability of the realm of documentality can be grasped by thinking of the various *grades of inscription*, which is to say the hierarchy that turns a mere trace into a document, and of the different *levels of validity* of documents, which may be underwritten by the intervention of a figure like a notary public or an attorney.

5.1.1.1 DOCUMENTS IN THE NARROW SENSE   As we have seen and swiftly verified, the question about the nature of documents in the narrow sense is complicated by the variability of the acts and the modalities of inscription in which the formula "inscribed act" can be realized. If, for instance, we can draw a theoretical line between individual registrations and inscriptions that involve more than one person, at what point does an inscription become a document in the narrow sense? There is nothing surprising, after all, about thinking that what today is a document may not be one in a hundred years or vice versa. Applied to the endless antiquity of writing this consideration makes a definition of "document in the narrow sense" almost impossible to find.

On the other hand, there are juridical traditions, such as that of the common law, in which any piece of paper on which are written the words, "I owe unto X the sum of Y," is a document in the narrow sense, which is what an IOU is. In Italy they do things differently; yet, since 1997 full documental value can be ascribed to self-certifications on plain paper,[5] which previously would not have been documents in the narrow sense in the Roman law, but mere inscriptions. If the criterion is variable, we will never find a set of axioms for documents in the narrow sense, but will have to settle for whatever is established practice as the only (though variable) authority on the matter. In other words, it is always and only starting from a social context that we can fix the conditions that an inscription must meet in order to be the vehicle of a document in the narrow sense.[6] Even so, such conditions are often explicitly spelled out in complex societies, supposing for the sake of argument that we can speak of a society that is genuinely simple.

Only one theoretical remark can be made about documents, namely that a document is an inscription that meets certain requirements. At least in contemporary societies, the requirements for something's being a document are in turn established by laws, and hence by other documents, which can therefore vary as the laws vary, or by customs and practice, which is to say by other inscriptions.[7] But, in this way, we have still not picked out the feature that is characteristic of documents in the narrow sense so that we can distinguish them from inscriptions. Fortunately, in most cases this is a problem only for theory, given that the difference between an inscription and a document intuitively stares us in the face, and it would be hard to pretend to misunderstand when an official requires us to "show me your documents." To a request of this sort we might offer a passport, an identity card, or a driver's license, according to the branch of state we have to deal with. It is unlikely that it would occur to anyone to offer a book he happens to be carrying, a letter, or a computer file. If we try giving the officer money, we will be making a clumsy effort at corrupting him.

5.1.1.2 THE SYMPTOMATOLOGY OF DOCUMENTS   In the absence of a definition, all we can do is run through some of the symptoms of being a document, in the spirit of Nelson Goodman's proposal for artworks: Symptoms are nothing but evidence; a patient can have the symptoms but not the illness or have the illness but not the symptoms.[8] On this basis, I propose four symptoms.

First, as we have seen, documents in the narrow sense stand in a close relation with the law insofar as they are representations of some juridical fact, such as the ownership of a house or the fact of having paid for a train ticket (which, after all, is a "travel document"). Nevertheless this criterion of recognizability becomes complicated when the realm of the law itself undergoes significant changes as it is now, under the pressure of technology, but also when the theoretical—for instance, historiographical—viewpoint shifts.[9] As an instance of technological transformation, consider what a "travel document" is when a traditional ticket, a computer printout, or an SMS on your cell phone will do equally well. This is an archetype manifested in various ectypes, or rather a single inscription with very different media. These are transformations that came about long go and more slowly with money in the moves from coin to banknote to electronic money, and that are now affecting the whole realm of documentality.

Second, building on what we have said about the intuitive understanding of documents, we should notice that there exist documents to all intents and purposes, but that turn out to be without legal value, such as the documents of a state that has ceased to exist, and that can receive such value only in specified cases. While, for instance, a passport seems immediately to have legal value, we would not be certain about placing passports and banknotes in the same ontological category. Even though banknotes have legal value (it is an offense to burn them), their documentality seems to be less strong because they are bearer instruments and are not decisively linked to any identity. A banknote is valid even though the signature of the secretary of the treasury is clearly *reproduced* and would thus seem to fall into the same documental category as train tickets. This is why it is so inappropriate to offer a banknote to a public official who asks for our documents. On the other hand, trying the same thing with a check is not a good idea; if the officer were corrupt, he would not accept it because it would leave traces. If he were not corrupt and were game for a bit of philosophy, he might say that he needed an inscription validated by the signature of the mayor, the police chief, or a minister, and not by mine; even if I were the mayor, the police chief, or the minister, then he would say that my signature is in the wrong medium.

Third, even a long and complex text can easily not be a document in the narrow sense, even if it is undoubtedly an inscription. Similarly, a registration need not be an inscription and a trace need not be a registration. An identity card surely says very little about us; yet, for all its terseness, it is a document in the narrow sense; a thousand-page biography of us can surely be more revealing, but it does not on those grounds counts as a document even though it is undoubtedly a prolix inscription.

Fourth, this highly schematic outline of our intuitions about documents allows us to pick out two elements that are to be found, though not necessarily together, in documentality. On the one hand, there is what we may call *idiographicity*, which is the fact of being a unique and irreplaceable expression of an identity or a right, as in the cases of identity cards, passports, and diplomas. On the other hand, there is *nomotheticity*, which is the fact of being in conformity with a formal reproducibility. Still at the intuitive level, idiographicity seems to be more important than nomotheticity, as when we think of an identity card as more fully a document than a banknote. But we are not entirely reliable in this, as can be seen from the ways that figures such as notaries and attorneys are called for to confer nomotheticity on idiographic writings. Idiographicity and nomotheticity, singularity and iterability are, so to say, the dialectical poles of documents. It is no surprise, as we will see in Chapter 6, that the quintessence of documents lies in the idiom, which is to say an iterable singularity.

5.1.2 *EU and other Initials*

I suppose that what I have said so far is exposed to an obvious objection: it may well be that documents are things that are used in social reality; indeed, in a society like ours, this is a mere banality; but it does not follow from that that documents have the power to construct social reality, as is posited by the law Object = Inscribed Act. In reply, I think that the example of the European Union is a proof of the fact that, in certain circumstances, we have complex social organisms whose origin derives exclusively from documents and that are in turn able to generate other documents, just as Baron Munchhausen pulls himself out of the mud by the scruff of his own neck or, to stick with a case close to that of inscriptions, like the boot-up of a computer, which is sometimes called *bootstrapping*.[10] To be sure, history offers many case in which states come into being on the basis of treaties and are often known by their initials, such as CH for Switzerland, UK for the United Kingdom, USA for the United States of America, or USSR for the ex-Soviet Union. These, then, are states in which documents played a crucial role right from the determination of their names, and such acronyms would be inconceivable without writing. The curiosity regarding Europe, however, is that, unlike the other cases, the new dispensation did not derive from a war of independence or of expansion, but took place on a purely documental basis, through the systematic application of the law Object = Inscribed Act. Let us examine the case a little more closely.[11] Anyone who is more interested in the upshot of the question might want to go directly to 5.1.3.

5.1.2.1 DOCUMENTALITY OR EUROPE   Some Euroskeptics call the European Union the "Belgian Empire," meaning by this that a group of bureaucrats in

Brussels rule, by means of norms and documents, over a range of nations and peoples that have quite another history, other destinies, and other interests. I think there is also a hint that there bureaucrats are a shade dim, like Belgians in French jokes, like Bouvard and Pécuchet, or like Otlet and La Fontaine. I would like to see things in another light. The Belgian Empire, the Europe of Bouvard and Pécuchet, the Europe of struggles over milk quotas, of paper shuffling and circulars, is historically united in being a state organism that was constructed entirely by the power of documents. This came about after so many attempts at continental unification, through blood and soil or through the spirit—whether it be the spirit of individual countries, the philosophical spirit, a generic "European spirit" or "common Christian roots"—had failed, and had failed all the more for having sought to impose unity by force. Suffice it to say that the last nonbureaucratic attempt to construct a united Europe from the Atlantic to the Urals, that of the Third Reich, ended with the most drastic partition known to the history of Europe.

What I want to articulate in the coming pages does not follow from any particular affection on my part for Europe, but rather from a very powerful theoretical leaning regarding bureaucracy. If Novalis's brief text *Christianity or Europe* was a romantic fantasy, I think that "Documentality or Europe" stands for an obvious truth that everyone can see. As I have said, Europe offers a unique case in which a continent has been unified by documents. It is a very different organism from the United States, where the Declaration of Independence was followed by wars against England, and from the procedures for the application of the rule of law in the postcommunist countries, which were already endowed with national unity and simply received a constitution from without. By contrast, in Europe, the point of departure was a set of increasingly committal documents that ended up with the document par excellence, namely the common currency. This was a process of great interest in itself. But it is all the more so for me, given that I mean to argue that it provides a palmary case for the law of the construction of social reality, which consists in inscriptions and documents.

To this end, I would like to point out an opposition between the ideal foundation, which I summarize as "foundation following the spirit," and the real foundation or "following the letter," which latter, of a bureaucratic and documental nature, was the effective process of European unification. When I speak of *ideal foundation*, I mean the fact that we very often encounter demands for a different Europe from the one we know—for instance, a Europe of the peoples, free from the snares of Brussels bureaucrats, or one founded on shared Christian roots. The prime feature of such demands is the desire for more soul in what appears to be an inert construction made of letters, laws, and documents; a construction that is based only on documents seems to be insufficient because the spirit enlivens and unifies where the letter divides and kills. This, however, is the theory; what experience shows is that the opposite is true: spirit kills and divides, while the letter unifies and enlivens, albeit in a prosaic sort of way. Let us briefly see how.

5.1.2.2 UNIFICATION FOLLOWING THE SPIRIT My objection to unification following the spirit is very simple: It has never really happened. It has often been talked about, in speeches in favor of unification following the spirit, about the Roman Empire and then the Holy Roman Empire as precursors of European unity. Nevertheless, what was unified in these supernational organisms was either much bigger or much smaller that what we call *Europe* today, and for very good but purely bureaucratic reasons so far as the argument for unification following the letter is concerned. The lack of coincidence is then taken to extremes by those who make claims for the Eastern Empire, despite the fact that it was mostly in Asia and in Africa and sometimes, as after the sack of Constantinople by Europeans and Christians, was limited to Anatolia, which is to say in Asia. This last consideration will, in all likelihood, be set aside when Turkey enters Europe thus showing that the change does not derive from the appeal to a geopolitical past, but rather from the application of bureaucratic acts.

Above all, what I want to bring to the attention relative to these European proto-organisms that are so often evoked as examples of unification following the spirit is that there is no trace whatever of spirit, whether that be the spirit of peoples or nations, or of Christianity as the "common root." The peoples were obviously different, given that the structures were supernational, as were the religions (paganism, Roman Catholicism, Orthodox Christianity, Islam). What made up the unity, then? Here too it was not a matter of spirit, nor yet some peculiar geographic nature of Europe, but rather a network of norms that had nothing to do with the European spirit but that depended on the latter, which is to say on bureaucratic and chancellery acts, whose fundamental form can be found in the Edict of Caracalla of 212 CE, which conceded Roman citizenship on all the free citizens of the

Empire. There is no difference whatever between this Edict and all the subsequent decrees that have conferred European citizenship on nations with the most various histories, traditions and languages.

We may draw out a consequence from our considerations of collective intentionality in 3.2.3.3 and 4.1.2. There is a resemblance between the idea that social reality is constituted by collective intentionality and the ideas that these forms of statehood are precursors of European unity. The point, however, is that the unity of the various empires does not seem to be based in the least on a unity of intentions of its citizens, but rather on working bureaucracies, which offer a guarantee of unity. On paper, the Roman Empire, which was based on conquest, had the same solidity as the Mongol Empire; but the former lasted for centuries, at least as long as the Chinese Empire or the Egyptian dynasties, both of which had the advantage of ethnic homogeneity as well as a bureaucracy, whereas the latter dissolved with the death of the military leader. The breakup of the conquests of Alexander the Great are not a counterexample to my claim, because here we are dealing with the division of ownership understood not as an empire but as a real estate, of which the Macedonian generals regarded themselves as the legitimate heirs.

Thus, the supposed examples of unification following the spirit are in fact examples of unification following the letter. To this historical fact, I add a theoretical point, namely the intrinsic obscurity of the notion of "spirit."[12] This is already clear as soon as one points to a religion, such as Catholicism, that has its raison d'être in a universality (*kat'holou*) that transcends every determinate circumstance. The basic idea is essentially this: Unlike Africa or America, Europe does not have stable and secure natural boundaries, but is rather a sort of promontory of Asia; this natural shortcoming is made up for by imposing unifications founded on the spirit.[13] These unification are that much easier for Europe which, precisely because of its limited natural resources, the unstable nature of its geographic limits and perhaps the peculiarities of its climate,[14] has been inclined to develop spirit to its highest level, through its vocation for liberty against despotism (already in evidence in the Greeks' wars against the Persians), for philosophy against myth (again the Greeks), and for scientific and political development which has been a consequence of what we might call, oxymoronically, a "natural disposition to the spirit."[15]

Setting these claims out and discovering their inherent contradictoriness are one and the same process. Spirit ought to be a volatile element that is nevertheless called on to make up for the inadequacies of nature (geography, resources), and at the same time it ought to be the representative of a national identity and a natural vocation. On the basis of this paradox, Fichte went so far as to claim that a national spirit—the German one—is by nature oriented toward a cosmopolitan and supremely European vocation, given that Germany is the material and spiritual heart of Europe.[16] It is pointless to ask how one might invoke the geographical centrality to justify a spiritual centrality that, in its turn, according to the notion we are expounding, is needed to establish the geographical boundaries.

This is a modest circularity by comparison with the other Fichtean theme that, since *German* is an essentially spiritual determination, everyone who believes in freedom and the progressive nature of the spirit is German in such a way that if someone who is empirically German is spiritually underendowed then he is not part of spiritual Germany and hence not part of Germany tout court.[17] The failure in this line of argument of the conclusion to follow from the premises, as well as the consequences that followed from its acceptance, have been rightly pointed out. But it recurs, a hundred years after Fichte, in Husserl, who, despite having himself been expelled from the German universities because he was a Jew, still maintained that the European spirit is a grand cultural organism, indeed the grandest there has ever been, one the goes beyond its geographical borders to include America and the British Dominions, but excludes those, such as the Rom and the Inuit (whom Husserl called "Gypsies" and "Eskimos"), who belong geographically to Europe, but are spiritually outside it.[18]

What I would like to draw attention to is that here we are not dealing with merely abstract utterances, but with considerations that found political expression, even if we leave the massacres of the Rom under the Third Reich to one side. To justify his voluntary enrolment in the "Frundsberg" SS-Panzer Division in March 1945, Günter Grass said in 2006 that it was a cosmopolitan army effectively representing Europe. After all, that was how it was at the time. At the beginning, the Waffen SS was rigidly limited to soldiers who were of pure German blood, which was then extended to the Volksdeutsche, those of German ethnicity but of different nationality; as the war dragged on divisions were founded to include the French, the Dutch, the Norwegians, the Danes, the Italians, the Ukrainians, the Russians, the Croats, the Bosnians (so that there were Muslim SS men), the Indians, and even—it seems—some Englishmen. These nationalities were explicitly represented in the troops' insignia, and the divisions were organized along national lines, unlike for instance the French Foreign Legion. To begin with, Hitler was opposed to this recruitment, but he had to change his mind, so much so that when, in 1944, he pinned a medal on Léon Degrelle, a Belgian officer of the Walloon SS division who had distinguished himself on the Eastern Front, he said that he would have wanted a son like him.[19]

Hitler's faith in the European Waffen SS was well placed, if we recall that the last defenders of the Chancellery bunker were French soldiers belonging (in one of the genuine ironies of history) to the "Charlemagne" division: French aristocrats and lumpenproletarians transported to Berlin to fight in the last battle against Bolshevism in the name of the European spirit. This was the interpretation that Hitler had given to the whole Russian campaign, which was itself an outcome of what he had maintained since the 1930s about a "common European home." Here we have a supposed unification that should have come about following the spirit and in the name of the spirit. Thus, Hitler's broadcast to the troops on June 21, 1941, the day of the attack on the Soviet Union: "My soldiers, I have taken the decision that I had to take not only as the responsible head of the German state, but *as a representative of European culture and civilization*"; likewise, in his last speech, on April 16, 1945, when the Battle of Berlin began on the Oder River: "Führer order! To the soldiers on the Eastern Front! Asia's final assault will fail!"

5.1.2.3 UNIFICATION FOLLOWING THE LETTER   Leaving to one side the myth of foundation through the spirit, it is better to pass to real history and to the foundation through the letter, which not only explains a unification that has actually taken place, the one we can all see, but, somewhat surprisingly, also presents itself as the genetic possibility of spirit.[20] The destitution of Europe and the progressive decadence of the spiritual continent, which many wanted to read as a sort of biological decline,[21] was in reality a destitution at the level of letters and documents, a relegation of inscriptions. We may pick out three signs among many others. First, the ascendancy of the dollar as the international currency, an event whose negative impact can be measured when we think how much prestige Europe gained by the introduction of the euro. Second, as Carl Schmitt pointed out,[22] after 1890 the idea that international law was European law fell out of favor. And third, the fact at the Versailles Conference in 1919, the language of negotiation was no longer

French, the continental language par excellence, at the explicit request of the American president, Woodrow Wilson, who did not speak it.

If the destitution took place on the level of documents, it is no surprise that, conversely, the constitution of Europe and the progressive construction of the Union is the history of essays and documents starting with Saint-John Perse's 1930 *Memorandum sur l'organisation d'un régime d'union fédérale européene* and proceeding from the prehistory of the Hague Congress of 1948 to history with a succession of declarations and treaties, initially and significantly of an economic nature, that have made Europe. This is a "making" that must be taken literally, given that we have here performatives: the 1950 Schuman Declaration; the Treaty of Paris in 1951; the modified Western European Union by the Treaty of Brussels in 1954; the Treaties of Rome in 1957; the Merger Treaty of Brussels of 1965; the Luxemburg Treaty of 1985; the Schengen Accords of 1985; the European Single Act of 1986; the Maastricht Treaty of 1992; the Ioannina Compromise of 1994; the 1997 Declaration on the Western European Union; the 1999 Amsterdam Treaty; the 2001 Nice Treaty; the 2001 Laeken Declaration; the European Constitution of 2004; the Berlin Declaration of 2007; and the Treaty of Lisbon that same year.[23]

The fact that documentality plays a prime role both in destitution and in construction confirms the intuition from which I began: Those who have their doubts about Europe in the name of the spirit of the peoples or of the nations, and who on that basis undermine the legitimacy of the social object that is *Europe* are in all likelihood appealing to the idea of a state that has a precise history and geography. This is the sort of national state that the nineteenth-century romantics yearned for though they could not always bring into existence. As we saw in 3.2.3.4, it is hardly wise to take this sort of being as a norm insofar as it turns out to be, if anything, a significant exception. In the end, states' being divided up as if they were ordinary real estate in the name of documents of inheritance has been more characteristic of European history. Even Charlemagne's empire was divided into three parts, into something that is now France, something that is now Germany, but also into something that is now a tongue of land stretching from the North Sea to the Jura mountains and that was known as *Lotharingia* because it was inherited by Lothario, and whose name survives in modern Lorraine (known to the Germans as Lothringen). Likewise, there was no spiritual, ethnic or territorial unity to unify Prussia before Napoleon. Documents are quite enough to make a state, and from this point of view, Europe has its papers in order.[24]

So far, so good, as regards exemplification, which could obviously be extended indefinitely, but whose meaning can be summarized as follows; when we speak about unification through the spirit, we are appealing to vague notions that nevertheless are not improved by being made precise, given that every attempt at determination leads to less than comforting results. Let us take the Italy that Manzoni dreamt of as "one in arms, in language, in altar / in memories, in blood and heart" ("March 1821"). After the events of the twentieth century, this sort of military, religious, ethnic, and religious unity has lost its charm even as an ideal, and Manzoni's desire might be a splendid ideological platform for a xenophobic political party. As to the memories, if we want to give a precise sense to an otherwise vague word, we have to do precisely with the sphere of inscriptions and documents.

One might object that if there is a unification after the letter, then it is linguistic, which holds equally well for money and for documents. But I do not think this is how things stand. However strange it might seem, a language is not necessarily a unifying factor. If Mark Twain ironically claimed that the Americans and the English are a single people divided by a shared language, it is a sad fact that Serbo-Croat was unable to guarantee the unity of Croatia and Serbia. And curiously, the only difference between the two languages is grammatological: Croat is written in the Roman alphabet and Serbian in the Cyrillic; and the conflict between them finds its roots in this divergence in documental history, the one belonging to the Western Roman Empire and the other to the Eastern Roman Empire. The point is not unimportant; China is not unified by language, which is broken up into myriad dialects, but by its writing system of shared ideograms that allow mutual understanding; likewise, the Islamic Umma is unified by Arabic that is written the same for all and divided by spoken languages that vary from nation to nation. It might be objected that I am talking about writing that is highly communicative and hence very close to the spoken language. But this is not so: From the point of view of the state structure, the fact of speaking the same language is a marginal phenomenon, as we can see from the occurrence of civil wars, relative to the documental unity of laws, dispositions and inscription as the experience of supernational empires shows; suffice it to think of the Austrian empire, which was held together by the land registry established by Maria Theresa and by the bureaucratic network allegorized by Kafka. But how is it possible for a document to do all this? The moment has come to set out the relations between documentality and governmentality.

5.1.3 Documentality and Governmentality

5.1.3.1 PAPERS   For us, Europe is something we see on maps at school, and it is not impossible that the reason why Husserl decided to exclude the Eskimos from the European spirit was that sometimes on those maps the Northern part of Scandinavia is not included, while Husserl's native city of Freiburg, now known as Pribor in the Czech Republic, is.[25] Now this is not a merely accidental fact. Political maps depend on decisions that are made "on paper," by means of inscribed acts in documents and treaties. In the case of states, such as Colorado, with fiat borders this is particularly visible; but even states with bona fide borders undergo the action of documentality on the territory. If, as we have just seen, the northern part of Scandinavia is often cut off the map of Europe, it often happens that the Canary Isles are inserted in a box even though they are physically off the coast of Morocco.

This can easily be explained. Considered as social objects, states depend much more on history than on geography and, contrary to the notions connected with "spirit," this dependence on history is not at all vague, but is in exact correspondence with the ways that the borders and the nature of states, the laws that regulate them and the institutions that characterize them are all established by documents. In this sense, maps *represent* the geography that is *determined* by other papers, the documents that constitute the inscription of acts that brought into being the social objects that are nations. The dominance of cultural inscription relative to nature is all the more evident in ancient maps, in which the size of things is often altered to indicate their political importance, or the orientation of the map is fixed by the position of the capital rather than by the cardinal points.[26]

In 4.3.3.3, I offered the example of the example of the identity of Poland, which was guaranteed less by the ever-shifting territorial identity than by documental identity. This principle can be extended to the whole of Europe in at least two senses: first, by showing that what is often indicated as the source of the spiritual roots of Europe has no basis in geography, but only in documents; and second, by recalling, what we have just seen, that the development of the European Union has not followed any sort of geographic or spiritual necessity, but has always and only been an sequence of inscribed acts that are much more important than any geographical coherence. In this connection, suffice it to think of Switzerland, which is at the heart of Europe but is not part of the European Union, whose members include or have included territories that are very far geographically from the continent, such as Greenland (from 1973 to 1985), the Portuguese Azores, or French Martinique, which are detached parts of states that themselves belong to the EU thanks to the signing of treaties. There is a further point to be made. While this might appear to be an anomaly no different from that of Husserl's European spirit, it is not so at all; neither the United States nor Australia belongs to Europe either physically or politically, but some Eskimos do belong, physically and politically, insofar as they are Norwegian or Finnish citizens.

What is made clear is the power of a document, which can transform a piece of Chinese territory into English territory for a hundred years, or make Gibraltar, which is part of Spain, politically English while, on the other side of the Strait, Ceuta, which is physically in Morocco, is politically Spanish. After all, the states of the ancien régime worked just this way, and, in this sense, it might be worth reconsidering Metternich's often-vituperated saying that Italy is just a geographical expression. Geography is insufficient to generate state unity; documents are called for. Nothing that I have said so far is at all surprising. For nations as much as for institutions, and even for individuals, a document is needed to give and to receive power: the driver's license that allows me to drive my car, the visa that allows me to go abroad, or the policeman's badge that allows him to give me a fine. The question, however, is what this power depends upon; and the answer I am proposing, developing what I said in 4.1.2.5, is that such documents are the formalizations of the ingredients that intervene in the construction of social objects, since there is a continuum that goes from a nod of understanding or a handshake to credit cards, passports, and contracts.

5.1.3.2 DOCUMENTAL ACTS   Let us now move from maps to the other pieces of paper that determine them. In Moscow in the autumn of 1944, Churchill and Stalin made informal notes on a sheet of paper of the percentages of influence they would have in Western and Eastern Europe once the war was over. That piece of paper determined the geography, and with it the destiny, of millions of people. Now, the construction of social reality obeys the law Object = Inscribed Act.[27] With a principle of this sort, it is worth distinguishing a *strict* application of it from a *broad* one. The broad application is what we encounter in the construction of social reality, where the inscription need not be rule-governed and may indeed not even be an inscription in the full sense. Thus, everyday social reality is made up of appointments, lunch invitations, bets, and threats; in all of these cases the inscription can be relatively informal, such as a handshake, an annotation in someone's memory or on their cell phone, a receipt, a restaurant bill, or a train or bus ticket.

But, as we can see, as inscriptions in the strict sense come into play, the pieces of paper, such as receipts with legal value, not to mention money, begin to take on the hue of an institutional reality, where the application of the law Object = Inscribed Act is strict and literal. This is not a matter of informal custom, but rather of genuinely codified inscriptions. It is in this sense that we need the distinction between archiwriting and writing, between registrations of traces in people's minds that generally recalls writing and what is in the full and strict sense writing. In this respect, archiwriting is memory, custom, ritual, etiquette, habit, and the famous "unwritten laws" that we discussed in 4.1.2.4 and 4.2.2; writing, on the other hand, is what we find on a piece of paper or in the file of a computer. As we saw in the last part, writing is a species of the genus "archiwriting." Archiwriting surrounds writing; in other words, the latter is nothing but a modification of the former; in set-theoretical terms, the set of writings is a subset of the set of archiwritings.[28]

5.1.3.3 INSTITUTIONAL OBJECTS An analogous relation to the one that holds between archiwriting and writing can be seen to hold between the realm of the social and that of the institutional. The basic hypothesis is that institutions are specializations of social reality, just as writing is a specialization of archiwriting:

Social
Institutional

If the law Object = Inscribed Act holds, then there is an underlying continuity between social objects and institutional objects, which derives from the inscription, while there is a discontinuity in virtue of the formalization and codification of the inscriptions, which is precisely at the point where archiwriting becomes writing. When we have to deal with institutional realities, the law Object = Inscribed Act is to be taken literally. To make this point less vague, we may illustrate the relations between the institutional and the social with a diagram like the following.

Institutional	*Social*
Linguistic	Not necessarily linguistic
Deliberate	Not necessarily deliberate
Historical	Not necessarily historical
Emendable	Unemendable

From this table it can be seen that institutional reality has some of the features of science, while the social has those of experience in the sense explained in 2.2.3. By this I mean that, while we cannot have science without language, without deliberation, without historical depth yet subject to constant renewal, we certainly can have experience that is nonlinguistic, that is undeliberate, that is ahistorical but that, considered as something that has happened, cannot be revised. Likewise, on the hypothesis I am suggesting, institutions are codified, deliberate, historical, and emendable structures within a social life full of tacit accords, customs, and events that need no linguistic expression and may even elude being put into words. There is thus a dissociation between words and things: the film mafioso who says, "Let us kiss hands," is not performing the equivalent of a hand-kissing. As regards the polarity between the emendable and the unemendable, it must be understood in a lax way to allow for a relative revisability of the institutional, which proceeds bureaucratically with norms and rules, and a relative unrevisability of the social, which proceeds by way of tradition, with "unwritten rules" that are hard to spell out and hence to modify.

In short, institutional objects are much more subject to codified norms than social objects are. From this it follows that institutional objects may, though they need not, produce further norms. A wedding does not produce other weddings; at most it may produce a divorce; but the title of mayor confers, among other things, the power to officiate at weddings. In this sense, the acts that underlie institutional objects are, in the terminology of Czeslaw Znamierowski, "thetic acts" which is to say acts that "would not exist if there were no norms,"[29] and for that reason appear particularly adapted for producing norms and thus creating ever stricter application of the law Object = Inscribed Act.

The details of the phenomenology of institutions relative to social reality seems to me a less important task than making clear the central point namely the role that documents play in social reality and, all the more so, in institutional reality. Thus, a theory of social objects and of their specialization in institutional objects evolves naturally into a theory of documents.

5.1.4 *The Theory of Documents*

In general, a theory of documents has to take account of at least seven entities.[30]

1. The different types of document, from informal notes to formal and solemn documents;
2. Their various physical realizations;
3. The different operations that can be performed on documents (filling in, signing, countersigning, stamping, copying, authenticating, transmitting, invalidating, destroying);
4. The various acts that can be executed thanks to documents (concessions, loans, declarations, and so on);
5. The diverse ways (both felicitous and infelicitous) in which those acts can be realized;
6. The institutional systems to which documents belong and their role in them;
7. The provenance of documents (the differences between original, copy and fake).

So far, I have looked into points 2–6, and the last part of the book is dedicated to point 7. As regards point 1, I think that the theory is satisfied by the individuation of the sphere of *documentality*, which includes both *strong* documents, which are inscriptions of acts within institutional realities and present themselves as documents in the full sense,[31] as well as *weak* documents, which include not only strong documents that have lapsed to the state of mere registrations (banknotes that are no longer current, expired passports) but also registrations of facts that need not be public or intentional, but that, in certain circumstances, can take on documental value even without being documents in the narrow sense (compare a fingerprint included in a passport and a fingerprint found on a safe). In this scheme, artworks are given their own place, as we see in 5.2, as documents in the strong sense—that is, as inscriptions and expressions of acts—but that, unlike the expired passport, never lose their purpose because they are conceived from the beginning as having an internal finality. Let us look at the two main types of documents.

5.1.4.1 STRONG DOCUMENTS AND WEAK DOCUMENTS   It is often said that a document is a representation, but it is not clear what is meant by "representation." It would seem that, in the literal sense, a document *attests*, a verb in which we should hear the resonance of the act that produced the document. Otherwise, it would be hard to explain how my identity card represents me, or my Italian citizenship, or that rather elusive thing that is my identity. Attesting is thus a basic activity of documenting, and, in line with the law Object = Inscribed Act, it comes as no surprise that attestation is properly speaking the inscription of an act. Attestation is permanent over time in virtue of the persistence of the physical medium, and it has social value in virtue of the disposition of its subjects.

As we have anticipated, a strong document is the *inscription of an act*, an attestation that endures in time and has social value, while a weak one is the *registration of a fact*. The registration of a fact can be unintentional, as when the forensic scientists discover a trace, an archaeologist unearths a find or a doctor notices a symptom of a disease in a clinical file, the last of which is a document in the weak sense but is clearly intentional. In this scheme, a document in the strong sense is mostly linked to writing, while one in the weak sense may be, as in the cases of traces and discoveries, connected rather to archiwriting, though it need not be so, because the notes in a clinical file are at least in part writing of a very traditional sort.

There is an important ontological difference between strong and weak documents insofar as the former is an *act*, while the latter is *evidence* that may be employed in an act, but need not be and indeed very rarely is. Conversely, it can happen that acts are used as evidence.[32] I can use the register kept at a degree ceremony to prove in court that one of the professors could not have committed a murder that took place at the same time as the ceremony. But characteristically, considered as attestations, documents hardly function as evidence of *what they attest* on pain of circularity. I can show my degree certificate in medicine to prove that I am not an impostor, but what makes it evidence is that it is a valid certificate, in such a way that if its validity were put in doubt, for instance in court, I would have to produce extra evidence to vindicate it. In other words, a document cannot be evidence for its own validity.[33]

Despite this peculiar difference between them, strong and weak documents have in common the fact of being valid only in a context. As I have said, I can make use of a strong medieval document, such as a will, as an attestation that the testator owned certain goods, and I can write it up in an article on local history. Though its legal function has expired, the strong document has found a new function as a weak document that is valid for the historian. In each case, however, there must be a tribunal of at least two persons that is ready to consider the document as such. This holds all the more for unintended documents, such as traces and findings, which never had documental value in themselves, but acquire it within a certain juridical, technical or political context, which can intervene to make the trace evident, as when the police discover a trace of DNA or of carbon-14, which are not visible to the naked eye.

5.1.4.2 DOCUMENTS AND PERFORMATIVES Sticking with strong documents, the fact that they are inscriptions carries with it three main features.

First, a strong document is not monological, and it is not the objectivization of an individual spirit, but it is rather the potentially public registration of an act that concerns at least two persons. In this framework, a document in the strong sense is generally characterized by the inscription of a declarative act; a status may be attributed (the award of a degree), conditions may be set for the acquisition of a status (laws in general), or the existence of an institution is established (statutes and the like).

Second, the documental function, which puts an act into form, inscribes it, and disposes it as an attestation is the true equivalent and the only concrete realization of Kant's schematism; the "art hidden deep in the human soul" is that of the notary, the bureaucrat, the registrar of births, deaths and marriages and so on, who gives form to documents. The form of a document is what makes it an *instrumentum*, which, for the Justinian Code, meant "written act," "written document," and "documental writ."

Third, a strong document is not descriptive but performative. It is not intended to be a bearer of knowledge, even though it can incidentally also do that; but it aims to produce effects, which is what often happens with the attestation of an act. These performative features are in large measure lost in weak documents, which are rather descriptive and vehicles of knowledge, and at best attest an individual's behavior (I leave my fingerprints while breaking and entering, and I keep a diary in prison to vent my despair). On the other hand, these features are to be found in artworks, where the representative as well as the performative rather than the descriptive are to the fore.

The fact that documents belong to the realm of the performative is ontologically decisive, and the fact that we are often inattentive to the theory of performatives explains why weak documents can easily be confused with strong ones. On the other hand, the fact that the theory of performatives has been traditionally applied to speech acts, without due consideration to written acts, which are basic to the construction of social reality, has led to very little recognition of the fact that, rather than being just one instance of the kind, strong documents are the paradigm case of the performative. Instead philosophers have sometimes regarded them as signs (and hence as weak, constative documents) of the fact that a performative, and hence an attribution with social value, has taken place. From this point of view, it is worth recalling what we argued in 3.1.1.3 and 3.3.2.5, namely that the classical theory of performatives, primarily regarding speech acts, seems not to take account of the way that these expressions could hardly reach the level of performatives in the absence of written registrations, of the sort that is typical of marriages, baptisms and wills. And we may note that lottery tickets demonstrate as well as anything could that even betting can be formalized in writing.

In this sense, the interpretations of documents as "objectivizations of the spirit"[34] turn out to be mistaken in two ways. On the one hand, strong documents are inscriptions of acts, which would not exist without the inscriptions, and not objectivizations of a spirit that could exist even without such objectivizations (we return to the point in 5.3). On the other, weak documents are not necessarily the manifestation of a spirit and often enough are not even the expression of an intention.

5.1.4.3 DOCUMENTAL PYRAMID   As will have become apparent, here we see a convergence among various documental hierarchies. The first was set out in 1.3.3.3, on inscribed artifacts, and consisted in the sequence *things, instruments, works, documents*. The second, which has been emerging as we have proceeded, consists in the series *traces, registrations, inscriptions, documents*. The third, which we have just been looking at, is the distinction between weak and strong documents. It might properly be asked how these hierarchies interconnect. In effect, they refer, respectively, to the socialization of objects, to the structure of the inscriptions that ensure that socialization, and to the inner hierarchy of documents. A thing is more socialized in proportion to its being more inscribed, so that an identity card has a greater social depth than a pebble used as a paperweight, which also enjoys a sort of inscription by the fact of being in a certain context. On the other hand, a thing is more socialized in proportion to the quality of the writing that figures on it, so that a pebble with a ritual inscription has greater social significance than the pebble used as a paperweight. The most important form of inscription is the inscription of an act. We may illustrate this with a documental pyramid:

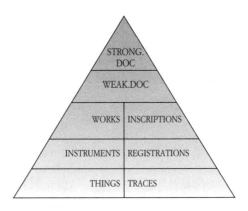

Characteristics of institutions

5.1.4.4 BARE LIFE AND GOVERNMENTALITY   A final consideration of the power of documents: The secret power of bureaucracy is that of producing acts, fixing them, making them available beyond the here-and-now that generated them, and making them transportable. In this respect, this power is like the power of science as registration and transmission. But there is one, in my view crucial, difference: here we are dealing not with the registration and the relaying of facts, but with, above all else, acts. Documentality thus comes to be the foundation of what Foucault called "governmentality,"[35] and of its developments in biopolitics.[36]

With the hypothesis of documentality, I would like to offer a paradigm capable of making sense of the fact that citizens feel themselves much more controlled, and hence subject to the multiple pressures of power, than they did in totalitarian regimes, and that this, much more that the idea of control of power over life, is the fundamental sentiment of technologically advanced states. Power is more capillary and effective today because we have seen a growth in the systems of registration, both in the weak documents (evidence gathering, control, hacking) and in the speed with which strong documents can be produced (delivery of acts, complex bureaucratic executions). Despite the illusions that once were fostered and the appearances of all times, the explosion of writing on which I have been insisting in the book has not led to an increase in emancipation but to a growth in control, where the upside is an increase in rights because they are better documented. The notion of *documentality* aims to capture and recognize the role of bureaucracy; bureaucracy is not an accident, and the paperwork is indispensable to live and to have power.[37] Biopolitics, the power over life and death, certainly can become capillary, but it can do so only through the increasing sophistication of the bureaucratic machinery, of the systems of registering and tracing, which is where, in 5.3.2.3 and 5.3.2.4, we look for the essence of politics.

5.2 WORKS

In 5.1 I tried to show the pragmatic power of documents in the ordinary sense, and in the next I propose a general theory of culture. Before doing so, it seems to me useful to offer a detailed analysis of another kind of documental inscriptions, namely artworks, that, here too, can be skipped by a reader who is in a hurry. Discussing "inscribed artifacts," I referred briefly in 1.3.3.3 to these objects that are so important in the social world: artworks do not answer primarily to practical needs but rather, in our culture (which is by no means universal) to values of pure prestige or entertainment or disinterested education. This is a realm that I have elsewhere highlighted with the metaphor of the "automatic girlfriend," meaning that the relations we establish with artworks can be likened to those we have with other persons.[38]

I think that the best was of expressing the difference between the documents we have been discussing so far and those to be discussed now is in terms of the fact that the former serve *negotium* while the latter are for *otium*. For all the advantages that may flow from an esthetic education and for all the turnover generated by the market in artworks, films, rock concerts, and literary best-sellers, the fact remains that the basic reference point is that of recreation, which is altogether different from the world of international treaties, driver's licenses, checks, supermarket receipts, and parking tickets. Artworks constitute so to say the futile peak of the documental pyramid that I set out in 5.1. They are inscriptions of acts that have no practical purpose and, at the same time, they are material objects that have no instrumental value.

There are two basic reasons for giving over space to artworks within my theory and for choosing to privilege them among the objects of the phenomenology of the letter that I propose in 5.3. On the one hand, artworks are the high point of social reality inasmuch as they are social objects whose value does not reside in the power that they directly procure (as in the case of documents), but rather in the hypersociality that is prestige or in their entertainment value. On the other hand, I suspect that, if we use documents and social objects as a key, we have a good chance of unlocking the phenomenon of artworks, which has traditionally been rather swathed in mystery. Here I would like to concentrate on two essential features that I have just mentioned: artworks as things and artworks as documents.

5.2.1 Artworks as Things

It seems very easy to understand an artwork as a thing, given that merely saying so seems a banality. But after all it is not quite so easy, if we recall that there is a strong pull to say that there is an ontological leap from a mere thing to an artwork.[39] Even the esthetic theories that have emphasized the way that an artwork is a thing have often concentrated on avant-garde productions,[40] as if the thingness of artworks were a recent discovery. And we should not forget that these thing-esthetics have generally focused primarily on the visual arts, which is a limitation of the claims they make. What I want to show is that thingness holds of all artworks and that the passage from the thing to the artwork depends on an increase in inscription in line with the second part of my theory regarding the relationship between artworks and documents.

5.2.1.1 HOW TO AVOID FRUSTRATION IN ART Let us begin with a banal thought. Frustration is one of the most common experiences in the face of contemporary art. Gallery owners are perfectly aware of this, and, by way of consolation, they put on their exhibitions in very elegant galleries and accompany the shows with white wine and nibbles. One of the most common explanations of this is that, being part of a market system in which the mass media play a decisive role, contemporary art goes in search of provocation and paradox. This seems to be a necessary explanation; but it is not sufficient because it runs the risk of making us lose contact with the essence of contemporary art, and indeed of art in general. So it is this false impression that I wish to correct with two consolations and one constructive suggestion.

The first consolation is that we should not assume that we understand or really like classical or beautiful art. When we see the *Mona Lisa* in the Louvre through a thicket of Japanese tourists, we are often disappointed. It may be that we are tired, that our feet hurt or that we want to sit down; but the fundamental point is that the pleasure we expected does not happen or, at best, it is exactly what we get from a postcard of the painting. The truth is that the fact that the *Mona Lisa* represents a lady's face does not make it any more understandable than a work by Duchamp or Francis Bacon. It is just that we are ashamed to admit it.

The second consolation is that, even though "contemporary art" is often used to mean avant-garde visual art, this is by no means the most typical sort. To be sure, it is the sort that is most difficult to understand but, happily, there a mass of other art that is pleasing and comprehensible as well as being, I add, equally esthetically worthy. I have in mind pop art and things like novels, movies, and rock concerts. In short, it is just not true that visual art is the only paradigm of modernity. Pop in all its manifestations is another paradigm and is not in the least incomprehensible; sometimes it is all too comprehensible.

The constructive suggestion is the question: Are we really sure that contemporary art is incomprehensible? After all, they are objects like any other and, as such, have a lot to learn from design, which has itself shuffled the line between instruments for use and artworks. We would do well to abandon the superstitious distinction between everyday things and these slightly sacred and slightly vain objects that are artworks. We would do well to look at the works not just of contemporary art but also at those of more traditional art as if they were coffee makers or iPods. We would probably understand them much better than if we went in some frustrating search for a secret meaning.

5.2.1.2 READY-MADES In this connection, it is perhaps not an accident that the consecration of Pop Art was Andy Warhol's 1964 exhibition in a New York gallery of a set of supermarket products: Kellogg's Corn Flakes, Del Monte peaches in syrup, Campbell's tomato soup, Heinz ketchup. But the laurels went to the box of Brillo Pads, which was decked out in the elegant design of the abstract expressionist James Harvey, who was making honest money out of commercial art.

Harvey is not much remembered today, which is a pity, but there is no doubt that it was Andy Warhol who had the fundamental intuition in deciding to select and literally to magnify (increasing the physical dimensions) those groceries. Given that the boxes in question were in any case handsome, Warhol made one concession to the canons of traditional art, but he picked up another insight taken from Marcel Duchamp who in 1917 had put an inverted urinal on display in an art gallery. Much has been made of the provocation, of the fact that the urinal suggested that anything whatever could become a work of art, so that the ontologically constructive point has been overlooked, namely that the gesture itself showed that *a work of art is essentially a thing.*

As we said in connection also with the Copernican Revolution, it is not so hard to see things as Kant saw them, once he taught us how—for we have noticed that the art world is a world of objects. And this seems to hold especially of contemporary art. In 2007 at the Venice Biennale, Sophie Calle put on her *Prenez Soin de Vous.* It was only fair to ask: Where is the work? Was it in the pavilion or in the accompanying book? For it would be wrong to call the book a *catalogue*, because it was not a reproduction, but the original. More radically, where were the works—in the national pavilions or in that international pavilion where they sell the catalogues, rubbers, penholders, fridge magnets, but alas no longer snow globes,[41] because they are regarded as kitsch?

This is what the ready-made has taught us, and it is most startlingly confirmed not in avant-garde galleries, but in more traditional venues. After all, seventeenth-century aristocratic galleries, the ancestors of the modern museum, would display alongside pictures also pistols and armor in a way no different from Duchamp. From the point of view of the ready-made, archeological museums are hypertransgressive because they gather tomb-stones, sarcophagi, amphoras, buckles, and whatnot. And then there is that variant on the ready-made that is body art, given that the exhibition of bodies are artworks is the norm in Egyptian museums that display mummies, not to mention Pompeii, where the show includes casts of human beings in the act of dying.

If this thought is surprising, perhaps it is because we do not reflect sufficiently on what is a "thing," "instrument," or "artwork," on what is a "museum," "catalog," "library," or on the slightly opaque laws that govern the distinctions among such entities. For instance, museums only rarely contain books, the exceptions being when they are visual poetry or—and here we are back with Duchamp's ontological intuition—destroyed books, bits of pages and a cover as in the *Mariée mise a nu*, which managed to get a book back into a museum. But the overwhelming majority of books in museums do not execute the *ergon* of the work, but rather have the role of *parergon*, of something that surrounds the work, as a frame surrounds a picture. We find them in the museum bookstore along with postcards, jute bags, diaries, erasers, and pencils; they are *parerga* that nevertheless have a role to play in the experience of artworks, of the *ergon*, just like the white wine and nibbles at the *vernissage*.

5.2.1.3 SIZES   To show that recourse to ready-mades does not mean that anything whatever can be a work of art we may note that, contrary to the conventionalist claim, there are objects fairly close to hand that *cannot* become artworks for various reasons, including mere considerations of size. For instance, a statue that is more than twenty kilometers tall cannot become a "work," and perhaps one that is a mere two kilometers tall is already too big. It is true that nano-art exists, with very interesting artifacts that can only be seen with a microscope, but the fact remains that the work in such a case is the ensemble of the nano-object and the microscope that makes it visible, just as Christo's wrapping of the Great Wall of China really finds its expression in the catalogs that document the "performance."

The size criterion shows that artworks share some features with things in common use, including the fact of fitting, by way of dimension and duration, into a human environment, in the way I tried to outline in 2.2.3.3. As Aby Warburg might have said, the good God is in the sizes; in the end, we are used to supposing that the question of dimension is extrinsic to art, but when a work cannot be seen all at once with the naked eye or calls for, for instance a trip to an orbiting space station, then we are outside the realm of works proper, while to say that a city is "on the human scale" is to praise it.

This holds not only for space, but also for time. At a certain time, people want to go to sleep, and I suppose that Aristotle had this in mind when he proposed that a tragedy should observe unities of time, place, and action. Let us imagine a novel that is a million pages long. Who would have the courage to launch themselves, at the age of fifty, on such an enterprise? And would even a youngster begin reading it, given that he has to plan on doing something else with his life? The duration of a work has to fit in with human live: we cannot imagine a symphony that lasts a thousand years; and if it calls for a certain stamina to listen to the more than eighteen hours of piano music that make up Erik Satie's *Vexations*, superhuman endurance is required by John Cage's *As Slow As Possible*, which would last 733 years. Time makes quite a difference. Andy Warhol's *Empire*, twenty-four hours of the Empire State Building taken from a single angle, tried the patience of film lovers, and even Wagner's *Ring* runs into serious production problems.

5.2.1.4 THINGS THAT PRETEND TO BE PERSONS   The continuity between things and works allows us to formulate an ontology of artworks under six headings.[42]

First, art is the class of the works. The common denominator of the practices that make use of different media and different materials at various times with the most various purposes is the fact that they end up with works that have the feature of *poiesis* as discussed in 3.3.2.1. This is a very broad but not infinite class. As we have seen, the fact of ready-mades does not mean that anything can be an artwork. Rather, a work of art is in the first instance a thing with definite physical features as regards size, duration, and perceptibility by the senses.

Second, despite the aspirations of conceptual art and those of the postmodernists who talk of art and reality as complementary fictions, works are above all physical objects. It is not a mere opinion that art has to do with *aisthesis*, but rather a fact that can be established by anyone who tries to replace a concert with a written account of a concert, an exhibition with a review of it, a novel with a summary or a poem with paraphrase.

Third, works are social objects. It is senseless to talk of works without referring to human beings who share our or a similar culture. We can easily imagine societies that do not create things like artworks, and indeed there are cultures in which the realm of art is not distinguished from that of religion or of folklore; but we cannot imagine that there would be artworks for a man left alone in the world. Like promises, bets, honorific titles, artworks exist only in a society, even one made up of only two persons.

Fourth, artworks produce knowledge only accidentally. While there are forms of art, such as narrative and portrait painting, that do transmit knowledge, there are some civilizations of which remain only artistic productions, which have thus become the only knowledge we have of them. But this does not at all mean that knowledge is the primary function of art. It is possible to learn something about Ireland by reading James Joyce, but it is much easier and more efficient to buy a guidebook or a history.

Fifth, artworks necessarily stimulate some sentiment. What we expect from works are sentiments and emotions, which are the same things that documents produce in us, except that they are generalizable and disinterested, where documents, such as a fine or a lottery win, are individual and interested.

Sixth, artworks are things that pretend to be persons. The judgments we pass on artworks are very similar to those that we formulate about persons. To say that a person leaves us indifferent is the same sort of negative comment that could be used of an artwork, while to say that a screwdriver or a telephone, considered from the instrumental point of view, leaves us indifferent is not a criticism, but just an odd thing to say.

5.2.2 Artwork as Document

What turns a thing into an artwork? The answer is: Inscription, which confirms the continuity between artworks. On these grounds, I believe that the best way of explaining that peculiar kind of object that is an artwork is *Work = Inscribed Act*, and this formula should be understood as a necessary but not sufficient condition: for there to be a work, an inscribed act is needed but it is obvious that there are many inscribed act that are not works.

5.2.2.1 WORK = INSCRIBED ACT   Let us see how this works. The work is the result of an act that involves at least one author and one addressee: even a person who writes "for himself" at least postulates a reader. On this understanding, works present themselves as a peculiar type of document, that is, as inscriptions that register social acts. In some cases, more often than with normal social objects, the object coincides physically with the inscription, as in the case of a painting or a novel, but not in that of a symphony.

The specific reason why I think that the rule *Work = Inscribed Act* is preferable to the formula "X counts as Y in C" is that it applies to all forms of art, where Searle's version is applicable only to ready-mades.[43] Francis Ford Coppola did not just take a load of celluloid and baptize it *Apocalypse Now*; if he had done so, perhaps a better title would have been *Laocoön*. But he did not. What he did was to compose the script, meet backers to whom he explained his project, ask for permissions, sign contracts with the actors and distribution houses, and so on; what he filmed, registering on celluloid, depended directly on those acts and the inscriptions that followed from them. The same goes for old artworks: Botticelli did not take a wooden board with colors painted on it and baptize it *The Birth of Venus*; rather, he planned a painting as such, did some preparatory sketches, and then applied paint within the context of commissions and cultural codes.

As will have been noted, artworks are perfect examples of the "documental pyramid" illustrated in 5.1.4.3. On the one hand, it is an object that sits atop the hierarchy that runs from things to works passing through instruments. It is in this respect that I have insisted on the way that ready-mades have a certain paradigmatic character; works share with things the medium size and the presence within the human world, and there is nothing surprising about the way that things and instruments can become works under certain conditions. But what determines this passage is what we might call the "increase in inscription." Trivially, it is enough for a weapon or a buckle to be placed in a showcase in a museum accompanied by an explanatory caption, which is a central factor whose significance is easily overlooked. This fact shows the central role played by inscription in the transfiguration of the ready-made. On the other hand, it is not surprising that there are works, such as literary and musical ones, that are inscriptions from the very start. in this sense, the law Work = Inscribed Act is a more general theory of which "X counts as Y in C" is just a particular instance.

5.2.2.2 STORIES AND TEXTS FOR NOTHING   So far we have been concentrating on the analogies between artworks and documents. Let us look now at the differences. Works are located in an institutional setting in that we cannot imagine a work without institutions, just as we found for documents, but they do not have the powers of documents; rather their power or prestige consists in their uselessness. The Kantian notion of "purposefulness without purpose" can be applied to this fact. Works seem to have an end or purpose, but then we discover that they do not or that, just as with persons on the Kantian understanding, they do have one, but it is in themselves or it is an internal purposefulness. Typically, when the development of firearms made armor useless, there began the esthetic contemplation of it in terms of it design and ornamentation.

Here we find a second difference between works and documents. While signatures and documents take the place of their authors, it would seem that works are much more similar to personas, and it is in light of this that they have privileged status in our culture. As we have seen, works are social objects, which exist as such and not as merely physical objects because humans think that they do, precisely as happens with those social objects that we call *documents*. On this scheme, the work is an idiomatic inscription that pretends to be a person. The work seems to address us and it seems to be the work itself and not its author that does this as if it had representations, thoughts, and sentiments.[44] Unlike documents, works, which are undoubtedly objects, present themselves as quasi-subjects, as instances in which the inscription seems to promote an intention on its own account.

A further reflection on the relation between art and documents. Some philosophers maintain that the question about the ontology of art is ill framed if it is of the form, "What is art?" Rather, we should be asking, "When is art?"[45] There is no dispute about that. There are historical conditions and circumstances of exhibition that make a document become an artwork or that make an artwork regress (or progress, according to one's point of view) to the status of mere document. An analysis of these conditions and circumstances does not mean, however, that there can be no ontology of art, but rather that the ontology of art does not have access to the highest level, so to speak, which determines the passage of the inscription to the status of document or artwork. This highest level calls for a very strong institutional input. For documents, there are parliaments and attorneys; for artworks, there are publishers, museums, and critics.

Thus, an artwork is a social object that is founded on institutional objects. But, it might be asked, what sort of institutional object is a museum? Or a critic? What constitutes their normative value? And the answer is fairly straightforward: They depend on other inscriptions. The social world is circular, and this is no surprise.[46] From this it does not follow that a critic's fiat suffices to turn a tropical hurricane into an artwork; it may be necessary, as we have seen in considering the thingness of works, that certain sufficient conditions of size and inscribedness be observed. But once these conditions are fulfilled, a critic may say that a given thing is a masterpiece; but that does not mean he will be believed. Let us look now at the features of artistic inscription.

5.2.2.3 CUTS In line with the law Object = Inscribed Act, an artwork is the result of an expression that involves at least two persons, such as a writer and a reader or a painter and a patron, and that is inscribed, which is to say fixed on some medium such as paper, wood, stone, or a computer chip, or even just in the heads of the persons involved, as in the case of a performance. Just as the ready-made seemed to illustrate particularly clearly the fact that a work is a thing, I think that Lucio Fontana's slashed canvases are a perfect illustration of, even the essence of, the work as inscription. Reducing painting to pure inscription Fontana achieves many things: He finds the element common to all forms of art; he offers works that are in effect somewhere between sculpture, painting, and literature (because after all, the model of the page is omnipresent); and he reduces to a single trace both figure and signature because Fontana's slashes are immediately recognizable and idiomatic, and they cannot be confused with anything figurative like a signature, which is often an illegible scribble and not merely the reproduction of the signer's name. In light of these considerations, we are in a position to offer a phenomenology parallel to that proposed in 4.3.3 for inscriptions in general.

Traces. The trace is the basic element of the work as it is for any inscription. A trace is out there in the world, the modification of a surface. A work without trace is strictly inconceivable, as follows from what we have said about the work as a physical object. Obviously, a trace is a necessary but not a sufficient condition of there being an artwork: not every trace is a work, indeed almost all traces are not; yet there can be no work without a trace: paintings, books, symphonies, songs, performances, films, and soap operas all need, in order to be realized, some possibility of inscribing something, even if it is only in the minds of persons. Think of a jazz jam session with no score and no recording; its only trace is in the minds of the spectators and the players. I do not think much need be added here, if not a simple thought experiment: Try to imagine a work without traces; from the fact that you cannot, you will understand that there is no work without traces.

Impression. There are two dimensions to a trace. One is the fact that something physical, a sound, a color, some ink, is present in the world; the other is that this event is registered in a mind (and in this case, too, we have an inscription that can be picked up by a brain scan). There are no traces except for the minds that observe them and register them as other traces. This follows naturally from the fact that the work is a social object, which is to say something that exists only because there are minds (not necessarily human minds) that are able to register it. Nevertheless, when a trace is in a mind, it is an impression, which is not of itself at all social, and hence is not at all artistic. I can have a childhood memory or a dream, but this is not by any means an artwork. The same applies if I look at a work and do not recognize it as such: it will be simply a physical object with certain characteristics for me and this is completely different from what happens when I know, or merely suspect, that the thing is art. In that case, I contemplate it with the supposition that other humans exist who are ready to share my sentiments; these are the humans who make the work what it is. Here is a possible case of collective intentionality, but also a demonstration of how little that sort of intentionality can explain about the working of society and especially about how indispensable documents, in this case artworks, are to bring it into being.

Expression. The decisive passage toward the status of the artwork lies with expression, which involves at least two people. The minimum condition for the existence of art is thus the same as what is required for the existence of a society: two persons, an addresser and an addressee, an artist and a client, a promissor and a promissee, a creditor and a debtor. At this point we have made the move from the level of impression to that of expression. I can give an order, make a bet, compose a poem in rhyming couplets, challenge someone to a duel. In all these cases, we see an essential difference between the purely psychological level of the impression and the social level of expression. If it is true that there is all the difference in the world between saying and doing, we should add that there is an even greater conceptual difference between thinking and saying, writing or showing. For the difference between thinking about giving an order and giving an order, between thinking about composing a poem in rhyming couplets and composing a poem in rhyming couplets is to all intents and purposes the difference between nothing and something. The mere thought has no social importance until it is expressed, even if it comes out as a slip of the tongue or an omission.

Work. If, as we have seen, an expression shares the formal features of a work, what makes an expression into a "work"? Nothing ontological, but lots of history, psychology, and social reality: taste, circumstances, the coordinates of an era, just as we find with documents. Just as a document can easily not be recognized as valid, or even not be recognized as a document, in a state different from the one that issued it, just so it can happen to a masterpiece that, with the passing of just a few decades, it becomes nothing more than evidence about the period in which it was made, and then be rediscovered as a result of the unpredictable fluctuations of taste. This has happened to Italian poet Giosuè Carducci, to Liberty style, to academic art, and to many other styles, movements, and works. But—and this may give pause for thought—it has never happened to ideal objects, such as numbers and theorems; nor to natural events, such as tsunamis or spring showers; nor yet to yesterday's dreams or artists' unexpressed thoughts. The reason for this is simply that in these cases we do not have to deal with inscribed acts, which are thus confirmed as the necessary but not sufficient condition for the existence of an artwork, as it is for the existence of any social object whatever.

5.3 THE PHENOMENOLOGY OF THE LETTER

5.3.1 *.Doc: the Revelation of the Essence*

Now that we have examined the two principal functions of documents, for their usefulness in life and their uselessness in art, the time has come to make sense of what we have been saying in passing from the catalog of the world to social objects, from there to the law Object = Inscribed Act, to the role of inscriptions in the construction of social and mental reality and so to the notion of *documentality*. This sense emerges from the contingencies of recent technological changes, but it reveals an essence that was at work long before these transformations came about.

5.3.1.1 DOCUMENTAL COMMUNITIES What is the real power source for this gigantic earthquake? Often enough, we hear it said that it all depends on the virtual, which can mean anything or nothing. For myself, I would propose a slightly narrower response: in line with what we said in 5.1.1, the true hero is the extension .doc, the abbreviation of document that has invaded our lives over recent decades. A number of elements are mixed together here to prove the basis of what we might call *documental communities*, which are built on the sharing of documents and protocols that take the place of words and physical proximity.[47] There is no good reason to suppose that such communities need be any less authentic than "natural" communities. To be sure, they involve a lot more dialog and a lot more documentalization of life; but this is by no means a novelty, given that Goethe's Werther and Foscolo's Jacopo Ortis did all their pining and whining in the chat rooms of the day. More seriously, religions have been founded on books, nations on the sharing of laws, and the birth of public opinion is closely dependent on the existence of newspapers.[48]

But, as always, the Web, that great network of writings and registrations, has led to a qualitative leap, not to mention the transformations in arrival from biotechnologies where, once more, the management of life is becoming ever more documental, from DNA to protocols for assisted fertilization, to families based on documents and not on heredity. If this is how things stand, then we are on the threshold of a change in which will be realized the rabbinical tradition that wanted the world to be made up of an aggregation of letters.[49] Here, then, is the point that has perhaps been hidden by the size and speed of the technological turn: *What this story unveils, for all the contingency of its particular passages, is not an accident, but the essence.*

5.3.1.2 THE *GEIST* MODEL AND THE .DOC MODEL   There is no doubt that we are witnessing mutations that are linked to technological contingencies. Yet what these innovations reveal is nothing that is radically new, but rather as old as history, namely writing and its power. But it is not the simple reemergence of an archaism. Instead, if the hypothesis I have been arguing for holds true, then what is making itself manifest, with all the force of the return of the repressed, is the essence of what we call spirit, which animates our individual and social lives. This essence is revealed as being determined by the letter, by the letters that are at the heart of the transformation that is underway. However important they may be, we may set to one side the historical contingencies and concentrate on reconsidering everything that has been traditionally regarded as belonging to the category of the spirit and on reconceiving of it as a modification of the letter.[50] I am aware that this claim appears to undervalue the role of spirit, or at least (given that derivation is not always subordination) it seems to impact frontally with the Pauline message that the letter killeth, but the spirit giveth life (2 Cor. 3:6). This is fair enough, but I wonder whether that message was not the expression of a prejudice, which expresses an ancient hatred of the written word, from Plato's condemnation of writing down to the curious anti-Semitism of writing manifested by Baudelaire when he writes in an astonishing fragment, "*Mon coeur mis à nu*": "A fine conspiracy to be organized for the extermination of the Jewish Race. The Jews, libraries and the witnesses of the Redemption."[51]

Why is there this hatred? On the one hand, it involves an anti-Semitic, and for that reason particularly shocking, version of a prejudice that in other cases may pass unnoticed: a certain disquiet or discomfort with technique, a cult of improvisation and spontaneity, the idea that immediacy and authenticity go together and above all that what appears to be immediate should really be so. All of these are notions that make us prefer, in an imaginary hierarchy, the voice to writing, except that we then appeal to writing in important business. Deep down, the attitude that finds its extreme in the anti-Semitism of the letter derives from the love we have for our own lives, of our demand to be at the beginning of a chain, to have at least a touch of something original and unique about us, to be anything but a robot. Except that we are then surprised by our own and others' banality and predictability, and by the answers we get from call centers.

It is a sort of repression that makes us prefer the spirit to the letter, as in the dialogue Plato presents between Solon and the priests of Sais.[52] Solon recounts the origin of the world in the Greek fashion, with the flood and Deucalion and Pyrrha throwing down stones to bring mankind back to life. So the priests make fun of him for thinking that he is describing the first flood, when it is just one of the many that have washed over the Earth and washed away the Greeks' archives (but not the Egyptians'), canceling all memory of them. *De te fabula narratur* (the story is being told about you): When you prefer the spirit to the letter, you believe (and demand) to be at the beginning, when in fact you are at the end, of the chain.

If things stand as I have tried to describe so far, my next task is to set out a phenomenology of the realms in which documentality intervenes, which I propose to call a *phenomenology of the letter*, by way of contrast with Hegel's

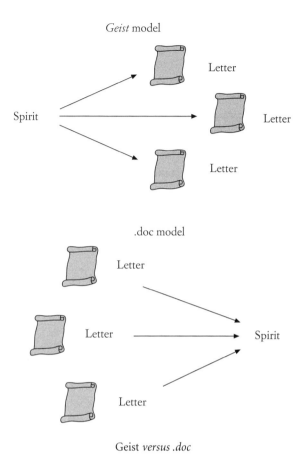

Geist *versus .doc*

phenomenology of the spirit. In the Hegelian notion of "spirit" there is the underlying assumption that there is an autonomous entity, free of any material foundation, which is objective in institutions or makes itself evident independently of them as an absolute. I think that we have left this notion behind us and abandoned it as one of the old relics of philosophy; yet, when we claim the existence of a European spirit or of an artist's original creativity or again of collective intentionality—and many more cases besides—there is an allusion to precisely that ghost that, unlike the one invoked in *The Communist Manifesto*, does not restrict itself to haunting Europe, but rather moves about freely, not merely unmolested but above all uninterrogated in so many philosophies that believe that they have nothing to do with the spirit.

Here we come to the heart of what I have been saying, which, despite appearances, is not a critique of spirit, but rather an effort to explain what is going on. On this scheme, what I propose is not so much an overturning of Hegel as a fulfillment of what he said about spirit and of what others have continued to say about its various declinations, which turns out to be concerned with the letter. Only when the conditions for this have been recognized will it be meaningful to talk about "spirit." Rather than think of spirit as something that descends on the world from on high like a divine flame and that is then solidified in documents, which is what I call the the *Geist* model, we should think of the letters that, within the world of a culture, a psyche, and a society, give life to as spirit that, as represented above, I call the .doc model.

5.3.2 Objective Spirit

To set in motion my rereading of spirit in terms of letters, I do not recur to the question of subjective spirit, which I hope to have resolved into letters in 4.2.3. I start, rather, with the realm of objective spirit, with the family, with civil society, and with the state, which are Hegel's three canonical forms, but which nevertheless, as I hope to show, culminate in the superconcept of bureaucracy.

5.3.2.1 FAMILY   J. L. Austin used to say ironically that marrying is just saying some words. In point of fact, marrying is a matter of the accumulation of documents before during and after a certain ceremony, and these documents are inscriptions of acts without which the marriage has no legal value. And the fact that, in recent social debates, other forms of union, such as the French pact of civil solidarity (PACS), aspire to documentality is as good a proof as there could be of the centrality of the documental function relative to naked life. For the issue underlying PACS has nothing to do with sharing a life, which is perfectly possible even without a PACS, but rather concerns the bureaucratically sanctioned rights, such as reversionary pensions and the like, that can only be assured by documentality. In the end, the campaign in favor of PACS or, conversely, the reaffirmation of the holiness of marriage, is a dispute that, quite legitimately, centers on paperwork.[53] And these considerations can be extended to a wide variety of unions, both those that are historically attested and those that are merely possible, that stand between the individual and society, and that are marked for their social recognizability by the appeal to inscriptions.

5.3.2.2 CIVIL SOCIETY   From the family we come to the other form of objective spirit that, for Hegel, is civil society. The passage to civil society, in those cultures where this term is applicable, is characterized by an increase in written titles, from identity cards to tax codes or ATM PINs. In line with the analysis offered in 4.2, we may recall that the economy is a typical expression of a civil society. Writing derives its origin from the economy; in its turn writing contributes to the invention of new technologies and to the division of labor; to the elaboration of administrative structures, such as tax systems and censuses, and of commerce; to the accumulation of capital; and to the transformation of individual transactions. It is in this sense that writing produces economic effects: financial wealth, stocks and shares, money. In particular, money appears as a document that performs an absolutely central role in economic transactions and, at the same time, brutally reveals the fragility of the documental realm, in the extreme ease with which it can become mere wastepaper, passing from the status of strong document to that of weak document.[54]

5.3.2.3 STATE   In the two centuries that separate us from Hegel, we have witnessed the state's succumbing first to bureaucratic documentality and then to informatic documentality, to which we return in the next section. Nevertheless, the state conserves its power in the management and the distribution of documents, even though it is under siege from other forces, such as banks, the telecom companies, supermarkets, airline companies, and hotels, which are of roughly equal power and sovereignty. The residual power of the state is manifested in the handling of rights such as tax breaks, permissions, and concessions, but above all in the management of the purely identificatory documents that are so sorely lacking to the *sans papiers*.

What I would like to stress here is that, in a perfectly obvious way, documentality generates political power—or, to put the point more strongly, documentality is a necessary condition for the existence of something like a society in which power can come into being. There is no better way to illustrate this than to think of images of Talleyrand dictating as many as six letters at once, of Napoleon dictating until midnight, of Louis XIV dividing his time and his formidable energy equally between those inscriptions in the broad sense that were parties, *levées*, and other spectacles, and those inscriptions in the narrow sense of the affairs of state. And it is not a wild idea to think that among the causes of the fall of the ancien régime was the incapacity of the sovereign to keep up with the documental demands of the practical administration of power in the face of the demands of rituals, entertainments, and the worldly display of power.[55] Documentality functions both at the level of internal administration (taxation, accountancy, censuses; numbers and the control of time; administrative correspondence in the form of letters, ordinances, and accords) and at that of external administration (international treaties, a realm that, with globalization, has been extended in a way that could hardly have been imagined in the past).[56]

In this framework, documentality is not just a matter of the production rights and of wealth, but it is also concerned with protection against other documental claims. The mere fact of possessing documents confers greater power not only on the individual but also on the collectivity. The fact that European colonialism had a greater and more devastating impact on Africa, America, and Oceania than it did on Asia is in a large measure attributable to the fact there were preexisting bureaucratic structures in Asia.[57] This point can be made even more strongly by comparing the almost total disappearance of the Indians of North America with the civilizations of Latin America, which had forms of writing and, in the face of everything, were able to imprint on the postcolonial states that emerged some trace of their specific civilizations. Furthermore, precisely in virtue of its use of writing as, bureaucracy allows a fundamental factor in the exercise and the nurture of power, namely the separation between an office and the person who exercises the role. And there is no doubt that the formation of archives contributes to the constitution of something like an office and, again, to the separation between the office and the individual.[58]

But writing does not serve the state only for archives and bureaucracy. Writing reinforces the social bond and property relations, by keeping track of genealogies and family relations, and on the other hand introduces a social stratification in terms of the various grades of literacy. Again, as regards the relations between writing and power, we may recall the points made in 4.1.2.5 about the powers of the recorder of minutes in a meeting, of the secretary, and of the attorney, all of them offices that delegate the exercise of writing. And we may bear in mind the value of the responsibility that is connected to writing; from the point of view of power, everything that is written is that much more binding than anything that is not, as is shown by the importance of written orders in every hierarchical structure. The development of documentality in recent decades has thus carried with it not only a growth in certification and control, but also in responsibility.

5.3.2.4 INFORMATIC BUREAUCRACY The analysis we have been presenting suggests a superconcept, which covers the three foregoing functions and which I dub *informatic bureaucracy*. Writing has exercised its power since time immemorial, but it has become particularly visible now because of the grammatological explosion that is at the same time the accidental occasion and the deep inspiration behind this book. Here the fundamental categories are those of right, which is the traditional basis of writing's power; of bureaucracy, which is its modern development; and of information science, which is its postmodern hypertrophy.

Right. As regards the law, the reference to documentality is pretty obvious. It seems that the very word *law* derives from a Scandinavian root that means to lay (*lie*) and the French *loi* comes from the Latin *lex*, which is perhaps related with the verb *legere*, to collect. The characteristic of the law, which differentiates it from custom, is the fact of being written: *legem figere* is to sculpt laws in bronze and exhibit them in the forum; exactly for this reason, in light of the material medium on which it is written, we have the expression "to break the law" (*legem delere*).[59] Obviously custom and habit can taken on documental features; as we saw in 4.1.2.4, when we talk about the "unwritten law," we always mean a "law that is written elsewhere and by other means," that is to say, registered as archiwriting rather than as writing.[60] In short, the medieval French distinction between Pays du Droit Ecrit, meaning the Roman tradition, and Pays du Droit Coutumier, meaning the Germanic usage, could be reformulated as one between Pays du Droit Ecrit (land of the written law) and Pays du Droit Archi-écrit (land of the archi-written law). Equally, the effort to provide a unified law, both Germanic and Roman, of German jurisprudence turns out to have been a way to represent in written form the traditions that were laid down as archiwriting. The very notion of law as something that endures stably, that sets limits and that requires execution presupposes that the law is registered, at least in the hearts of the citizens; the principle that ignorance of the law is no excuse means just this. From the logical point of view, the connection between law and registration (whether written or archiwritten) is just as binding as the connection between language and code; there cannot be a language whose syntax, grammar, and word meanings are in continual flux, and a law that was not fixed and stable over time would not be a law.

Bureaucracy. As a point of consistency, a bureaucrat ought simply to carry out regulations decided on elsewhere. In fact, the possession of the means for inscription constitutes power exactly like the ownership of the means of production and allows the bureaucracy to take the lead over the political or legal authorities to which it is formally subordinated. In other words, the spirit of the law is concretely applied in the letter of the bureaucracy. This point was recognized by Max Weber, whose student Carl Schmitt interpreted the whole problem of totalitarianism as the outcome of the spread of bureaucratic power. In his account, Hitler's rise to power is not to be understood as an effect of collective intentionality bewitched by the leader's charisma, but rather as a development of a cycle that was already under way in the Weimar Republic. After the legitimacy of the German Empire had crumbled after 1918, all that was left was the legal system guaranteed by the bureaucracy. This apparatus had been significantly empowered by the procedure of *ordinances* (laws by decree), which speeded up the legislative process and translated into greater power for the offices that were in effect the producers and managers of the lawmaking activity.[61] The totalitarian state of the Third Reich was not a deviation but rather a reinforcement of this line, which identified bureaucracy with legality, which in turn explains bureaucratized extermination. The naked life of the concentration camps presupposed an intense labor of paper shuffling, of getting documents in order, in such a way that it identified bureaucratic correctness with legality.[62]

Informatics. It would be a mistake to see this identification as characteristic of totalitarian regimes, given that it was already under way in the Weimar Republic. It does not come to an end with the Third Reich, but rather has received new impetus with the revolution in information sciences. Here we find a new phenomenon, to which we have already made allusion, namely the fact that power and its sovereign prerogatives are extended, and in the case of weak states transferred, to other agencies that possess the instruments for registration. In the front rank of these are the banks and the communications industries that have brought to life a whole new and very powerful bureaucracy, whose emblem is the call center.[63] As a matter of politics and morals, this no more speaks against writing than pollution speaks against industry or the atomic bomb speaks against physics. The potentialities of registration have existed ever since the Sumerians, and certainly do not excuse individuals from their responsibilities. This may be made clearer if we pass to the action of the letter in the realm of the absolute spirit, which is to say in the realms of art, religion, and philosophy, considered as the areas traditionally connected to conscience, to action, and to individual responsibility.

5.3.3 Absolute Spirit

Over the two centuries that separate us from the formulation of his system, absolute spirit is probably the part of Hegel's system that has had the worst press. The reasons for this discredit are very various, but Hegel's point is hard to counter. We all see in our lives that there are functions that have a purpose and others that seem to be valuable in themselves, independently of the practical advantages that they may—and in many cases do—secure us. These functions are those of art, religion, and philosophy (this last understood as the realm of knowledge in general). For all that art can make money for collectors, religion can guarantee financial and temporal power, and philosophy can make a job for a professor, it would be embarrassing to justify one's choices in favor of an artwork, a religion, or knowledge on the sole basis of practical usefulness. By contrast, there is nothing wrong about saying that one went to the post office to pay the gas bill. The embarrassment in question derives from the fact that art, religion, and philosophy possess an immanent purpose that transcends all determinate objectives. It may not be of any use to discover a galaxy millions of light years away, but this is nevertheless a perfectly respectable objective for an astronomer.

Now, as with the objective spirit, here, too, what is called "spirit" is a modification of the letter. This does not in any case take anything away from the dignity of spirit, but it rather does not regard it as a sort of breath that circulates in our heads like the flies in the heads of the madmen in Teofilo Folengo's *Domus Phantasiae*. What I once more wish to stress is that it is a matter of viewing the spirit as a result of the letter and, from this point of view, the case of art is particularly telling given that, as we saw at length in 5.2, art is the field in which we cannot speak of works in the absence of perceptible expressions and manifestation. That is to say, there is no spirit without the letter.

5.3.3.1 ART A few words will suffice about art, given that I have discussed it at length in 5.2. In a tale by E. T. A. Hoffmann, a musician claims to be able to give violin lessons to anybody, but, when he takes the instrument in hand, all he produces are caterwauls that no one can stand. It is hard to claim that the violinist is a violinist, that someone who claims to have a whole novel in his or her head but who has not yet written a word is really a novelist, or that someone who asserts that he or she has only the idea of a picture is really a painter. Even the most conceptual of artists cannot live by spirit alone, but must come to terms with the letter, lest everyone who is in a poetic frame of mind should be counted as a poet (obviously it is not enough to write poems to be a poet, given that this is a merely necessary but not sufficient condition, but that is another story). In line with the law Work = Inscribed Act, the manifestation and fixing of a letter are indispensable elements in an activity that normally, and rightly, is considered spiritual: There is no art without a work, which means that there cannot be any spiritual activity without the letter, and the works are inscriptions.[64]

5.3.3.2 RELIGION

In the religions deriving from Abraham, revelation is the letter that precedes and constitutes the spirit. It is something external, such as a burning bush, which makes itself present to the conscience, which, as a result of that revelation and of the prescriptions that flow from it, becomes a believing conscience.[65] In the end, the revelation is deposited in a book. For this reason, it is hard to think that it is entirely accidental that the religions of the spirit are also and at the same time in the highest degree religions of the book. In the religious realm, writing contributes to fixing and generalizing norms, which are themselves conditions for the creation of universal religions: if therefore it is possible to have something like a universalistic requirement, this cannot depend on the spirit, but only on the letter. This in turn gives rise to ethical norms that are often alternative to or, often enough, in competition with the demands of the law; in such cases, writing comes to help or to replace rituality. Especially in the monotheisms, we see an identification between religious power and temporal power. Here, the book has the double function as the basis of the objective spirit and as the foundation of absolute spirit.[66]

As regards the priority of the letter, it does not seem to be accidental that religious faith is consubstantial with the performance of rites and in some cases is manifested through public acts that have nothing to do with the spirit. The death of Christ on the cross has nothing spiritual about it; it is a series of actions that are mostly undergone. In the course of those actions, no theological discussion is carried forward. If anything, in the dialog with

Pilate we have an interrogation that concerns a political situation, to find out whether Christ proclaims himself King of the Jews. Yet it is on this series of events and on the miraculous act of the resurrection (which after all is irrelevant from the theological point of view, and which has everything to do with the state of a body) that is founded the New Testament's *kerygma* (from the Greek for an announcement, like that of a salesman), since, as Saint Paul says, if Christ be not risen, our faith is vain.[67]

This priority of the letter over the spirit cannot be discounted by interpreting it as a form of superstition or at least as a religious behavior of simple people, as distinct from the religion of the learned. On the one hand, the religion of the learned is surely more lettered, and it would seem to be all the more linked to the letter than that of the simple. But aside from that fact, which holds for all forms of culture, I would like to offer an example that seems illuminating because it involves Saint Augustine, a saint and philosopher, who, in the *Confessions*, asks at a certain point why we confess our sins to God, who already knows everything. This is a question to which Augustine gives an answer very similar to the one we found in connection with telepathy in 4.2.3.3. As in the case of telepathy, we excluded the idea that communication without letters and codes would be better, so Augustine writes that he confesses in words and in writing because it is in precisely this way that he means to *make the truth*, with what seems thus to be an inscribed performative, not just before God but also, Augustine writes, with the pen and in front of many witnesses.[68]

5.3.3.3 PHILOSOPHY   Last, we have the third term of Hegel's absolute spirit, philosophy. I say "philosophy" though I ought perhaps to say "science" in the sense of "knowledge taken as a whole," including what is called (or used to be called) "the world of culture." In Eustache Le Sueur's painting *Saint Paul Preaching at Ephesus* (1649),[69] we have an allegory of the role of the letter for the spirit and of books for philosophy. Saint Paul is standing on some steps like the philosophers in Raphael's *School of Athens*, and he is pointing to heaven with one hand and holding the new book in the other; the old books are piled up at the foot of the steps, and a servant is setting fire to them. Now, to ask how much letters count for the spirit is a question that wavers between banality and impertinence. On the one hand, it is taken for granted that books serve culture. At least traditionally, it is obvious that a cultured man is one who has read many books, just as it is obvious that in the sciences at large, documentality sets the conditions for the transmission of knowledge, for the progress of the sciences, for appointments of university chairs, and for the awarding of Nobel prizes and Field medals. Nevertheless, if we ask whether writing in general—of the sort that we were taught in primary school and that has invaded our lives through computers, cell phones, and the Web—has anything to do with philosophy, at least an initial reaction is less obvious.

Eustache Le Sueur, St. Paul Preaching at Ephesus *(1649), Louvre, Paris*
(© 2009, White Images/Scala, Florence)

Characteristically, in 1978, Richard Rorty wrote an article, "Philosophy as a Kind of Writing,"[70] in which he divided philosophers into two families: the Kantians, or scientific philosophers, whose ideal it was to do without writing, and the Hegelians, or literary philosophers, who could not do without writing. At first glance, this looks convincing, if we compare, for instance the semi-ascetic dryness of Wittgenstein's *Tractatus* with the nearly hundred books that Derrida wrote. In practice, it is not possible to do without writing, even though one might dream of getting rid of it so as to show the world with an act of pure ostentation. In Rorty's view, this was the Kantians' dream. But then anyone who has beheld the thirty volumes of the Akademie edition of Kant's works, with their thousands of pages of treatises, correspondence, unpublished material, and lecture notes, will begin to wonder whether the Kantians write so little after all; and if we think that a philosopher so attached to the idea of philosophy as a rigorous science as Husserl was should have left an endless pile of manuscripts, we might ask whether the "Kantians" really think they can get rid of writing.

As I have tried to argue in the foregoing pages, writing is not an accessory for the spirit, and the best proof of this is given by efforts to do without it. As I recalled in 4.2.3.3, Plato is credited with one of the most famous condemnations of writing, in which he accuses it of ruining memory and imposing a culture that is mere parroting, and which is so similar to the criticisms we hear of the Internet today. Yet not only is it evident that Plato has to write his accusation down, but then, when he comes to define the features of the soul, he likens it to a book inside which an inner scribe fixes sensations and thoughts, and when he characterizes legitimate reasoning, he says that it is written on the soul. Here, then, external writing is condemned, but only in the name of an internal writing, which turns out to be thought. But to what extent can we do without external writing if we are aiming at knowledge and science? After all, if we know what Plato had in mind, we owe that knowledge to the fact that he wrote it down. Likewise with Paul, who encourages consigning books to the flames but holds on tight to the Gospel.

To be sure, it happens often enough that theories are passed on by imbeciles or by enemies,[71] but the best situation is the one described by that manic scribbler Husserl, who in any case did not want to tell the story of the birth of literacy but rather that of geometry as the primordial and exemplary model of science. If, when the first geometer discovered the first theorem, he had not fixed it in his mind, had not communicated it to others, and above all, had not written it down somewhere, his discovery would have fallen back into nothingness. These are the themes around which Derrida constructed his philosophy of writing,[72] and on which, in my view, is based the role of culture, considered as a system of organized and selected traces that possess a meaning that goes beyond themselves,[73] expressing a life and its survival after death, and in the end representing the permanent value of what is perishable.

On this scheme of things, writing becomes, so to say, philosophy's transcendental. On the one hand, it is the quintessence of technique: between the ape in *2001: A Space Odyssey* that flings its bone club in the air and the spaceship, the intermediate passage is represented by the techniques of inscription that, as we saw in 4.1.1.2, now represent the true future much more than spaceships do. On the other hand, these technologies come to make up not just a world of tools but also (if, indeed, a hard and fast distinction can be drawn) what we have been calling the *world of spirit*. This is a world that concerns not just knowledge, but also our happiness and our wisdom; in the end, it concerns our attitudes to life and death, which would doubtless be very different indeed if we did not have writing.

6

IDIOMS

After having tried to reformulate the objective spirit and the absolute spirit in terms of a phenomenology of the letter, I would like to return to where this book began and to what Hegel regarded as the subjective spirit, as subjects and their characteristics. At the outset, I concentrated on those representations that never escape from the sphere of the subject, and I sought to individuate the moment in which subjectivity, in exiting from itself, constructs social objects by means of expressions and inscriptions. Now I would like to respond to the question, What establishes the link between those objects and the subjects that bring them into being? On the Geist *model, this is supplied by intention. On the .doc model that I have tried to set out, it is a trace that is called on to express subjectivity as absolute individuality. This is the idiom, which has many manifestations, of which the most common in our culture is the signature, whose importance in a social ontology it is hard to overestimate.*

To get some idea, suffice it to think of Van Eyck's Arnolfini Portrait. *In the foreground, there are the newlyweds. Behind them and in the middle of the room there is a mirror that reflects the witnesses, among whom in all probability is the painter himself. Above the mirror there is a signature: "Johannes de Eyck fuit hic 1434." It is a painting that distills all the valences of social objects, as much the work itself, which is an act inscribed before our eyes, as the representation of the wedding, which is the document of an inscribed act, with all its ingredients—the spouses, the witnesses and the signature, which is a valid testimony to the marriage: "I, Van Eyck, was present at this act on this date" as well as an attribution of the painting itself: "I, Van Eyck, am here in this exact moment and I leave this trace which is mine alone."*

Relative to the general discussion hitherto of the role of traces in the constitution of social objects, I would like now to concentrate on a specific feature of the situation. This is the fact that certain traces have an individualizing func-

tion, which is to say, they signal the presence and intentions of a person who gives rise to and is involved in a social object. At one and the same time, these traces reflect our desire and need to leave traces behind us as well as the necessity of making use of these to attest publicly our individuality in a process that encompasses a range of phenomena from tattoos to the world of fashion.[1] In this framework, if we consider ornaments and tattoos as signs of barbarism, we will be forgetting that that inscriptions on the body are one of the first forms in which the social bond makes its presence felt.[2]

I propose to call this sort of trace an idiom, in the sense that it is the idion (what is "proper" or "private" in Greek) that constitutes what is unique to a person. By idiom, I thus mean that specific mode of presentation an inscription (expressive sign, trace, registration, or even writing in the full sense) that links it to an individual. Its aim is to individualize the object, and, insofar as it succeeds, it plays a decisive role in validating social objects, which fix an intention by way of a signature. In this sense, the signature is the representative of individual intentionality, and a number of signatures at the foot of a document (whether it be the minutes of a condominium meeting, a petition, or the Declaration of Independence) are representatives of a plurality of individual intentionalities that are unified in the document. There are myriad ways in which an idiom can be manifested. It can be a document in the highest sense, such the autograph of a papal bull; or a part of a document, such as the signature on a contract or a check; or a characteristic feature present in serial documents, such as the differences between Turin tram tickets and those in Naples or Lisbon, which thus turn out to be idiomatic; or a tone of voice or, in the natural world, someone's DNA, and in the world of culture, an artist's style or a person's way of dressing and behaving. And so on. To be sure, there are many such things, perhaps too many; but the social world has come up with an idiom that is convenient, portable, and susceptible to analysis: the signature.

6.1 WHAT DOES A SIGNATURE MEAN?

The fax is a technological relic that survives for one purpose and one purpose only: the transmission of signatures and idioms. A person today could pass his or her life without taking a pen in hand. It is enough to type on the keyboard of a computer or of a cell phone or to click on a website; everything can be done by these means—except for the signature, which appears just a shade less archaic than a tattoo and, from a philosophical point of view, a concentration of very special properties. It is a blend of singularity and iterability, of intimacy and sociality, which associates it not only with an animal's tracks or fingerprints, but also with the realm of idioms that includes styles, copyrights, trademarks, and logos.[3]

When we put our signature, we give rise to something that is *absolutely unique*: the signature should be just that, put in that moment on that day; *in principle repeatable*: if I were to be forever changing my signature, I could not sign anything, which is why the bank asks us to deposit a signature; *wholly private*: unless I give my explicit authorization, no one can sign my signature in my place; at most, a power of attorney can allow him to sign for me with his; *essentially public*: if I were to create a signature that I use only for myself, while I used another in public, only the latter would really be a signature. Robinson Crusoe had no use for a signature, at least until Man Friday came along.

These features recur also in the performances, such as a handshake, that can in some circumstances take the place of a signature. When two statesmen establish an agreement, even a verbal one, they may very well shake hands on it. The hands in question are their own; it would be very odd if they made their assistants or interpreters shake hands. Then, when they come out of the conference chamber, they repeat the act for the television cameras; and all these public repeat performances are authentic, because it is them doing the handshaking, even if the first handshake in public was a repetition of the private one (which, in any case, could have been dispensed with because it is the public one that counts), and the others were iterations for the benefit of the television.

Like a handshake, a signature has to be done by hand, and the efforts to find a way of having a digital signature have not yet been able to perform all the duties that the natural signature covers. A digital signature is just a numerical code, like a password, and so much less idiomatic than a handwritten scribble, so much so that my digital signature can be stolen, where my scribble cannot (though it can be counterfeited, which is a different matter), just as happens with a fingerprint. The only way to steal a fingerprint is to cut off a finger, as we see at the movies and that at some time may have happened in real life; but one cannot steal a scribbled signature that way. Nevertheless, the ideal to which a PIN code aspires is the exact reproduction of the features of a signature, of being unique and indefinitely repeatable, of being totally private and essentially public, where the privacy is protected by secrecy, which is obviously not so necessary for the signature, and the public realm is that of such things as ATMs, to which everyone has physical access, but without which we would not need a PIN.

Just as a hand is always somebody's hand, so a signature is a unique and idiomatic trait of an individual. It expresses and manifests before it designates: as I shall elaborate soon, a signature is not a name. I can write anybody's name as many times as I like, but I cannot reproduce another person's signature, which does indeed reproduce his name but in an idiomatic way and often illegibly. Herein lies the paradox of the request that we sometimes find on forms, namely to put down a *legible signature*. It calls for us to self-falsify our own signature if it turns out to be illegible. But why make such heavy weather of signatures?

6.1.1 *Identity*

The first and most obvious reason for the social value of the idiom, and of the signature in particular, is the manifestation of identity, which is represented by a certain deviation. After all, a signature is essentially a greater or lesser imprecision relative to the norms of handwriting: in general, the signature "John Doe" is less legible than the name "John Doe" written by hand. This imprecision nevertheless has to be codified; if we continually changed our signatures, they would be names or mere scribbles. Thus, the signature is a survival of documents that were originally all autographs, a custom that persists in some cases.

For sure, kings made use of secretaries; but it is interesting to note that the documents produced by the chancellery of Charlemagne, who was himself both illiterate and a reformer of documents and writing, were drawn up in a script, known as Merovingian cursive, which was very different from and less legible than the Carolingian miniscule. The reason for this archaic practice was to assure the idiomaticity undergirded by tradition. A page written in a different hand, even when it was easier to read (and the Carolingian miniscule was quickly taken up for books), would not have been taken seriously. This is the reason for the curlicues and ornaments that appear apparently disorderly and incoherent on chancellery texts and, until not so long ago, on those of notaries public.[4] The use of singularity can also be found in the arabesques employed as security devices on the Internet. In particular, these are nothing but letters of the alphabet that have been deformed and individualized so as to make them unreadable by an OCR and resistant to copy-and-paste procedures. These observations throw light on the nature of idiomaticity. What makes an idiom idiomatic? Perhaps influenced by thoughts about artworks, one might hazard the answer: perfection. But the right answer is *imperfection*.

Signatures are irregularities and imperfections of the calligraphic norm. And their general form is that of the shibboleth, a Hebrew word that means a "stream of water," or perhaps "ear of corn." The word is explained by the following story. In order to distinguish the Ephraimites from the men of Gilead (who pronounced "s" as "sh"), the Ephraimites (who did not) were made to pronounce the word *shibboleth*, so that anyone who said "sibboleth" was killed. In short, it is a story like that of the Sicilian Vespers, when the French, who were made to pronounce the Italian word *ceci* (chickpea) and said "*sesì*," met the same end as the Ephraimites. As we shall see, imperfection is not just a feature of the signature, but it also attaches to the signatory.

6.1.2 Origin

As I have said, among the properties of a signature is one that can be defined as a blend of the idiographic and the nomothetic: the signature is mine alone (idiographic) and yet has to be always the same (nomothetic). So far as I know, and can imagine, this is the sole case in which the law, instead of generalizing, individualizes.

As regards individualization, Saul Kripke introduced the notion of a "rigid designator," by which he means a name that indicates univocally a single object and tracks just that object across all the counterfactual situations in which it exists; typically, proper names are rigid, while definite descriptions and common nouns are not[5]. Nevertheless, if I look up "Maurizio Ferraris" in the phone book, I find that there are seven in Piedmont and sixteen in all Italy, and you can imagine what would be the result of a search for "Mario Rossi," the Italian correlate of "John Smith." Conversely, fingerprints, manual and digital signatures, e-mail addresses, and even cell phone numbers, which are in some situations regarded as valid identification documents, would satisfy Kripke's notion of rigidity.

Apart from the empirical fact, there is the philosophical point; in the theory of idiomaticity that I am proposing, Kripkean rigid designation could be regarded as a regulative ideal: we want signatures, both analogical and digital, to come as close as possible to being rigid designators in such a way that idiographicity and nomotheticity reinforce each other. In a certain sense, the idiomaticity of a signature, the fact that my signature cannot be anyone else's, is analogous to the idiomaticity of a biological or material origin: I could not have had different parents from those I actually have; this particular table could not have been made from any material other than what it was actually made from. And the analogy seems to be confirmed by the identification and documental use of DNA, which is a sort of biological super-signature in which idiomaticity and origin are one and the same things as in no other case. Here, then, is why signatures are so important for validation, a point to which we return. For an object to be the very object it is, it can change some or even all its properties, except one: its origin.

6.1.3 Uniqueness

A person's DNA is unique, even if it is replicated in every cell. A signature, as a cultural idiom, tends toward recreating this situation: The signature is always unique in that no one can sign in another's stead, and yet the uniqueness must be repeatable infinitely often. A uniqueness that was not accompanied by regularity would, from a logical point of view, be much more "unique," since it would have a single exemplification, but it would not have the idiomaticity that is attributable to a signature (or to DNA) as a repeatable uniqueness, where "uniqueness" should be understood to mean not something that is unique, but rather something that makes something unique. This may seem to be verging on a pun, but a signature has just this function: it is unique as a type, but is repeatable in many tokens. In the exam registers, my signature is repeated who knows how many times, after so many years of teaching; yet the signature makes that document unique because it is the only one that, in a given moment, was signed. This also reminds us that, next to a signature, a date is called for.

6.1.4 Presence

But what did it mean to put one's signature onto a document? One thing is certain: It did not mean "My name is such-and-such." The meaning was something else. In the first instance, it meant, "I was physically present while

I was signing the check, the minutes, the receipt." "I was there," as we have seen paradigmatically in the Van Eyck painting. In the case of the signature by hand, this aspect of presence is connected to one of the features of traces, namely, the material element that underlies the documental pyramid. As such, a trace can be deputed to mean anything at all, but it also possesses the value of a certain and irreplaceable provenance. Thus, a pigeon's footprint can, if we want, be used also represent the Mystery of the Trinity, but it will always nevertheless be a pigeon's footprint and, moreover, the footprint of that particular pigeon. In line with the proposal made in 4.3.1.2, we thus have two uses of the trace: one as a conventional sign, the other as an individual mark that we find also in the digital imprint and in the signature.

As a matter of idiographicity and nomotheticity, there is not much of a difference between a digital imprint and a signature. If it were feasible to sign by means of a smell, much as animals mark their territory, we would have the same result as we obtain by means of a signature, which reprises one of the features of a digital imprint or an odor: the fact of attesting the presence of a particular body. What even an electronic signature is called on to do is guarantee that a mind, with certain intentions and inside one body rather than another, has given its assent. But, strictly speaking, we have here one of the first cases in which I attest that I am myself without there being any uninterrupted physical link between myself and what I am using to make the attestation.[6] We may recall that, at least for the time being, had there not been any other documents on which I had put my traditional signature, it would not have been possible to constitute the electronic signature precisely because it would not have been possible to be sure of its validity, which is to say, its connection with an individual. Perhaps it would be possible to replace the signature with a DNA profile; but then, to guarantee that the profile was really mine, I suspect that the signature of a doctor, of an administrator, or of a laboratory technician (or maybe of all three) would be called for.

Nevertheless, a signature does not just mean, "I was there." It also means, "I was conscious, was not asleep, and knew what I was doing." This does not hold for mere footprints, for footprints are rarely intentional: a person chooses to sign, but not to leave traces while walking. After all, there are many more footprints than there are signatures. For sure, in Hollywood, a pavement bears the stars' handprints along with their autographs; in this case, the application of the hand has the same intentional value as a signature. Nevertheless, the inimitable imprint of an anonymous cat in wet cement will consign it, as much as stuffing would, to something close to immortality. So far, the imprint serves the function of the idiom, but, because it is not intentional, it is not a signature.

6.1.5 Code

Discussing the relation between a signature and its origin, I suggested an analogy between codes, such as telephone numbers, and signatures, but now we can make out something specific and exclusive to a signature, which as is irreplaceable as we assume that persons, considered as persons and not as functions, are. This should not surprise us, precisely because a signature is the social representative of a person. Because of this, the uniqueness of a signature is different from the uniqueness of a code.[7] A signed social object is more fundamental than an unsigned social object; this can be seen in clothing or in the difference in price between a print that has the authentic signature of the artist and one that does not. The divergence at point of sale reflects an ontological distinction: the garment or the print that carries a signature is the more powerful social object because both are closer to their authors than unsigned ones are. At the end of this process of moving away (viewed negatively) or of liberation (viewed positively) from the signature, and hence from genesis and origin, there are the ideal objects, which are so far from being generated that they can appear to be discovered rather than created, as I suggested earlier.

Of course, one might object that all the features of a signature can also be found in a username that a person chooses online. That, too, is essentially unique, in that the system will tell you if someone else has already taken it and will ask you to choose another; it is in its nature repeatable, given that it is repeated every time you log in; it is private because it is linked to a password; and it is essentially public because it is associated with your online profile. Nevertheless, unlike a signature, a username can be imitated to perfection by anyone who knows it.

As I remarked at the beginning of this chapter, a manual signature preserves its authenticity by the fact of not being imitable, at least in principle. No one should be able to reproduce my signature but me. This requirement is first of all metaphysical, and only secondarily juridical. If this were not so and a signature were reproducible by other people, the concept of *signature* would no longer have any sense. An electronic signature with PIN or a digital one where the PIN is in code for greater security obviously cannot rely on inimitability, because a string of letters and numbers is the most imitable thing there can be, but it must depend on secrecy: Only the signatory should, in principle, have access to the code.

Two major differences between the manual and the digital signature derive from this fact. The first is that, unlike the manual signature, everyone who has access to the code can sign with equal validity, even if not necessarily with equal legitimacy. The other is that, while a natural or manual signature has a certain appearance and is a phenomenon that obeys the laws of inscription, including being smaller than its medium, an electronic signature consists rather in a system of validation of a document and has no location in the validated document.

To summarize, then, we have three sorts of signature: the manual one, which is inimitable; the electronic one, with a secret PIN; and the digital one, with secret and encoded PIN. Secrecy takes the place of inimitability. Where the reproduction of a manual signature, such as a photocopy, is not a signature, the reproduction of a digital signature is a signature to all intents and purposes; the distinction between copy and original is not applicable. As regards the counterfeit signature, we are faced with a halfway point between conformity of the inscription and individual intentionality, in that I can perfectly well decide to declare my assistant's imitation of my signature on a document to be valid, because it really did correspond to my will. But the fact remains that, for a graphologist, that signature is false, even though it is not for a lawyer.

There is a further consequence of inimitability to be drawn. We do not think that a code or a telephone number can tell us anything about the person with whom they are associated. Such codes are purely accidental, while we suspect that a signature and handwriting in general can reveal something about the person, and perhaps that the signature tells us about the image someone wants to project of himself. Here we grasp the centrality to social reality of what we might call *style*.

6.2 *LE STYLE C'EST L'HOMME*

We allow quite naturally that handwriting reveals something about a person's psychology, which is why graphological tests are in use. Just so, we assume that the style of a work says something about the personality of its author. These are assumptions above discussion. A rather stronger claim is that *le style c'est l'homme*, by which is meant not that a person can be reduced to his or her style, but that it is style that individualizes a person.

Now, what do we mean by *style*? Conceptually speaking, style is what we may call *form*, meaning by that a form that is produced intentionally. It makes no sense to speak of a shell's style, and if someone says that a shell has baroque spirals, this is a metaphorical way of speaking. Etymologically, style is in some intimate way bound up with inscription, with the *stylus* with which wax tablets were inscribed. Thus, we speak of a fine or ugly style, of a sophisticated or rough style, but what we want to know is what we are referring to when we speak of style.

To understand better, it may be useful to return to the distinction between act, content, and object. As we saw in 1.2.2, this distinction is attributed to the Polish logician Kazimierz Twardowski, but for the purposes of my theory, I would like to make a modification to it. Twardowski spoke of the processes that happen on in people's thoughts, but I am more concerned with things that are in the world, even though in some cases their inscriptions may be only in the heads of persons, such as when I make an informal promise to someone. For Twardowski, the content was a small physical object in an individual's brain; mine may be a more physically robust object, such as a signature on a document or indeed the whole of a manuscript document.[8] There are some differences, but the essence remains the same; the inscription that may be but need not necessarily be external has the feature of being idiomatic: I promise something with my voice, I sign with my signature, and so on.

Is it possible to assimilate the internal content to the external inscription? Yes, it certainly is. The style is precisely this, and on these grounds, I propose to call the equivalent of the content in the social world *styleme*.

6.2.1 Stylemes

The first and most obvious function of stylemes is esthetic, and this is connected to what we saw in 5.2.2.3 and 5.3.3.1. It seems fairly straightforward that the act cannot become a work: Admirers of Rodin's *Thinker* are not appreciating any inward acts on the part of the statue, but the outer representation of what looks like a mental effort, which is not helped by the subject's nakedness nor by the uncomfortable posture he has adopted.

On the other hand, neither can the object, the common idea, become a work. Perhaps this is a little less obvious, though in reality it is as clear as the exclusion of the act. No one has ever thought of accusing Bach or Caravaggio of plagiarizing the Gospels, even though we have here a set of specific events, whether they are historical or mythological, regarding the passion and death of Christ. It would make even less sense to accuse Mondrian or the architects of the pyramids of plagiarizing geometrical forms, and not just because it would be rather hard to determine who the legitimate copyright holder might be.

Once we have excluded acts and objects, in the sense we are using here, there is nothing left but the styleme. Here there is good reason to think that there is some connection with the work. I can look at Monet's *Rheims Cathedral*; it is a styleme, a specific mode of presentation of that object in Monet's style, and it does not correspond to an act by Monet (who is now dead and, even before dying, was not always thinking about it), nor to the object, for I can say "*Rheims Cathedral*" and you will understand even without thinking of Monet—all the more so that the cathedral is there even if I am not thinking about it. Yet, if I decide to go to a museum to see the *Rheims Cathedral* painted by Monet, what I want to see is precisely the styleme; otherwise I would rest content with a memory or with a photograph. For the same reason, if I want to hear the *Marriage of Figaro*, it is in order to relish that styleme, which certainly concerns the contents that passed through Mozart's head.

It is worth noting that, with the same object, the stylemes or expressed forms can vary. Think of Flaubert's *Madame Bovary* and the same story (the same object) recounted by another writer; this is what happens, for instance, in classical tragedy or in historical novels that have the same object. Likewise, two paintings of the same object, for instance, Antony and Cleopatra or the Flight into Egypt, can turn out to be completely different. But this does not happen to ideal objects: The Pythagorean theorem remains the same irrespective of the medium, of the chalk or pen used to draw the figures, of the colors, of how precisely it is executed or the size of the representation.

It is irrelevant to observe that this also holds true with social objects, such as the Italian Constitution or Manzoni's novel *The Betrothed* (in paperback, hardback, or audiobook). To be sure, the physical medium is less important for allographic works such as novels or constitutions than for autographic works like paintings. But there is no doubt that a novel with the same plot as *The Betrothed* but a different style and author would be a different novel, albeit one that could be accused of plagiarism. Even when the author is the same, a difference of style makes different objects, as we find in Manzoni's earlier work *Fermo and Lucia* and in the two editions, of 1827 and 1840, of *The Betrothed*. As regards the Italian Constitution, the text that we can find on the Internet is valid because it is presented as a faithful reproduction of the signed original in a certain medium in a certain moment. That is not at all true of the Pythagorean theorem.

Thus, when we read a book, watch a film, or look at a painting, what we recognize as belonging to the artist in the essential sense and as constitutive of the work in all its individuality (though perhaps not in its value, because we are concerned with attribution not with judgment) is precisely the specific and exclusive manner of representation. We are interested in Goya's dog for the way that Goya represents it, and not for how we might find a dog in an illustrated dictionary. This explains the centrality for art of style, which is of the essence in a way that it is a merely dispensable adjunct in geometry. Here, then, is why style is important and why a theorem cannot be a work, though perhaps a transcription by a conceptual artist might be; and even in such a case, we do not have the realization of the theorem but a styleme.

6.2.2 Individuation

Stylemes are constitutive not just of art but also, though in a different way, of documents. Here we must distinguish three requirements: that of inscription, that of conformity, and that of individuation.

First, there is the question of inscription, which I have discussed at length in this book. As I have said several times, the mere performance of a speech act is not enough to have a marriage. One has to put one's signature, together with one's spouse's signature and the signatures of witnesses, in a register; otherwise, nothing whatever is produced. But from that it does not follow that I have to be forever thinking of the social act. It is enough if I remember it, and even if I do forget it, there are still the inscriptions. I know that I promised something to someone two days ago, but just at the moment I am not thinking about it. Yet, I know about it, so that the promise is an attitude that philosophers call *dispositional* meaning that I have the potential to recall that I promised if only the conditions are favorable. It is in this sense that the promise is in force even when I am sleeping or (so long as it has been recorded) if I am in a coma, or even after I am dead: That is what a will is.

In the second place, the styleme comes into play in the need for conformity. The decisive act in a wedding is the "I do" or "yes," according to the rite in question. Yet, if instead of saying "yes" someone were to say "certainly," the marriage would not be valid because of the difference from the required styleme, despite the same object; it would not be valid, either, if someone were to pronounce the ritual formula in a falsetto voice or put on a regional accent, because of the difference between the oral styleme, despite the same written styleme. In short: Could I really get married while doing an impersonation of Don Vito Corleone? Moral: For a social act to be performed, whether it be an order in the bar or the ordination of a priest, there must be an inscription, which in turn must be idiomatic, which is to say in conformity with a ritual and with an identity.[9]

In the third place, there is the requirement of individuation. Someone might say: Once it is registered, we have the object—*that* marriage or *that* promise. That is true, but what differentiates that marriage from another or that promise from another? What defines the singularity of that specific object? Answer: the fact that it passed through the heads of those two agents and not those of others, coming into being on a determinate occasion, and with this styleme and not another. Thus, it becomes clear that the mode of individual presentation of the act and the specific form of its registration is decisive. Stretching the point a little, a styleme can also be characteristic of a modus operandi. It is sometimes said that the thief left his signature, which obviously is not a calling card, unless he is Arsène Lupin, or fingerprints, but rather a certain style that repeats itself, even while the legal object (a bank job, breaking and entering, burglary) varies.

6.2.3 *Authorship*

Inscription, conformity, and individuation underscore the close connection between art and documents, which share a common core in what we might call *authorship*. There is in the end no really crucial difference between a banknote, with certain ornaments and a reproduced signature, a check, with the identifying curlicues of the bank and an authentic signature by the depositor, a painting, executed in accordance with the author's manner and signed at bottom right. In each case, we have a document of a certain degree of idiomaticity to such an extent that, if we view the matter formally, there is no essential difference between a holographic will and a painting.

This is why we are so powerfully led in social life by forms and styles. Why do people want designer clothes? Let us try to imagine a society that really knows where esthetics begins and ends. Would it be a society that regulates itself only by the act and the object, leaving stylemes for, as we once said in Italian, Sunday idling? Not at all, as we can easily show.

A certain gentleman goes to a *vernissage* and appreciates the artist's style. He is free to do so because he is in an art gallery and not in a law court or an office: no one can criticize him for his deplorable penchant for the style, since he is in precisely the place set aside for the exhibition of stylemes. Everything is in order, then, because this is Sunday idling. However, something rather embarrassing happens, and then the theory of stylemes can be set aside. If he likes an painting a great deal and his bank account allows him, the gentleman can pull out his checkbook and write first a number (which is surely an object) and then the name of the artist or, more likely, the gallery owner (and here too we have an object); at this point, he will add at bottom right something like his own name, but not in any old fashion, because what he will trace is precisely his signature. In that moment, he will become the owner of the painting, which is another idiom, itself validated by its author by a signature at bottom right. If there is any disagreement, a court, which is anything but indifferent to signatures, will decide. Suppose that the gentleman in question has all that money because he is a manager of a firm. There will be more signatures there, not to mention the strange survival of the medieval blazon that is the logo and to which we will return in 6.2.5.

Imagine instead that our rich collector made his money with a patent or, less likely, with a book.[10] There are stylemes here, too. In the case of the book, what is protected is not the object, but the styleme. The phrase "that branch of Lake Como" is Manzoni's; but the story of two fiancés who are persecuted by a country squire is not so exclusive to Manzoni, and it could even be by Walter Scott. The expression is protected in the various languages into which a book can be translated and independently of the medium by which it is reproduced: a book in any font or kind of print, radio, CD, or obviously cinema and television. For it is supposed that what is reproduced is not just the plot, but also the characters, the form of the dialog and so on, so that a television version of *The Betrothed* in which Lucia is a giantess, Renzo a midget and Father Cristoforo a drunkard with green hair would be a parody.

All this is precisely the protection of a styleme, which is what we find also in trademarks, which are a sort of signature.

Let us concentrate now on the apparently more problematic case of patents, which involve the ownership of an idea, or of an ideal object. Suppose our art collector made his pile because he invented and patented the Tetra Pak. He could not protect the idea, any more than he could privatize the parallelogram, but he could get rich precisely through the idiomatic application of a geometrical solid, making the most of the peculiarities of size, of the material used, and of the way the thing is opened. It is probably because of this that certain fruit juices have such baroque and complex tops: they are getting around our collector's patent, which applies not to the object but to the styleme. It might be objected, in favor of patenting ideal objects, that it is possible to protect "quasi-ideal" objects such as computer programs and the "concepts" of television programs. I respond that this can be done because they deal with objects that are only *quasi*-ideal or, more exactly, *pseudo*-ideal, given that there is an evident difference between a parallelogram and *Celebrity Survivor*. Rather than ideal objects, we have here fully social objects, which have a beginning in time and one or more authors. The only difference between an installment of *Celebrity Survivor* and the "concept" of the program is that the latter is what I called in 1.3.3.1 "Archetype₂," presenting itself like the rules of a game, such as Monopoly. In short, single shows or novels are definite inscriptions, while the "concepts" or the programs are, at different levels of detail and unlike books, inscriptions to which no definite inscription corresponds.

6.2.4 Validation

What I have said about stylemes helps us to understand why signatures are so important in the validation of social objects. Kant maintained that a hundred real dollars are identical in their concept to a hundred ideal dollars. What, then, is the difference? In the inscription and its peculiarity. For the ideal object to become a social object what is necessary is that an inscription intervene so as to manifest the hundred dollars both on the outside and intersubjectively. At this point, however, must we conclude that any piece of paper with "hundred dollars" written on it is worth a hundred dollar? Or indeed that merely uttering the two words "hundred dollars" is worth a hundred dollars? Obviously not. What is required is that the expression and the inscription come about in a way that is in conformity with a styleme and that is underwritten by the crucial idiom of the secretary of the treasury's signature.

This is why autographs are modern surrogates of holy relics. If we think about the creation of artworks, we see in the ready-made the object becoming a work by means of the signature. In a painting, the status of work changes according to whether the work is signed or not, or merely initialed, or bears a false signature, not to mention cases like that of some of De Chirico's, where the signature is real but the painting is not.[11] In certain circumstances the requirement that a document be an autograph can depend on the solemnity that the act is endowed with, where the solemnity derives simply from the fact of being written by me with my handwriting. But being written by me means something very simple: that the act is true. Thus, the idioms serve to distinguish true social acts from simulated ones. The signature has a function like that of formulas such as "hereby," "*hiermit*," or "*con questo*," with which a social act is underwritten and declared valid, authenticating it with the expression of our full intentionality. Even if the intentionality is not full, the act can be valid in any case, while an unsigned check is void.

In this sense, a signature responds to one of the requirements of written performativity that is absent from speech acts, which do not contemplate anything corresponding. Speech acts can be expressed in oaths, benedictions, or spells. These are all codified: if I say "Open Sasame!" the door will not open. The only difference is that there is no doubt about who is producing it; he is there speaking with his own tongue in his own mouth. In the case of written acts, the same importance is given to the hand, as is recognized in the phrase "with his own hand,"[12] with this idiom, which should be unmistakable, and precisely because it is so it exercises enormous power in the validation of the act. The role of the autograph and of the holograph, like that of style, in the process of validating documents shows the falsity of the idea that style has a merely ornamental function.

Thus validation depends on the rightholder's placing his irreplaceable (at least in principle) mark in conformity with the current laws, protocols, and customs, which may themselves vary over time. And the value of this unsubstitutability resides in the way that it sets up a link between the physical person and the social person. A check is worthless unless it has a signature, yet it is a surely a document—but only in the weak sense, because it is a print that observes certain formal canons: it becomes a strong document capable of being exchanged for money, goods, or services only when the signature connects by convention with the will of a person with a body; and this holds for any form, which is just an empty model until it is signed. From the substantial point of view, then, the signature is called on to attest unmistakably the physical presence of the signatory; and it is for this reason that it is reconnected to its individualizing function, which we have recognized as a property of traces that establishes a complete equivalence between biometric data (the fingerprint, or simply a mark left on the ground by a foot) and signatures.

Two further points about validation. The first concerns a peculiarity of the signature-function, which is not identical to the signature-fact. On the one hand, as we have seen, there are many realizations that can give rise to a signature: a stamp, an imprint, an oath, or the use of biometric procedures. On the other hand, there can be signatures of the classic kind that are nevertheless not validations, but appear to be more like quotations: typically an autograph, whether Maradona's or John Lennon's or the one that Derrida put at the foot of *Margins of Philosophy*, has no legal value and should, in terms of the full intentionality, be counted rather as a sort of citation. The second point is this. It can always turn out that the hundred dollars are false, but that is humankind's fault, not the theory's. It is simply that the counterfeiters have put on the banknotes names that are not theirs; they have signed in the place of another person, namely the only one who is legally authorized to do so, and this is the reason why the banknotes are false. If, on the other hand, they had signed with their own names, they would have done something absurd but not intrinsically illegal (though I imagine they would be prosecuted, because not everyone checks the signatures on banknotes).[13]

6.2.5 Proper Names

The meaning of authorship and validation is clear enough. If signatures are so important and omnipresent, it is because they bind social objects to subjects or to what we call *persons*. An initial impression is that this binding derives from the fact that the signature is the name of the person, but I have indicated that this impression is misleading. A common practice that highlights the difference between a signature and a name is the collection of signatures on a petition, which is obviously a different thing from collecting names, though the signatures are similar to names. So what exactly makes this difference? Let us begin with a very normal situation. Let us consider these four tokens of my name:

Maurizio Ferraris
Maurizio Ferraris
Maurizio Ferraris
Maurizio Ferraris

This is the same name, written once in normal type, once in bold, once in cursive, and once in a font that resembles handwriting. Suppose, however, that the last was my signature. In that case, we would have an inscription that, from the viewpoint of social ontology, is quite different from the name, to such an extent that no one thinks it strange to sign documents with one's own name.

In line with what I said about origins, signatures mark a continuity with their author much more than a proper name does; they seem to give us a part of him, just like a relic, which is a part of a body or of some tissue that has been in contact with that body. It is what we are after when we ask for a footballer's autograph: no one would be satisfied if the footballer simply dictated his name.

The same applies to a firm's logo. This is quite different from the *names* Fiat, IBM, or Pirelli. It seems that behind the logos' precise form of presentation there is lurking an intention on the firms' part, which is not necessarily present in the mere mention. For Fiat, IBM, or Pirelli to become more than a mention of the firm, we can see that what is needed is another idiomatic presentation, which is to say a signature. And it is not by chance that the Italian for signature is *firma*, presumably to evoke the sense in which a right to sign undergirds those actions that constitute the identity of the business. Nevertheless, a logo can easily be a mere symbol, like the five rings of Audi or the Mercedes sign, which have no direct relation with the name, just as we find in medieval blazons, where only in some cases, such as the tower and the badger in the coat of arms of the Turn-und-Taxis family, the elements are a sort of rebus whose solution is given by the family name.

In another case, a signature can carry the name of the signatory, but not be written in his handwriting, as in the case of the calligraphic monogram or *tughra* of the Ottoman sultans or the cartouches used by the Egyptian pharaohs, where a court scribe made up the design. Yet these are idioms that attest an origin by way of a sort of stamp. Stamps are secularized versions of seals and are ideal for the illiterate, including emperors such as Charlemagne. Because he was unable to do so himself, the document was drawn up by someone else and then folded in two (*diploma*) and closed with wax lacquer. The emperor then used his monogrammed ring to put his signature, which in less heroic times would become the stamps that make themselves heard in so many offices. In the last resort, then, we have a signature. The stamp is an attempt to standardize and multiply signatures even absent the legitimate signatory; in this respect, it is a sort of proxy or, more often, a way to propagate the signature of a juridical person in pre-computer times. The Italian Republic, the Interior Ministry, and the Philosophy Department do not have a signature, but they do have a stamp, which is at least in principle idiomatic.

In some cases, however, the stamp can be, so to speak, the original, of which the signature is a copy. In Japan, here as in other things against the grain, a signature is a substitute for a stamp. Each child is given a stamp, which starts to have legal value at the age of sixteen and hence has the function that signatures have for us. One interesting consequence is that when a Japanese person signs a check in a Western bank, it is like a Westerner using a stamp. In any case, we can obtain the effect of a signature even absent, in part or whole, the name. This confirms the hypothesis that it is accidental that we use our names as signatures, given that once it was possible to sign with a cross and, anyway, in many signatures the name is illegible.[14] In a monogram, the signature may not be wholly illegible, and all the more so in initials, not to mention the fact that a national anthem or a television signature tune is only conventionally connected to the name in question; the notes of the Marseillaise are something like the signature of France, something absolutely characteristic, just as a jingle can become the recognizable opening signature of a radio or television program.

6.2.6 Individuals

So we reach the conclusion. As we have seen, the way that a signature is connected to the signatory has little to do with the name and can do without it altogether. It is idiomatic insofar as it makes use of a styleme, which is a deviation from the norm and, so, much closer to an error. After all, what is typical about a person's accent if not an undertone of dialect, a mild pronunciation error or a deviation from the norm? Now, it is this very error, this shibboleth, that picks out the individuality of individuals and characterizes their uniqueness.

In fact, this claim is far from obvious, but it follows from a straight choice. There are two ways of explaining the uniqueness of persons. One is hifalutin and solemn, and it insists on our positive exceptionalness because we are infinite and ineffable. Leibniz himself, the defender of the principle of the identity of indiscernibles, said that the individual is ineffable. If there were two drops of water that were exactly alike, they would be the same. But this is not possible, because every drop is different from every other; and the same goes in spades for persons. This story does not convince me. I do not feel myself to be at all infinite, it does not seem to me that I have an infinity of masks, I feel that in the overwhelming majority of my behavior, thought, and emotion I am just like the rest of humankind. And in any case, travel agencies, restaurants, filmmakers, and so much else besides, all presuppose the perfectly reasonable notion that the individual is anything but ineffable and infinite, but can rather be encompassed in just a few traits.

The problem is quite different. Uniqueness is rather a negative exceptionalness, a production error so to say, at least a speech defect or a shibboleth. When we are right, we are not individuals but universal, because anyone in our situation would think the way that we do. But we are most ourselves when we go wrong. It is error, or at least imprecision, that individuates us. Otherwise, we could not explain why a scribble, a signature as an allegory of our imperfection, should be called on to individuate us. There is nothing surprising in this. We know perfectly well that the only way to be loved is to be loved for our defects, given that our (supposed) merits make us like thousands of others. And it is with this conviction—or rather this encouragement—that I take leave of the patient reader.

6.3 EPILOGUE: ELEVEN THESES

By way of conclusion, I would like to summarize the underlying theses that I have sought to expound in this book.

1. **Ontology catalogs the world of life.** The philosophy that I propose is a descriptive metaphysics of a realist type, which aims to account for the social world and everyday experience, which is to say the world

that stands outside the range of the natural sciences. Its model is the catalog. The sort of understanding I propose requires in the first instance the identification, classification, and distinction of what there is in this world, how it is ordered, and how it is to be distinguished from the other things that there are. From this perspective, I claim that the world is the totality of individuals: stones, organisms, artifacts, and persons both physical and juridical. The salient characteristic of individuals is that of belonging to classes (the class of corkscrews, that of emperors, that of symbolist poems) as *examples*, both in the sense that they can serve as principles of classification and in the sense that they are members (or samples) of a class, which does not itself preexist the individuals but is derived from them.

2. **There are three types of objects: natural, ideal, and social.** Examples are divided into subjects and objects. Subjects have representations, while objects do not. In turn, objects are divided into three classes: natural objects, ideal objects, and social objects. Natural objects exist in space and time independently of subjects; ideal objects exist outside space and time independently of subjects; social objects exist in space and time and are dependent on subjects. For all that the principal characteristic of subjects—that of having representations—is of central importance for social ontology, the difference between subjects and objects should not be taken to be a basic categorial difference. Indeed, subjects are also a type of natural objects (they are a subcategory of them) insofar as they are biological entities and (if they find themselves in society) they are also social objects. From the point of view of a theory of lived experience, social objects are the most important of all, because much of our happiness or unhappiness depends on them.

3. **Ontology is distinct from epistemology.** As a point of methodology, I propose to mark a distinction between ontology and epistemology. The former concerns what there is independently of how we know it and of whether we know it or not. The latter is knowledge of what there is, or rather, what we are justified in believing in a given context. These two dimensions have often been confused, as we can see from the way that we often make the existence of objects depend on our knowledge of them. This, which I call the *transcendental fallacy*, makes the external world derive from language and thought, and so

presents itself as a form of logocentrism. I maintain that this is not how things stand. In the world of natural objects, what there is has the essential characteristic of unemendability: It cannot be corrected by the mere force of thought. What we know about what there is, on the other hand, can be emended, and this process of cumulative correction constitutes progress and the ultimate sense of knowledge. For, what we are justified in believing can change and be emended as science progresses.

4. **Social objects depend on subjects, but they are not subjective.** The external world, understood in the first instance as the world of natural objects, is independent of conceptual schemes and of perceptual apparatuses. Just as there is no continuous and necessary link that leads from perception to experience and from that to science, neither, on the other hand, does knowledge make up the main activity within our experience. In the world of social objects, by contrast, belief determines being, given that these objects depend on subjects. This does not mean that things like promises and money have a purely subjective dimension. Rather, it means that, unless there were subjects capable of recognizing social objects, such social objects would not exist. The upshot of this observation is that while transcendentalism is not applicable to natural objects, it fits social objects perfectly. The Kantian thesis that intuitions without concepts are blind does not apply to lakes and storms (which remain as they are independently of our conceptualizations), but it does apply to mortgages and conferences.

5. **The constitutive rule of social objects is Object = Inscribed Act.** It thus becomes possible to develop an ontology and an epistemology of social objects. The epistemology renews the tradition of the sciences of the spirit, defining itself rather as a "science of the letter," given the importance that inscriptions are endowed with in the construction of social reality. The ontology is a theory of social objects, namely those that obey the constitutive rule "Object = Inscribed Act." That is to say, social objects are the result of social acts (and involve at least two persons) characterized by the fact of being inscribed: on paper, in a computer file, or even simply in the heads of persons.

6. **There is nothing social outside the text.** The importance attributed to inscription is the characteristic feature of my theory. The underlying idea is that it is not enough that the act be performed so as to

produce an object; it is necessary that it be registered. A marriage or a promise that was not inscribed would not be an object, whereas a mountain can easily exist without being mapped. In this sense, we do not hold that "there is nothing outside the text" (given that natural and ideal objects exist without inscriptions), but only that "there is nothing social outside the text."

7. **Society is not based on communication but on registration.** Because nothing social exists outside the text, papers, archives, and documents constitute the fundamental element of the social world. Society is not based on communication but on registration, which is the condition for the creation of social objects. Man grows as man and socializes through registration. Naked life is nothing but a remote starting point, and culture begins very early making for a clothed life, which is manifested in registrations and imitations: language, behaviors, and rites. This explains why writing is so important—and even more so *archi-writing*, which is the realm of registration that precedes and encircles writing in its proper or current meaning.

8. **The mind is a surface that collects inscriptions.** As regards a theory of mind, social ontology is based on ichnology, which is to say, a theory of traces. The representation of the mind as a *tabula* or a writing surface is not a mere metaphor, but captures the fact that perceptions and thoughts come to us as inscriptions in our mind. But the mind is not just an inscribed surface; it is also capable of grasping inscriptions, namely the traces that there are in the world, on the surface that is before us in experience. We can make out an ascending hierarchy that takes in traces (any incision on a background), registrations (traces in the mind as a *tabula*), and inscriptions in the technical sense (traces available to at least two persons).

9. **Documents in the strong sense are inscriptions of acts.** Considered as a theory of society, the ontology of social objects presents itself as *documentality*, which is to say as a theory of documents as the highest form of social objects, which can in turn be divided into documents in the strong sense as inscriptions of acts, and documents in the weak sense as registrations of facts. Documents can have practical purposes, or they can be mainly directed at the evocation of sentiments. In the latter case, we have artworks, understood as those things that pretend to be persons.

10. **The letter is the foundation of the spirit.** Considered as a theory of culture, the ontology of social objects presents itself as a phenomenology of the letter. It aims to recognize in every work of the spirit the result of inner and outer inscriptions, making use of the results reached by ichnology and documentality. This holds as much for the subjective spirit (the soul considered as *tabula*) as for both the objective spirit (the world of institutions) and the absolute spirit (art, religion, and philosophy). No product of the spirit could exist without the letter, registration, and the document; and, more radically, spirit itself finds the condition of its possibility in the letter and in the inscriptions that constitute us as social beings.

11. **Individuality is manifested in the signature.** Considered as a theory of the subject, the ontology of social objects develops into a theory of the idiom, of style, and of the signature. The sense of the uniqueness of each subject derives from its own peculiar deviations from the norm. This is exactly what we find with a signature, which is a way of representing publicly one's own presence and identity, and consists in writing one's own name in a way that differs more or less from the calligraphic norm. This principle of individuation applies to artworks (which are characterized by their style) as much as to the recognizable signs that we find in documents. The individual is ineffable and can never be captured in an ontology or an epistemology, but the sign of this individuality is shown in its style.

NOTES

INTRODUCTION

1. Earlier partial versions of the theory can be found in "Documentality or Why Nothing Social Exists Beyond the Text," in *Cultures, Conflict-Analysis-Dialogue*, ed. C. Kanzian and E. Runggaldier, *Proceedings of the 29th Ludwig Wittgenstein Symposium in Kirchberg, Austria* (Publications of the Ludwig Wittgenstein Society, 2007), pp. 385–401; "Ontologia dell'opera d'arte e del documento," in *Ontologie regionali*, ed. A. Bottani and R. Davies (Milan: Mimesis, 2007), pp. 141–163; "Documentalità: ontologia del mondo sociale," *Ethics and Politics* 9, no. 2 (2007): 240–239, online at www.unit.it/-etica/ferraris.pdf; "Science sociali," in *Storia dell'ontologia*, ed. M. Ferraris (Milan: Bompiani, 2008), pp. 475–489. See also the conference proceedings of the Centro interuniversitario di ontologia teorica e applicata, *Documentalità. L'ontologia degli oggetti sociali. Rivista di estetica* n.s. 36, no. 3 (2007), edited by D. Tagliafico.

2. In Greek, *ichnos* means "trace, track, footprint" both in the material sense ("follow in the tracks" for instance in the *Phaedrus* and in the *Theaetetus*) and in the spiritual sense ("the trace of speeches" Aeschylus, *Prometheus*, 854). The term echoes in the Greek name for Sardinia (Hyknusa), the "footprint" which is the aerial view of the island's shape, *ichneusis* is the search for traces; *ichneutés* is a researcher; "*ichnéuo*" is to search (*Parmenides*, 128c); and *ichnographia* is a map or sketch. I gave the title "*Ichnology*" to an article of mine in 1995 ("Ichnologia" in *Interpretazione ed emancipazione. Studi in onore di Gianni Vattimo*, ed. G. Carchia and M. Ferraris (Milan: Cortina, 1995), pp. 103–135) and to the closing chapter of *Estetica razionale* (Milan: Cortina, 1997). Using what I believed to be a neologism (and I had to take care not to let the word be corrected to *iconology*), I meant a general theory of traces, a sort of semiotics broadened to include also thought processes, and which a strong emphasis on registration over communication. Years later, I learned that that there is a scientific discipline called *iconology*, which studies traces, tracks, footprints, ruts, tunnels, and in general all the imprints that leave information about the lifestyles of organisms ancient and modern. In this sense, it is misleading to think of it as just a branch of paleontology, given that, in addition to paleoichnology, which is concerned with ancient traces, there also exists neoichnology, which studies recent traces, often taking clues from the experience amassed in paleoichnology. This field of study dates back to the beginning of the nineteenth century but has grown enor-

mously in recent years. There are university courses in ichnology (mostly in Earth Sciences), ichnotheques, and, in the last fifteen years, the journal *Ichnos: An International Journal for Plant and Animal Traces*. The scientists who study ichnology, predictably enough, call themselves *ichnologists*.

1. CATALOG OF THE WORLD

1. P. Otlet, *Traité de documentation* (1934), reprinted *Traité de documentation: le livre sure le livre. Téorie et pratique* (Liège: Centre de lecture publique de la communauté française de Belgique, 1989). Otlet's biographer, W. B. Rayward, has published an annotated translation of a selection of his writings: P. Otlet, *International Organization and Dissemination of Knowledge: Selected Essays,* (Amsterdam: Elsevier, 1990).

2. I am grateful to the archive's director, Stéphanie Manfroid, for supplying me with a copy.

3. M. Foucault, *Discipline and Punish: The Birth of the Prison* (New York: Random House, 1977).

4. He dissociated telereading, as a particular application of television, and telewriting, as a particular application of telemechanics; see Otlet, *Traité*, p. 390.

5. *Don Giovanni*, Act I, scene v.

6. P. F. Strawson, *Individuals: An Essay in Descriptive Metaphysics* (London: Methuen, 1959).

7. Obviously, there were alternative solutions. In particular, I could have divided individuals into objects in the full sense, which have no representations, and subjects, which are objects that have representations. In that case, I would have had among natural objects those with representations (which are subjects) and those without representations, which are a subset of objects proper. But it seemed to me that the distinction between subjects and objects was clearer.

8. The launching pad for these attitudes is Kant's principle that "intuitions without concepts are blind," which I discuss at length in connection with philosophical constructivism in Chapter 2.1.

9. In particular, Nelson Goodman, *Ways of Worldmaking* (Indianapolis: Hackett, 1978).

10. After the classical ontologists such as Wolff and Baumgarten, the English philosopher C. D. Broad held that the task of science is to draw up catalogs of the world (*Scientific Thought* [New York: Harcourt Brace, 1923]). More recently, the idea of metaphysics as a catalog of the world has been reproposed with vigor and acumen by A. Varzi in *Parole, oggetti, eventi e altri argomenti di metafisica* (Rome: Carocci, 2001), followed by P. Valore, *L'inventario del mondo. Guida allo studio dell'ontologia* (Turin: Utet, 2008).

11. A slightly different case is presented by those material interventions, deriving from acts of conscious deliberation, that concern the realm of natural and social

objects. Here, the inquiry is genetic and, as such, can be a useful supplement to ontology, though it is distinct from and inessential to it.

12. Among the supporters of ontology as a theory of objects, and hence of the fundamental identity of entity, object, and thing, I cite P. Natorp, *Einleitung in die Psychologie nach kritischer Methode* (Freiburg: Mohr, 1888); K. Twardowski, *On the Content and Object of Presentations: A Psychological Investigation*, trans. R. Grossmann (The Hague: Nijhoff, 1977); A. Meinong, "The Theory of Objects," trans. Isaac Levi, D. B. Terrell, and Roderick Chisholm, in *Realism and the Background of Phenomenology*, ed. Roderick Chisholm (Atascadero, Calif.: Ridgeview, 1981); H. Pichler, *Über Christian Wolffs Ontologie* (Leipzig: Dürr, 1909), a book that would have a great influence on Hartmann. For the centrality of the object in classical ontology, see P. Kobau, *Essere qualcosa. Ontologia e psicologia in Wolff* (Turin: Trauben, 2004).

13. In his *Metaphysik* (Leipzig: Weidmann, 1841) Hermann Lotze made the powerful claim that things are laws.

14. C. E. von Hoften and E. S. Spelke, "Object Perception and Object-Directed Reaching in Infants," *Journal of Experimental Psychology* 114 (1985): 198–211.

15. Richard N. Nisbet in *The Geography of Thought: How Asians and Westerners Think Differently* (New York: Free Press, 2003) has picked out different tendencies in Westerners and Asians in the selection of objects, but these are minimal differences relative to those that show up in language, concepts, and customs.

16. On this point, I refer the reader to my "Inemendabilità, ontologia, realtà sociale," *Rivista di Estetica* 19 (2002): 160–199.

17. Thus Reinach: "How Ontology or the A Priori Theory of the Object Concerns the Analysis of All Possible Types of Objects as Such," in *The A Priori Foundations of Civil Law*, trans. John Crosby, *Aletheia* 3 (1983): 1–141 at p. 6. The main change I make to this way of looking at things is that I do not reduce the analysis to a priori theories but include also the realm of the a posteriori, or what is concretely to be found in the world.

18. G. Berkeley, *Treatise concerning the Principles of Human Knowledge* (1710), Introduction §13.

19. *Hamlet*, Act I, scene v.

20. W. O. Quine, "On What There Is" (1948), reprinted in *From a Logical Point of View* (Cambridge, Mass.: Harvard University Press, 1953), p. 4.

21. I am thinking of the "Ockhamizing zeal" that Ryle chose to characterize his own philosophical youth: G. Ryle, *Collected Papers* (London: Hutchinson, 1971), p. 7.

22. The expression "Meinongian jungles" is due to R. Routley, *Exploring Meinong's Jungle and Beyond* (Canberra: Australian National University Press, 1980).

23. G. W. Leibniz, *New Essays on Human Understanding* (1705), trans. Peter Remnant and Jonathan Bennett (Cambridge: Cambridge University Press, 1996), ch. IV §1.

24. And that Roberta De Monticelli calls "the thesis of the existence of nonempirical data"; see R. De Monticelli and C. Conni, *Ontologia del nuovo. La rivoluzione fenomenologica e la ricerca oggi* (Milan: Mondadori, 2008). I have discussed the logic

of the exemplarity of the sample at length in "Kant e l'esemplarità dell'esempio," *Filosofia* 94, ed. G. Vattimo (Rome: Laterza, 1995), pp. 147–172; in *Estetica razionale*, pp. 302–318; in *L'altra estetica*, ed. M. Ferraris and P. Kobau (Turin: Einaudi, 2001), pp. 5–107, esp. pp. 41–6. I come back to the point in 1.3.3.2.

25. The prototype of this sort of argument can be found in Goodman, *Ways of Worldmaking*.

26. [Translator's note: The Italian word for *sample* here also means a champion, someone who is exceptional because he or she sets, for instance, sporting records.]

27. I discuss this matter in my introduction to the Italian translation of Strawson's *Individuals* (*Individui*, trans E. Bencivenga [Milan: Mimesis, 2008]).

28. This is the terminology suggested by Roberto Casati in his "Scienze cognitive," in *Storia dell'ontologia*, ed. M. Ferraris (Milan: Bompiani, 2008), pp. 437ff.

29. Achille Varzi has brilliantly argued the point in "Il catalogo universale," in *Forme della ragione*, ed. R. Finzi and P. Zellini (Bologna: Clueb, forthcoming), online at www.columbia.edu/~av72/papers/CatalogoUniversale.pdf.

30. Jonathan Schaffer has rightly questioned the idea of a fundamental level of description: "Is There a Fundamental Level?," *Nous* 37 (2003): 498–517.

31. In this framework, the notion of dependence can play an important role, because it turns out to be more respectful of the descriptivist principle than are other notions (such as appearance) that can undertake similar theoretical work. When I say that color is dependent on chromatic waves, I mean something true without on that ground reducing color to a mere appearance, that is to something that should have no place in our catalog of the world.

32. W. O. Quine, *Word and Object* (Cambridge, Mass.: MIT Press, 1960), p. 11.

33. J. L. Austin, *Philosophical Papers* (Oxford: Oxford University Press, 1961), p. 178.

34. I reuse this example from my *Tunnel delle multe. Ontologia degli oggetti quotidiani* (Turin: Einaudi, 2008), pp. 207–208. In that book I propose also a theory of objects that underlies what I have been saying so far. On the importance of objects or things, see R. Bodei, *La vita delle cose* (Rome: Laterza, 2009), and F. Rigotti, "Il pensiero delle cose," *Sole* 24 Ore, July 5, 2009.

35. J. L. Austin, *Sense and Sensibilia* (Oxford: Oxford University Press, 1962), p. 8.

36. This is in agreement with the phenomenology offered by Aristotle in the *De Anima*: "the soul never thinks without images" (413a16–7), and images are essential to deliberation and desire.

37. F. Brentano, *Psychology from the Empirical Standpoint* (1874), ed. and trans. L. McAlister et al. (London: Routledge, 1973).

38. I have developed this line of thought in my *La fidanzata automatica* (Milan: Bompiani, 2007), pp. 193ff.

39. On the various ways one might define consciousness, see D. M. Rosenthal, "Two Concepts of Consciousness," *Philosophical Studies* 49 (1986): 329–359, reprinted in Rosenthal, *Consciousness and Mind* (Oxford: Oxford University Press, 2006),

pp. 22–45; see also P. Bieri, "Why Is Consciousness Puzzling?" in *Conscious Experience*, ed. T. Metzinger (Exeter: Imprint Academic, 1995), pp. 45–59.

40. This distinction was introduced by the Polish logician and philosopher Kazimierz Twardowski in *On the Concept and Object.*

41. The allusion is to Giordano Bruno's *De Umbris Idearum* (1582), which proposed a memory technique.

42. See the analysis in Aristotle's *De Memoria et Reminiscentia.*

43. I have discussed the matter at length in my *L'immaginazione* (Bologna: Il Mulino, 1996), pp. 27 ff.

44. See G. Frege, "The Thought, A Logical Inquiry" (1918–19), trans. A. Quinton and M. Quinton, *Mind* 65 (1956): 289–311.

45. "The voice that escapes from the breast / cannot be recalled; / the arrow cannot be held back / once it has left the bow," Metastasio, Aria 51. Schopenhauer tells the following anecdote: Napoleon was riding his horse and his hat fell on the ground. An officer picked it up and gave it back to him. Napoleon, who had looked at him distractedly, said "Thank you, captain." The officer, who was in fact a lieutenant, had the wits to ask him, "In which regiment, sire?" Napoleon could not take his words back, so the man was promoted on the spot.

46. "Man is this night, this pure nothingness, which encloses everything in its simplicity—an endless wealth of representations and images of which none stands before him or are not insofar as they are present. What exists here is the night, the inside of nature—a *Pure Self,* in phantasmagoric representations all around the night, suddenly a bleeding head leaps out here and there a white figure, and equally suddenly they disappear. We can see this night when we look into a man's eyes—we penetrate into a night that becomes *frightful;* here everyone is suspended against the night of the world," G. W. F. Hegel, *Hegel and the Human Spirit: A Translation of the Jena Lectures on the Philosophy of Spirit,* trans. L. Rauch (Detroit: Wayne State University Press, 1983), p. 87.

47. In his *Intervista a un suicida,* Vittorio Sereni wrote, "You who, from the heart of the city / Talk about the heartless city / Think about what a man can be in a town," and continued "under the pen of the scribe a rustling sheet/and then / in the dust of the archive / nothing no one no place never."

48. Here I take up the classification I first proposed in 2005 in *Dove sei? Ontologia del telefonino* (Milan: Bompiani, 2005), pp. 69ff.

49. Unlike, for instance, the process that realizes them, where the space occupied is that of the participants in the process and the time is that of the duration of the process.

50. See D. von Hildebrand, *What is Philosophy?* (Chicago: Franciscan Herald Press, 1973).

51. Aristotle, *Metaphysics,* V, vi. Among the moderns, see Strawson, *Individuals;* W. O. Quine, "Speaking of Objects," *Proceedings and Addresses of the American Philosophical Association* 31 (1958): 5–22; and Quine, *Word and Object.*

52. Frege, "The Thought," pp. 299ff.

53. J. Derrida, *Edmund Husserl's Origin of Geometry: An Introduction*, trans. J. P. Leavey (Lincoln: University of Nebraska Press, 1978).

54. S. Awodey, "An Answer to Hellman's Question 'Does Category Theory Provide a Framework for Mathematical Structuralism?'" *Philosophia Mathematica* 12 (2004): 54–64.

55. In line with what we have said so far, the thesis is put forward by Husserl and developed by Derrida in his *Introduction* to Husserl's *Origin*.

56. "This is no longer a working number, please redial your call."

57. House numbers, like telephone numbers, are codes and so social objects rather than ideal objects. Add Via Melezet, 18, Turin to Corso Cristoforo Colombo, 8, Milan to am Kastanienberg 12, Neckargemünd to 6, rue de l'Arbalète, Paris to the junction of 119th Street and Morningside Drive New York, and what do you get? Fortunately, no one has ever asked. The difference between a number as an ideal object and a number as a social object can be seen in various fields, to which we may dedicate a note.

Ordinal numbers. In his lecture on phenomenology of 1914 (in his *Sämtliche Werke*, ed. K. Schumann and B. Smith [Munich: Philosophia, 1989], Reinach denies for good reasons that ordinal numbers are really numbers (esp. pp. 1:538–9). Numbers considered as social objects have a great deal to do with the difference between ordinals and cardinals, to which we generally pay little attention, forgetting that ordinals are not really numbers or at least are not arithmetic numbers. At best, we notice this when we have to make that little effort to remember that the twentieth century is the century that begins in 1901. The calculation becomes a muddle when, mixing in the base-twelve measure of the hours, we wonder whether by chance the fourteenth century is that of the years beginning with 1200. Dates have a very weak arithmetic value, representing rather the quintessence of the social world. The Bastille was stormed in 1789, America was discovered in 1492, and so on. If I add 1789 to 1492, what do I get? Nothing, except perhaps a fine date for setting a science-fiction novel. And the names of several months are ordinal numbers, even though the number in question is wrong: September (7th) is the ninth month and so on. Likewise in Portuguese the names of the days of the week are numbered to avoid paganism; and also here the numbers are wrong: Segunda-feira (2nd) is the first day and so on.

Measures. Measuring units are a typical example of the social use of ideal objects. Lengths, breadths, and weights, in the various kilometers and deciliters, in gallons and feet and yards, in miles and versts, in parsangs and knots. Temperatures measured in Celsius or Fahrenheit. Earthquakes on the Richter scale or the Mercalli scale. Minutes and hours, which are counted on the Babylonian base of 60 and 12, which no one would use in arithmetic. As if the body were the origin of all the measures and calculations, we have inches, palms, feet, and spans. Numbers as social objects also play a role in disproportion. There were counting systems in which there were only one and two, then three indicated everything else; this remains in the French *très* and the Italian *troppo*. If you say "*très joli*" or "*troppo bello*" you are not counting but are rather saying that what you are referring to goes beyond all quantification. By the same logic, to refer to a troop is not to count, but to use the Sanskrit root, which also gives us "trans." Nor again is the biblical phrase "seventy times seven" an arithmetic expression.

Common nouns and proper names. Not in order to avoid paganism, as in the case of the Portuguese day names, but because we cannot find a name for everything, the toes have numbers as their names. In such cases, the numbers stands in for a common noun or may indicate, for instance, a model of automobile, either ordinal, as in the case of the Fiat Uno, or in reference to the engine size, as in the case of the Fiat Cinquecento (500cc), or again with models of pistols or guns, such as P38 or M16. M16 is no more an arithmetic number than is Kalashnikov, and Kalashnikov, when used of the machine gun rather than of its designer, is no more of a proper name than M16 is. But there is also the opposite direction, in which, once they have become names, numbers acquire nicknames, even among those who have the good sense not to talk about florins or tournois: twenty-five cents becomes a quarter and ten cents a dime. The Romans never stopped counting: Quintilia or Quintilian for a fifth child, Sextus for a sixth, and Septimus for a seventh. The reason was simple: only the first four children had the right to a name that was not a number, such as Titus, Caius, or Sempronius (which are the names used in modern Italian for Tom, Dick, and Harry). But probably once they got to Octavia or Octavian (numerous families), they gave up counting. Even though there was Decimus, often they used Numerius—numerous.

58. *Ontologia sociale. Potere deontico e regole costitutive,* ed. P. Di Lucia, (Macerata: Quodlibet, 2003); R. Sacco, *Antropologia giuridica* (Bologna: Il Mulino, 2007).

59. P. Di Lucia, *L'universale della promessa* (Milan: Giuffré, 1997).

60. In his *Nunc Pro Tunc. Temporal Aspects in Social Ontology,* 2008, ms. (online at www.labont.com/public/papers/torrengo/NuncProTunc.pdf), Giuliano Torrengo distinguishes among the individual tokens, the eternal types (corresponding to my Archetypes$_1$) and the temporal types (my Archetypes$_2$). Eternal types can be understood as possibilities that do not need to be inscribed but correspond to what Torrengo calls "documents that institute types" (for instance, the laws that govern marriage unions in a given state), and to the individual token, there correspond "documents that institute tokens" (such as a particular marriage certificate).

61. This is the claim of Amie Thomasson (*Fiction and Metaphysics* [Cambridge: Cambridge University Press, 1999]).

62. Obviously in a literate society. We can perfectly well imagine a preliterate society in which marriages are registered by means of a rite or a custom, but this, in depending on a tradition (whether explicit or implicit), reveals its connection with what, in Chapter 4.2, I discuss under the heading of "archiwriting."

63. I examine this problem in detail in *Goodby Kant! Cosa resta oggi della Critica della ragion pura* (Milan: Bompiani, 2004), pp. 117–126.

64. At least in the standard formulation of the *Critique of Pure Reason*, the relation that applies to the determining judgment and that goes from the rule to the case. Things are rather different in the *Critique of Judgment*, where Kant speaks of the "reflective judgment" that rises from the case to the rule. As we shall see, this applies very neatly to the phenomenon of social objects.

65. In my review of the Italian translation of the *Critique of Judgment* by E. Garroni and H. Hohenegger (Turin: Einaudi, 1999) in *Il Sole* 24 *Ore*, April 4, 1999, p. 29.

66. This is a differentiation that Meinong expressed in terms of the difference between existing and ex-existing objects, but that I propose to reformulate in terms of the distinction between *ontic* social objects and *historical* ones. Ontic social objects are all the social objects that are actually present as states and not merely as acts: for instance, the act of promising at 6:00 in the evening that I will pay five euros tomorrow is not a social object, but rather a social act, while the state of the promise began to obtain from 6:01 and is a social object. Obviously, there is a problem of establishing when a social object is actually present, whether or not the conditions for its coming into being are in conformity with the rules or legitimate; this issue is at the heart of many judicial disputes. On the other hand, historical social objects are those that survive only as inscriptions, such as the Roman Empire. Here, too, the idea of appealing to an ancient right is a sign that the distinction between the ontic and the historical is not hard and fast, but can be determined by contextual considerations.

67. As I mentioned in 1.1.5, Austin is right to think that things are "moderate-sized specimens of dry goods"; likewise, A. J. Ayer wrote of "familiar objects" in *The Foundations of Empirical Knowledge* (London: Macmillan, 1940), p. 2. The reference to size and familiarity may be useful also in capturing some typical features of social objects, whose temporal career is in many cases measured by bodily extension and the length of a human life.

68. B. Brown "Thing Theory," *Critical Inquiry* 28 (2001): 1–22.

69. M. Heidegger, *Being And Time*, (1927) trans. J. Stambaugh (Albany: SUNY Press, 1996), §§21 and 69b (*Vorhandenheit*) and §§15–18, 22 and 69a (*Zuhandenheit*).

70. "Man is the wisest of animals because he has hands," Diels-Kranz 59A102

71. "The soul is like the hand, for the hand is the instrument of instruments, and the soul is the form of forms," *De Anima*, 432a1–3. In the *Parts of Animals* (687a10–33) Aristotle objects to Anaxagoras: "Anaxagoras holds that man is the most intelligent of the animals in virtue of having hands; it is reasonable to maintain instead that he gained hands because he is the most intelligent. . . . To him who is able to master the largest number of techniques, nature has given in the hand the instrument adapted to use the largest number of instruments."

72. "The hand is the ensouled artificer of human happiness; it may be said of it that it makes man what he is, that in the hand, the active organ of his self-perfecting, man is present as an animating force; and, being originally his destiny, the hand expresses this in itself. G. W. F. Hegel, *Phenomenology of Mind* (1807) trans. J. B. Baillie

(London: Allen & Unwin, 1961), pp. 342–343. It is thanks to the hand that we grasp our destiny. But, continues Hegel, the hand, like writing and not unlike the voice, is also the expression of individuality, the exteriorization of the inner: "The simple features of the *hand*, like the timbre and volume of the voice as the individual determination of language—and in its turn language itself, inasmuch as it receives from the hand a firmer existence than it does from the voice, become writing and, in particular, *handwriting*—all that is an expression of the inner state" (ibid.). The literal and explicit reference to the Aristotelian formula of the hand as the "universal instrument" is in *Encyclopedia of the Philosophical Sciences*, trans E. Behler (New York: Continuum, 1990).

73. On the theory I am proposing and that I have developed at length in *La fidanzata automatica* (pp. 65–128), artworks are both social objects and physical objects: this excludes from the register of potential works the whole enormous territory of ideal objects. Amie Thomasson's view is similar to mine and she has coined a new ontological category to capture physico-social objects, which she calls "abstract artifacts" (*Fiction and Metaphysics*, 117–120), whereas I prefer to account for social objects in terms of documentality.

74. Cf. the analysis offered in G. Lorini, *Dimensioni giuridiche dell'istituzionale* (Padua: Cedam, 2000).

75. Giovanni della Casa, *Galateo overo de' costumi*. [Translator's note: in Italian, *costumi* has been adopted as a common word for etiquette.]

2. ONTOLOGY AND EPISTEMOLOGY

1. I coined the phrase in *Il mondo esterno* (Milan: Bompiani, 2001), and discussed it at length there, especially at pp. 97–106.

2. I introduced the concept of the *transcendental fallacy* in ibid. and developed it in *Goodbye Kant!* pp. 65–72.

3. A (certain sort of) constructionist might dispute this description of his position, saying something like, "I would not dream of claiming that reality depends on our conceptual schemes; I only want to say that certain formats (such as that of objects) and structures of experience are imposed by the mind on the flux of information that comes our way from the external world, which I really believe exists quite independently of our minds." To this constructionist, who is after all very similar to the one we met in 1.1.2, I reply pretty much as I did there: To think that the external world is there but that it is amorphous and is determined by our conceptual schemes seems a timid kind of acosmism. In a sense, more robust positions, such as skepticism about the external world, seem to be preferable insofar as they correspond more closely to our experience. I do not find it particularly hard to suppose that life is a dream. But I do find it hard to explain how come the swarms of elementary particles that make up the external world come together so well to create a world that submits with perfect timing and harmony not merely to my conceptual schemes, but also to

my neighbor's and to those of my dog Fido. This seems a genuine miracle, and I cannot manage to understand how two diners who are so harmoniously synchronized as to see the same table and the same food should then find themselves in disagreement about the flavors they are tasting and a wide range of other topics of conversation.

4. M. Ferraris, "Logocentrismo: 3 0 4 Taglie," in *Rudolf Arnheim. Arte e percezione visiva*, ed. L. Pizzo Russo (Palermo: Centro Internazionale Studi di Estetica, 2005), pp. 81–97.

5. R. Descartes, *Meditations on First Philosophy* (1641) trans. J. Cottingham, R. Stoothoff, D. Murdoch and A. J. P. Kenny, in *The Philosophical Writings of Descartes* (Cambridge: Cambridge University Press, 1984–91), vol. 2. I develop this point in "24 modi per dar torto a Cartesio," in *L'identità empirica*, ed. I. Bianchi and U. Savardi (Milan: Angeli, 2005), pp. 138–146.

6. R. Descartes, *Rules for the Direction of the Mind* (1628), in ibid, vol. 1.

7. Regarding this use of "naturalization," Diego Marconi, reviewing my *Goodbye Kant!* ("L'esperienza non è scienza," *Il Sole 24 Ore*, December 19, 2004) observed that, because we normally mean by "naturalization" the reduction of a discipline to a natural science, we cannot understand how physics can be naturalized, given that it is already a natural science. The observation is very apt, but the fact is that Kant proposes a naturalization that is raised to a power of at least two: the natural science that is physics is not just a theoretical construct but corresponds exactly to the conceptual schemes and perceptual apparatus that, for the most part, human nature is endowed with.

8. Quine's *From Stimulus to Science* (Cambridge, Mass.: Harvard University Press, 1995) presents a perfect paraphrase of the transcendental fallacy.

9. This agrees with the proposal of R. Casati and A. C. Varzi, "Un altro mondo?" *Rivista di Estetica* 19 (2002): 131–159.

10. C. Becchio and C. Bertone, "Neuroscienze," in Ferraris, ed., *Storia dell'ontologia*, pp. 458–459.

11. E. Gombrich, *Art and Illusion* (London: Phaidon, 1960).

12. A. Jacomuzzi, N. Bruno, and P. Kobau, "Molyneux's Question Redux," *Phenomenology and the Cognitive Sciences* 2 (2003): 255–280.

13. G. Kanizsa, *Vedere e pensare* (Milan: Il Mulino, 1991); and Kanizsa, *Grammatica del vedere. Saggi suall percezione* (Milan: Il Mulino, 1980). I have set this point out in full in *L'ermeneutica* (Rome: Laterza, 1998), pp. 62–66, and in *Il mondo esterno*, pp. 188ff.

14. Taken from V. Costa, *L'estetica trascendentale fenomenologica: Sensibilità e razionalità nella filosofia di Husserl* (Milan: Vita e Pensiero, 1999).

15. Hamlet: "Do you see yonder cloud that's almost in shape of a camel?" Lord Polonius: "By the mass, and 'tis like a camel, indeed." Hamlet: "Methinks it is like a weasel." Lord Polonius: "It is backed like a weasel." Hamlet: "Or like a whale?" Lord Polonius: "Very like a whale." Hamlet, Act III, scene iii.

16. F. Nietzsche *Posthumous Fragments* 1886–7, 7 [60].

17. See my *L'ermeneutica*, pp. 17–20.

18. [Translator's note: In Italian, the change of only the first letter of *fatti* produces this effect with *matti*, *patti*, and *gatti*.]

19. Let us see how it works: (a) there are no facts; (b) it is a fact that there are cats; (c) there is no such fact as that there are cats; but then (d) there are no cats. Given the absurdity of the conclusion (d), we are authorized to reject premise (a). If the supporter of pragmatism were to claim that the argument does not go through because (c) does not imply (d), he would owe us an explanation of what he means by "fact." To claim that from the nonexistence of the fact that there are no cats *it does not follow* that there are not cats makes the premise (a) vacuous; but to claim that the implication does no hold is plain false.

20. L. Wittgenstein *Philosophical Investigations*, trans G. E. M. Anscombe and G. H. von Wright (Oxford: Blackwell, 1953), §217.

21. Quine, *Word and Object*, p. 41.

22. J. L. Borges, "Averroes' Search," in *Labyrinths*, trans. D.A. Yates (Harmondsworth: Penguin, 1964).

23. Now it is true that I (and it is probably an idiosyncrasy of mine) never really understand the arrows on the roads (it seems to me, for instance, that the turning signs on Swiss roads are inviting one to swerve off the road, given that they are pointing not just to the right, but also upward at 45 degrees), but in the end I get by. If I had to behave as Quine thinks I should, I would be long dead by now, and not just on the Swiss highways.

24. J. Derrida, *Of Grammatology*, trans. G. C. Spivak (Baltimore: Johns Hopkins University Press, 1998).

25. R. Rorty, *Philosophy and the Mirror of Nature* (Oxford: Blackwell, 1979).

26. J.-F. Lyotard, *The Postmodern Condition: A Report on Knowledge*, trans. G. Bennington (Minneapolis: University of Minnesota Press, 1984).

27. J. Ratzinger, *Europe Today and Tomorrow* (Minneapolis: Ignatius Press, 2004).

28. My friend Alessandro Salice sends me the following comment, for which I am grateful: "The world really has changed. Gramsci, on the other hand, blamed the league of (not only philosophical) Neo-Thomists in Civiltà Cattolica for the orthodox materialists Plekhanov and Bukharin. Against the two fronts, which Gramsci accused of metaphysics (Catholic creationism and Aristotelian essentialism), he defended a form of historicism derived from Benedetto Croce!."

29. In *Il mondo esterno*, p. 90, I called it the "slipper argument," but it seems to me to be clearer to speak of an *experiment*.

30. "'The world is my representation': here is a truth that holds good for every living and thinking being, though man can come to only an abstract and reflexive knowledge of it. And when man has in fact arrived at that knowledge, the philosophical spirit has entered into him. Then he knows with clear certainty that he does not know either the sun or the earth, but only an eye that sees the sun and a hand that feels contact with the earth." A. Schopenhauer, *The World as Will and Representation*, trans. E. F. J. Payne (Indian Hills, Colo.: The Falcon's Wing, 1958), §1.

31. This reproduces, with minor variants, as do the other schemes in this chapter, those presented in *Il mondo esterno*, pp. 89, 159, 160.

32. "Without man, being would be mute: *it* would be, but it would not be *true*." A. Kojève, *Introduction to the Reading of Hegel* (Ithaca, N.Y.: Cornell University Press, 1980), p. 188. This condition should not be read only negatively, but also as a positive resource: there is a being that is fortunately mute and indifferent to our reasonings, but capable (if need be) to make them true.

33. Following D. Reina, *Quale realismo per la realtà social*, PhD diss., University of Turin (Italy), 2008.

34. The phenomenology of the lived world also seems to be a realm apt for defining a layer of experience that is immune to science, and that is prior or independent of it. Thus the notion of a "proto-physics" in Heinrich Rickert, *Der Gegenstand der Erkenntnis. Ein Beitrag zum Problem der philosophischen Transcendenz* (Freiburg: J. C. B. Mohr, 1892); on this see A. Donise, *Il soggetto e l'evidenza. Saggio su Heinrich Rickert* (Naples: Loffredo, 2002), as "background" in J. Searle, *The Construction of Social Reality* (Harmondsworth: Penguin, 1995), and as the "hard core" in U. Eco, *Kant and the Platypus* (New York: Harcourt, 1997). All the same, it is worth noting that Kant himself, in the first edition of the first *Critique*, introduces the enigmatic notion of the "synopsis of sense" (A 97–8), which is the order that experience has before the I-think and the categories intervene.

35. R. Nozick, *Invariances* (Cambridge, Mass.: Harvard University Press, 2001).

36. W. Metzger, *Psychologie: Die Entwicklung ihrer Grundannahmen seit der Einführung des Experiments* (Darmstadt: Steinkopff, 1954).

37. And it picks up the notion of the material a priori that many philosophers discussed at the beginning of the last century. In Reinach's version: "Aprioriness does not refer in the first instance to knowledge . . . but to the state of affairs, whether it is 'posited,' judged or known. . . . The 'universality' . . . is founded on the essence of the object." Reinach, "The A Priori Foundations of Civil Law," trans. John Crosby, *Aletheia* 3 (1983): 1–141 at 48 n. 5. For his part, Emil Lask proposed reformulating the Kantian slogan that "concepts without intuitions are empty, intuitions without concepts are blind" in the following terms: "form without content is empty, and content without form is naked": *Logik der Philosophie* (1911), in his *Gesammelte Schriften* (Tübingen: Mohr, 1923), p. 2:74. Years later, Husserl writes that judgment is the *clothes* of a thought that is thrown over the world of intuition (*Experience and Judgment: Investigations in a Genealogy of Logic*, trans. J. S. Churchill and K. Ameriks (Evanston, Ill.: Northwestern University Press, 1973).

38. I draw on the proposal of Y. Berio Rapetti and D. Tagliafico, "Teorie ingénue," in Ferraris, *Storia dell'ontologia*, pp. 273–293.

39. P. S. Churchland, *Neurophilosophy: Towards a Unified Science of the Mind/Brain* (Cambridge, Mass.: MIT Press, 1992); R. Casati, "Scenze cognitive," pp. 437–451; A. Goldman, *Liaisons* (Cambridge, Mass.: MIT Press, 1992), chap. 2.

40. The leading Italian exponent was the late Paolo Bozzi; see his *Fisica ingenua* (Milan: Garzanti, 1990), and *Scritti sul realismo. Un mondo sotto osservazione*, ed. L. Taddio (Milan: Mimesis, 2007).

41. Such a view may be found in Husserl's essay on the Copernican theory in *Experience and Judgment*.

42. J. J. Gibson, *The Ecological Approach to Visual Perception* (Boston: Houghton Mifflin, 1979).

43. G. Piana, *Elementi di una teoria dell'esperienza* (Milan: Il Saggiatore, 1979); C. Gabbiani, *Per un'epistemologia dell'esperienza personale* (Milan: Guerini, 2007).

44. See Casati, "Scienze cognitive."

45. Strawson, *Individuals*. I do not labor the point because I have set it out more fully in 1.1.4.

46. Bozzi, *Fisica ingenua*, pp. 23–65.

47. I have offered a detailed analysis of this phenomenology in the second part of *Mondo esterno*.

48. As Husserl writes: "The not true, the not existent, is already eliminated in passivity" (*Analysen zur passiven Synthesis, aus Vorlesungs- and Forschungsmanuskripten 1918–26*), and this is thanks to the benefits of disappointment: "'Now I *see* that it was an illusion' is itself a mode of evidence" (*Aktiven Synthesen: Aus der Vorlesung "Transzendentale Logik,"* 1920–21).

49. This is the starting point for the basic theoretical proposal in my *Estetica razionale*, esp. pp. 1–35.

50. For detailed analysis, see my *Mondo esterno*, pp. 193–201.

51. This aim may make sense in certain very specific fields, such as that of a wine or food taster or of a chicken sexer, which call for discriminations that are not useful in everyday life. Even in such cases, there is no expectation that the sensitivity can be sharpened to infinity.

52. I have set these distinctions out in detail in my *Mondo esterno*, pp. 143–157.

53. It might indeed be objected that if ontology is called on to say what there is, then the framework I am suggesting is very badly off because it is forced to deny the existence of things that are there, such as quarks and indeed everything that we are not currently perceiving, and because it is forced to assert the existence of things that are not there, such as stars that exploded millions of years ago and the pink elephants of *delirium tremens* and so on. To this I reply that, in the first instance, I am proposing a distinction among experience, technique, and science. My table, like that in the next section, certainly does not mean that there are only the things that we experience, and that ontology is nothing but a matter of the ecological-empirical realm. Galaxies and atoms exist, even though we have no direct experience of them, and they make up the ontological foundation for epistemology, considered as the knowledge that is able to formulate true assertions about galaxies and atoms.

54. This distinction is proposed by F. Dretske, *Seeing and Knowing* (Chicago: University of Chicago Press, 1969). R. Casati and A. C. Varzi, in *Un altro mondo?* suggest instead that we should distinguish between the "referential function" and the "attributive function." The sense is the same: We can have even complex experiences without having full competence, more or less as we can use a hand, a computer, or an elevator without knowing how they work.

55. Gibson, *The Ecological Approach to Visual Perception.* For in-depth analysis, see P. Kobau, "L'eredità di Gibson e lo 'enactive approach,'" in *Estetiche della percezione*, ed. F. Desideri and G. Matteucci (Florence: Florence University Press, 2007), pp. 101–121.

56. Goodman, in *Ways of Worldmaking*, p. 95, seems to confuse reading with seeing as if they were simply equivalent when he says that, when we read, we normally extract fragmentary evidence which we integrate. By contrast, it seems that when we read what we do is add a sense, which is a sort of thinking, not a sort of seeing; after all, we leave errors in a text that we are proofing because we did not *see* them, rather than because we did not *read* them.

57. It is no objection to say that there are Molotov cocktails, matches, and cyanide capsules. For sure, there are instruments, such as cotton buds, that can be used only once, but this is for extrinsic (in this case, hygienic) reasons, and it is no accident that things of this sort are not sold singly. During the French atomic tests on Mururoa, it was reported—quite plausibly—that, next to the bomb, they had installed a very expensive meter whose sole function as to collect data and send it to a central computer before being dissolved by the explosion. In this case, the noniterability also seems to be a purely extrinsic matter. If they had been able to build an indestructible meter for the same cost, they probably would have done so.

58. Articulated more in full in my "Inemendabilità, ontologia, realtà sociale," discussed (in conjunction with A. C. Varzi) in "Che cosa c'è e che cos'è," *Nous* 2002–3: 81–101.

59. I have presented this argument in "Matrix e la mozione degli affetti," in *Dentro la matrice. Filosofia, scienza e spiritualità*, ed. M. Cappuccio (Milan: Albo Versorio, 2004), pp. 55–72, and in *La fidanzata automatica*, pp. 187–189.

60. It is again Goodman, in *Ways of Worldmaking*, p. 7, who claims that to speak of unstructured content, of nonconceptual data or of a propertiless substrate is self-defeating, for to speak is already to impose structure, to conceptualize, to attribute properties.

61. E. Cassirer *Philosophy of Symbolic Forms*, trans. R. Mannheim (New Haven: Yale University Press, 1955), to which Goodman refers.

62. *Mondo esterno*, pp. 163–174.

63. B. Russell, *Human Knowledge: Its Scope and Limits* (New York: Simon & Schuster, 1948).

64. P. Legrenzi, *Credere* (Bologna: Il Mulino, 2008).

65. For analysis and historical reconstruction, I refer the reader to my "Analogon rationis," *Pratica filosofica* 2 (1994): 5–126, and to *Estetica razionale*, pp. 70–120.

66. J. Lacan, *De la psychose paranoïaque dans ses rapports ave la personnalité* (Paris: Seuil, 1975).

67. As I suggest in *La fidanzata automatica*, pp. 129–158, the failure to notice this sort of case often leads us to identify art with science, thinking that in art there are peculiar sorts of knowledge, when in fact the intervention of knowledge is art, which is always distinct from science, is by definition accidental. I return to the point in 5.2.

68. As I sought to explain in *Una ikea di università* (Milan: Cortina, 2009), there is an intrinsic contradiction in the setting up a PhD in communication sciences. Because these are practical disciplines aimed at doing, not at knowing, a doctoral program would justify the state in which someone who cannot find a job finds himself.

69. In the case of the incompatibility between quantum and relativity physics, it may be noted that one of the major challenges of modern theoretical physics is precisely that of finding a unifying theory of the sort that string theorist claim to have done (or to have begun doing); see the fine popular exposition by Michio Kaku, *Hyperspace: A Scientific Odyssey Through Parallel Universes, Time Warps and the 10th Dimension* (New York: Anchor Books, 1994).

70. See *Estetica razionale*, pp. 39ff., and *Estetica sperimentale*, pp. 30–33.

71. We might therefore doubt the validity of Goodman's claim on the last page of *Ways of Worldmaking*, when he says that judgments about the Parthenon and about the *Book of Kells* have not been more subject to variation that those about the laws of gravitation.

72. N. Carroll, "Identifying Art," in *Philosophy of Art: An Introduction* (New York: Routledge, 1999), pp. 249–264.

73. "*Sermo opportunus est optimus*": timely speech is best. But working out when it is "timely" involves an undoubtedly constative element.

74. I discuss this more at length in *Piangere e ridere davvero. Feuilleton* (Genoa: Il Melangolo, 2009).

75. Michael Lynch argues against the idea that truth is the exclusive property of scientists and in favor of its strongly practical value (for instance, in answer to the questions, "Do you love me?" "Are you betraying me?") in *True to Life* (Cambridge, Mass.: MIT Press, 2004).

76. M. Weitz, "The Role of Theory in Aesthetics," *Journal of Aesthetics and Art Criticism* 11 (1956): 27–35.

77. J. L. Austin, "A Plea for Excuses," in *Philosophical Papers* (Oxford: Oxford University Press, 1979), pp. 175–204.

78. In his posthumous *Examen de la philosophie de Bacon* (Paris: Puossielge-Busand, 1836) Joseph de Maistre criticizes this epistemologism with rigor and wit: "Words are not at all made for expressing things, but only the ideas we have of them; otherwise we would not be able to speak. Would the moderns, whom here I contradict frontally, perhaps like to condemn the human species to silence until the essences of things are known?" (p. 1:131). "I ask of the chemistry that preceded ours: 'What is an acid?' and Maquer replies: 'It is a salt that excites the taste that I call *acid*,

and that turned blue certain blue or violet vegetable dyes.' I ask the same question of today's chemistry, and Cadet replies: 'It is a substance that, when united to *oxygen*, takes on an acid taste and the property of reddening many blue vegetable dyes and so on.' At bottom, the two definitions are equivalent. 'Acid is what excites the taste we call *acid*,' which, after all is none too enlightening. Except that in the second one, we find the word 'oxygen,' which is just a further mystery" (pp. 1:141–142). De Maistre was a reactionary thinker, but in this case his philosophy turns out to be progressive. I have summarized this stylistically and doctrinally powerful book in "Come stanno le cose tra scienza, antiscienza e senso comune," *Kéiron* (April 2000): 50–59.

79. Plato, *Phaedrus*, 268a–c.

3. SOCIAL OBJECTS

1. The earliest occurrence of the term *social ontology* is in C. Znamierowski, "The Basic Concepts of the Theory of Law, Introductory Remarks," in Z. Ziembinski, ed., *Polish Contributions to the Theory and Philosophy of Law* (Amsterdam: Rodopi, 1987).

2. David Lewis, in *Convention: A Philosophical Study* (Cambridge, Mass.: Harvard University Press, 1969), says explicitly that conventions are a sort of norm. For discussion of this theme, see F. Guala, "Esistono le convenzioni di Lewis?" *Rivista di Estetica* 44 (2009).

3. W. Dilthey, *Formation of the Historical World in the Human Sciences* (1910), ed. R. A. Makkreel and Frithjof Rodi (Princeton: Princeton University Press, 2002). For exposition of these methodological problems, see my *Storia dell'ermeneutica* (Milan: Bompiani, 2008), pp. 115–223.

4. W. Windelband, "History and Natural Science," trans. G. Oakes, *History and Theory: Studies in the Philosophy of History* 19 (1980): 165–185.

5. On the back of structuralism, semiotics came into being in the twentieth century with a view to facing this problem. Its great merit in the 1960s and 1970s was its concentration on everyday life. This was a perspective that was at least potentially richer than the investigations of ordinary language. But there was a dash of Kant also in semiotics; with also a dash of irony, Umberto Eco himself defined his own *Theory of Semiotics* as a sort of *Critique of Semiotic Reason*. With the retreat of structuralism, it was easy for the rising hermeneutics to say that there are no facts, but only interpretations, to deride excesses of method, and to calumniate or pity the sciences. What was emphasized was subjectivism, the Heideggerian Dasein that does whatever it wants with the world (which in turn accounts for why at a certain point people began to talk about a "philosophical impressionism" on a par with Simmel's "sociological impressionism"). The upshot of these approaches has already been examined in 2.1.2 and 2.1.3.

6. In the opposite position there is the designer or project director, who is often torn between two desires: on the one hand, to make a sensible product, and on the

other to make a splash with something that is memorable even if only for its extravagance. Sometimes this leads to the creation of objects like the projects for the monument to Italy's first king, Victor Emmanuel II, which Carlo Dossi made fun of in his 1884 book *I Mattoidi al primo concorso per il monumento in Roma a Vittorio Emmanuele* (The Madmen in the First Competition for the Monument in Rome to Victor Emmanuel), which should be read by anyone who feels the afflatus descending on them. In the end, the winning design was a sort of ready-made avant la lettre, in the shape of a typewriter rather than of an altar to the Fatherland. By a mysterious alchemy, the form was already there waiting from the start, encapsulated in an object that was in any case more powerful than its subject and than the project, and indeed than all possible meanings: parchment? [Translator's note: The Italian word for parchment is the name of the ancient city of Pergamum.] No: Remington. This happens more often than you might think. The Zanotta beanbag chair was designed in 1968 and presumably aimed to express an unconventional and relaxed way of life, but instead became the emblem of the humiliation of Ugo Fantozzi, the clerk who had no inkling of '68. [Translator's note: the reference is to a successful series of comic films starring Paolo Villaggio.]. Because of the undignified position that one has to adopt to sit on this pillory-chair, it has become common to call these pieces of furniture "Fantozzi armchairs," despite the intentions of the designers.

7. D. A. Norman, *The Psychology of Everyday Things* (New York: Basic Books, 1988).

8. I. Kant, *Critique of Pure Reason*, A 81–2, B 107.

9. "We do not describe any chance quantity as 'mutilated'; it must have parts, and must be a whole. The number 2 is not mutilated if one of its 1's is taken away—because the part lost by mutilation is never equal to the remainder—nor in general is any number mutilated; because the essence must persist. If a cup is mutilated, it must still be a cup; but the number is no longer the same," Aristotle, *Metaphysics*, V, xxvii, 1024a10–17. Here we note a fine distinction between ideal objects and natural objects.

10. As regards specifically the discovery of social objects, I refer to *social objects* in *Sistemi Intelligenti* (2004): 441–466. This is a special number, edited by R. Casati, on ontologies.

11. See *Third New Science* (1744), in G. B. Vico *Selected Writings*, ed. L. Pompa (Cambridge: Cambridge University Press, 1982), pp. 250ff.

12. Despite what Vico thought, phenomena such as recessions, economic cycles, and systems of power show that, for all that it is dependent on our beliefs and is thus "made by us," social reality is anything but transparent. On this opacity, see D. H. Ruben, *The Metaphysics of Social Reality* (New York: Free Press, 1985); A. Goldman, *A Theory of Human Action* (Princeton: Princeton University Press, 1970); M. Gilbert, *Living Together: Rationality, Sociality and Obligation* (Lanham, Md.: Rowman & Littlefield, 1996).

13. T. Reid, *Essays on the Active Power of the Human Mind* (1785), in *Philosophical Works* (Hildesheim: Olms, 1967), essay I, chapter VIII: "Of Social Operations of the Mind."

14. J. L. Austin, *How to Do Things with Words* (Oxford: Oxford University Press, 1962).

15. A. Reinach, "A Priori Foundations of Civil Law"; see also *Speech Act and Sachverhalt: Reinach and the Foundation of Realist Phenomenology*, ed. K. Mulligan (The Hague: Nijhoff, 1987). The concept of "social objects" is obviously analogous to that of moral beings (as distinct from physical things) discussed by Samuel Pufendorf in the seventeenth century, and to that of "social collections" (Félix Kaufmann) and "juridical beings" (Sante Romano).

16. J. Derrida, "Signature Event Context" (1971), in *Margins of Philosophy*, trans. A. Bass (Chicago: University of Chicago Press, 1982).

17. I here take up anew a theme I first discussed in *La svolta testuale. Il decostruzionismo in Derrida, Lyotard, gli "Yale Critics"* (Milan: Unicopli, 1986).

18. To be sure, a particularly subtle philosophy might want to rewrite (1) as the proposition: "The fact that mountains, lakes, beavers, and asteroids are subsumed under the concept (ontological category) of *objects* depends on our conceptual schemes." But in either case there is the collapse of being on knowing, because at this point one may as well rewrite (1) as "The fact that mountains, lakes, beavers, and asteroids are subsumed under the concept (ontological category) of *objects* depends on the fact that there is someone about." In one sense, this is true enough, but it is irrelevant to the ontology of mountains, lakes, beavers, and asteroids.

19. I thank my friend Giuliano Torrengo for suggesting that this limitation applies even if we imagine that there are magical social objects, created by spells. In Tim Burton's film *The Corpse Wife*, the son of rich fish merchants wanders in the forest in despair at having miserably failed in the rehearsals for the marriage that the parents of his betrothed have imposed on him because they are aristocrats who have come down in the world. In trying and retrying the ritual that he had clumsily bungled, he places the wedding ring by mistake on a dry branch while pronouncing the fateful words, only to find that it is the hand of the corpse who rises up and follows him until they complete the rite. The spell is cast, and the two find themselves in the world of the dead, where they are welcomed as a married couple. Now, being transported into the underworld is wholly magical, but the wedding does not seem all that different from a normal wedding. Even setting aside the fact that the ritual is identical in substance, the point is that, if no one beyond the grave has a memory of the fact of being married, then magic would have no effect. Turning someone into a husband is completely different from turning him into a pig; however powerful the spell might be, it would be wholly inefficacious to perform the first transformation if it had no effect on the minds of others. In short, a magic wand can change a man into a pig but not into a husband.

20. In the following, I refer to A. Collier, "L'ontologia sociale del realismo critico," and repropose parts of my "Commento a Collier," both in *Realismo sociologico*, ed. A. M. Maccarini, E. Morandi, and R. Prandini (Genoa: Marietti, 2008), at pp. 14–42 and 43–54 respectively.

21. This is the conclusion of Rousseau's *Discourse on the Origin and Basis of Inequality Among Men* (1754), trans. P. Gay in *The Basic Political Writings of Jean-Jacques Rousseau* (Indianapolis: Hackett, 1987).

22. I. Kant, *Critique of Practical Reason* (1788) trans. T. K. Abbott (London: Longman, 1889).

23. I. Murdoch, *The Sovereignty of Good* (London Chatto and Windus, 1970); M. C. Nussbaum, *Upheavals of Thought: The Intelligence of Emotions* (Cambridge: Cambridge University Press, 2001).

24. I refer to my *Ermeneutica di Proust* (Milan: Guerini, 1987), pp. 107ff.

25. R. Barker, *Ecological Psychology: Concepts and Methods for Studying the Environment of Human Behavior* (Stanford: Stanford University Press, 1968).

26. Here too we follow A. Collier, "L'ontologia sociale del realismo critico." For a clear presentation of the philosophical theories on value, see A. Donise, *Valore* (Naples: Guida, 2008). For a reassessment of hermeneutics within the restricted realm of social objects, see P. G. Monateri "Deep Inside the Bramble Bush: Complex Orders and Humanities," *Cardozo Electronic Law Bulletin* (2007).

27. Letter from K. Marx to F. Lassalle, 22 February 1858, referring to the *Critique of Political Economy*: "The work in question is a critique of economic categories or, if you like, the system of bourgeois economics expounded critically. *And at the same time it is an exposition of the system and a critique of it by way of an exposition.* . . . After all, I have the foreboding that now, when, after fifteen years of study, I am on the point of putting my hand to the business, stormy movements from the outside with probably begin to interfere. Never mind. If I arrive too late to find a world still attentive to these things, the fault is evidently my own" (in K. Marx, *Letters on "Capital,"* trans. A. Drummond [London: New Park, 1983], pp. 51–52, emphasis added).

28. An extended account of these positions is set out in *Dove sei?* pp. 179–268.

29. R. Sacco, "Criptotipo," *Disgesto IV* (Turin: Utet, 1989), pp. 5:39–40, and his *Che cos'è il diritto comparato?* ed. P. Cendon (Milan: Giuffrè, 1990); see also his "Il diritto muto," *Rivista di Diritto Civile* 1 (1993): 689–702. The notion of a "cryptotype" corroborates the claim that law *preexists* linguistic expression: "The law does not need the word. The law preexists the articulated word. Even today, the law recognizes the dichotomies that are freighted with meaning, which are due to the continued actuality of instruments with which it operated even before man had the word and did not yet use the word to create juridical facts" (Sacco, *Che cos'è il diritto comparato?* p. 14).

30. A. Reinach, "The a Priori Foundations of Civil Law": "If there are free-standing juridical beings in this world, then a new territory opens up for philosophy. Considered as ontology or the a priori theory of objects, is the analysis of all the possible types of objects as such. . . . Here philosophy encounters a wholly new species of objects, objects that do not belong properly speaking to nature, objects that are neither physical nor psychical, and at the same time are distinct, in virtue of their temporality, from ideal objects."

31. Following the lucid reconstruction of A. Salice in "Obbligazione e pretesa in Adolf Reinach: Due relazioni sociali," *Rivista di Estetica* 39 (2008): 225–240, it is a triadic relation, which is to say a state of affairs involving more than one element.

32. M. Foucault, *The Order of Things: An Archaeology of the Human Sciences* (London: Tavistock, 1970).

33. M. Foucault, *History of Madness*, trans. J. Khalfa (London: Routledge, 2006).

34. J. R. Searle, *Speech Acts* (Cambridge: Cambridge University Press, 1969).

35. J. R. Searle, "Minds, Brains and Programs," in D. Hofstadter and D. Dennett, *The Mind's I* (Harmondsworth: Penguin, 1982); *Intentionality: An Essay in the Philosophy of Mind* (Cambridge: Cambridge University Press, 1983); *The Rediscovery of the Mind* (Cambridge, Mass.: MIT Press, 1992).

36. J. R. Searle, "Rationality and Realism: What Is at Stake?" *Daedalus* 122 (1993): 55–83; "The World Turned Upside Down" and "Reply to Mackey," in *Working Through Derrida*, ed. G. B. Madison (Evanston, Ill.: Northwestern University Press, 1993), pp. 170–184 and 184–188; "Postmodernism and Truth," in *Two Be: A Journal of Ideas* 13 (1998): 85–87.

37. J. R. Searle, *Mind, Language and Society* (London: Weidenfeld and Nicholson, 1999).

38. I have criticized this aspect of Searle's theory at length in *Dove sei?* pp. 214–255. The first formulation of this notion is not, however, Searle's, but that of the Finnish philosopher Raimo Tuomela, *The Importance of Us: A Philosophical Study of Basic Social Notions* (Stanford: Stanford University Press, 1995).

39. C. Schmitt, *Political Theology: Four Chapters on the Concept of Sovereignty*, trans. G. Schwab (Cambridge, Mass.: MIT Press, 1985).

40. V. Gallese, "La molteplice natura delle relazioni interpersonali: La ricerca di un comune meccanismo neurofisiologico," *Networks* 1 (2003): 24–47; L. Fogassi et al., "Parietal Lobe: From Action Organization to Intention Understanding," *Science* 307, no. 5722 (2005): 662–667; N. Nakahara and Y. Miyashita, "Understanding Intentions: Through the Looking Glass," *Science* 308, no. 5722 (2005): 644–645.

41. Furthermore, we need a way to handle propositions such as "*we* build a house," in which it is not I (alone) nor you (alone) who builds the house, but the two of us *together*. Whatever collective intentionality may be, it has to be able to explain how it is possible for there to be actions that are done together. Another class of propositions that it ought to explain are those that take in institutions: "Abkhazia has seceded from Georgia," but who is Abkhazia? It is clear that behind all this there stands the notion of a social group, which must be either the *definiens* collective intentionality or its *definiendum*.

42. R. Miraglia, "Osservazioni per una fenomenologia delle *We-Intentions*," *Rivista di Estetica* 39 (2008): 171–188.

43. He did so in the course of a seminar held at the University of Turin in May 2008. Compare J. R. Searle, *Consciousness and Language* (Cambridge: Cambridge University Press, 2002).

44. C. Menger, *Investigations Into the Methods of the Social Sciences*, trans. L. H. White and L. Schneider (New York: New York University Press, 1985): "The origin of money can be fully explained only if we know how to see in the social institution its unreflective product, the involuntary result of the specifically individual activity of the members of a collectivity" (p. 155).

45. [Translator's note: In Italian, the word for head, *testa*, differs in only in the final letter from the word for text, *testo*.]

46. Searle, *The Construction of Social Reality*, pp. 39–41.

47. I refer to my *Sans Papier. Ontologia dell'attualità* (Rome: Castelvecchi, 2007), pp. 62–63; cf. D. Grasso, "Memoria e conservazione. La *Rückfrage* delle istituzioni," *Rivista di Estetica* 36 (2007): 149–166.

48. Searle, *The Construction of Social Reality*, p. 41.

49. On the distinction between objects, confines, *fiat*, and *bona fide*, see my "Oggetti *fiat*," *Rivista di Estetica* 20 (2002), special number on social ontology edited by L. Morena and A. C. Varzi.

50. B. Smith, "Un'aporia nella costruzione della realtà sociale. Naturalismo e realismo in John R. Searle," in Di Lucia, *Ontologia sociale*, pp. 137–152.

51. Leibniz, *New Essays*, book II, chapter XIII.

52. It is perhaps worth making the law I have just announced a little bit more precise. If we take the formula Object = Inscribed Act literally, we have an identity relation. According to Leibniz's law, everything we can say about the object can also be said about the inscribed act. Yet it is not quite so in all cases. To be sure, in the case of *Mona Lisa* the object and the inscription do coincide, but let us look at the case of the Fiat. The Fiat is not its buildings, nor its employees, nor yet the automobiles it produces, and so on. Moreover, the Fiat could not exist without tons of paper: registrations. The relation between the inscribed acts and the object is rather one of (1) *existential dependence* (if the papers go out of existence, so too does the social object, even though the physical objects remain); and (2) *representation* (the papers represent the Fiat). But this is not yet identity: the documents could be drawn up badly, but the Fiat could not; the documents may be located in a computer, but the Fiat could not. More properly, then, the law should be represented by the formula Object ← Inscribed Act. But I fear that this would be less clear, and one might in any case object that, insofar as we have to capture the fact that the inscribed act is a necessary but not sufficient condition for the object (there can be no object without the inscribed act, but it is possible for there to be an inscribed act without an object), the formula would then have to be represented by Object → Inscribed Act. Once these observations have been made, I am inclined to hold on to the formula Object = Inscribed Act, which as clarity on its side.

53. In his *lectio magistralis* presented May 19, 2008, in the Modern Art Gallery of Turin.

54. Smith approvingly cites De Soto (*The Mystery of Capitalism* [New York: Basic Books, 2000]) where he says that capital is born representing *in writing*—a bond, a

guarantee, a contract or some other record of that sort—the most useful social and economic qualities, so that when you pay attention to the title deed of a house rather than to the house itself, you are automatically stepping out of the material world and into the conceptual world that is inhabited by capital.

55. See M. G. Turri, *La distinzione fra moneta e denaro. Ontologia sociale ed economia* (Rome: Carocci, 2009), specifically pp. 7–13 (the role of signs and traces in the constitution of the social object *currency*), p. 23 (writing and social objects), and pp. 84ff. (writing in De Soto and Derrida); see also her "Possedere denaro senza possedere neppure una moneta. L'ontologia del denaro e la metafisica della moneta," *Rivista di estetica* 37 (2008): 195–238.

56. Achille Varzi acutely remarks that Searle's social theory is a generalization of Goodman's theory of art; see A. C. Varzi, "Il denaro è un'opera d'arte (o quasi)," *Quaderni dell'Associazione degli Studi di Banca e Borsa* 24 (2007): 17–39.

57. For further confirmation of this point of view, see Niall Ferguson, *The Ascent of Money: A Financial History of the World* (Harmondsworth: Penguin, 2008).

58. For the background to this section, see Di Lucia, *Ontologia sociale*; Ferraris "Oggetti sociali"; M. Gilbert, *On Social Facts* (New York: Routledge, 1989), and her "Group Membership and Political Obligation," *The Monist* 76 (1993): 119–131; I. Johansson, *Ontological Investigations: An Inquiry into the Categories of Nature, Man and Society* (London: Routledge, 1989); J. Kim and E. Sosa, eds., *Metaphysics: An Anthology* (Oxford: Blackwell, 1999); M. S. Moore "Legal Reality: A Naturalist Approach to Legal Ontology," *Law and Philosophy* 21 (2002): 619–705; B. Smith, "Ontologie des Mesokosmos: Soziale Objekte und Umwelt," *Zeitschrift für philosophische Forschung* 52 (1998): 521–540, his "Les objets sociaux," *Philosophiques* 26 (1999): 315–347, as well as his "Ontology of Social Reality," http://ontology.buffalo.edu/smith//articles/searle/PDF; R. Tuomela, *The Philosophy of Social Practices* (Cambridge: Cambridge University Press, 2002); A. Thomasson, "Foundations for a Social Ontology," *Protosociology*, 18–19 (2002): 269–290.

59. Paolo Di Lucia (in his "Idealtypen per una tipologia degli atti istituzionali," *Rivista di Estetica* 39 [2008]: 133–145) distinguishes social acts from nonsocial acts and spoken acts from mute acts. I prefer to speak of speech acts or linguistic acts (as against nonlinguistic acts) as an allusion to Austin and to recall the performative value of the acts.

60. [Translator's note: In Italian the verb *fare* covers both "to make" and "to do" and is used for what one does with a walk.]

61. A. Reinach, "Nichtsoziale und soziale Akte," in *Sämtliche Werke*, ed. K. Schuhmann and B. Smith (Munich: Philosophia Verlag, 1989), pp. 1:355–360; P. Di Lucia, "Tre specie di entità giuridiche: oggetti, enti, figmenti," in *Documentalità*, pp. 97–111; also M. Mandelbaum, "Societal Facts," *British Journal of Sociology* 6 (1955): 305–317.

62. This analysis should certainly be refined by examination of single cases. For instance, Reinach regarded forgiveness not as a social act but rather as a psychological one. On the other hand, I assume (supported in this by Norberto Bobbio in his

Introduzione alla filosofia del diritto [Turin: Giappichelli, 1948]) that forgiveness may be a psychological act, but that that act is nothing but a reflection of forgiveness as a social act or indeed institutional act. Forgiveness enters into the catalog of a subject's psychological attitudes beginning with highly ritualized ceremonies of purification and sacrifice, which cancel the wounds opened among the members of the society. The fact that forgiveness is in the first instance an institutional act, then a social one and only finally a psychological one can be seen from the way that institutional forgiveness is easier to obtain than psychological forgiveness. Institutional forgiveness is a daily occurrence. Social forgiveness is rarer: I can accept that unlicensed building works can be regularized by an amnesty, but my friends and I will remain wary of the perpetrator. Personal forgiveness is the rarest of all, and one might wonder whether it has ever happened at all and whether it is not more apt to speak merely of forgetting or of a change of interest. If we do not bear this in mind, it becomes very hard to explain how a person might, at one and the same time, forgive genocide but not forgive an unfaithful husband.

63. P. Grice "Logic and Conversation," in *Studies in the Way of Words* (Cambridge, Mass.: Harvard University Press, 1989), pp. 22–40; see also C. Bianchi, *Pragmatica del linguaggio* (Rome: Laterza, 2006).

64. In Reinach's view, the essential characteristics of social acts are spontaneity and punctuality; the requirement that they be perceived and understood; and the linguistic clothing. See "A Priori Foundations of Civil Law," pp. 18–21.

65. Ibid., p. 20.

66. In considering offices and roles, we saw that some animals can fill roles, or social functions, but they cannot fill offices, which are institutional functions because the realm of institutions requires human agents. Caligula's horse Incitatus was not really a senator, and the queen bee is not a real queen. We can individuate some less certain cases. For instance, there is Inspector Rex, the German shepherd dog who helps the Vienna murder squad. With this function as beneficent dog, he is the heir of a dynasty that also includes such figures a Rin Tin Tin and Lassie; in the particular business of resolving obscure cases, he is also a relative (despite the difference in size) of Tintin's dog Snowy. There are two questions to be asked. One is easy: is Inspector Rex really an inspector (office). Here the answer is probably not. A dog cannot be an inspector any more than a horse can be a senator; our intuitions refuse this sort of possibility precisely because the title inspector or senator apply to an institutional reality, which excludes creatures such as dogs and horses because they do not speak and do not have the category of social objects. Unless we are thinking of a reality like that of Orwell's *Animal Farm* or Disney's Mouseton: but in Mouseton, the chief of police, Seamus O'Hara, is a police chief in the fiction, while Rex is an inspector in a series that pretends to be realistic. We may also reflect on the difference between Goofy (a dog who is human in the fiction) and Pluto (a dog who is a dog in the fiction). The second question is different: whether he is an inspector or not, is Rex really an actor? Does he know that he is acting? Here the situation is more complicated and

the answer less obvious. Animals do know how to make believe, and some can make believe to make believe; so why should they not know in some sense that they are acting even if they do not know what an actor is? So: Rex is not an inspector (he cannot fill an office), but he can be an animal that makes believe (he can fill a role), and in making believe, he follows the script attributed to an inspector.

67. M. Sbisà, *Detto non detto. Le forme della comunicazione implicita* (Rome: Laterza, 2008).

68. C. Bianchi, "Recording Speech Acts," in *Pragmatics as Basis for Semantics*, ed. R. Giovagnoli and G. Seddone (Leiden: Brill, 2011).

69. Plato, *Theaetetus*, 191 c–d.

70. On the abstract and idealized character of speech acts and ordinary language as a whole in Austin, see S. Rosen, *The Elusiveness of the Ordinary: Studies in the Possibility of Philosophy* (New Haven: Yale University Press, 2002).

71. We may take the example of the Italian declaration of war against France and Britain in June 1940. According to Curzio Malaparte's 1944 novel *Kaputt*, we have a hypergrammatological detail of this inscribed act. Italian Foreign Minster Galeazzo Ciano read the declaration to the British ambassador Sir Percy Lorraine. Sir Percy exclaimed "Ah!" and then said, "May I have a pencil?" "Yes, certainly." Count Ciano gave him a pencil and a sheet of Foreign Ministry letterhead. The British ambassador folded the sheet and, using a paperknife, carefully cut off the letterhead, looked at the point of the pencil, and then asked Count Ciano: "Would you be so kind as to dictate to me what you have just read?."

72. [Translator's note: The reference is to an incident involving Prime Minister Silvio Berlusconi.]

73. This is also what we find in advertising recorded on the telephone, which is in every way identical to a fax, a flyer in a letterbox, or an email. As Plato said, writing always says the same thing, and this is undoubtedly true of the recorded message. The cases can be multiplied: prayers, magic formulas, every kind of rite, poems that have been learnt by heart, actor's performances, safety instructions on airplanes, which are the same whether they are on the leaflet "in the pocket on the back of the seat in front of you," in a recording or in the demonstration that the steward makes. And we should not forget conversations with a call center, which are determined by a protocol, or the explanations of a tourist guide. A preacher or a professor can talk for hours without thinking, and we are often, as Nietzsche said, "embodied compendia." And there is a part of us, the part that deals with greetings, set phrases and even precooked sentiments, in which we have a situation like that of *Fahrenheit 451*, in which books pile up in our memories as on the shelves of a library.

74. In this sense, intrinsic exteriorizations of an act should be distinguished from extrinsic ones. For instance, when a professorship is announced, the deliberation of the faculty board and, in Italy, publication in the *Official Gazette* are intrinsic, while the publication of an advertisement in newspapers is extrinsic. Conversely, in a pub-

lic tender, publication of an announcement in the newspapers may be intrinsic, if the law so disposes. The document that is exteriorized must also be registered. The extreme convenience of writing for the documental function resides in the fact that it allows exteriorization and registration to be performed in a single act.

75. J. Derrida, "Signature Event Context," pp. 321–327.

4. ICHNOLOGY

1. This is the theme of my *Mimica. Lutto e autobiografia da Agostino a Heidegger* (Milan: Bompiani, 1992).

2. I owe this observation to Umberto Eco in private conversation about the reasoning on the point in *Dove sei?*

3. A lucid critique of the "communication society" can be found in Mario Perniola's *Contro la comunicazione* (Turin: Einaudi, 2004) and in his *Miracoli e traumi della comunicazione* (Turin: Einaudi, 2009).

4. Just a few years ago, there was a great deal of talk about the disappearance of the paper edition of the *New York Times*, which was scheduled for 2013. Yet, for all that it has symbolic significance, this piece of news was not so very shocking. After all, for every *New York Times* that stops coming out on paper, whole forests are being cut down to print free weeklies, which are now possible because of computerization. Is this not curious? We can do without paper because of the computer, but when will we lose the print function in word processors? I hazard to guess that it will never be removed, and this on the basis of the moral to be drawn from another piece of news: the International Air Transport Authority has ordered its last batch of paper tickets. Soon there will no longer be paper tickets but codes. It is really so? I am not sure it really is. We should say rather that the codes will be written on Post-Its or printed in the office, as has been happening for years with the electronic tickets for the train and the plane. Paper is hard to kill. It seems that one of the reasons for the collapse of the Twin Towers was the immense heat produced by the tons of paper that filled those postmodern offices, in which, if they had been logical, the only paper should have been Kleenex. Why? Why is it that at just the moment when writing, archiving, and communicating are being dissociated from paper, the world is filling up with paper? There are at least four reasons. (1) Before there were computers, texts had to be filled in laboriously letter after letter, line after line, and, if need be, boringly photocopied in another room. Now, with "cut and paste" and downloading from the net, there is nothing to the production of court orders that are 1,600 pages long. Giving the print command for a hundred copies of those 1,600 is no trouble at all; we do not even have to stand up, and in no time we have more than a million and a half sheets of A4 paper, all neatly collated. (2) Even if we are not bothered with subversive uses of it, paper has to its credit the fact that it needs no special technology to be read. A pair of glasses will do at the outside. We do not have to switch on a computer, the batteries do not run down, and a simple gesture is sufficient to show our ticket to the inspec-

tor; and if the ticket falls on the floor, it is not the end of the world. (3) Paper takes up space. This may seem a disadvantage, but it is also a strength. You do not so easily lose a chunky file as you do a memory stick. There they are taking up room, hard to transport and so hard to leave by mistake in the pocket of the pants you have sent to clean. And the laundry bill, on paper, may end up in the edition of your complete works, while the masterpiece you wrote in WordStar 3.0 is destined to oblivion, unless you are quick to get the file converted. (4) Above all else, and a point that we will return to at length in Chapter 6, paper is an excellent medium for the curlicues and signatures that documents need. Today it is very common to receive contracts and forms by email. But, once we have received them, we have to send them back by surface mail: the original, the authentic, the absolute value of the signature remains ink on paper; and the electronic signature is, after many years, still a rarity that is viewed with diffidence.

5. We should bear in mind that, until the end of the 1970s, TV archives were regularly "wiped." The BBC did so systematically until 1978, and even now its statutes do not impose the requirement to keep recording; see http://en. wikipedia.org/wiki/Wiping.

6. See J. Habermas, *Theory of Communicative Action,* trans T. McCarthy (Boston: Beacon Press, 1984).

7. Elementary test: Is the number to get information by phone 411 or 441? The uncertainty is increased by the fact that there are twenty other numbers that you can call to have information or at least hear the words, "I'm Cynthia, how can I help you?"

8. Despite appearances, YouTube does not fulfill Andy Warhol's prophecy; it does not give fifteen minutes of fame to everyone because it is so big that you get lost in it. Claiming that someone is famous because they are on YouTube is like thinking that every house photographed in Google Maps is a monument. Everything has changed since the era of only two or three television channels, when even the program announcers were celebrities. The real effect of YouTube is quite different: a sort of suppression of time because it presents simultaneously all the pictures, films, and recordings that crowd the world. Previously this was the prerogative of only the most secret and sophisticated archives, but now it is there to be seen from any computer. On YouTube, there are forty centuries of history that are looking at us or that we are looking at. Or at least there is the last century, the post-Lumière century, that has taken on the ambition of recapitulating all the preceding centuries at all levels, from the lowest to the most sublime, from the masterpiece to the foolery recorded on the mobile phone.

9. From this follows the variety of social pathologies connected to the different ways of losing memory: in Christopher Nolan's *Memento* (2000), the lead character has lost his short-term memory, but not his long-term memory, so that he has to continue fixing and structuring his own actions by means of inscriptions (including tattoos on his body). In Umberto Eco's *The Mysterious Flame of Queen Loana* (2004)

the protagonist has lost his autobiographical memory but not his semantic memory, so that he has to reconstruct his own past with papers and conjectures. Not forgetting (so to say) Pirandello's *The Late Mattia Pascal* or, above all, Proust's *In Search of Lost Time*, where the problem is not even amnesia, but rather the awareness that the texture of our social being is nothing but memory.

10. J. Derrida, *Writing and Difference*, trans. A. Bass (London: Routledge, 1978).

11. J. Derrida, "Différance," in *Margins of Philosophy*, trans. A. Bass (Chicago: University of Chicago Press, 1982), pp. 1–28.

12. [Translator's note: The effort is less in Italian than either in English or in Derrida's French.]

13. In his *Western Passage* (2003), Giacomo Marramao has rightly stressed the importance of "global electronic mediation" in the constitution of the globalized world.

14. To clarify the point, I propose two simple experiments: (1) hold onto all the tickets and pieces of paper you receive in the course of a single day; (2) try the same thing on a weeklong journey. So much paper and so eloquent: a whole network of rights, duties, possibilities, institutions and payments that is laid down in documents, whether they be solemn like the Magna Carta or modest and everyday like a tram ticket.

15. In his book *Perché laico* (2009), Stefano Rodotà has vigorously argued for the centrality of consciousness and memory in the definition of life. In general, many of the considerations put forward in the present book on the role of inscriptions and documents in the constitution of individuals as social objects are inspired by Rodotà's analyses.

16. The centrality of mimesis in the animal world was already a theme in Darwin's work: see his *Expression of Emotion in Man and Animals* (London: John Murray, 1872); more recently A. Whiten and R. Ham, "On the Nature and Evolution of Imitation in the Animal Kingdom: Reappraisal of a Century of Research," *Advances in the Study of Behavior* 21 (1992): 239–283.

17. As W. J. Verdenius reminds us in *Mimesis: Plato's Doctrine of Artistic Imitation and Its Meaning for Us* (Leiden: Brill, 1949), visible forms are imitations of eternal forms (*Timaeus*, 50c), thought is an imitation of reality (*Critias*, 107, *Timaeus*, 47b–c), words are imitations of things (*Cratylus*, 423e–4b), sounds imitate the divine harmonies (*Timaeus*, 80b), time imitates eternity (ibid., 38a), the laws mimic the truth (*Politics*, 300c), human government imitates the true and divine government (*Politics*, 297e) and the pious man imitates his gods (*Phaedrus*, 252d, *Laws*, 713e).

18. J. Piaget, *Play Dreams and Imitation in Childhood*, trans. C. Gattengo and F. M. Hodgson (London: Routledge, 1951); and, more recently, G. Butterworth, "Neonatal Imitation: Existence, Mechanisms and Motives," in J. Nadel and G. Butterworth, eds., *Imitation in Infancy* (Cambridge: Cambridge University Press, 1999), pp. 63–88.

19. G. Tarde, *The Laws of Imitation*, trans. E. C. Parson (London: H. Holt, 1903), p. 74. On the basis of this assumption, Tarde proceeds to explain the working of

society in terms of imitation. Theses and texts on imitation are collected in M. Lavelli, ed., *Intersoggettività* (Milan: Cortina, 2007). The role of imitation and repetition has been highlighted by G. Deleuze in *Difference and Repetition*, trans. P. Patton (London: Athlone Press, 1994), which I discuss in "Proust, Deleuze et la répétition," *Littérature* 2 (1978).

20. Thus, in particular, René Girard's claim that society is directed by mimetic desire (by mutual envy), which is cyclically unleashed on scapegoats; *Violence and the Sacred*, trans. P. Gregory (Baltimore: Johns Hopkins University Press, 1977). For historical presentation of the political role of mimesis, see B. Fuchs, *Mimesis and Empire: The New World, Islam, and European Identities* (Cambridge: Cambridge University Press, 2003); see also G. Gebauer and C. Wulf, *Mimesis: Culture, Art, Society*, trans. D. Reneau (Berkeley: University of California Press, 1995), and their *Jeux, rituels, gestes. Les fondements mimétiques de l'action sociale* (Paris: Anthropos, 2004).

21. M. Weber, *Die Börse* (Göttingen 1894–96); text at http://www.textlog.de/6140. html.

22. S. Nichols and S. Stich, *Mindreading: An Integrated Account of Pretence, Self-Awareness and Understanding Other Minds* (Oxford: Oxford University Press, 2006). I am grateful to Daniela Tagliafico for very useful clarifications on mindreading and empathy.

23. V. Gallese and A. I. Goldman, "Mirror Neurons and the Simulation Theory of Mind-Reading," *Trends in Cognitive Science* 2 (1998): 493–501; G. Rizzolatti and C. Sinigaglia, *So quel che fai. Il cervello che agisce e i neuroni specchio* (Milan: Cortina, 2006); M. Iacoboni, *I neuroni specchio. Come capiamo ciò che fanno gli altri* (Turin: Bollati Boringhieri, 2008).

24. H. G. Gadamer, *The Relevance of the Beautiful and Other Essays*, trans. N. Walker (Cambridge: Cambridge University Press, 1986).

25. A point that I discuss in *Mimica*, esp. pp. 5–24.

26. E. Auerbach, *Mimesis: The Representation of Reality in Western Literature*, trans. W. Trask (Princeton: Princeton University Press, 2003).

27. This objection has been made by D. Sperber, *Explaining Culture* (Oxford: Blackwell, 1996).

28. In this way, the financier George Soros has been able to claim rightly that he is one of Karl Popper's most coherent followers—and he was indeed his pupil for some months—because of his application of the principle of falsifiability: On the stock exchange, the agent who can manage to act both against the current (that is, falsifying others' expectations) and yet rationally has a good chance of making gains. See G. Soros, *The New Paradigm for Financial Markets: The Credit Crisis of 2008 and What It Means* (New York: Public Affairs, 2008).

29. Lewis, *Convention*, pp. 118–121.

30. This story reelaborates and integrates the scheme $IC_1 \rightarrow II \rightarrow IC_2$ proposed in 3.2.3.3.

31. See T. L. Chartrand and J. A. Bargh, "The Chameleon Effect: The Perception-Behavior Link and Social Interaction," *Journal of Personality and Social Psychology* 76 (1999): 893–910.

32. As claimed by Jacques Lacan in "The Function and Field of Speech and Language in Psychoanalysis," in *Écrits*, trans B. Fink, H. Fink, and R. Grigg (New York: Norton, 2002), pp. 197–267.

33. R. Dawkins, *The Selfish Gene* (Oxford: Oxford University Press, 1976).

34. D. Sperber, "An Objection to the Memetic Approach to Culture," in *Darwinizing Culture: The Status of Memetics as a Science*, ed. R. Aunger (Oxford: Oxford University Press, 2000), pp. 163–173.

35. S. Dehaene, *Les neurons de la lecture* (Paris: Odile Jacob, 2007).

36. H. G. Gadamer, *Truth and Method*, trans. J. Weinsteiner and D. G. Marshall (New York: Crossroad, 2004).

37. I am in debt to Giuliano Torrengo for the following report: "In India, the bureaucracy is truly mighty (any 'official' action calls for lots of forms and letters of presentation and calls forth as many more), and the bureaucrats (the so-called babu)—who make up 10% of the population and often come in whole families—really exercise serious power, because by delaying or refusing even one passage in the elephantine bureaucratic process they can hold you up quite literally for days (and suppose that all you want to do is book a train for the following day). From this there follows not just a mixture of reverence and hatred on the part of the non-babu population, but also a sort of code of behavior of 'submission' to the clerk whose job it is merely to make the bureaucratic machine work. The golden rule is never to annoy the clerk you have in front of you because it will do you no good; you must always say that he is in the right, and apologize for the trouble you are giving him."

38. It is worth noting in this connection that there is in any case what we might call the traditionalist version of tradition, which takes it as a guide to living. Traditionalism runs together two senses of tradition: (1) custom and idiom, what is transmitted mimetically within a family, a community and so on, and (2) authority, whether it be political or epistemic. It is clearly only in sense (1) that tradition can be accepted; (2) is altogether an improper transposition.

39. We are thus generalizing De Soto's thesis about the arising of capital as formulated in *The Mystery of Capital*. Indeed, De Soto stresses a crucial point about property in real estate and terrain. Unless it is adequately documented (in the terms I am suggesting, registered), this sort of property cannot be easily and quickly converted into capital; real estate and terrain cannot be put on a market outside a narrow local circuit within which the people know and trust each other; since they do not take on an impersonal character, they cannot be used as a surety for loans or as part of an investment. In advanced economies, on the other hand, everything about goods is accompanied by writing, by some document that attests and affirms ownership and that sets up a system of representations, which is a visible dimension parallel to the

hidden life that connects the material existence of goods to the rest of the economy. In the United States, it was the mortgages on real estate that underlay the generation of wealth as well as (a point we take up in the next note) the current economic crisis, which was principally owing to the implosion of this system. The ex-Communist countries and what used to be called the Third World do not have this formal system of representing property so that many of them have economic systems that are undercapitalized. The enterprises of the populations of the so-called Third World turn out to be similar to those of the firms in developed countries that are unable to issue shares to obtain fresh investments. Thus, in the absence of registrations—writing— these holdings are "dead capital."

40. In describing writing as a *pharmakon*, a remedy but also a poison, Plato prophesied, with arguments that still hold good today, the invasion of toxic paper with which postmodern governments have to deal. De Soto has recently maintained—in an interview ("Slumdogs vs Millionaires") and an article ("Toxic Paper"), both in *Newsweek* for March 2, 2009—that the central feature of the crisis is precisely the fact that no one is able to quantify the number of toxic documents in circulation in the world. Christopher Cox, an ex-president of the US Securities and Exchange Commission, calculates that the sum of toxic bonds is one or two trillion, while the secretary of the treasury says it is three or four. In fact, no one knows how many or which financial organs, banks and insurance companies hold them. Thus there is at least one point in common between the Manhattan banker and the favela dweller: this latter has no title to property and is without paper, while the former has papers but they are not reliable and this uncertainty spreads to the whole realm of documents. I do not find it easy to agree with De Soto that everything in the United States—with the exception of derivatives—is legally documented, if it is true that, in December 2008, a journalist with the *New York Daily News* was able to steal the Empire State building with false documents, and that, there being no notaries public in the United States, sixty thousand properties change hands on the basis of false documents. Without considering—as Joseph Stiglitz, a Nobel Prize winner for economics, has written (with L. Bilmes) in *The Three Trillion Dollar War: The True Cost of the Conflict in Iraq* (New York: Norton, 2008)—the particular laxity of documental controls allowed the financing of the public debt in favor of the American military.

41. P. Bourdieu, *Distinction: A Social Critique of Judgment of Taste*, trans. R. Nice (Cambridge, Mass.: Harvard University Press, 1984).

42. G. Agamben, *Homo Sacer: Sovereign Power and Bare Life*, trans. D. Heller Roazen (Stanford: Stanford University Press, 1998). The phrase itself owes to Walter Benjamin.

43. See my *Sans papier*, pp. 47–113.

44. On the role of registration in the concentration camps, see the witness of the commandant at Auschwitz: Rudolf Höss, *Kommandant in Auschwitz* (Bonn: Deutsche Verlags-Anstalt, 1958).

45. Plato presents the myth in the *Phaedrus*. See Derrida's analysis in "Plato's Pharmacy," trans. B. Johnson, in *Dissemination* (Chicago: University of Chicago Press, 1981), pp. 63–171. I refer also to my *La filosofia e lo spirito vivente* (Rome: Laterza, 1991), pp. 97–120.

46. I offer the following example from the recent Italian political scene. In November 2008, at a moment of tension between the majority and the minority in Parliament over the designation of the Oversight Commission for Public Television (RAI), the name of Riccardo Villari was voted for, though he belonged to the minority but was not the minority's candidate for the post. The minority asked him to resign. Villari refused to do what he was asked on the grounds that he had been voted for (*scripta manent*) and if, in any case, he never said he would resign, then he saw no reason why he should. Now, if we look at the question in Searle's terms, we have: the physical object X (in this case, the Riccardo Villari's body) counts as the social object Y (in this case the president of the RAI Commission) in C, namely a certain context in which collective intentionality dominates so that the social objects are what we believe them to be: euros are currency, identity cards are documents, and Villari is the president. The point is that the last social object, President Villari, is not believed in by anyone, except by Villari himself. Yet Villari did not resign for a long time, despite widespread dissent; which shows that Searle's law does not work, at least for Villari, whose case on the other hand does confirm the law Object = Inscribed Act. That is to say: the social object (Villari as President) is the result of a social act, namely an act involving at least two persons (in this case, many more, given that it was a parliamentary vote) and that is registered somewhere. This is what happened to Villari, and the proof that the social object *president* depends on the inscription of the act and not on the intentions of people lies in the fact that Villari did not resign and there was no way to make him do so. For once an act has been written, it cannot be annihilated; it cannot be treated as if it had never happened; at most, it can be revoked. But if the interested party does not want to, there is nothing to be done. To remove Villari, the Oversight Commission itself had to be dissolved: no commission, no president.

47. In this connection, I am reminded of an anecdote that Barry Smith recounted to me recently about the Hungarian phenomenologist Aurel Kolnai (on whom see F. Dunlop, *The Life and Thought of Aurel Kolnai* [Brookfield: Ashgate, 2001]). Kolnai was an upper-class Jew who had to leave Hungary in 1938 because of the racial laws passed by Admiral Horthy and take refuge in France. After the German invasion, he tried to flee once more, and he had more luck than Walter Benjamin; Benjamin committed suicide at the Spanish border, fearing that he would not cross, but Kolnai was taken prisoner and interned in a camp guarded by German soldiers. We may note that Benjamin's death can be traced to an inscription: the border between France and Spain: on one side he would have been saved and on the other doomed, and this latter possibility led him to accelerate things in the most improvident of ways. On the other hand, in the camp, Kolnai was faced with a physical barrier in the shape of the

barbed wire, yet he managed to escape by overcoming a social barrier and making clever use of conventions; marching up to the gate of the camp, he used the aristocratic tones of one who, like him, had been an officer in the Austro-Hungarian army and ordered the guards to let him pass, which they duly did. Having freed himself by manipulating conventions, he managed to flee to London, where he was joined by his wife (who was not a Jew) with whom he had several difficult months. They were staying in a boarding house where most of the little money they had went to pay for the room and there was almost nothing left for food, so that every morning they looked greedily at the bacon and eggs, the toast and the fruit juices of the English breakfast. It was a daily torture and it was only at the end of their stay that they learned that the breakfast was included in the price of the room. An invisible barrier had kept them for months from the simple and legitimate chance to be fed.

48. I am grateful to Davide Grasso for this observation, as for much else.

49. Lucretius, *De Rerum Natura*, III, 998–1002. Luciano Canfora's *La natura del potere* (Rome: Laterza, 2009) discusses these Lucretian themes.

50. In the 1997 science fiction film *Gattaca*, DNA is transformed into a document in a society in which genetic makeup has a social role; individuals whose genetic potential is low are designated invalid and destined to menial tasks; by manipulating the DNA of a perfect specimen, an invalid manages to take on his social role using hair and skin samples left at his work station by way of documents.

51. It is not possible to live without documents; and both the Soviet and the Chinese armies, which had abolished ranks, found they had to reinstate them as a matter of necessity, so that the Chinese took to using the number of pens in the breast pocket of the uniform as a way of indicating seniority, which is a splendid allegory of inscription. See S. Stafutti and G. Ajani, *Colpirne uno per educarne cento. Slogan e parole d'ordine per capire la Cina* (Turin: Einaudi, 2008).

52. *Hamlet*, Act I, scene v. In addition to other comments and observations, I am grateful to my friend Alfredo Ferrarin for the following gloss from Purcell's *Dido and Aeneas*: "In one of the most beautiful arias in the opera, Dido sings, 'When I am laid in earth, may my wrongs create no trouble in thy breast. Remember me but forget my fate.' It is a wish, not an oath, for nothing is written on the heart."

53. As suggested by Dehaene, *Les neurons de la lecture*.

54. P. Tullio, "La forma naturale delle lettere dell'alfabeto," *Bollettino della Accademia Italiana di Stenografia*, 1931; I. A. Gelb, *A Study of Writing: the Foundations of Grammatology*, rev. ed. (Chicago: University of Chicago Press, 1963); A. Kallir, *Sign and Design: The Psychogenetic Source of the Alphabet* (London: Alfred James Clarke, 1961); E. A. Havelock, *Origins of Western Literacy* (New Haven: Yale University Press, 1986); G. R. Cardona, *Storia universale della scrittura* (Milan: Mondadori, 1986). For further analysis, I refer the reader to my *Estetica razionale*, pp. 469–514.

55. W. Warburton, *The Divine Legation of Moses Demonstrated* (New York: Garland, 1978).

56. A. Leroi-Gourhan, *Gesture and Speech*, trans. A. Bostock Berger (Cambridge, Mass.: MIT Press, 1993).

57. A wide-ranging set of case studies on the connections among traces, numbers, and alphabets can be found in G. Ifrah, *Universal History of Numbers: From Prehistory to the Invention of the Computer*, trans. D. Bellos (New York: Wiley, 2000).

58. Aristotle had already grasped the value of registration and inscription on money: "For the future exchange—if we do not need a thing now, we shall have it if ever we do need it—money is as it were our surety. . . . Money, then, acting as a measure makes goods commensurate and equates them; for neither would there have been association if there were not exchange, nor exchange if there were not equality, nor equality if there were not commensurability. Now in truth it is impossible that things differing so much should become commensurable, but with reference to demand they may become so sufficiently. But then there must be a unit, and that fixed by convention (*nomos*) (for which reason it is called money (*nomisma*)); for it is this that makes all things commensurate, since all things are measured by money." *Nicomachean Ethics*, V, v, 1133b10–25 (trans. Ross with amendments).

59. J. Goody, *Logic of Writing and the Organization of Society* (Cambridge: Cambridge University Press, 1986), pp. 91–92.

60. Derrida, *Grammatology*. I have suggested an analysis of this in my *Introduzione a Derrida* (Rome: Laterza, 2003), pp. 62–67.

61. G. Celli, *La mente dell'ape. Considerazioni tra etologia e filosofia* (Bologna: Compositori, 2008). I have developed the argument that animals do not speak but do write (in the sense of archiwriting) in *Estetica razionale*, 295–302.

62. Thus we have structures, like those of African, Polynesian, and American kingdoms which, even without writing, still had forms of registration; see Goody, *The Logic of Writing*, p. 109.

63. Goody describes how, in simple societies communication and the "informative" element of ceremonies and mass rituals tends to mark the whole of the ceremony because it is in that moment and at that place that decisions are made, news is passed on, information is exchanged, relationships are reaffirmed and conflicts break out (*The Logic*, p. 125).

64. J. Assmann, *Cultural Memory and Early Civilization: Writing, Remembrance and Political Imagination* (Cambridge: Cambridge University Press, 2011).

65. It might be objected that it is unclear which archiwritings are relevant to social reality, and it might be wondered whether the appeal to archiwriting is not just another way of invoking collective intentionality. On this point, I think it worth stressing that, while collective intentionality is, as we have seen, an occult factor, a sort of hypothesis about the arising of social reality, archiwriting, and its upshot in writing, is an omnipresent and plain fact, one that everyone has in front of his eyes in the shape of documents, signals, accountancy, traditions, and so on; in short, it is the form of social reality in general.

66. "Thought is already itself the organization of representations, engrams or whatever. . . . Our inner life is already mental writing": Cardona, *Storia universale della scrittura*, p. 18.

67. J. Sutton, *Philosophy and Memory Traces: Descartes to Connectionism* (Cambridge: Cambridge University Press, 1998).

68. On the mind as a reader and writer, see C. M. Turbayne, "Metaphors for the Mind," in *Logic and Art: Essays in Honor of Nelson Goodman*, ed. R. Rudner and I. Scheffler (Indianapolis: Bobbs-Merrill, 1972). On the extended mind, see D. Chalmers and A. Clark, "The Extended Mind," *Analysis* 58 (1988): 10–23.

69. "Hades is the great judge of the men in the underworld and surveys all things in the tablets of his mind." Aeschylus, *The Eumenides*, 273–275.

70. M. M. Sassi, *Tracce nella mente. Teorie della memoria da Platone ai moderni* (Pisa: Edizioni della Normale, 2007).

71. As Steven Pinker aptly points out in *The Blank Slate: The Modern Denial of Human Nature* (Harmondsworth: Penguin, 2002).

72. I describe in detail the function of the tablet in the history of philosophy in *Estetica razionale*, esp. pp. 234–240.

73. Plato, *Philebus*, 38e–39b.

74. Ibid., 39b; in *De Memoria*, Aristotle likens the memory trace to a *zographema*, a portrait (450a29–30).

75. Aristotle, *De Anima*, III, iii, 429b30–430a3.

76. J. Locke, *Essay on Human Understanding* (1690) I, ii, 15; II, i, 2.

77. Leibniz, *New Essays*, Book II, chapter I.

78. As a cure for this, there is the search for an *ars oblivionalis*, to help us forget rather than remember: see U. Eco, *Dall'albero al labirinto* (Milan: Bompiani, 2007), pp. 79ff.

79. S. Freud and J. Breuer, "Studies on Hysteria," trans. J. Strachey et al. in *Complete Psychological Works of Sigmund Freud* (London: Hogarth Press, 1953–74), 2:188n.

80. S. Freud, "Project for Psychology," in ibid., 1:283–397.

81. S. Freud, "The Magic Notebook," in ibid., 19:227–233.

82. S. Freud, *The Interpretation of Dreams*, in ibid., 5:512ff.

83. S. Freud, *Beyond the Pleasure Principle*, in ibid., 18:67–143.

84. Both Kant and Hegel drew attention to this, the former in *Anthropology from a Pragmatic Point of View*, trans. R. B. Louden (Cambridge: Cambridge University Press, 2006) §28; and the latter in *Aesthetics: Lectures on Fine Art*, trans. T. M. Knox (Oxford: Clarendon Press, 1975), pp. 128–129.

85. G. Simondon, *Du mode d'existence des objets techniques* (Paris: Aubier-Montaigne, 1958). I examine the articulation of this hypothesis in Hegel, Peirce, and Derrida in *Estetica razionale*, pp. 250ff.

86. I think that it is to this double power of iteration to give and to take sense that D'Annunzio is referring when he writes in one of his last poems: "Here lie my

dogs / My useless dogs / stupid and shameless / ever new and always old / faithful and faithless / to Idleness their master / not to me, a worthless man. / They chew underground / in the endless dark / they gnaw the bones that are their bones, / they do not cease gnawing their bones / whose marrow has been scooped out / and I could make / a panpipe from them / as with seven tubes / I could without wax or linen / make Pan's flute / if Pan is everything and / if death is everything. / Every man in the cradle / sucks and dribbles on his thumb / every man buried / is the dog of his nothingness" ("Qui giacciono i miei cani," 1903).

87. See the presentation and discussion in Derrida, *Of Grammatology*.

88. Aristotle, *De Interpretatione*, 16a3.

89. G. W. Hegel, *Encyclopedia*, annotation to § 459. Hegel observes that ideograms are fitting for an immobile culture like the Chinese one. He could not have imagined how dynamic that culture would become and took no account of how ideograms agglutinate in such a way that new meanings are represented by the coupling of previously existing characters and not by creation *ex novo*.

90. Appealing to the pragmatist reflections of George Mead as well as to Derrida, Carlo Sini has proposed, in a series of important writings, on a scheme and for a purpose slightly different from mine, an alternative to this "Cartesian grammatology"; see his *Filosofia e scrittura* (Rome: Laterza, 1994) and *Etica della scrittura* (Milan: Mimesis, 2009). I discuss Sini's views in *Estetica razionale*, pp. 495ff.

91. E. Bonnot de Condillac, *Essay on the Origins of Human Knowledge*, trans. H. Aarsleff (Cambridge: Cambridge University Press, 2001); J. J. Rousseau, *Essay on the Origin and Basis of Inequality Among Men*, in *Basic Political Writings*, trans. P. Gay (Indianapolis: Hackett, 1987).

92. C. Darwin, *The Expression of the Emotions*; W. Wundt, *Elements of Folk-Psychology*, trans. E. L. Schaub (London: Allen, 1916).

93. M. C. Corballis, *From Hand to Mouth: The Origins of Language* (Princeton: Princeton University Press, 2002).

94. The point is stressed by Corballis in ibid., pp. 46–48.

95. R. Sacco, *Antropologia giuridica* (Bologna: Il Mulino, 2007); G. Cocchiara, *Il linguaggio del gesto* (Turin: Bocca, 1932). Vico distinguishes three kinds of languages: "Of which the first is the mental language for silent religious acts or for divine ceremonies" (*New Science*, Book IV § 5).

96. G. Lakoff and M. Johnson, *Metaphors We Live By* (Chicago: University of Chicago Press, 1980). This serves also for thinking about the role of metaphor, which is very strong in the representation of thought.

97. Corballis, *From Hand to Mouth*, pp. 110ff.

98. Ibid., pp. 82ff.

99. Ibid., pp. 213ff. According to Corballis's periodization, the first graffiti date to about 30,000 or 40,000 years ago, while phonetic writing emerges about 5,000 years ago.

100. J. Jaynes, *Origin of Consciousness in the Breakdown of the Bicameral Mind* (Boston: Houghton Mifflin, 1976), pp. 129–138.

101. Leibniz, *New Essays*, Book II, chapter IX.

102. F. Bacon, *The Proficience and Advancement of Learning*, 1605.

103. C. Lévi-Strauss, *World on the Wane*, trans. J. Russell (New York: Criterion Books, 1961), pp. 288–289; see also Derrida, *Grammatology*, pp. 107ff.

104. The great theoretician of primary orality was Walter Ong in *Orality and Literacy: The Technologizing of the World*, 2nd ed. (New York: Routledge, 2002). The great theoretician of secondary orality was Marshall McLuhan in *Understanding Media: The Extensions of Man* (Cambridge, Mass.: MIT Press, 1994). I offer further thoughts on the matter in *Dove sei?* pp. 77–110.

105. Plato, *Phaedrus*, 275c–6b.

106. "We owe it to writing if we can have a mental image of language as something that is 'thinkable.'" Cardona, *Storia universale*, p. 24.

107. Rousseau complained about this when he deplored the fashion at Paris to pronounce "vingt" as it is written and to call Lefèbvre "Lefèbure," mixing "u" and "v."

108. I develop this theme in *L'immaginazione*, pp. 7ff, and *Estetica razionale*, pp. 240ff.

109. Aristotle, *De Memoria*, 449b31–50a5.

110. In *Estetica razionale*, I analyze the modern developments of this theme, with particular reference to the Kantian schematism. See pp. 350ff. For extended examination, see my "Origini della immaginazione trascendentale," *Annuario Filosofico* 10 (1994): 133–226.

111. For a lucid account of the relations between thought and depiction, see V. Giardino and M. Piazza, *Senza parole. Ragionare con le immagini* (Milan: Bompiani, 2008).

112. G. Frege: "For one can hardly deny than mankind has a common store of thoughts which is transmitted from one generation to another" ("On Sense and Reference," trans. M. Black, *Philosophical Review* 57 (1948): 209–30, at 212.

113. This point has given rise to some curious misunderstandings. For instance, when, in the wake of romanticism, writers insisted on translating the Greek word "logos" as "language," thus suggesting an identity between thought and word (a point I examine at length in *Storia dell'ermeneutica*, pp. 318ff.), little attention was paid to the way that this equivalence was late and specific, or to the fact that the most usual and original sense of *logos* was to mean "relation," which is to say something that cannot be had without inscription and registration (I give references in support of this claim in *Estetica razionale*, pp. 421–432.)

114. Wittgenstein, *Philosophical Investigations*, I, §§ 243–315.

115. I develop this question in relation to artistic production in *Fidanzata automatica*, pp. 70ff.

116. A. Ferrarin, "Immaginazione e memoria in Hobbes e Cartesio," in Sassi, *Tracce nella mente*, pp. 159–189.

117. Kant, *Critique of Pure Reason*, A33, B49–50.

118. On this interaction, see Leroi-Gourhan, *Gesture and Speech*, pp. 250–251, writing at the dawn of the computer revolution in the early 1960s. It was then true that it was only in the preceding twenty years that the mimetism of artificial objects had reached a high level of imitation. This had needed almost a century of familiarization with electricity and the emergence of machines that synthesized the preceding steps. While mechanical movement was powered by energy sources, it was set in motion by a program whose medium was a tickertape. The essential transformation was the introduction of a nervous system for transmitting orders and controls by the central organs.

119. H. Bergson, *Matter and Memory*, trans. N. M. Paul and W. Scott Palmer (London: Sonnenschein, 1911), pp. 77ff.

120. In some case, such as those of DNA and electronic memories, we are dealing with modifications in volumes, of physical and chemical states, and not necessarily with a surface, but the fact remains that the ways in which these modifications operate are the same as a trace on a surface.

121. On the various types of ontological dependence, see K. Fine, "Ontological Dependence," *Proceedings of the Aristotelian Society* 95 (1995): 269–289.

122. *Estetica razionale*, pp. 204ff.

123. See G. Torrengo, "Documenti e intenzioni. La documentalità nel dibattito contemporaneo," *Rivista di estetica* 42 (2009): 157–188.

124. Aristotle, *Posterior Analytics*, 100a4–14.

125. For all that they draw too much attention to themselves, the scare quotes are necessary, since registration is never an entirely passive happening; in order to able to collect impressions, the recipient must have certain properties, as with the wax that must not be too hard nor too soft. I develop the point in *Estetica razionale*, pp. 318ff.

126. Here, too, the scare quotes are called for, for the same reasons as for "passive."

127. Suppose I was given a parking fine today. If I think that the fine was not legitimate because the policeman made a mistake, I will take some legal action to have the fine revoked. My aim is to change the institutional status of a certain event, namely my parking my car in a certain place at a certain time. I can succeed if I am able to bring it about the documents that are collectively held to be valid are revoked or transformed by means of a procedure that is legitimated by other documents that I myself (along with the collectivity of which I am part) regard as valid (such as the laws that permit an appeal). The example can be applied also to more dramatic cases, in which whole collectives refuse to recognize as valid documents that are much more important than parking fines. In such cases, legitimation is given by appealing to other inscriptions that are held to be valid, such as the Constitution (though this is rare in Italy) or merely to shared ideals (which are not inscriptions in

the technical sense). I look at such circumstances in 5.3, looking at the phenomenology of the letter.

128. On the basis of studies of the malleability of memory and the possibility of manipulating it ("Our Changeable Memories: Legal and Practical Implications," *Nature* 4 [2003]: 231–234), the American psychologist Elizabeth Loftus has confirmed the need for registration on an external support above all to guarantee (up to a certain point) the absence of distortions and the unambiguousness of the registered information.

129 In the best cases, three: the two parties and a third, a witness—even a nonhuman one such as a video camera in a bank or a recording in a call center.

130. C. Da Ponte, *Don Giovanni*: "With his marble head he does thus . . . thus," Act II, scene xii.

131. For instance, on the site of an airline company or a bank. Daniela Tagliafico informs me, and I am grateful to her for it, that there is a specific online site for promises: http://www.pledgebank.com.

132. Da Ponte, *Don Giovanni*: "You invited me to dinner / Now you know your duty," Act II, scene xvii.

133. The locus classicus for the distinction is C. S. Peirce, *Collected Papers of Charles Sanders Peirce*, vols. 1–6 ed. C. Hartshorne and P. Weiss, vols. 7–8 ed. A. W. Burks (Cambridge, Mass.: Harvard University Press, 1931–58), pp. 4:537. On the current status quæstionis, see L. Wetzel, "Types and Tokens," online at http://plato.stanford.edu/archives/win2008/entries/types-tokens.

134. I reproduce the case as it is presented in *Dove sei?* pp. 256–257, basing the account on a project by Davide Fassio.

135. T. Hobbes, *De Corpore*, Book II, chapter 11, § 7. More recent discussion is to be found in R. Chisholm, *Person and Object: A Metaphysical Study* (London: Allen & Unwin, 1976), pp. 89–113; P. Simons, *Parts: A Study in Ontology* (Oxford: Oxford University Press, 1987), pp. 194–204; D. Wiggins, *Sameness and Substance Renewed* (Cambridge: Cambridge University Press, 2001), pp. 76–106; A. C. Varzi, "Entia successiva," *Rivista di Estetica* 22 (2003): 138–158. See also the monographic number of *Rivista di Estetica* on "Ontologie analitiche," 26 (2003), edited by M. Carrara and P. Giaretta.

136. G. Evans, "The Causal Theory of Names," in *The Philosophy of Language*, ed. P. Martinich (Oxford: Oxford University Press, 1985), pp. 271–283, offers an argument against Kripke's theory in *Naming and Necessity* (Oxford: Basil Blackwell, 1980), which, with a different application in the more codified context or monetization, will be useful to me shortly.

137. It applies also to Enron. Among the comments that surrounded the meltdown, a financial daily put at the top of its list of things to do with Enron shares: "Use it for sanitary purposes and other bathroom activities."

5. DOCUMENTALITY

1. Within this framework, the appeal to the spirit against the letter, the fusional and vitalistic paradigm that hermeneutics inherits from idealism and, more broadly, from Christianity, is highly problematic. Staring from this reflection, we might develop a critique of Heidegger's philosophy; the problem of his joining the Nazis is not an incidental matter but brings out a substantial feature of Heidegger's thought, which, in defining truth as the fruit of a decision and as a historical opening, rather than as the conformity of a proposition to a thing, appears to offer a philosophical justification of the *Führerprinzip*. I have developed this line of thought in *La filosofia e lo spirito vivente*; in "Cronostoria di una svolta," in M. Heidegger, *La svolta*, trans. M. Ferraris (Genoa: Il Melangolo, 1990), pp. 35–115; and, in a broader theoretical context, in "Déduction d'une herméneutique," *Études de lettres* 1–2 (1996): 189–207.

2. A. Candian, "Documentazione e documento (teoria generale)," in *Enciclopedia del diritto* (Milan: Giuffrè, 1964), 13:579.

3. V. Crescenzi, *La rappresentazione dell'evento giuridico. Origini e struttura della funzione documentaria* (Rome: Carocci, 2005).

4. All this is in line with Otlet's principle, discussed in Chapter 1. Thus, even the hair the barber sweeps up can in certain circumstances count as a document and raise problems of privacy. Even limiting ourselves to the sphere of what is more commonly understood to be a "document," documentality includes a variety of manifestation that runs the gamut from memory to notes (reminders that can but need not have a social value) to international treaties; it can be realized in the most various media (writing on paper, electronic writing, photography, and so on); and it can refer to the most diverse activities (from borrowing a library book to getting married, from receiving a name at the registry office to declaring war).

5. This was the law of March 15, 1997: "Government Delegation for the Reform of the Public Administration and for Administrative Simplification," otherwise known as the "Bassanini Law" after the minister responsible for it.

6. Diplomatics is the science that studies documents, both in the narrow sense of those that have explicit juridical value and in the broader one of letters and mandates as well as those acts, such as official correspondence and witnesses that pave the way for the preparation of documents. It is no surprise that the core notion that connects these apparently diverse objects is precisely that of inscription; the very word for the study derives from the Greek *diploma*, literally "folded in two," which was the name given to any writing by an authority competent to assign a function or status.

7. For instance, in Germany, stationers sell sheets appropriate for drawing up a will, and in America a simple deed, a little red stamp, an echo of the wax seal, confers documental value to the yellow sheets in a legal pad commonly used for all sorts of inscriptions. What is known as protocol paper in Italy had a similar function and became stamped paper when an excise stamp was stuck on it. These material features

are never accidental and aim at a peculiar idiomaticity as well as conformity to rules (to a protocol).

8. Goodman, *Ways of Worldmaking*.

9. Referring to J. Glénisson, "Una história entre duas erudições," *Revista de História* 110 (1977); Jacques Le Goff, in "Documento/Monumento," *Enciclopedia Einaudi* (Turin: Einaudi, 1978), 5:41–42, refers, as a point of historiography, to a "documentary revolution": "It is at once a quantitative and a qualitative revolution. The interests of collective memory and of history no longer crystalize on great men, events, history that rushes headlong, the history of politics, diplomacy and the military. Now it is concerned with all men, which carries with it a new and more or less implicit hierarchy of documents, which places for instance the parish register, which conserves the memory of everybody, at the forefront of modern history. . . . The parish registers in which births, deaths and marriages parish by parish represent the entry onto history of the 'slumbering masses' and opens up mass documentation."

10. My friend Enrico Ferrone brought to my attention that the bootstrap is based on an inscription, given that the program (Bios) is registered on the read-only memory (ROM) within the mother chip of the computer. It is thus the only program that can run when the computer is switched on, since the main internal memory, the RAM, is volatile and loses the data when the computer is switched off.

11. This is developed in *The Monist* 92, no. 2 (2009), the monographic number edited by M. Ferraris and L. Morena and devoted to Europe.

12. This duplicity is analyzed with particular reference to the connection between spirit, nationality, and nationalism by J. Derrida in his *De l'esprit* (Paris: Galilée, 1987) and in *L'autre cap*, (Paris: Minuit, 1991). I refer also to the developments suggested in my introduction to the Italian translation "L'Europa in capo al mondo," in *Oggi l'Europa* (Milan: Garzanti, 1992).

13. P. Valéry, *La crise de l'esprit*, in *Oeuvres*, ed. J. Hytier (Paris: Gallimard, 1957), 1:988–1014.

14. "If Europe had been as rich as India, as flat as Tartary, as warm as Africa, as isolated as America, none of this would have come about. . . . The two great rich continents, Asia and Africa, embraced this poor little brother and sent it their goods and inventions, from the ends of the earth, from the towns of the most ancient and long-lasting civilizations, and so spurred its ingenuity and its spirit of invention. The climate and the remnants of the ancient Greeks and Romans also contributed to help its development and, thus, the greatness of Europe is founded on *the activity and the spirit of invention, on science and the effort of emulation*." J. G. Herder, *Reflections on the Philosophy of the History of Mankind*, trans. F. E. Manuel (Chicago: University of Chicago Press, 1968). The theme returns also in Hegel, *Lectures on the Philosophy of World History*, trans. H. B. Nisbett (Cambridge: Cambridge University Press, 1975), and Heidegger, *Introduction to Metaphysics*, trans. G. Fried and R. Polt (New Haven: Yale University Press, 2000).

15. This disposition seems so natural as to have a biological cycle, as with the decadence of the West described by Oswald Spengler in *The Decline of the West*, trans. C. F. Atkinson (New York: Knopf, 1926); and, in the same years, by Valéry: "*nous autres, civilisations, nous savons maintenant que nous sommes mortelles.*"

16. J. G. Fichte, *Addresses to the German Nation*, trans. G. Moore (Cambridge: Cambridge University Press, 2008).

17. Ibid.

18. E. Husserl, *Crisis of European Sciences and Transcendental Phenomenology*, trans D. Carr (Evanston, Ill.: Northwestern University Press, 1970), p. 273.

19. It has been discovered recently that this Degrelle was the model for Tintin, the character invented by that eminent Brussels resident, Hergé. He had the same round face, the same blond hairdo, the same red cheeks, and the same plus-fours. There are various knock-ons from this discovery, and in particular this: that Hitler would have liked Tintin for a son. On the personality and psychology of Degrelle, see Jonathan Littell's *Le sec et l'humide. une brève incursion en territoire fasciste* (Paris: Gallimard, 2008).

20. This is in line with the intuition already expressed by Montesquieu in *The Spirit of the Laws*, trans. A. M. Cohler, B. C. Miller, and H. S. Stone (Cambridge: Cambridge University Press, 1989), Book XIV, chapter III), which places climate alongside "religion, laws, maxims of government, traditions and customs" at the origin of the formation of the "general spirit."

21. The analogy with the organic is not in conflict with the spirit; indeed, it goes hand in hand with the reference to the sprit understood as "living spirit," as I have tried to show in my *La filosofia dello spirito vivente*, where I made much of the totalitarian trend of the appeal to the spirit; with particular reference to Heidegger, at pp. 197–222.

22. C. Schmitt, *The Nomos of the Earth in the International Law of the Jus Publicum Europaeum*, trans. G. L. Ulmen (New York: Telos Press, 2003).

23. Obviously I cite only the main treaties: Wikipedia carries at least two hundred, and the European Union's site carries pages and pages of such accords.

24. It was in this spirit that, along with Barry Smith and Leo Zaibert in an Ifomis seminar at Leipzig in 2004, I elaborated a project for a unified terminology for everything of bureaucratic or administrative importance in Europe, as a further contribution to unification through the letter. The basic idea is that, if we admit that the monetary union is a good thing, then a unified terminology for the administration and the legal system is an even more primary need. This may seem like one of those pipe dreams that Umberto Eco recounted a few years ago in *The Search for the Perfect Language*, trans J. Fentress (Oxford: Blackwell, 1993)—a book published simultaneously in French and the "original" Italian. But when we talk of a "unified terminology," we do not mean the recovery of some Edenic language or a word that covers "dog," "chien," "Hund," "cane," "perro," and so on. There is already Esperanto for that. Rather, this takes on a different guise when we think about legal questions

(is there a unified concept of "contract" in the various juridical traditions?), medical ones (is there a unified and statistically helpful terminology?), administrative ones (what is the Slovak for differentiating trains into "local," "express," "intercity," and "Eurostar"?), or university affairs (are the various degrees really correspondent?) or again military designation (does the concept of a "division" have a uniform application? Are there "brigades" in every military system? And, if not, where do we put the officers commanding them in case of unification?). The consequences for daily life, for the economy and for information flow of this sort of dispersion are fairly clear. And ontology, as a principle of rational cataloging of the world, seems to offer the right path toward solutions by going beyond the words and finding the underlying conceptual structures.

25. But everything is open to question. Once Gadamer told me, by way of justification of Husserl's scarce use of the word, that he "came from those lands where Europe shades into Asia."

26. F. Farinelli, *I segni del mondo. Immagine cartografica e discorso geografico in età moderna* (Florence: La Nuova Italian, 1992).

27. In this way, we can formalize the dependence relations of a theory of documents following the suggestion in Torrengo, "Documenti e intenzioni": (a) For every social object O, there exists a document (or more generally an inscription) D from which O depends specifically; (b) For every document D, there exists an instituting act (or event) E such that D and E depend specifically on each other; and (c) For every document D from which O depends specifically, O depends generically on subjects ready to recognize D as valid and to act accordingly.

28. I thank Luca Morena for this suggestion and for having pointed out that also in Searle the relation between the social and the institutional is one of inclusion.

29. C. Znamierowski, "The Basic Concepts of the Theory of Law," in *Polish Contributions to the Theory and Philosophy of Law*, ed. Z. Ziembinski (Amsterdam: Rodopi, 1987).

30. See Smith, "Document Acts," online at http://ontology.buffalo.edu/document_ontology.

31. See F. Carnelutti, "Documenti—teoria moderna," in *Novissimo Digesto Italiano* (Turin: Utet, 1957); Le Goff "Documento/Monumento"; V. Crescenzi, *La rappresentazione dell'evento giuridico. Origini e struttura della funzione documentaria* (Rome: Carocci, 2005).

32. Crescenzi, *La rappresentazione*, p. 19.

33. The self-certifications offered by a document appeal to idiomatic features such as watermarks and the like. Typically, their features call for other documents, or at least for customs that attest their validity. Here there is clearly a whiff of the infinite regress (the validity of a document requires a *valid* document to attest it), but the regress is blocked by practical limits. The case of identity is even more complex, because in general we are interested in finding out *who is* the person with certain

features (for instance, that of having performed certain actions) or *whether* a given person has certain features (such as his nationality or his family relations).

34. E. Betti, *Teoria generale della interpretazione* (Milan: Giuffrè, 1990), p. 68.

35. M. Foucault, "Governmentality," in *Ideology and Consciousness*, pp. 5–21. By "governmentality" Foucault means the ensemble of institutions, procedures, analyses and reflections, calculations, and tactics that allow this specific and fairly complex form of power to be exercised, that has the population as its main target, whose privileged form of knowledge is that of political economy and whose essential technical instruments are security devices; see also *Security, Terror, Population (Lectures at the Collège de France 1977–1978)*, trans. G. Burchell (New York: Picador, 2009).

36. Agamben, *Homo Sacer*; R. Esposito, *Bios. Biopolitica e filosofia* (Turin: Einaudi, 2004). I have discussed these views in the first part of my *Sans papier*.

37. It can even happen that the bureaucratic mindset manifests itself in the most unthinkable ways. In February 2008, there was a bank heist with a banker's order, a splendid meeting of bureaucracy and illegality. A lady from the town of Grado held up a bank in Trieste, pointing a knife at the cashier's throat. She was not interested in banknotes, which are hard to transport and may be marked. What she wanted was a banker's order to the tune of 400,000 euros credited to her current account. To speed the operation up, the robber had taken care to assault another branch of the bank where she had her account; that way it would be much easier. But the branch manager managed to trick her. He gave her an order, but a false one. In this way, the legalistic robber was up against a counterfeiting manager, who did what he did for the best, or at least for the interest of the bank; for it transpires that, if the banker's order had not be false, perhaps the 400,000 euros would have ended up on the bureaucratic robber's account. Dostoevsky once said that the French are infatuated with pieces of paper, with the supplementary irony that the French really were ruined by the stocks issued to pay for Russia in World War I. But I do not understand why Dostoevsky limited his observation to the French. After all, this particular heist took place in northeastern Italy and could have come off anywhere in Europe or indeed in the world. After all, if we are so secure that all our money (pieces of paper after all) is safe in the bank, where they do not let us see it, but only tell us, with other pieces of paper, that it is there, it is not clear why the infatuation with paper is a French disease, or what is wrong with the lady's action, given that she had urgent need of a free grant.

38. See my *La fidanzata automatica*, pp. 193ff.

39. M. Heidegger, "On the Origin of the Work of Art," in *Off the Beaten Track*, trans. J. Young and K. Haynes (Cambridge: Cambridge University Press, 2002), pp. 1–55.

40. A. C. Danto, *The Transfiguration of the Commonplace* (Cambridge, Mass.: Harvard University Press, 1981).

41. I have set out the fundamental features of this most kitsch of objects in *Il tunnel delle multe*, p. 181.

42. The following sketch is filled out in *La fidanzata automatica*.

43. For instance, when Piero Manzoni signed seventy-one living sculptures, including Umberto Eco, he performed a transformation of Eco not so very different from the one carried out by the examination board of the University of Turin in 1954, when they conferred on Eco the title of doctor of philosophy.

44. "Why do you not speak?" is a question apocryphally attributed to Michelangelo in front of his statue of Moses (if he had really said it, he would have been sick in the head); and doubtless, when Heidegger said of a painting by Van Gogh that "it was that painting that spoke," he was speaking metaphorically (no one could sensibly say, for instance, "it was the CD that spoke"). In *The Truth in Painting*, trans. G. Bennington and I. MacLeod (Chicago: University of Chicago Press, 1987), J. Derrida examined the limits of the metaphor of the painting that speaks, suggesting that has more to do with writing, in agreement with the documental theory I am proposing. Nevertheless, artworks do have what Arthur C. Danto calls, in his *Transfiguration of the Commonplace*, "aboutness," which is not so very different from "telling us about."

45. Goodman, *Ways of Worldmaking*, and, commenting on Goodman, Varzi, "Il denaro è un'opera d'arte (o quasi)."

46. D. Hume "Of the Standard of Taste," in *Philosophical Works*, ed. T. H. Green and T. H. Grose (London: Longman, 1874–75), vol. 3. On the nonconventional (because a convention is not enough) but accidental nature of the work, see S. Fish, *Is There a Text in This Class? The Authority of Interpretive Communities* (Cambridge, Mass.: Harvard University Press, 1980).

47. Of late, there has been a great deal of talk about social networks such as Facebook and people debate about whether or not it is worth entering them and, above all, they wonder in anguish about whether, once inside, it is possible to get out again. But this is the tip of an iceberg in a world of the web that makes possible betrayals, pilgrimages to Fatima, shopping in London and even confessions by email (with absolutions sent by ordinary post). This is where the new world is, not with journeys to Mars. A leading Italian philosopher who teaches in New York and has his family in Italy has for years been having his groceries delivered from an American supermarket where his wife shops for him. For all its simplicity, this situation brings to light possibilities that were inconceivable just a few years ago and suggests questions that science fiction has never raised. For instance, are cloistered nuns who surf the net really cloistered? For sure, a prisoner who had access to Second Life would not really be in prison, which is why penitentiaries do not allow Internet access. The whole enormous bureaucracy of the service industry, the antistate uses of texting in Eastern Europe and the Middle East, and of the Internet in China, the governments' desire to control the web and the widespread "archive ache" that grows out of the power and, at the same time, the fragility of the systems of registration are all political and economic reflections of a transformation that touches everyday life, which I discuss in *Sans papier*, pp. 193–229; but above all J. Derrida, *Archive Fever*, trans. E. Prenowitz

(Chicago: University of Chicago Press, 1996). Once we started talking about telecommuting, we did not think that we would soon have telefriendship, telefamily, and telelife, but this is indeed what is coming about. What are being created or being transformed are *communities*, not just circuits of shared knowledge on the model of Wikipedia, as was predicted not so long ago for instance with the notion of *collective intelligence* (see P. Lévy, *Collective Intelligence: Mankind's Emerging World in Cyberspace* [New York: Perseus, 1999]). The transformation affects not just what we know (for all that that is important) but what we do and how we live.

48. J. Habermas, *Structural Transformation of the Public Sphere*, trans. T. Burger (Cambridge, Mass.: MIT Press, 1989).

49. G. Scholem, *Die Geheimnisse der Schöpfung* (Berlin: Schocken, 1935).

50. In addition to the theoretical justification offered in Chapter 4, I have proposed historiographical examples in *La filosofia e lo spirito vivente* and *Estetica razionale*.

51. Derrida stresses this passage in *Given Time*, trans. P. Kamuf (Stanford: Stanford University Press, 1992), noting that Benjamin cited it in the *Arcades Project* but dismissed it as a "*gauloiserie*." Baudelaire's editor in the Pléiade edition, Pichois, after saying that the passage is "difficult to interpret," concludes that "all anti-Semitism is to be rejected."

52. Plato, *Timaeus*, 22b–3c. I have proposed a detailed analysis of this aspect in *La filosofia e lo spirito vivente*, pp. 97–120.

53. Conversely, the irritation with paperwork and even the dream of an unencumbered life is a tribute to the spirit, that impalpable entity that Don Giovanni invokes when he invites Zerlina to a most secret marriage ("That little house is mine: we shall be alone / and there, my jewel, we shall be wed") without witnesses, papers, registers or officials: in short a truly spiritual marriage of a sort that was not so long ago evoked in the obituaries pages of Italian newspapers where, after the announcement of the death of the dear departed and the condolences of relatives and friends, we might find a declaration from a certain lady describing her relation to the late gentleman as that of his "wife before God." This little had to suffice for the spiritual wedding, if she felt impelling but belated need to publish following the letter and in a newspaper. But what we should really be asking is: is this bereft and saddened lady so very different from the thinkers and politicians who privilege the spirit over the letter?

54. Obviously, as observed in 3.2.4.3, writing *alone* is not enough to produce wealth or to confer political power. It is true that an important difference between North America and Latin America does not lie in the goods, but in the fact that in North America there are documents and in the South there are not; yet, we have to take into account also other factors that add up to a much more complex scenario. For instance, the United States has taken control of South America but not of Russia, not because the Russians had more documental instruments to protect private property (very likely, in the first years after the end of the Soviet Union, there were fewer

than in South America), but because Russia had an army and a relatively efficient administrative machine. By all this I do not mean to say that the army has nothing to do with documental transmission; on the contrary, it is one of the areas where documentality is of vital importance, as we can see from the way that all the first applications of registration and interception systems, of email, Internet, and cellular phones, were military.

55. H. Taine, *The Ancient Regime*, trans. J. Durand (Gloucester, Mass.: Peter Smith, 1962).

56. J. Goody, *Logic of Writing and the Organization of Society* (Cambridge: Cambridge University Press, 1986), pp. 92ff.

57. Ibid., p. 86.

58. Nevertheless, a change has occurred in the last few years in this respect; the fact that archives are held on the personal computers of employees has led to a reduction of this separation and to a weakening of the idea of an "office." After all, the office that was the station ticket office has now been delocalized into the passenger's computer, and into the ticket collector's printer when he prints a receipt after putting in the code.

59. Goody, *Logic of Writing*, p. 128.

60. Certainly, a custom can be internalized to such an extent that it appears spontaneous and even hard to verbalize by the agent. In short, it can become something like an ability. But, apart from the fact that only rarely is what is called "unwritten law" a matter of ability, even if it were, it would be hard to think that it could be a matter of custom without memorization (which itself need not be verbal or conscious). Of course, however, the intervention of writing in the full sense brings about transformations. The written law is more susceptible to interpretation than custom is, but at the same time is more detailed. The same holds for documental acts relative to customary ones: marriages, contracts, mortgages, wills. In the specific case of a will, it is worth noting that originally a will was drawn up only when there was an intention to break with the customary disposition; the same is true today, though the default dispositions are written. In general, the fact that writing confers a peculiar solemnity on the act is a sign that it is intrinsic to the nature of the law that it is, so to say, on the road toward writing.

61. "Legislative activity is 'motorized' by simplifications and accelerations; but every motorization of the legislative procedure meant an increase in the power of the offices from which those orders emanated." C. Schmitt, "Das Problem der Legalität," in *Verfassungsrechtliche Aufsätze aus des Jahren 1924–1954* (Berlin: Duncker & Humblot, 1958), p. 441.

62. "In a system that is modern, which is to say industrialized, highly organized and specialized, based on the division of labor, *legality means a determinate method of offices' operating and functioning.* The procedures for putting affairs through, the routine and the habits of the office, the partially predictable functioning, the care to preserve this sort of structure and the need to have 'cover' against the calls of respon-

sibility: all these features belong to the complex of legality, conceived in functional-bureaucratic terms. If a sociologist like Max Weber can say 'bureaucracy is our destiny', then we ought to add: legality is the way this bureaucracy works." Schmitt, "Das Problem," p. 444.

63. There are few places in which the justification "I was following orders" holds good as much as in a call center. The fact that this function, which is apparently a matter of the spoken word, is in reality wholly written is shown both by the way that before one gets through to an operator he is guided by registered messages, and by the way that the operator's reply (recorded, like our questions) is highly stereotyped: it follows protocols, has a fixed length and in the end provides only responses that are empty and procedural. After all, there is no difference between a conversation with a call center and the purchase of a train or plane ticket on a website, and the call center in all probability is nothing but a staging post in a process that is destined to manage all interactions with clients in a purely scriptural way.

64. Even the nonpossession of an external end allows the work to manifest in the highest degree the fact that spirit is not prior to inscription and does not become objective in it but is rather the product of it. The plot of a novel is not a novel; the subject of a painting is not a painting, and it is not at all surprising that a novel can change plot and title in the process of being produced, that a poem can come into being beginning with a line which the poet himself does not fully understand, or that a painting can be given a title only once it is finished. The fact that the genesis of such works is often presented as accidental by the artists themselves, because they emerge from an image, a hook, a jingle, or a sketch traced without thought, is an important clue to why the works can be regarded as the "sensible appearance of an idea," but only on condition that the idea is a function that comes on the scene at a later stage and is often recognized only with hindsight: first there is the trace (Poe's "nevermore" in the "The Raven" or the "nothing no one nowhere never" in Vittorio Sereni's "Intervista a un suicida").

65. Then again, the prescriptural manifestation is often itself scriptural in the full sense, as in Moses's tablets, which prescribe mostly external behaviors that evolve (or should evolve) into spiritual attitudes.

66. From this point of view Catholicism passes directly, with great dynamism, to a bureaucratic community, the church apparatus, which imposes it own system of roles, titles and inscriptions irrespective of any precise spiritual content. I elaborate this point in *Babbo Natale, Gesù adulto. In cosa crede chi crede?* (Milan: Bompiani, 2006), pp. 123ff.

67. This can be found in many witnesses to the life of faith, which, especially in Catholicism, consists in assiduous attendance at rites, and which finds its highest expression in the kind of witness that ends in death and martyrdom (a word that in Greek means simply "witness"). Unless one has it clearly in mind that the spirit is derived from the letter, participation in prayer meetings, processions, masses, and

other rituals will seem like a futile activity, which does not in any way bear witness to faith. In this framework, martyrdom in itself is only a voluntary renunciation of life (accompanied by the involuntary death of others, in the case of the kamikaze); if we tried to ignore the role of the letter in the constitution of the spirit, we would find it hard to recognize it as a function that is connected to religion as the moment of absolute spirit.

68. "*In stilo autem meo coram multis testibus,*" St. Augustine, *Confessions*, X, 1.1.

69. I put this painting on the cover of my *Estetica razionale*, and Umberto Eco and Jean-Claude Carrière comment on it in *Non sperate di liberarvi dei libri*, ed. J.-P. de Tonnac (Milan: Bompiani, 2009), p. 198.

70. Reprinted in his *The Consequences of Pragmatism* (Minneapolis: University of Minnesota Press, 1982).

71. As Eco and Carrière aptly remark, "our knowledge of the past is due to cretins, imbeciles, and enemies." *Non sperate*, pp. 147ff.

72. The overall sense of Derrida's philosophy is the rehabilitation of the role of the letter in spirit. In the introduction to the French translation of Husserl's *Origin of Geometry* (trans J. Protevi, at http://www.protevi.com/john/DH/PDF/ITOG1-3.pdf), Derrida stresses, in the wake of Husserl, the role of registration in constituting the world of ideal objects. The Pythagorean theorem cannot be identified with its discoverer. But that there should be an ideal and noncontingent entity such as the Pythagorean theorem depends on the fact that a real and contingent entity like Pythagoras existed; if Pythagoras had straightaway forgotten his discovery, it would have returned to nothingness; and if he had not communicated it to someone by means of language, it would have disappeared with him; for the discovery to go beyond the bounds of the community in which it arose, it needed to be written down. As I explained in 1.3.2.3, this claim does not fit the case of ideal objects, but is surely true for social objects. In *Speech and Phenomena* (1967) Derrida generalizes this intuition: Without writing, without traces, memories, signs and marks in general, not only would there be no history, there would not even be its structure, the idea. For, in general, what we call structure or, in Kantian vein, the "transcendental," which is the condition of the possibility of knowledge, is in the final analysis writing. This theme is discussed in *Grammatology* (also of 1967): Derrida transposes the categories that, for Kant, mediate our relation with the world into the notion of archiwriting that I picked up in 4.2. Nevertheless, Derrida has little interest in being systematic. Grammatology, which is Derrida's transcendental philosophy, is less concerned with showing the role of signs in the construction of social reality than with emphasizing that, both in philosophy and in everyday life, that role is subject to a repression that is itself systematic. For further details, refer to my *Introduction to Derrida*.

73. R. Nozick, *Philosophical Explanations* (Cambridge, Mass.: Belknap Press, 1981), pp. 472ff.

6. IDIOMS

1. "Bodily lesions are like cries, shouted by the flesh every time language falls short. . . . Faced with the spread of emotions that they are unable to control, some adolescents beat their heads against the wall, break their hands on a door, burn themselves with cigarettes, cut themselves, beat themselves and mutilate themselves—all in the effort to contain a suffering that drags along everything in its path." D. Le Breton, *La peaux et la trace. Sur les blessures de soi* (Paris: Éditions Métailé, 2003), p. 37. This is the transition from the word to archiwriting: Whereof we cannot speak, we cannot write either. Tattoos, wounds, awards, borders, and rites all obey this logic, which has a very strong element of identity-formation. Some people have tattoos that they will carry with them all their lives, while others etch on their arm the name of their boyfriend or girlfriend and show it off, in reality to protect a relationship that they feel is under threat (ibid., pp. 68–69), which is not that different from someone who commits himself to a thirty-year mortgage or brandishes a check, a banknote or a document. Also by Le Breton: *Signes d'identité* (Paris: Éditions Métailé, 2002).

2. I have in mind the famous text in which Adolf Loos associates ornament with crime. I discussed this in an early essay, "Metafora proprio figurato. Da Loos a Derrida," *Rivista di Estetica* 12 (1982): 60–73, reprinted in *Tracce. Nichilismo moderno e postmoderno*, new edition (Milan: Mimesis, 2006), pp. 119–134.

3. I have tried to give a first overview in *Dove sei?* pp. 260–268.

4. Likewise, the use of archaic formalisms is accepted as a natural peculiarity whose role is make the document seem old and give it an aroma of authenticity.

5. See Kripke, *Naming and Necessity*.

6. European Community Directive 1999/93 governs the use of electronic signatures. The signature must (a) be connected in a unique way with the signatory; (b) be apt to identify the signatory; (c) be created in such a way that the signatory can keep exclusive control over it; (d) be connected to the data to which it refers so as to allow the identification of any subsequent change in the data.

7. In this sense, the pair signature/code displays important similarities to Goodman's distinction between autographic and allographic works of art, where an "autograph" is a signature.

8. This latter is the case, for instance, in France, where the guarantees for rental agreements have to be written by hand in full copying from a model, in such a way as to subject the poor guarantor to a punishment that, in its small way, puts one in mind of Kafka's "In the Penal Colony."

9. Obviously, this does not hold only for marriages. If we try to imagine that Mussolini had made the announcement of Italy's entry into World War II on June 10, 1940, putting on a Piedmont accent, or that General Badoglio had made the announcement of the armistice on September 8, 1943, putting on a Romagna accent. [Translator's note: Mussolini was from Romagna, while Badoglio was from Pied-

mont.] Would these have been serious social acts, able to be felicitous (in the technical sense of a 2.3.2.1), which is to say, to have the consequence they did in fact have?

10. Albeit in a different theoretical key, I have analyzed this point in detail in "Problemi di ontologia applicata: La proprietà delle idee," in *Significato e ontologia*, ed. A. Bottani and C. Bianchi (Milan: Angeli, 2003), pp. 104–115.

11. See F. Carnelutti, *Teoria del falso* (Padua: Cedam, 1935), and *Rivista di Estetica* 31 (2006), a special volume edited by P. D'Angelo.

12. "Handwriting acquires a special weight as indicative of 'character,' and the equivalent of the oral oath is the signed confession. The signature effectively becomes a substitute for the person, at least at the bottom of cheques. But it is not only a card of identity, as individual as the print of the finger or the hand, but also an assertion of truth or of consent." Goody, *Logic of Writing*, p. 152.

13. I think this provides an answer to an important objection that was raised on a philosophical blog (www.lestinto.it/articolo/truffa): "Either a social act is inscribed or it does not exist. Yet inscriptions can be simulated; hence, inscription is not sufficient. One of the examples that Ferraris chooses is that of the rubber check, which is nevertheless a *social act*, though it is different from what is expected. Socially speaking, a rubber check and frauds more in general, exist. The problem is that the rubber check is identical to a normal check. A simulated marriage is identical to a non-simulated marriage, where by 'simulated' I do not mean the recital but the intentions of the bride and groom, as provided by the civil code. A false document is identical, or at least very similar, to an authentic one: if the differences are very big, then we have a badly done reproduction rather than a false document. In short: a given registration can determine different social objects. Inscription is surely one of the ingredients of social objects, but that is all there is to it: social objects do not consist in registrations. Obviously, this is not a serious problem: Ferraris's analyses remain sound and his weak textualism remains a fine and interesting theory. Only it does not explain what social objects are: it is a phenomenological rather than an ontological analysis. He cannot have it both ways: either we continue looking for an ontology of social objects or we leave ontology alone and make do with phenomenology."

14. Goodman, too, falls into the confusion of name and signature when he claims that bearing the signature of Thomas Eakins or Benjamin Franklin is not stylistically identifying property and that, for all that a style is metaphorically a signature, a literal signature is not a stylistic trait (*Ways of Worldmaking*, p. 41). What is problematic about this comes out as soon as we try to explain what is *metaphorical* and what *literal* in this context.

INDEX

Aesculapius, 80,157

Aeschylus, 321n2, 354n69

Agamben, G., 350n41

Agnelli, G., 242

Ajani, G., 352n51

Alexander the Great, 137, 257

Anaxagoras, 53, 328n71

Angela, A., 108

Angela, P., 106–9

anticipations of experience, 99–100

apperception, 25–26

archetype, 44–48, 141–42, 166, 240, 252, 311

archive, 1, 4, 7, 9–10, 15, 29, 174, 180–81, 209, 233–34, 284, 288, 319

archiwriting, 4–5, 176–7, 197–200, 205–10, 214, 217–25, 237, 241–42, 250, 264–67, 289, 319

Aristotle, 11, 53, 76, 80, 126, 167, 188, 208, 212, 220, 232, 276, 324n36, 325n42, 325n51, 328n71, 337n9, 353n58, 354nn74–75, 355n88, 356n109, 357n124,

artifact, 36, 46, 49–54, 123, 126, 161, 270–71, 275, 317

artwork, 1, 17, 21, 33, 51–53, 163, 252, 267, 271–73, 275–82, 291, 301, 312, 319, 320

Assmann, J., 353n64

Auerbach, E., 348n26

Augustine of Hippo (St.), 215, 249, 293, 368n68

Austin, J. L., 20, 113, 114, 127–29, 146, 171–72, 286, 324n33. 323n35, 328n67, 335n77, 338n14, 342n59, 344n70

authoriality, 42–43, 212, 277–79, 304, 308–11

authority, 105, 109, 170, 193–94, 251, 290, 299, 313

Averroes, 76, 331n22

Awodey, S., 326n54

Ayer, A. J., 328n67

Bach, J. S., 307

Bacon, F. (Viscount Verulam), 217, 356n102

Bacon, F. (painter), 273

Badoglio, P., 396n9

Bargh, J. A., 349n41

Barker, R., 339n25

Baudelaire, C., 284, 365n51

Baumgarten, A. G., 13, 322n10

Bayle, P., 109

Becchio, C., 330n10

Bellarmino, R. F., 80

Benjamin, W., 72, 350n42, 351n47, 365n51

Bentham, J., 9

Bergson, H., 223, 357n119
Berio Rapetti, Y., 332n38
Berkeley, G., 15, 131, 146, 323n18
Bertone, C., 330n10
Betti, E., 363n34
Bianchi, C., 343n63, 344n68, 370n10
Bianchi, I., 330n5
Bieri, P., 325n29
Bilmes, L., 350n40
Bobbio, N., 342n62
Bodei, R., 324n34
Bonaparte, N., 30, 52, 87, 137, 148, 187,
    242, 260, 287, 325n45
Borges, J. L., 13, 57, 76, 209, 331n22
Bottani, A., 321n1, 370n10
Botticelli, S. (A. Di Mariano di Vanni
    Filipepi), 278
Bourdieu, P., 350n41
Bozzi, P., 89, 333n40, 333n46
Brentano, F., 324n37
Breuer, J., 354n79
Broad, C. D., 322n10
Brown, B., 328n68
Bruno, G., 325n41
Bruno, N., 330n12
Bukharin, N., 331n28
bureaucracy, 5, 32, 193, 195, 197, 255, 257,
    270–71, 280, 288–90
Burton, T., 338n19
Butterworth, G., 347n18

Cage, J., 276
Caligula, 343n66
Calle, S., 274
Candian, A., 359n2
Canfora, L., 352n49
Cappuccio, M., 334n59
Caravaggio (M. Merisi da Caravaggio),
    307
Carchia, G., 321n2
Cardona, G. R., 352n54, 354n66, 356n106

Carducci, G., 282
Carnelutti, F., 362n31
Carrara, M., 358n135
Carroll, N., 335n72
Casati, R., 324n28, 330n9, 332n29,
    333n44, 334n54, 337n10
Cassirer, E., 334n61
catalog, 7–13, 15–16, 24, 274–75, 316–17
Celli, G., 353n61
Chalmers, D., 354n68
Charlemagne, 260, 300, 315
"Charlemagne" Division, 259
Chartrand, T. L., 349n31
Chisholm, R., 323n12, 358n135
Christo (C. V. Javasev and J. C. D. de
    Guillebon), 275
Churchill, J. S., 332n37
Churchill, W. L. S., 263
Churchland, P. S., 332n39
Clark, Alfred, 352n54
Clark, Andy, 354n68
classification, 9–15, 18–21, 34, 135, 317
Cocchiara, G., 355n95
code, 42–43, 131, 173, 176, 184–85, 210,
    243, 251, 278, 287, 289, 293, 299, 304–5
Collier, A., 338n20
common sense, 18, 20, 58, 104–5, 116–17,
    189, 192–93, 211
communication science, 110, 181–82
conceptual scheme, 2, 13, 18, 35, 55,
    58–60, 64–66, 78, 81–82
consciousness, 25–29
constative, 111, 113–14, 128–29, 269
Condillac, E. Bonnot de, 355n91
Conni, C., 323n24
constructionism, 13–15, 39–40
construction of social reality, 50, 53, 148,
    153, 160–61, 187, 190, 193, 203, 206, 208,
    211, 228, 230, 255, 263–64, 269, 318
content (pure), 102–3
Copernicus, N., 63–64, 200, 274

Coppola, F. F., 278

Corballis, M. C., 355n93, 355n94, 355n97, 355n98, 355n99

Cortese, P., 190

Costa, V., 330n14

Cox, C., 350

credit card, 1, 195, 227, 233, 250, 263

Crescenzi, V., 359n3

Crusoe, R, 5, 36, 179, 203, 299

Cunimund, 50

D'Angelo, P., 370n11

D'Annunzio, G., 354n86

Danto, A. C., 363n40, 364n44

Darwin, C., 347n16, 355n92

Davies, R., 321n1

Dawkins, R., 349n33

De Chirico, G., 312

De Maistre, J., 335n78

De Monticelli, R., 323n24

De Soto, H., 341n54, 342n55, 349n39, 350n40

Degrelle, L., 259, 361n19

Dehaene, S., 349n35, 352n53

Deleuze, G., 348n19

DeLillo, D., 183

Della Casa, G., 329n75

Dennett, D., 340n35

Derrida, J., 4, 39, 56, 60, 121, 128, 138, 159, 174, 185, 206, 212, 238, 295, 296, 313, 326n53, 326n55, 331n24, 338n16, 342n55, 345n75, 347nn10–12, 351n45, 353n60, 354n85, 355n87, 355n90, 356n103, 360n12, 364n44, 364n47, 365n51, 368n72

Descartes, R., 12, 18, 24, 60–62, 74, 90, 208, 222–23, 330n5–6. *See also* archi-writing and *hors–texte*

Desideri, F., 334n55

Di Lucia, P., 327nn58–59, 341n50, 342nn58–59, 342n61

Dilthey, W., 123–25, 336n3

document, 1–6, 7–9, 32–34, 46–54, 137, 154–57, 174, 193–97, 199, 205–6, 224–27, 229, 231–32, 235–38, 242–45, 249–55, 264–71, 277–82, 286–90, 301–3, 305, 312, 314–15, 319

documents (strong vs. weak), 4, 110, 165, 267–68, 319

documentality, 1, 5, 160, 249–55, 264–71, 282, 286–90, 319

documental pyramid, 165, 270–72, 278, 303

Donise, A., 332n34, 339n26

Dönitz, K., 169

Dossi, C., 337n6

Dostoevsky, F., 363n37

Dretske, F., 334n54

Duchamp, M., 52, 163, 273–75

duck–rabbit, 53, 69–70

Dunlop, F., 351n47

Dylan, Bob (R. A. Zimmerman), 116

Eco, U., 332n34, 354n78

ecological world, 21, 34, 37–38, 88–89, 96–98, 101, 152, 166

ectype, 44–49, 141–42, 240, 253

eide, 34–35

epistemology, 2, 13–15, 24–25, 34, 55, 58–61, 64–66, 69, 76, 81, 84, 88–89, 101–3, 112, 118–19, 121–22, 132, 132–34, 136–37, 317

Esposito, R., 365n36

esthetics, 13, 21, 89–91, 112, 272, 310

experience (contrasted with science), 12, 17–22, 56, 60, 62–69, 72–74, 84–89, 93–97, 99–104, 117–18, 129–30

expression, 29–32, 71–72, 127–28, 167–69, 235, 237, 253, 265, 267, 274–75, 280–82, 287, 289

European Union, 2, 4, 156, 161, 245, 248, 254, 260–63

Evans, G., 358n136
facts ("there are no facts but only inter-
    pretations"), 19, 56, 61, 70–75
Farinelli, F., 362n26
Fassio, D., 258n134
Ferguson, N., 342n57
Ferrarin, A., 352n52, 357n 116
Fichte, J. G., 258, 361n16
Fine, K., 357n121
Finzi, R., 324n29
Fish, S., 364n46
Fleming, A., 95
Fogassi, L., 340n40
Fontana, L., 280
Foucault, M., 9, 144, 271, 322n3,
    340nn32–33, 363n35
Franz Josef I of Austria, 238
Frege, G., 42, 220, 325n44, 325n52,
    356n112
Freiser, R., 80
Freud, S., 209–11, 231, 354nn79–83
Fuchs, B., 348n20

Gabbiani, C. 333n43
Gadamer, H. G., 348n24, 349n36, 362n25
Galilei, G., 80
Gallese, V., 340n40, 348n23
"gavagai," 75–78
Gebauer, G., 348n20
Gelb, I. A., 352n54
Giardino, V., 356n111
Giaretta, P., 358n135
Gibson, J. J., 333n42, 334n55
Gilbert, M., 337n12, 342n58
Giovagnoli, R., 344n68
Girard, R., 348n20
Glénisson, J., 360n9
Goethe, J. W. von, 189–90, 283
Goldman, A., 332n39, 337n12, 348n23
Gombrich, E., 330n11
Goodman, N., 252, 322n9, 324n25,

334n56, 334nn60–61, 335n71, 342n56,
    360n8, 364n45, 369n7, 370n14
Goody, J., 353n59, 359nn62–63, 366nn56–
    59, 370n12
Google, 13, 118, 346n8
Goya, F. J. de, 308
Gramsci, A., 331n28
Grass, G., 258
Grasso, D., 341n47, 352n48
Grice, P., 343n63
Guala, F., 336n2

Habermas, J., 346n6, 365n48
Ham, R., 347n16
Hamlet, 15, 199, 200, 208, 239, 330n15
Harvey, J., 274
Havelock, E. A., 352n54
Hegel, G. W. F., 5, 24, 31, 53, 124, 150,
    212, 217, 249, 285–87, 291, 293, 295,
    297, 325n46, 328n72, 354n84, 354n85,
    355n89, 360n14
Heidegger, M., 11, 53, 59, 113, 328n69,
    336n5, 359n1, 360n14, 361n21, 363n39,
    364n44
Herder, J. G., 360n14
hermeneutics, 19, 73–75, 79, 81, 124, 174,
Herzl, T., 245
Hesiod, 133
Hildebrand, D. von, 34–35, 325n50
Hitler, A., 9, 137, 259, 290, 361n19
Hobbes, T., 196, 244, 358n135
Hoffmann, E. T. A., 291
Hofstadter, D., 340n35
Hoften, C. E. von, 323n14
Homer, 133
Honecker, E., 155
hors–texte, 4, 56, 75, 78, 80, 93, 121, 138,
    145, 238, 319
Horthy, M., 351n47
Höss, R., 350n44
Hume, D., 60, 62, 134, 178, 364n46

Husserl, E., 141, 184, 258, 262–63, 295, 326n55, 332n37, 333n41, 333n48, 361n18, 362n25, 368n72

ichnology, 4, 42, 121, 160, 175–76, 198, 224, 227, 247, 319. *See also* trace

identity, 32, 38, 136, 153, 156, 170, 178, 195, 207, 221, 229, 236, 242–45, 250, 252–55, 258, 262–3, 270, 300–1, 309

Ifrah, G., 353n57

imagination, 28–29, 31, 84, 87, 90, 108, 123, 158, 219

imitation, 4, 133, 143, 154, 157, 178, 187–97, 200, 215, 249, 305, 319

induction, 62, 87, 91

inscribed act, 2, 4, 30, 39, 43, 47, 50, 120, 121, 127–28, 136–37, 159–60, 164, 165, 172–73, 186, 197, 199, 203, 205, 230, 232, 236–37, 243, 246, 247–49, 251, 254, 262–67, 277–82, 292, 297, 318

inscriber, 45–46

inscription, 1, 4–5, 24, 29–32, 41–44, 49–54, 93–94, 127–28, 140, 150, 156–69, 171–74, 178, 183, 187, 192–204, 206–11, 221–27, 235–43, 245, 249–55, 264, 266–72, 277–82, 290, 305–6, 308–9, 311–12, 314, 318, 319

instrument, 50–53, 96–99, 124, 161, 164, 180–81, 234, 269–70, 273, 275, 278

interpretation, 19, 25, 61, 70–72, 108–9, 120

"intuitions without concepts are blind," 55, 60–61, 65–70, 97, 131, 219, 318

Italian Republic (laws of), 1, 122, 135, 171–72, 207, 251, 308, 315

Jacomuzzi, A., 330n12

Jastrow, J. (duck–rabbit), 53, 69–70

Jaynes, J., 356n100

Johansson, I., 342n58

Johnson, M., 351n45, 355n96

Jovanotti (L. Cherubini), 116

Joyce, J., 277

Kafka, F., 126, 193, 262, 369n8

Kaku, M., 335n69

Kallir, A., 352n54

Kanizsa, G., 69

Kant, I., 3, 11, 12, 17, 21, 32–33, 45, 47, 49, 53, 56, 57, 59–64, 66–69, 74, 99–102, 111–13, 118, 121, 123–26, 129–31, 143, 147, 219, 222, 268, 274, 279, 295, 311, 318. 322n8, 328n64, 330n7, 332n34, 332n37, 336n5, 337n8, 339n22, 354n84, 356n110, 357n117, 368n72

Kanzian, Ch., 321n1

Kaufmann, F., 338n15

Kim, J., 342n58

knowledge, 13–14, 16, 19, 37, 52, 54–64, 73, 73–74, 76–78, 80–81, 88–93, 102–11, 132–33, 221, 232, 269, 277, 291–95

Kobau, P., 323n12, 324n24, 330n12, 334n55

Kojève, A., 332n32

Kolnai, A., 351n47

Kripke, S. A., 301, 358n136, 369n5

Kubrick, S., 180

La Fontaine, H.–M., 7, 9, 255

Lacan, J., 335n66, 349n32

Lakoff, G., 355n96

Lask, E., 332n37

Lavelli, M., 348n19

Le Breton, D., 369n1

Le Corbusier (C. E. Jeanneret), 9

Le Goff, J., 360n9, 362n31

"Lefèbvre" (J. J. Rousseau), 356n107

Legrenzi, P., 334n64

Leibniz, G. W. von, 11, 16, 20, 100, 106, 158, 196, 209, 216, 316, 323n23, 341n51, 354n77, 356n101

Lennon, J., 313

Leporello, 10–11

Leroi–Gourhan, A., 353n56, 357n118

Lévi–Strauss, C., 217, 356n103

Levi, I., 323n12

Levi, P., 23

Lewis, D. K., 336n2, 348n29

Littell, J., 361n19

Livy (Titus Livius Patavinus), 12

Locke, J., 208–9, 354n76

Loftus, E., 358n128

logocentrism, 60–61, 65, 92, 160, 217, 318

Loos, A., 369n2

Lorini, G., 329n74

Lotze, H., 323n13

Lucretius T. Carus, 196, 352n49

Lynch, M. P., 335n75

Lyotard, J. –F., 78–79, 331n26

Maccarini, A. M., 338n20

Machiavelli, N., 12

Madison, G. B., 340n36

Malebranche, N., 14

Mallarmé, S., 10

Mandelbaum, M., 342n61

Manfroid, S., 8, 322n2

Manzoni, A., 25, 105, 187, 261, 307–8, 310

Manzoni, P., 364n43

Maradona, D. A., 313

Marconi, D., 330n7

Marinetti, F. T., 179

marriage, 1, 5, 29, 33, 44–48, 53, 127,
    130, 164–67, 171–73, 234–37, 240–41,
    268–69, 286, 308–9, 319

Martinich, A. P., 358n136

Marx, K., 138, 339n27

mathematics, 39–41, 45, 63, 110, 118, 141,
    203

McLuhan, M., 356n104

Mead, G., 355n90

Meinong, A., 16–17, 32–33, 323n12,
    323n22, 238n66

memory, 4, 25, 27–32, 50, 59, 90, 109,
    123, 131, 140, 158, 160–61, 164–65, 169,
    171, 173, 175–77, 187, 194, 197, 199,

    204, 207–10, 220–31, 233–34, 236–39,
    244–45, 260–61, 264, 281, 284, 289,
    295, 307

Mengele, J., 50

Menger, C., 152, 341n44

Merkel, A. D., 71

metaphysics (descriptive vs. revisio-
    nary), 18–20

Metastasio (P. Trapassi), 105, 325n45

Metternich, K. W. L. von, 263

Metzger, W., 87, 332n36

Metzinger, T., 325n39

Michelangelo (M. Buonarroti), 364n44

Miraglia, R., 340n42

Miyashita, Y., 340n40

Mondrian, P., 307

Monet, C.,

money, 1, 33, 44, 50, 71, 73, 78, 105, 120,
    131, 145, 148, 151–52, 155–64, 178, 183,
    186, 195–96, 199, 202–5, 227 253, 261,
    264, 274, 287, 291, 310, 313, 318

Montaigne, M. E. de, 12

Montesquieu (Ch.–L. de Secondat),
    361n20

Moore, G., 361n16

Moore, M. S., 342n58

Morandi, E., 338n20

Morena, L., 341n49, 360n11, 362n28

morphic unities, 34

Mozart, W. A., 116, 307

Müller–Lyer illusion, 65

Mulligan, K., 338n15

Mundaneum, 7–10

Murdoch, I., 339n23

Mussolini, B., 9, 369n9

Nadel, J., 347n18

Nakahara, K., 340n40

Natorp, P., 323n12

Newton, I., 21–22, 39

Nichols, S., 348n22

Nietzsche, F. W., 12, 56, 61, 72, 74–76, 80, 137, 196, 330n16, 334n73

Nisbett, R. N., 360n14

Nixon, R. M., 163

Nolan, C., 346n9

Norman, D. O., 337n7

Novalis (G. P. F. von Hardenberg), 255

Nozick, R., 332n35, 368n73

Nuremberg rallies, 189

Nuremberg Trials, 1

"Object = Inscribed Act", 2, 4, 30, 39, 43, 50, 120, 121, 127–28, 137, 159–60, 164, 165, 175–77, 186, 197, 199, 203, 205, 230, 232, 236–37, 243, 246, 247–49, 251, 254, 262–67, 277–82, 292, 297, 318

objects (natural, ideal and social distinguished), 27, 29, 30–34, 317

objects, ideal, 2, 32–33, 38–43, 45, 47, 57, 77, 89, 99, 101, 118, 126, 128, 140–44, 160, 202, 223, 236, 240, 282, 304, 307, 311, 317

objects, natural, 2, 24, 32–38, 42, 50–51, 76–77, 89, 101, 120, 123, 130–32, 134–35, 139, 144, 198, 317

objects, social, 1, 2–4, 13, 24, 27, 29–37, 39–54, 57, 67, 75–77, 89, 101–2, 110, 116, 118–19, 120–48, 151, 154–65, 173–74, 176–78, 183, 185, 198–99, 203, 205–7, 224, 226–29, 232, 234–46, 260, 262–63, 265–66, 272, 277–79, 281–82, 297–98, 304, 307, 311, 313, 317–20

Ockham, W., 16, 135

Ong, W. J., 356n104

ontology, 2, 10–13, 24–25, 34–35, 38, 40, 55, 58–60, 69, 79, 81, 84–85, 88–89, 92, 101–2, 112–13, 121–22, 129, 132, 144–48, 159–61, 226–28, 236–38, 249, 276, 279, 314

origin, 36–38, 42–42, 126, 153, 155, 161, 163, 187–91, 201, 204, 211, 254, 284–87, 301–3, 314–15

Otlet, P., 7–10, 255, 322n1, 322n4, 359n4

panopticon, 7–9,

Pasteur, L., 80

Peirce, C. S., 354n85, 358n133

perception, 25–27, 59–62, 67, 90–92, 318

Perec, G., 2

performative, 30, 103, 110–14, 118, 127–29, 146, 155, 166, 171–72, 185, 220, 260, 268–69, 293

Perniola, M., 345n3

phenomenology, 5, 21, 24–25, 32, 76, 88–89, 102, 109, 111, 149, 160, 205, 228, 249–50, 266, 272, 282–85, 320

Piaget, J., 347n18

Piana, G., 333n33

Piazza, M., 356n111

Picasso, P., 12

Pichler, H., 323n12

Pinker, S., 354n71

Pizzo Russo, L., 330n4

Plato, 38–41, 45–47, 59, 106, 109, 133, 142–44, 172, 181, 184, 188, 208, 218–19, 284, 295, 336n79, 344n69, 344n75, 350n40, 351n45, 354n73, 356n105, 365n52

Plehanov, G., 331n28

Poe, E. A., 247, 367n64

Popper, K. R., 348n28

postmodernism, 3, 12, 56, 60–61, 70, 72, 75, 78, 80, 120, 132, 144, 148, 180, 182, 194–95, 276, 289

power (of documents), 137, 154, 162, 165, 169–70, 185, 193–97, 204, 233–34, 148, 250, 254–55, 263, 270–72, 287–92, 318

pragmatics, 168, 241–42

pragmatism, 3, 56, 61, 70–78

Prandini, R., 338n20

promise, 1, 30–34, 45–46, 84, 98, 111, 114,
    122, 127–28, 135–42, 146, 163–68, 173,
    185, 204, 236–37, 239, 241, 277, 306,
    308–9
Proust, M., 12, 115, 116, 133, 196, 347n9
Ptolemy, 69, 80
Pufendorf, S., 338n15
Purcell, H., 352n52
Pythagoras (his theorem), 33, 39, 41–42,
    307–8, 368n72

Quine, W. V. O., 15–16, 20, 59, 75–78,
    323n20, 324n32, 325n51, 330n8, 331n21,
    331n23

Ratzinger, J., 80, 331n27
Rayward, W. B., 322n1
realism, 33, 34, 78, 81–82, 123, 125–26,
    130–32, 138–43, 145–48, 156, 160, 197,
    226–27, 316
registration, 1, 4–6, 44, 47, 50, 54, 93–94,
    99, 110, 132, 136–37, 158–59, 163, 165–
    66, 171, 173–74, 175–79, 181, 183–87,
    192–95, 197, 202, 205, 207, 211, 213–27,
    230–38, 242–45, 253, 264, 267–71, 283,
    289–90, 309, 319–20
Reid, T., 127–28, 167, 172, 337n13
reification, 125, 135
Reina, D., 332n33
Reinach, A., 128, 140–46, 166, 168–69,
    240, 323n17, 326n57, 323n37, 338n15,
    339n30, 340n31, 342n61–62, 343n64
relativism, 78–82, 102–3, 122
representation (mental), 11, 22–27,
    130–31, 208
representation (inscribed), 152, 156,
    158–59, 160–61, 222, 230, 307–8
Rickert, H., 322n34
Rigotti, F., 324n34
Rizzolatti, G., 348n23
Rodin, F. A. R., 306

Rodotà, S., 347n15
Romano, S., 338n15
Rorty, R., 78–79, 295, 331n25
Rosen, S., 344n70
Rosenthal, D. M., 324n39
Rousseau, J. J., 133, 203, 339n21, 355n91,
    356n107
Routley, R., 323n22
Ruben, D. H., 337n12
Rudner, R., 354n68
Runggaldier, E., 321n1
Russell, B., 104, 334n63
Ryle, G., 323n21

Sacco, R., 139–40, 327n58, 339n29, 355n95
Saint–John Perse (A. Léger), 260
Saint Paul, 293
Salice, A., 331n28, 340n31
sample, 7, 10–13, 15–18, 40, 48–49, 317
Sarkozy, N., 71
Sartre, J.–P., 11
Sassi, M. M., 354n70, 357n116
Satie, E., 376
Savardi, U., 330n5
Sbisà, M., 334n67
Schaffer, J., 324n30
Schmitt, C., 150, 259, 290, 340n39,
    361n22, 366nn61–62
Scholem, G., 365n49
Schopenhauer, A., 66, 85, 87, 108, 255n45,
    331n30
science (contrasted with experience), 12,
    20–21, 30, 35, 56–65, 71, 73–75, 81–82,
    84–102, 104–10, 115–18, 122–25
Scott, W., 310
Scott Palmer, W., 357n119
Searle, J. R., 3–5, 145–63, 223, 278, 332n34,
    340nn34–38, 340n43, 341n46, 341n48,
    341n50, 341n56, 351n46, 362n28
Seddone, G., 344n68
Sereni, V., 325n47, 367n64

signature, 2, 6, 45, 160, 174, 188, 202, 205, 225, 229, 235–37, 243, 251, 253, 279–80, 297–316

Simenon, G., 7

Simmel, G., 336n5

Simondon, G., 354n85

Simons, P., 358n135

Sini, C., 355n90

Sinigaglia, C., 348n23

skepticism, 59, 62, 76, 124, 329n3

slipper experiment, 82–84

Smith, B., 158–61, 326n57, 341n50, 341n54, 342n58, 342n61, 351n47, 361n24, 362n30

socialization, 35, 36–37, 39, 41–43, 51

society, 4, 24, 36, 42, 45, 76–79, 121, 124, 127, 132, 136–38, 140, 142, 151, 154, 159, 164, 166, 169, 176, 178–83, 192, 194–97, 202, 211, 220, 223, 231–33, 236, 238–39, 250–52, 277, 281, 286–87, 310, 317

Socrates, 115, 117, 157

Soros, G., 348n28

Sosa, E., 342n58

space and time, 2, 11, 33, 37, 41, 43, 52, 183, 240, 317

speech acts, 146–47, 168, 173, 239, 250, 269, 312

Spelke, E. S., 323n14

Spengler, O., 361n15

Sperber, D., 348n27, 349n34

spirit (*Geist* as opposed to letter), 4, 5, 21, 25, 31–32, 44, 79, 102, 123–25, 129, 149–50, 175, 210, 215, 221, 228, 247–49, 255–63, 269, 283–87, 290–96, 318, 320

Stafutti, S., 352n51

Stalin, I. V. D., 263

Stich, S., 348n22

Stiglitz, J., 350n40

Strawson, P. F., 322n6, 324n27, 325n51, 333n45

styleme, 306–8

subject (of experience), 11–15, 22–31, 34–35, 43–44, 51–52, 122–24, 137–38, 143–45, 166–67, 306, 313, 317

Sutton, J., 354n67

Svevo, I., 29

Taddio, L., 333n40

Taine, H., 366n55

Talleyrand (C. M. de Talleyrand–Périgord), 287

Tanzi, C., 246

Tarde, G., 189, 347n19

technique, 5, 48, 77, 95–96, 98–99, 175, 177, 189, 210–11, 216, 219–20, 224, 227–28, 237, 284, 296

telephone, 42, 173, 176, 180–83, 185–86, 194, 214, 233, 243, 277, 304–5

television, 9, 107, 180–81, 183, 186, 214, 216, 235, 237, 245, 299, 310–11, 315

textualism, 4, 72, 121, 128–29, 132, 136, 138–40, 143–47, 156, 159–60, 169

Thomasson, A., 327n61

Tintin, 7, 201, 343n66, 361n19

Tintoretto (J. Comin), 52

Tolstoy, L. N., 116

Torrengo, G., 224, 327n60, 338n19, 349n37, 357n123, 362n27

trace, 1, 4–6, 28, 42, 44, 50, 121, 155–63, 172, 175–78, 186, 197–212, 216–17, 222–35, 251, 253, 256, 264, 267–70, 280–81, 288, 296

transcendental fallacy, 56, 57–84

Tullio, P., 352n54

Tuomela, R., 340n38, 342n58

Turbayne, C. M., 354n68

Turri, M. G., 162, 342n55

Twain, M. (S. L. Clemens), 261

Twardowski, K., 306, 323n12, 325n40

unemendability, 35, 55, 85–92, 100, 107–8, 265, 318

uniqueness, 284, 298–304, 316, 320

Valéry, P., 72, 360n13, 361n15
validation, 46, 77, 172, 174, 195, 229, 232,
    235–37, 240, 250–53, 266, 268, 282,
    301–5, 308–13
Valore, P., 322n10
Van Eyck, J., 297, 303
Van Gogh, V., 364n44
Varzi, A. C., 322n10, 324n29, 330n9,
    334n54, 334n58, 341n49, 342n56,
    358n135, 364n44
Vattimo, G., 324n24
Verdenius, W. J., 347n17
Vermeer, J., 115
Vico, G. B., 94, 126–28, 337n11, 355n95
Villari, R., 351n46

Wagner, W. R., 276
Warburg, A., 275
Warburton, W., 201, 352n55
Warhol, A. (A. Warhola), 274, 276, 346n8
Weber, M., 290, 348n21, 367n62

Weitz, M., 335n76
Wetzel, L., 358n133
Whiten, A., 347n16
Wiggins, D., 358n135
Wilson, W. T., 260
Windelband, W.,
Wittgenstein, L., 72, 126, 215–16, 295,
    331n20, 356n114
Wolff, C., 7, 322n10
writing 4–6, 10, 25, 30–31, 39, 41–41, 47,
    50, 93–94, 99, 131, 140, 159–61, 164–65,
    171–74, 176–77, 179–86, 192–209,
    211–25, 227, 233, 236–37, 239, 241–42,
    250–51, 254, 261, 264–70, 283–84,
    287–96, 319
Wulf, C., 348n20
Wundt, W., 355n92

"X counts as Y in C" (Searle), 3, 4, 146,
    157, 227, 278

Zaibert, L., 3Zellini, P., 324n29
Znamierowski, C., 266, 336n1, 362n29